P9-CDH-842

PRESIDENTIAL LEADERSHIP OF PUBLIC OPINION

ELMER E. CORNWELL, Jr.

Presidential Leadership OF Public Opinion

GREENWOOD PRESS, PUBLISHERS
WESTPORT, CONNECTICUT

Library of Congress Cataloging in Publication Data

Cornwell, Elmer E
Presidential leadership of public opinion.

Reprint of the ed. published by Indiana University Press, Bloomington.
Includes bibliographical references and index.
1. Presidents--United States--Press conferences.
2. Government and the press--United States. I. Title.
[JK518.C63 1979] 353.03'5 78-11946
ISBN 0-313-21076-4

Reprinted in 1979 by Greenwood Press, Inc.
51 Riverside Avenue, Westport, CT 06880

Printed in the United States of America

10 9 8 7 6 5 4 3 2 1

For B. M. C.

PREFACE

No one ever writes a book alone, whatever the title page may assert. Responsibility rests with the author exclusively, but gratitude is inevitably due to many helpers along the way, institutional and individual.

Both Princeton University and Brown University generously made possible various research trips to Hyde Park, Independence, Washington, and Northampton, Massachusetts, in quest of material. The George A. and Eliza Gardner Howard Foundation played the indispensable role of enabling the author to take a year of leave from teaching to prepare a first draft of the manuscript, and hence earned a special portion of deep gratitude.

Libraries and their staffs play crucial roles in any scholarly endeavor. Herman Kahn and Elizabeth Drewry at the Franklin D. Roosevelt Library, Philip C. Brooks at the Harry S. Truman Library, together with their devoted and efficient associates, were helpful beyond the call of duty. Numerous individuals at the Princeton University Library, the Widener Library at Harvard University, the John Hay Library at Brown University, the Forbes Library in Northampton, the Library of Congress, and the National Archives spent much time and effort making the work of the itinerant scholar pleasant and fruitful. A special word must be said about the tact and helpfulness of the personnel of the Indiana University Press, especially Miriam S. Farley, whose skill as an editor and enthusiasm for the project eased immeasurably the toils of publication.

My wife, like all women so lacking in foresight as to marry a poor school teacher, made the greatest single contribution by far. She endured with surpassing patience many hours of proofreading and index preparation, was always my most helpful and candid critic, and did much to sustain morale as we both waited for the light to appear at the end of the tunnel. Of the children less can be said save that both we and they survived the ordeal.

Countless other individuals made contributions of all sorts. Needless to say, I owe a special debt to the following people who gave willingly of their valuable time in interviews, and in supplying material only they could make available: Eben A. Ayers, Ben H. Bagdikian, Kenneth Barnard, Sevellon Brown, III, Louis Brownlow, Hadley Cantril, Douglass Cater, Frederic W. Collins, George A. Graham, James C. Hagerty, Bryce N. Harlow, Andrew Hatcher, Ken Hechler, Emmet J. Hughes, E. W. Kenworthy, Fletcher Knebel, David D. Lloyd, James Reston, James H. Rowe, Pierre Salinger, A. Merriman Smith, Murray Snyder, Harry S. Truman, Roger W. Tubby, Grace Tully, and Lincoln White.

The following fellow laborers in the political science vineyard deserve special mention for numerous acts of kindness and services rendered: Samuel H. Beer, and the late and sorely missed V. O. Key, Jr., both of Harvard; James MacGregor Burns of Williams College; J. Roland Pennock of Swarthmore College; and my valued colleague and friend at Brown, C. Peter Magrath. McGeorge Bundy, though now a practitioner, really belongs in the same list.

Howard F. Sachs, Jack Samuels, and Lois Jean Wilson deserve mention for special kindnesses rendered. At various stages I had the able assistance of Joan Edgley Webster, Gilbert P. Cohen, and William Brisk in doing research; and I was singularly blessed with the typing service of Carol Kellam and Florence Murphy, who have few rivals in skill and accuracy.

ELMER E. CORNWELL, JR.

Providence, R. I.

ACKNOWLEDGMENTS

The following articles by the author, first published in the journals indicated, have been incorporated in the chapters, in whole or in part, with the permission of the copyright holders:

"The Press Conferences of Woodrow Wilson," *Journalism Quarterly* (Summer 1962).

"Coolidge and Presidential Leadership," *Public Opinion Quarterly* (Summer 1957).

"Wilson, Creel, and the Presidency," *Public Opinion Quarterly* (Summer 1959).

"The Presidential Press Conference: A Study in Institutionalization," reprinted from the *Midwest Journal of Political Science* (November 1960) by permission of the Wayne State University Press, copyright, 1960.

Material from the Franklin D. Roosevelt Library, the Harry S. Truman Library, the Princeton University Library (Swem Papers), The Forbes Library (on Coolidge), and the National Archives has been used with the permission of the respective directors or authorizing officials. Permission was granted to use the Wilson papers in the Library of Congress by Mrs. Wilson; and to use the Coolidge papers, also in the Library of Congress, by Mrs. Coolidge.

Passages from the following articles and books are quoted with the indicated permission:

"Mr. President: II: Ten O'Clock Meeting" by John Hersey, published in *The New Yorker*, April 14, 1951, with the permission of the author and of *The New Yorker*, which holds the copyright, dated 1951.

"How Woodrow Wilson Won His Nomination" by Frank P. Stockbridge, published in *Current History*, July, 1924, with the permission of *Current History*.

"The Building of the Four Freedoms Speech" by Laura Crowell, published in *Speech Monographs*, November, 1955, with the permission of the author and of the Speech Association of America.

A portion of a Roosevelt speech taken from *The Public Papers and Addresses of Franklin D. Roosevelt*, Vol. III: *The Advance of Recovery and Reform, 1934*, published by Random House, New York, 1938, with the permission of Random House.

My Hero by Donald Richberg, published by G. P. Putnam's Sons, New York, 1954, with the permission of Putnam's and Coward-McCann Company.

The author expresses his gratitude to all of the foregoing for their cooperation.

CONTENTS

TABLES

ILLUSTRATIONS

PRESIDENTIAL LEADERSHIP OF PUBLIC OPINION

☆☆☆☆☆☆☆

Chapter 1

☆☆☆☆☆☆☆

INTRODUCTION

It is the office of the presidency that makes American democracy unique in the democratic world. It has been the presidency, more than any other part of the system, that has enabled American democracy to succeed and flourish for a century and three quarters. And it has been the relationship between President and public that has given this office its power and importance.

Sweeping assertions? Yes, but defensible—if not provable in an ultimate sense. The uniqueness of the presidential institution in a world of free nations that have most often followed the British cabinet model is obvious, and hardly less so in light of de Gaulle's assumed role under the Fifth French Republic. That the presidency has made the constitutional system workable is perhaps less obvious, but can be persuasively argued in light of the roles played by Jackson and Lincoln, Wilson and the Roosevelts.

But why insist that the President's key relationship is with the public rather than with his party, or with Congress? Popular government by definition entails close links between governors and governed, whatever the constitutional forms. Likewise all freely elected officials must cherish their popular base of support. In a very real sense, however, the American President finds in the populace not only his base of electoral support, but the very essence of his power to influence the process of governance. Were he the British Prime Minister and were American parties like British parties, Presidents could govern as party leaders. But American parties have rarely lent themselves to anything approaching "party government."

The separation of powers and the constitutional allocation of legislative authority to Congress shape the President's relation with that body. Save for the veto, the occupant of the White House has no means of either setting major policy himself or forcing the legislative branch to do his bidding. Apparently the framers did not intend the chief magistrate to be a policy maker except in crisis situations. The leverage the President has acquired in the lawmaking process has been indirect, based on use of the arts of persuasion, and ultimately grounded in the popular support he can claim or mobilize. Hence his link with the public is his key relationship.

The President, in the nature of things, must deal with the citizenry largely through the media of communication. Hence the evolving relationship between President and media will claim primary attention here. The impact of the revolution in communications on the presidential office during the present century has obviously been tremendous. Presidents have found in the mass circulation daily newspaper, radio broadcasting, and recently, television unprecedented channels for exerting leadership of opinion in the making of national policy. But not only does the Chief Executive now have the technical means to reach his clientele with an ease and rapidity unknown in the last century, he has also achieved an omnipresence in the general flow of news and in the awareness of the average citizen which in itself has vast implications for the shaping both of national opinion and of public policy.[1]

The presidency has always had a pervasive significance in national life beyond politics and policy alone. Presidents and their families have symbolized national values and the homey American virtues, as well as setting or confirming patterns of taste and fashion. Today the whole national sense of security and well-being depends to an alarming degree on the President's buoyancy or depression, his vigor or hesitancy. The psychological impact on the nation of the assassination of President Kennedy was awesome, and even frightening, in its implications. And the mass media, as they have developed, represent the major cause of this intensified preoccupation with the presidential office. Again the television coverage of the Kennedy tragedy underscores this point.

Unlike the other branches of government, the President is "news" as a person, as well as in his official role. Congress or the Supreme Court rarely make news save in their corporate capacity. Walter Bagehot's shrewd observation is in point: "The best reason why Monarchy is strong government is, that it is an intelligible government . . . the action of a single will, the fiat of a single mind, are easy ideas. . . ."[2] A public increasingly used to watching the daily round of the President and his family through the modern news media becomes a ready audience for his official pronouncements.

In short, a process of interaction between the developing media of communication and their generalized impact, on the one hand, and growing presidential use of them, on the other, has altered both the center of gravity of the national governmental system, and the frame of reference of the public in viewing government. Progressively, during this century (and episodically, during the last), the President has become *the* source of initiative and stimulus for action. He has done so by exploiting his unequaled platform for popular leadership. This fact, with a powerful assist from the burgeoning commercial news media, has virtually transformed the White House occupant into the personification of the national government.

Much of the foregoing, contemporary students and observers will willingly accept on the basis of the superficial evidence readily available. However, problems arise—of approach and method—that give pause to the researcher who would penetrate the surface and analyze these developments in detail. The central problem lies again in the nature of the presidential office and the kind of power it must wield. The President's role in relation to policy making is "hortatory" rather than "determinative." He has neither the legal-constitutional nor the party-political base to command action, or even attention, in the legislative process. He must persuade, bargain, exhort, and on occasion, bribe. Above all he must win and channel public support.

Tactics of this sort are in their very nature more difficult to study—and even the materials for their analysis are more difficult to find—than is the case with the "determinative" actions of a legislature or a court. Acts of presidential persuasion, or bargains with Congressmen for support, rarely leave more record than the questionable recollections of participants. Fortunately, when the President deals with the public, at least his utterances become part of the record, if not the processes whereby they were planned and prepared. Thus the pattern of public utterances will be the basic data for analysis, plus the ways in which the media were used for their transmission, and as much of the context and staff work from which they evolved as can be discovered or inferred.

This volume, along with recent studies of presidential power,[3] the President's Cabinet,[4] and other similar efforts is designed to help fill a long-standing vacuum in the literature about the presidency. Most previous writing has dealt broadly with the presidency in all of its phases and throughout the whole period of its development. Little effort has been made to isolate particular facets or crucial periods for the kind of intensive investigation that cumulatively leads to a sophisticated understanding of any institution. Far more of this kind of study is needed.

The focus here will be on the interaction between the President and the media, and on the mechanics of Executive leadership of public opinion, as one facet—perhaps the crucial one—of the presidential role, as it has evolved during this century. The implication here that the President can and does and probably should shape popular attitudes, and not just respond to them passively, inevitably raises questions of political theory and political values. Such questions, though lying beyond the scope of this book, deserve at least passing mention and frank acknowledgment.

Classic democratic theory makes little provision for leadership by rulers. The usual image of the policy making process depicts a welling up of "policy" from the people, which is filtered and then confirmed by the legislature. Leadership by executive authority is thus viewed as perhaps illegitimate if not potentially tyrannical. One recent critic of current trends talks of a growing threat of executive Caesarism, and insists that the American presidency is "already endowed with powers of truly Caesarian magnitude."[5] With modern totalitarianism's emphasis on the techniques of mass manipulation through monopoly control of the media in mind, critics can be pardoned if they view with alarm the array of public relations skills and tools which contemporary White House occupants have at their command.

Though these developments will not be treated here as a normative problem, the reader is entitled to know where the author stands on the questions of democratic values involved. In general, it seems apparent that democratic theory needs to make more room than it traditionally has for the ingredient of leadership in the political process. Specifically, though, does the preeminent position occupied by the President for influencing public attitudes pose a clear and present danger to American democracy? I do not think so. Unless this preeminent position is tranformed into exclusive monopoly, Presidents will always face competition for public attention. Actual control of the media is and doubtless will remain decentralized in private hands. Furthermore, we can safely assume that American pluralism will long preserve its built-in diversity of interests and viewpoints against efforts to override these with one set of homogenized opinions, from whatever source. Finally, and to this we shall return in the last chapter, the dispersed pattern of constitutional power in America represents the ultimate safeguard if one is required.

It can be persuasively argued that *without* this presidential role as opinion leader for the nation, the Republic would actually be in grave danger. If the presidency had remained passive and inarticulate, the vaunted dispersion of the power to govern might long since have destroyed the system itself. In the twentieth century, tyranny (even in Germany) has been less the problem than chronic inability of democratic governments to govern. But for the development of the presidency, this would be America's problem, given her constitutional structure. Thus Presidents must wring every legitimate advantage they can out of the "bully pulpit" of the White House. If they do not, governmental vigor will certainly flag, and they will be abdicating their responsibility to their office, to the nation, and perhaps to the free world.

The chapters to follow fall naturally into two groups. In each group roughly half of the period of presidential history since 1900 will be considered. Chapters Two through Five comprise a chronological discussion of the administrations of the first Roosevelt, Taft, Wilson, Harding, Coolidge, and Hoover. Since so much of the story during these years centered on the single factor of the newspaper press and its exploitation by the White House, a straight chronological account was appropriate.

For the most recent decades, the administrations of Franklin Roosevelt, Harry Truman, Dwight Eisenhower, and the brief but eventful tenure of John Kennedy, a change of format and approach was made. An analytical approach was substituted for chronological treatment. Chapter Six, which launches this portion of the book, is a case study, drawn from the watershed administration of the Democratic Roosevelt. It is designed to illustrate the combination of techniques and media that were by then available to a President, including F.D.R.'s innovations, and to relate the whole to one substantive policy problem. The remaining chapters then trace developments in the period from 1933 to the end of the Kennedy administration, with a few words on President Johnson. Since change came rapidly and covered an ever widening range of communication channels and ways of using them, each of three major areas of development has been isolated for separate treatment: the newspaper and the press conference (in Chapters Seven and Eight), the development of presidential public relations staff (Chapter Nine), and the evolution of the electronic media of radio and television (Chapter Ten). The final chapter seeks to set the patterns adduced in tentative perspective.

☆☆☆☆☆☆☆

Chapter 2

☆☆☆☆☆☆☆

BEGINNINGS: ROOSEVELT AND TAFT

Theoretically, democracy is impossible without the free expression of citizens' views which the press makes possible. Less frequently emphasized is the use of the news media by government itself to inform the electorate and to win their approval of its acts. The means of doing this must be organized in such a way as not to violate fundamental freedoms. In the United States, since roughly the middle of the last century, the prime vehicle both for free expression by citizens and for essential government publicity has been a privately owned, independent newspaper press, now increasingly supplemented by magazines and electronic media.

Presidents are peculiarly dependent upon the mass media for the exercise of their essential function of leadership. The growth of the "opinion leadership" and "policy leadership" aspects of the presidency has been paced by developments—both technical and organizational—in the media of communication.

The turn of the present century offers an appropriate starting point for examination of the roots of presidential leadership as it has come to be exercised in the twentieth century.[1] Two crucial developments culminated in this period. The first was the rapid evolution in the preceding two or three decades of the practices and technology of the modern newspapers; the second was that unique political phenomenon, Theodore Roosevelt.

The newspaper trade as practiced before Reconstruction was a very different thing from what it rapidly became between the 1870s and 1900.[2] Before the war, the daily or weekly paper was manufactured essentially by hand from relatively expensive materials and it served a small market (the demand for reading material was small even in relation to the population). Hence the scale of newspaper enterprise was tiny in comparison with that of today. In addition, the truly independent press had not yet emerged. Newspapers were often frankly organs of a particular party, faction, or candidate. During these years the line between the government and the media upon which it relied to publicize its actions was blurred almost to the point of the former having its own propaganda agencies.

Before the 1890s the "party organ" type of journalism and the limits of primitive technology tended to complement each other. Small circulations and slowness of manufacture were not serious handicaps to highly partisan journals of opinion with restricted audiences. On the other hand, cheap and rapid manufacture made possible and even necessary a *mass* market beyond the confines of one faction, party, or following. The press inevitably became large-scale enterprise, and journalistic independence followed logically.

This technological revolution in newspaper manufacture began with the application of steam power to the operating of presses in the mid-1830s and of electricity in the 1890s. The telegraph made possible the beginnings of the wire services, starting in the 1840s, and the ensuing rapid availability of news fostered the development of evening editions during the 1870s and 1880s. The evolution of typesetting techniques began with the invention of stereotyping processes in the 1860s, the linotype in the late 1880s and 1890s, and the monotype process shortly thereafter. Newspaper illustrations became possible on a lavish scale with the development of photoengraving in the eighties.

Press speed increased rapidly during this period, folder-cutters were built into presses in the 1870s, and other refinements. The tempo of news gathering and transmission accelerated with the advent of the telephone in the same decade and the typewriter in the next. Declining costs accompanied this mechanization and the transition to wood-pulp paper in place of rag paper. By the late eighties, 75 per cent of the rag had been replaced, and the price of newsprint dropped from about 12 cents per pound in 1872 to 3 cents in 1892. The whole financial structure of journalism changed. Prices declined along with costs of production, while advertising soared and took over an increasing share of the total costs. (Capitalization also increased sharply and it became less and less possible to start a paper on a shoe string.)

The contemporary mass circulation daily had emerged by the turn of the century. The technical ingredients were by then present. It was left to a group of "press lords" (as their English counterparts were called) to put them together and supply the formulae for a new age in newspaper publishing. Joseph Pulitzer (1847-1911) was one of the first of these, followed by Hearst, Scripps, and others. Circulations rose astronomically. Between 1870 and 1890, daily circulation went up 222 per cent while the population was increasing only 63 per cent. Increased literacy as well as the increased availability of cheap newspapers in attractive formats accounted for this rise. Average daily circulation doubled again between 1892 and 1914. Riding the crest of this wave, "yellow journalism" was born around the turn of the century.

The mass-produced, mass-circulation daily unquestionably broke down the isolation from the main stream of national events in which much of the population had always dwelt. (The newer media like the motion picture, radio, the mass-circulation magazine, and television have continued the process of molding one integrated mass society.) At the same time the demand for news increased enormously. The reading public's demand for material increased by leaps and bounds, and the efforts of the press to satisfy this demand developed proportionately.

The consequences of these two interrelated developments for government were that public awareness *of* government, of its activities and personnel, became progressively greater. The muckrakers, progressivism, and the like around the turn of the century suggest this. The citizenry was being informed and was reacting to its new awareness of developments in public life.

Besides reformist zeal, the new journalism unquestionably fostered a great deal of plain curiosity about government and its personalities, as well as about the world in general. The newspapers of the new era throve on mounting circulations which would attract advertising revenue. Circulation, in turn, could be acquired by presenting interesting news to titillate and entertain as well as inform, and by doing so in an ever more attractive format. This meant increased press discussion of public policy—often sensationalized, as with the Spanish War—and also meant increased preoccupation with the human interest side of government, clashes of personality, and the like.

These changing patterns of public attention had obvious implications for the conduct of government. While the Congressman was becoming less isolated from his constituents and more responsive to their demands, radically new possibilities were now available for leadership by the President. In fact, it was probably the President who benefited most of all from this new curiosity about government and from the accompanying possibilities for molding popular attitudes.

The decline of the partisan press and rise of the independent newspaper after the Civil War did not immediately bring changes in the behavior of the White House occupants of the period. Congress was in the ascendancy and Presidents remained more or less aloof from the public and from the working press.[3] What contacts there were with the journalistic fraternity tended to be with a few editors and publishers who were strong supporters or personal friends, plus random contacts with occasional reporters. Individual interviews or appointments were sometimes granted to one or to a small group.

Presidents were usually passive objects of reportorial and public curiosity, reflecting their passive approach to their role. Rather than attempt to use the press for some positive objective, the White House occupant was far more likely to give his attention to editorial comment and view the correspondents with either resigned patience or hostility, depending on their treatment of him and his immediate family. All relations between the President and the media remained extremely unformalized and casual. Channels for informing the public about White House activities were also lacking, in part because traditionally, conduct of the office was screened from public gaze, at least far more than the activities of Congress.

Episodes which foreshadowed things to come in White House press relations did occur from time to time. Garfield's assassination in 1881 was one of these. After being shot, he lingered on for some eleven weeks, hovering between life and death, with the papers covering his minute changes of condition avidly for their readers. In 1885 there was the prolonged illness and subsequent death of former President Grant, which again filled the press with a plethora of medical and sentimental details.[4] A year later there was the spectacle of the wedding of President Cleveland to his young, attractive ward, Frances Folsom, in the White House. The wedding itself, and particularly the honeymoon at Deer Park, Maryland, were covered by the correspondents with a completeness that would be taken as a matter of course today, but which many found shocking and uncouth at the time.

Then as now "human interest" subject matter made the best kind of copy, and the Chief Executive, by virtue of his office and the natural interest that attached to even the trivial doings of prominent personages, was a natural for this kind of exploitation.[5] Implicit, however, in this concentrated attention on Presidents was an opportunity for them to exploit: an avid and expectant audience to address, as well as a cross to bear.

I

Theodore Roosevelt was a phenomenon of unique and startling proportions on the American political scene. The time was ripe for another Jackson-like reorientation of the office which would lay the groundwork for meeting the demands of the twentieth century. In the new journalism, a new and powerful tool for political leadership had become available. As Jackson had made the President the tribune of the people, so some new President must develop the techniques for turning the emerging mass media to account. This was the role played by Roosevelt.

When Roosevelt's dynamic personality and ebullient energy were brought to bear on the presidential office following his chance elevation upon the death of McKinley, the result was a dual one. Prime attention was now focused on the White House as a source of news and action in government. T. R. also elaborated a kind of "model" for future executive exploitation of the mass media for opinion leadership. To the general outlines of this model his successors added surprisingly little. The changes and adaptations which did come later were functions of the technological development of the media and the vast increase in the scale upon which the presidency was conducted.

Oliver Gramling, historian of the Associated Press, writes that "Washington's emergence as the news center of America was one of the notable journalistic phenomena in the first decade of the twentieth century." Among the major causes for this was "the vigorous news personality of President Theodore Roosevelt, who seemed able to dramatize himself or a platform plank with equal ease."[6] According to Mark Sullivan: "Roosevelt's fighting was so much a part of the life of the period, was so tied up to the newspapers, so geared into popular literature, and even to the pulpit . . . as to constitute, for the average man, not merely the high spectacle of the Presidency in the ordinary sense, but almost the whole of the passing show, the public's principal interest."[7] Seldom, if ever, has any individual maintained so strong and persistent a hold on the attention and enthusiasm of the American people.

T. R. did not just provide bully entertainment for an enthralled public, but dramatized the potential of the office for affecting the course of public policy by means of a dynamic relationship with the electorate via the mass media. Presidents, particularly since the decline of the party press in the last century, have had few channels of communication under their own control. Democracy generally, and certainly American democracy, has jealously guarded against the Executive providing himself with any means of reaching a mass audience beyond the familiar "swing around the circle." The very idea of an official ministry of propaganda has been abhorrent. As a result, Presidents have been dependent almost exclusively upon commercial, privately controlled media.

The journalistic fraternity, both the working press and the owners and editors, therefore play the role of intermediary between the President and his audience. As a consequence, the President is faced with a much more complex problem than merely the phrasing and timing of announcements and appeals to the public. He must enlist the willing cooperation of the working press, in the first instance, or at the very least avoid alienating them. Hopefully, he will also have the sympathetic understanding of some of the owners, but whether he does or not, he must weigh carefully the merits of front page coverage versus editorial support and favor. He must, in short, become preoccupied with the mechanics of getting his utterances transmitted in an effective manner—without the power to *command* such cooperation—as well as give attention to content. The more sensitive an understanding he has of the publicist's art and the newspaper trade, the better off he will be.

Presidents before Theodore Roosevelt rarely felt that the press must be catered to or wooed. T. R.'s overriding contribution was a vivid realization of the potentialities of leadership via the newspapers, and, hence, realization that access to this potential must be pursued actively and continuously. Rather than merely releasing information and letting the press make the best use of it they could, or leaving it up to the reporters to dig out the news, he took the offensive and made news himself, calculating carefully the best ways and means and timing for its release.

Mark Sullivan quotes a critic of the President: "Roosevelt has the knack of doing things, and doing them noisily, clamorously; while he is in the neighborhood the public can no more look the other way than the small boy can turn his head away from a circus parade followed by a steam calliope."[8] Nor could the press turn its head, he might have added. Sullivan goes on to say that the heart of Roosevelt's method was to inspire headlines. One technique for doing this was to take advantage of the thinness of the Monday paper after the quiet of the traditional Sabbath by releasing something on Sunday in time to be seized eagerly by the news-starved editor making up his front page for the next day.[9]

Sullivan catches one of the subtleties of this "headline making" thus: "To the headlines and news dispatches that he especially devised and timed for the direct purpose of promoting the matter he had in hand were added the dispatches that arose spontaneously from his multifarious collateral activities, the investigations he ordered, the indictments he incited, the prosecutions he pursued, the denunciations he uttered."[10] A President can make at least two kinds of news: that which is deliberate and geared by him to the achievement of some policy goal, and that which he makes simply by going about doing and saying interesting things in an attention-arresting way. The latter enhances the receptivity of the public for the former, and the whole process is reinforced by the interplay between the publisher's compulsive quest for circulation and the increased appetite he thus engenders in his readers.

These are the first elements in the model for presidential opinion leadership that Roosevelt supplied. The passive approach to the press must give way to an active one in which every effort is bent toward using the news media rather than being used by them, molding their output in ways favorable to the current White House objective. Since the relation between the President and the newspaper press is not one of command and obedience, it must be compounded of tact and skillful exploitation of areas where objectives overlap while avoiding areas of inherent conflict.

T. R.'s grasp of the potential of the existing media is underscored by the use he is said to have made of the mass circulation magazines. He was a voracious reader of all forms of literature. He made it a point to get acquainted with magazine staffs, knew traits and biases, and, it is said, even knew the ins and outs of office politics as he knew the internal frictions of party committees. He did not hesitate to both praise and disagree with things he read, or explain his policies in detail, by letters to the editor. Partly by inspiring articles by intimates, and partly through the sheer magnetic attraction of his personality and ideas, he "kept the pages of the popular magazines glowing with support" of his crusades.[11]

The second element in the model has to do with the all-important working relationship which a President develops with the news correspondents. T.R. took the initiative in having quarters provided for them in the White House itself. A couple of decades earlier reporters first began to haunt the executive mansion in quest of news. Until early in the Roosevelt administration, their technique was to waylay presidential callers outside as they entered or left. During the McKinley administration the press representatives had the use of a table and chairs in the outer reception room, but that was the limit of the facilities allowed them inside.

The story is that Roosevelt one day noticed reporters plying their trade outside the White House in particularly unpleasant weather and gave instructions that a small anteroom be set aside for their use in the building. Then when the executive office wing was added later in his administration, he made sure that it included an appropriately equipped press room.[12] Symbolically, this act both suggested his interest in the working press as human beings, and, more important, initiated the formalizing of the President-reporter relationship. For the first time, a kind of organic link had been forged between the two, in place of the casual contacts of the past.

He also cultivated a warm and at times intimate rapport with many of the individual reporters. "Cultivate" must be used with care here. There is little doubt that he was fully aware of the usefulness of these ties of sympathy and friendship. At the same time, it would probably be incorrect to imply that they were contrived or forced. T. R. was a warm and gregarious individual who loved good conversation and stimulating companionship.[13]

David Barry describes a meeting with T. R. called at the President's own initiative only hours after he had returned from the McKinley funeral, with four wire service representatives. In the course of a lengthy discussion of his intentions regarding the press, he said certain reporters "have always possessed my confidence and shall continue to have it. I shall be accessible to them, shall keep them posted, and trust to their discretion as to publication."[14] He left no doubt, in other words, that he would talk freely and frankly at least with those in whose discretion he had confidence.

In general, throughout his period in office, his contacts with the reporters were frequent. They ranged all the way from casual meetings with individuals, or appointments with them, to at least a few occasions on which the word was sent out for all interested to foregather at an appointed time. For example, Sullivan wrote that during the fight over railroad rate legislation, the press gallery at the Capitol was notified that the President would be available at three that afternoon. Some thirty-six appeared to hear what he had to say.[15] Perhaps the most consistent pattern was the "audience" granted while the President was being shaved in the late afternoon. Often five or six or more reporters would meet with him then, drawn both by the opportunity to question the Chief Executive and by the skill of the barber who managed to work in spite of the fact that his client would frequently spring from his chair to emphasize a point or stride up and down the room expanding on a subject for minutes at a time.[16]

Several special techniques were used by Roosevelt. He was by no means above leaking a bit of strategic information in such a way that it would do his current cause the most good. He revealed information confidentially to some newspaper men which would undercut opposition in Congress and the country to his bill to establish a Department of Commerce, in January, 1903. He authorized the reporters to use it but said they must not reveal the source. When it appeared it created the desired reaction and contributed to the success of the legislation.[17] He used the leak device in 1905 to threaten a special session on revision of the tariff in order to keep the standpatters in Congress aware that the issue was not dead.[18] The trial balloon was another instrument he is reputed to have put to good use. He would mention something he was thinking of doing to the reporters, and repudiate the idea if public reaction was unfavorable.[19]

He cemented his cordial relations with the reporters by his extreme frankness. He would talk with them for their own information on the understanding that what he said would not be printed. "Off the record" statements can be used to muzzle correspondents. If the President does not want something discussed publicly, mentioning it "off the record" effectively seals the lips of his hearers. Even if they get the same information from another source, they are still pledged to silence. Roosevelt probably did this on occasion. On the other hand he could, when he wanted to, enlist the cooperation of the newsmen not to publish something by the much more forthright method of simply asking them. He was also known to give out information that could not be printed simply because he knew the reporters would be enlightened and perhaps amused to learn what had happened behind the scenes.[20]

There was mutual advantage for both President and press in this kind of device. When the President can explain privately to reporters the whys and wherefores of a pending proposal or decision, he can enhance their own understanding, and prime them with material for use when the time is ripe for publication.[21] At the very least, he can expect his programs to be discussed with intelligence, and in a few cases may enlist personal approval and agreement, which will further color reporting. Oscar King Davis, one of the President's reportorial confidants, suggests the importance of "off the record" discussions:

> You might have an hour with the President, and talk all around the horizon, politics, diplomatic affairs, military, naval or congressional situation, money trust, labor, undesirable citizens, or what not, and yet not get out of it all a word that you could write that day. Then, within a week, something might happen that would be trivial and unimportant to one who had not had such a talk with the President, but which furnished a good story to one who had.[22]

For Roosevelt the news columns were far more important than the editorial page, and he knew access to the news columns depended more on direct relations with the journeyman reporter than with the publisher. A reporter may represent a hostile newspaper, but his private beliefs are his own, and above all, he must get the news. A source who helps to make this task easier and pleasanter, and who evokes his respect and admiration, often earns a buffer against the publisher's animus. It should be noted that T. R. had one perhaps unique advantage in dealing with the reporters. He was able to get away with his policy of seeing only those press representatives that he wanted to see and ignoring others, of singling out a few for a discussion, or one for an interview, and rarely welcoming all comers. He could play favorites in this manner because the precedent had not yet been established that all must be treated alike by the White House. Once this became the normal expectation, the flexibility Roosevelt enjoyed was far less available to his successors.

Another major element in the model is the matter of staffing. To a considerable extent, a President must be his own press agent—though as the burdens of the office have mounted, this has become far more difficult than it was in the days of the first Roosevelt, or even the second. At the same time, any modern President must equip himself with some office assistance in his dealings with the media. At the very least he must have a secretary wise in the ways of the press to carry out instructions with understanding and finesse, while doing his bit to cement personal relations with the reporters on behalf of his boss. Ideally, the President should have near him a skilled and sensitive student of public relations who can act as his alter ego in this area. Not that he needs a "press agent" in the Hollywood sense. He should never be so disinterested or so lacking in skill that he must put himself wholly into the hands of an image maker. He does need, however, supplements to his own eyes and ears, and a source of suggestions and cogent criticism.

William Loeb, Jr., who had been closely associated with Roosevelt at Albany, became at first assistant secretary to the President and then, with the elevation of George B. Cortelyou to the Cabinet, secretary in his own right.[23] Loeb's background was primarily as stenographer and secretary to political figures, rather than journalistic, but he had come in contact with many newsmen as well as politicians before going to Washington, and had an excellent grasp of the problems he was to face in press relations. Not until the Hoover administration was the position of press secretary to become formalized in the White House, but according to Louis Koenig, "Loeb was in all but name the President's press secretary."[24]

Koenig goes on to summarize Loeb's work in this role: "To the press, Loeb was a sympathetic collaborator and gentle pacificator of ruffled feelings. The kindly secretary issued statements to reporters and conducted press conferences in which he was customarily helpful, although, when necessary, he could be as bland and discreet as a polished diplomat."[25] He also handled the demand for news about private and family happenings in the White House. This demand was itself a reflection of the new journalism and of the insatiable interest the public had developed in "Teddy" and his family.[26] Loeb too had his close friends among the reporters and there were those with whom he would have nothing to do.

It is difficult at best to secure documentation for the relationship between the President and his press secretary. Such business is either handled orally or at most jotted down in a brief note with indifferent chances of survival. The following note to Loeb in T. R.'s own handwriting is probably illustrative, however, of countless oral discussions:

> Mr. Loeb, Can't the Republican papers of N. Y. N. J. Conn, Indiana and Ill. be asked to republish the Post's editorial on the attack on me this morning; & it's headlines "Parker fails to furnish proofs [sic]"[27]

In a letter to Mark Hanna that followed a conference between the Senator and the President, T. R. wrote: "I did not see any newspapermen last night, but I did this morning. Mr. Loeb last night, by my direction, told the Associated Press, Scripps-McRae, and *Sun* people that we had had a most pleasant interview, of course. . . ."[28] Again there is here a glimpse of the Loeb-Roosevelt partnership in press relations.

O. K. Davis, the *Times* Washington Bureau chief, wrote regarding a special message the President was preparing to send Congress:

> Of course I knew, from all the talk I had had with him [T.R.], just about what that message would contain. So I told Mr. Loeb, right away, that I would send a story to the *Times*, that night, giving the substance of the special message. Loeb warned me, earnestly, to look out, or the Associated Press would fine the *Times* heavily for premature publication of a document delivered in advance, and under confidence until released.[29]

Note the intimate relationship between Loeb and a correspondent, the former's knowledge of the mechanics of the newspaper business, and his concern over a detail that actually affected the reporter and his paper much more than the President. One also glimpses here again the importance of the "off the record" sessions which T. R. had with his journalistic friends.

One final aspect of the role of Secretary Loeb. The speeches, statements, and contacts with the press of Cabinet members and other administration officials at times impinge on matters of immediate concern to the President, and may help or hinder the achievement of some presidential objective, either intentionally or by inadvertence. No final institutionalized means of coordinating over-all administration public relations will probably ever be found. However, Presidents with more highly developed publicity sense have usually informally arranged for a degree of coordination via their press secretary or through some other individual in the White House.

Koenig describes the role of Loeb in this connection, assumed, undoubtedly, at the behest of the President:

> In certain respects, Loeb was the equivalent of press secretary for the entire Executive Branch. He dealt extensively with the departments in press matters. As daily routine, he collected editorials from the nation's press dealing with various aspects of Administration policy. Sometimes, he, with the President, would draft a reply, to be issued as a White House statement, and circulate both the editorial and draft reply to the departments for their comments.[30]

The secretary also kept in touch with the departments about reporters who had fallen from presidential favor to insure that they did not bypass the White House and get news elsewhere.

Another way of coordinating administration news is to centralize as much control as possible over what is to be released. In a letter to Postmaster General Payne in 1903, relating to some departmental matter, T. R. wrote: "Meanwhile I should advise against your issuing any further statements whatever." He continued that when the matter was settled, "*we* can make one clear-cut definite statement issued [sic], which shall recapitulate the whole matter, showing what has been done."[31] In 1902 he sent a one-sentence letter to Secretary of Agriculture Wilson: "Before taking any action or allowing any publication or statement in the newspapers in connection with our economic troubles with Germany over borax, consult me in full."[32] Nothing infuriated Roosevelt more than to discover that information was being leaked at the departmental level against his wishes. Here Loeb would be put on the trail to discover if possible the source of the leak.

On the positive side, there is an example in T. R.'s *Autobiography,* doubtless not unique, of a publicity campaign put on by an agency in support of one of the over-all objectives of the President: "[The] Bureau [of Forestry] undertook, through the newspaper and periodical press, to make all the people of the United States acquainted with the needs and the purposes of practical forestry. It is doubtful whether there has ever been elsewhere under the Government such effective publicity. . . ."[33] In general, much care was taken during the Roosevelt administration to get the maximum benefit out of publicity emanating from the White House *and* from the agencies, in support of the presidential program. Staff aides including Secretary Loeb and personnel in the departments became adjuncts to the efforts of Mr. Roosevelt himself.

The final aspect of T. R.'s model of presidential public relations really dates back to the days of George Washington. Yet he used the speaking tour or "swing around the circle" with consciousness of purpose and flair that set his activity apart even in this rather hackneyed area. In October, 1907, for example, according to the President's own account, he made a trip down the Mississippi River with the members of the Inland Waterways Commission which he had appointed:

> This excursion, with the meetings which were held and the wide public attention it attracted, gave the development of our inland waterways a new standing in public estimation. During the trip a letter was prepared and presented to me asking me to summon a conference on the conservation of natural resources. My intention to call such a conference was publicly announced at a great meeting at Memphis, Tennessee.[34]

This is the presidential junket as a calculated publicity device.

He made frequent trips throughout his presidency. In August,

1902, he departed on a tour of New England and the Middle West. As Pringle notes, "Vast numbers heard Roosevelt's speeches and absorbed, by listening, ideas which they never would have read."[35] In the spring of the next year he made a tour westward which brought him to the Pacific coast. "He . . . made many speeches on the journey, partly in support of the legislative program he hoped to force through Congress and partly to make more certain the presidential nomination in 1904."[36] Then in the fall of 1905, following his triumphant reelection and inauguration as President in his own right the preceding March, he made a lengthy tour of the South. His object here was to do all he could to further conciliate that section, and he was received enthusiastically.

In the age of radio and television, it is a bit difficult to see the full importance of these "swings around the circle" in Roosevelt's day, and, in fact, down to the Coolidge administration. The press aside, there was then literally no other way for the President to get himself seen and heard by the electorate. Also, there was *no* way other than this for the Chief Executive to get his message across directly to the public without the intermediary role of the press and the risks of distortion or misinterpretation involved. By going directly to the people, at least those in his immediate audience saw and heard him without any such "filter," and presumably, the press would quote *in extenso* his actual phraseology and ideas as he stated them—which would not necessarily happen in the ordinary course of White House press coverage.

As a summary of the Roosevelt publicity technique, a case study of a particular policy will show the President combining virtually all of these devices. He went all out in his effort to mobilize public opinion to force Congressional passage of the Hepburn Act tightening railroad regulation. He had first won the support of Speaker Cannon in exchange, it is thought, for an agreement not to push tariff reform. The problem then was to get the legislation through the Senate. The lame duck session of Congress (December, 1904, to March, 1905) had adjourned without the necessary Senate agreement.

Roosevelt prepared to take his case to the people. Already in January, 1905, he had spoken to, of all groups, the Union League

Club of Philadelphia on the subject. "From then until the rate issue was finally settled eighteen months later, Roosevelt maintained his fire. . . . In April and May, he campaigned through the Middle West and Southwest while en route to the annual Rough Riders' reunion at San Antonio. . . . Early in the fall he even went into the Southeast where he . . . declaimed on the need for railroad legislation."[37] Interspersing these direct appeals to the people, he rang the changes on his various techniques with the press. The "press conference," mentioned earlier, to which some thirty-six reporters came in May, 1906, had been called to hear a presidential discussion of an acceptable amendment to a key provision of the bill.

Mark Sullivan devotes a good many pages to the press aspects of T. R.'s battle for his Hepburn bill. One chapter subhead reads, "Roosevelt Takes to Head-Lines" and contains a detailed account of the drumfire of stories emanating from the President and also from agencies of the federal government, all concentrating on the railroad control problem. One headline, appearing on December 11, 1905, read: "Attorney-General Moody Directs All United States Attorneys to Prosecute All Railroads Shown to be Giving Rebates." As this campaign progressed, Sullivan writes: "The cannonade of head-lines took on cumulative frequency—occasionally, indeed, two or more jostled each other on the same front page, the general saturation of the atmosphere causing *Life* to remark, plaintively, that 'there are a few solvent and respectable persons left in the country who have not yet been investigated.' "[38]

Supplementing what he calls "the superb art [T. R.] had of stirring up sentiment through the newspapers,"[39] Sullivan goes on to discuss "Roosevelt's Literary Allies." "Roosevelt, in marshalling public opinion for the railroad rate bill, had, as always, help from the magazine writers."[40] Articles berating the railroads and parading their sins and shortcomings or supporting the proposals of the administration appeared in *McClure's* for March, 1906, and *The Outlook* for April 7. An article in *The World's Work* by Henry Beach Needham, "the most devoted of Roosevelt's 'fair-haired boys,' " attacked directly the recalcitrant Senate group. In short, the President clearly and deliberately was bringing to bear here the full range of weapons in his arsenal for stirring public opinion and focusing it upon a reluctant Congress. The swing around the country, his contacts with the working press, his fabled ability to create news, and his invaluable influence with the popular journals of the day and their writers were all exploited. Here was full utilization of the tools of publicity and the new journalism, as Theodore Roosevelt had fashioned them.

II

Roosevelt had done more than set a new tactical pattern for presidential leadership of opinion. He unquestionably left the office bigger and more important and more a focus of attention in the eyes of the public than it had been before him. This had long-term consequences for all of his successors, and a particularly poignant meaning for his chosen heir, the affable and slow-moving William Howard Taft. Throughout the latter's term of office, he was forced to live under the shadow of his predecessor. The public had become habituated to the activism and pyrotechnic displays of Roosevelt, and Taft either could not or would not (probably both) attempt to duplicate them. In short, there had to be a letdown. One of the morals of Will Taft's unhappy situation was that though the office of President is highly plastic in the hands of each succeeding holder of it, precedent *does* shape and fix some of its broad contours in a way that is difficult, if not impossible, wholly to alter in the future.

Taft's personality and his attitude toward the presidency were in sharp contrast to Roosevelt's. The faithful Archie Butt, who served both men, and had opportunity to observe them closely, put the difference succinctly: "Mr. Roosevelt understood the necessity of guiding the press to suit one's own ends; President Taft has no conception of the press as an adjunct to his office."[41] This was the matter in a nutshell. Taft to this extent was an anachronism in the office. Though miserable and out of place in the period 1908-1912, he might well have ranked among the successful Presidents if he had had the good fortune to precede T. R. rather than follow him. Henry F. Pringle, who had also written a biography of Roosevelt, emphasized Taft's "inability to popularize or make exciting his accomplishments."[42]

The Taft administration represented a hiatus in the development of presidential leadership of opinion, if not actually a retrograde step. Some who have written on presidential press relations maintain that it was Taft and not his successor Wilson who originated the regular press conference open to all accredited newsmen. The weight of the evidence, however, seems to suggest that Taft behaved much as Roosevelt had done. He did, unquestionably, see large groups of reporters on at least a few occasions. The veteran correspondent, Bascom Timmons, wrote: "I attended only one press conference in the Taft administration."[43] Major Butt wrote regarding the reporters that had followed the President to Beverly, Massachusetts, during his summer holiday in 1909, that he had spent most of the day fending them off and finally persuaded Taft to meet them in a group.

The evidence is so persuasive that Taft did not like meeting with reporters, made himself inaccessible whenever possible, and often made serious missteps when he did see them, that it seems unlikely he held many general press conferences.[44] The assertion that he did may have come from Gus Karger, the one correspondent who had been close to Taft personally. Writing a decade later in the rosy afterglow of hindsight, he published an article in 1919 in *Editor and Publisher*[45] in which he mentioned "regular conferences." Other writers perhaps merely repeated a statement which it seemed possible to take at face value. Fred Essary, himself a longtime Washington correspondent, makes the same assertion, rather surprisingly, since he, more than most, should have been in a position to check the facts.

This difference of view on the origin of the regular press conference points up a major difficulty in studying the presidency in general, and press relations in particular. Much that goes on is not likely to be committed to paper at all. Obviously, in those days, press meetings were not quoted in full in the newspapers, and reporters were not even allowed to attribute to the President much of what they were told. Even within the White House, systematic transcription of the exchanges and their preservation in White

House files had not begun. Examination of the *New York Times* for the first months of the Taft administration turned up only one reference to a meeting of the President with reporters, and that was on his second day in office—quite possibly the courtesy call which O. K. Davis remembered as coming on inauguration day itself. Nor were the stories written about administration happenings put in such a way as to suggest that the information had come directly from the President.

If Taft did not pioneer the mass press conference, what were his relations with the correspondents? Arthur Dunn, who was in the group that followed the presidential party to Beverly, claims to have overheard the President, in the course of reluctantly agreeing to see the reporters, say impatiently: "Must I see those men again! Didn't I see them just the other day?"[46] Taft, as President, soon lost his former good nature and "had a manner of snarling in the presence of newspapermen."[47] Archie Butt wrote: "I met a number of correspondents. . . . They were each one of them complaining bitterly of the fact that they could get no news these days from the White House. 'Only this afternoon,' said (O. K.) Davis, 'he killed four good stories. . . .' "[48] Clearly the President did not seek to cultivate or even cooperate with the working press, nor did he sense the need for discretion in their presence, and above all, far from creating news favorable to himself, he hampered their work, perhaps unintentionally.

Taft's personal failings as a publicist seemed to extend to his secretariat as well. It was said of Fred Carpenter, the first of the several presidential secretaries who came and went during the Taft regime:

> He was a shy, reserved, quiet chap, who had been private secretary to Mr. Taft in the War Department, after serving with him in the Philippines. There had been nothing in his experience to develop any political instinct he might have had, and, if there had been, Mr. Taft was not the man to permit the same sort of relations between himself and his secretary that Mr. Roosevelt had fostered between himself and Mr. Loeb.[49]

By 1910 Charles D. Norton, a former assistant secretary of the Treasury, had replaced Carpenter. Davis surmises that Norton had talked over the whole situation thoroughly with the President when he took the job, "for there was an immediate and distinct improvement in the relations between the President and the newspaper men." It was no longer such a rare thing to get an appointment with the President, even on short notice.[50]

Actually, it appears that the most valuable "press relations" work done for Taft was not done by his secretaries at all but by others, including his military aide, Major Butt, and his reporter confidant, Gus Karger. It has been said of Karger that he "had access to the Executive at all times, was permitted to examine the White House mail daily, and to know all that went on behind the scenes." He did not, however, use his entree for his own advantage alone, but "gave to every newspaper man interested every line of news which he drew from White House sources during the whole Taft period. He was an extremely valuable aid to Mr. Taft in getting the Taft viewpoint before the public. . . ."[51] Fred Essary goes on to wonder why, with five secretaries to the President during his four years in office, Karger had never been appointed.

Archie Butt had served a year or two as aide to Roosevelt and Taft kept him on as his aide. Butt acquired a considerable gift as presidential confidant and adviser—almost a proprietary interest in the welfare of Taft—as well as the role of leisure companion, which from 1909 on meant many hours on the golf course. He saw clearly Taft's deficiencies as a publicist and did all that he could in subtle and sometimes not so subtle ways to help the President put himself across to the public. He knew many of the reporters well and did what he could in individual conversations with them. For example, he would persuade the President to go to a baseball game in Washington, and then maneuver him into sitting in the bleachers where he would be in view of the crowd and appear a "regular fellow" with the common touch, rather than in a box, where he wanted to sit. Neither Karger nor Butt, from their positions, however, could substitute for a skillful presidential secretary. But no secretary could have done the job without more willing cooperation from the President himself.

A comparison of the Roosevelt "swing around the circle" with the considerable traveling that Taft did is revealing. Basically,

T. R. enjoyed these jaunts hugely and made the most of them, while his successor went, on advice from his intimates, with considerable reluctance. Not that he did not like to travel, because he did, on any pretext. Travel for Taft was escape from the chores that confronted him in Washington more than anything else. His reaction to a speaking tour was quite a different matter. "If it were not for the speeches, I should look forward with the greatest pleasure to this trip," he told his military aide, just before a tour in the fall of 1909. Butt predicted accurately that when the journey started, Taft still would not have put pen to paper on a single speech preparation, for all his good resolutions to do so well in advance.

Furthermore, this particular tour had a kind of *ex post facto* quality about it that was quite uncharacteristic of Roosevelt's journeys. It was undertaken on advice of the Republican leaders to undo some of the reputed damage done to the party by the passage of the Payne-Aldrich tariff, before the 1910 mid-term elections.[52] Undoubtedly swings around the country are more valuable to stimulate favorable public opinion toward pending policies than as fire brigade operations after the damage has been done. Butt mentions another problem—one of detail, to be sure, but symptomatic of Taft's difficulty in making public appearances generally. He could not be persuaded to return the greetings of a crowd, or even to turn his head and notice that people were there hoping for a sign of recognition from the Chief Executive. That he should be unaware of the need for so elementary a gesture, or unwilling to give it if aware, suggests how far he was from being able to exploit the potential of the office under the conditions that had obtained since the advent of the new journalism and the White House incumbency of the redoubtable Rough Rider.

☆☆☆☆☆☆☆

Chapter 3

☆☆☆☆☆☆☆

INNOVATION: WOODROW WILSON

Woodrow Wilson came to the presidency at a period when more attention had been focused upon the office than, perhaps, ever before in its history. The new journalism was reaching its peak as a channel for communicating Washington news to an ever widening circle of readers. Progressivism, the muckrakers, the contemporary campaigns for governmental reform, etc., had focused attention on national political figures as never before. Then there had been Roosevelt himself. Since before the turn of the century he had remained a fount of colorful copy, in office or out. In short, one can assume that there existed an unprecedented awareness of matters political, and particularly of the presidency, personified in the individuals who occupied this office. The other side of the same coin was no doubt a public receptivity to leadership from the White House which could hardly have been matched in earlier history.

In this sense, then, Wilson was in a position to make his administration a kind of watershed in the development of the presidency. In the cyclical pattern of major reform, the Wilson administration does represent an important landmark. It also represents a landmark in the development of the office itself, and, particularly, in that of presidential leadership of opinion. The career and administration of T. R. had paved the way. The Great War, as the greatest news event to date in the history of the new journalism, and in many ways the greatest challenge yet to face the national government and its executive arm, was also bound to leave the office permanently changed. Wilson was both the beneficiary of these developments and the creator of techniques and precedents of great future importance.

The Wilson administration falls naturally into two major segments. The first corresponds with the peacetime period of domestic reform and involves exploitation of the newspaper press. The second embraces the war years and includes an attempt to devise means for the White House to communicate with the public *directly*, bypassing the press as intermediary. The early period saw the President inaugurating mass press conferences held on a regular basis and open to all eligible reporters; the latter centered on the spectacular activities of George Creel and the Committee on Public Information.

The frank acceptance by Roosevelt of the realities of the press as it had been developing, and his skillful cultivating of the journalistic fraternity, were unlikely to recommend themselves to Wilson as either desirable or legitimate. Wilson's attitude toward journalism and its minions contrasted sharply with Theodore Roosevelt's. The former was reserved, rather shy, and his Southern upbringing and deep commitment to the rather austere Presbyterian faith fostered a natural dignity which forbade the easy camaraderie in which T. R. reveled.[1] Wilson was also an academician and an intellectual. Aside from involvement in campus politics as president of Princeton, his election to the New Jersey governorship in 1910 was his first immersion in the rough and tumble of public life. The transition from cloister to State House and White House meant his first continuing contact with the press. It meant also the shift from a world in which ideas were savored for their own sake, where precision of expression was valued, where a measure of intellectual sophistication was taken for granted, and where issues were settled characteristically if not invariably through more or less rational discussion into the hurly-burly of politics. In politics most of these assumptions are frequently reversed. An academic career of studying government, especially in Wilson's day, did not necessarily fully prepare one for the brutally pragmatic and seemingly sordid realities of political practice.

The President had always had an academic appreciation both of the leadership potential of the White House and of the great importance and potency of publicity. One surmises, though, that what he really meant by publicity for an idea or policy was closely akin to a "lecture" presentation of it.[2] That is, he seems to have been concerned almost exclusively with the *content* of a public utterance. As a result of this preoccupation he was largely oblivious to the problem of the means of *conveying* ideas to the public, and the manipulation of these means; also he refused to believe that news about a public figure should contain anything except matter relating to his ideas and beliefs.[3] Finally, he assumed that such ideas and beliefs should and would be transmitted to the public intact without either alteration or distorting commentary.[4]

These generalizations emerge clearly from the voluminous literature about Wilson's public life. Ray Stannard Baker, for example, describes the candidate's reaction to the descent upon his summer quarters at Sea Girt, New Jersey, of the swarm of news hungry reporters, at the time of his nomination. He assumed initially that they should be greeted in his small study as social rather than business callers. He began the first session with a far more than perfunctory apology for the lack of sufficient chairs. Baker's account then goes on:

> 'Well, Governor,' remarked a New York police reporter. 'You've got the first page now. Hang on to it. You've got the edge on Teddy and we want a lot of good stuff from you.'
>
> Another chimed in: 'We are all on space down here, Governor, and the more we can play you up the more we can increase our checks at the end of the week.'
>
> The Governor looked over at the first man and smiled: he thought it was a joke. He did not smile quite so broadly at the second man.[5]

Several things emerge from this exchange. The President-to-be was here dealing, obviously, with a sample of the working press that heavily overrepresented the "sob-sisters" and hack reporters, while underrepresenting those with whom he might have dealt on terms of equality and confidence. Yet the fact that his only reaction to these rather bold suggestions was to recoil in disgust underscores his inability to understand and accept the realities of the new journalism and especially its insatiable appetite for human interest material. Nor could he grasp the extent to which this appetite can be turned to one's own account.

Even earlier, the speaking tour Wilson was persuaded to undertake as a means of furthering his candidacy furnished insight into his reactions to the demands of the press. To quote Frank Stockbridge, who accompanied him:

> On the way to Denver, examining the schedule for the stop there, he [Wilson] noted the time set apart to receive the press. 'Do I have to go through that again?' he asked. 'Everywhere we stop, Governor,' I assured him. It took a deal of explaining to make him see the difference between himself as local news feature and himself as a man with a message. The message would be telegraphed, but in every town he would be a personality of current local interest and would have to resign himself to that fact. He learned to do this with outward grace, but with much inward protest.[6]

Stockbridge here puts his finger on the nub of the matter. Wilson, throughout his career, could not bring himself to accept the fact that he and his family were news, in addition to the obvious news value of his public utterances as such. The occasions when he took the reporters to task for invading the privacy of his family, reporting false information about the loves of his daughters, and the like, are well known. His daughter Eleanor, writing many years later, said her father "resented almost fiercely the attempts to pry into family affairs and tried to protect us as much as he could. I have always believed that the first rumors of his 'aloofness' and 'unfriendliness' were the result of his annoyance at this first onslaught upon us."[7]

A good example of the failure of the President to understand or at any rate to comply with one of the mechanical requirements of good press coverage is in the matter of the advance distribution of speech texts. The importance of advance circulation before delivery is obvious. Wilson's habits and inclinations here to some degree paralleled Taft's, though not, one assumes, from slothfulness. Stockbridge again writes: "Governor Wilson had agreed to dictate the outlines of his addresses in advance, but ten days before the date set for the beginning of the [1911] trip he had not written a word of them. On my insistent urging he hurriedly prepared the first two. . . . These were immediately put in type and delivered to the press associations, to be mailed to their constituent newspapers subject to telegraphic release when delivered."[8] He goes on to note that this had to be done at least a week in advance to insure the broadest circulation.

Stockbridge then describes the elaborate preparations he had to undertake to provide stenographers at each stop for Wilson to use, in order to achieve the kind of dissemination for the Governor's words which alone would wring the most from the trip. "This was all new and extremely irksome to Mr. Wilson," he noted.[9] Baker, discussing the same swing around, has the would-be candidate complaining, regarding advance speech preparation: "But it is not my way, . . . I cannot make speeches to a stenographer."[10] Even in the latter phases of his presidency Wilson never seems to have reconciled himself to this urgent publicity requirement. Baker notes an episode during the war in which George Creel requests the advance text of a speech to insure "proper world circulation" and is told that he can have it if it is finished in time. Wilson also accepted in his reply to Creel the latter's promised guarantee of secrecy but implied that this concern had been another major reason for refusing advance texts in the past. Here the President's mistrust of the working press rather than speech writing habits was uppermost in his mind.

Though most of Wilson's attitudes toward the press and publicity remained more or less constant during all of his public career, Eleanor Wilson McAdoo, in the passage quoted above, hints that there was a kind of traumatic disillusionment involved in those first encounters with the correspondents, which colored his dealings with them thereafter. James Kerney also makes a parallel observation. Noting the accessibility of Wilson to the press while Governor, he writes: "In the closing days at Trenton the President-elect displayed unusual irritation at the newspapers. It was at this juncture that there began the amazing transformation from the Wilson pitiless publicity to that of the Wilson closed door."[11]

In spite of the fact that he had grown less sanguine about the journalistic trade by the time he took office in Washington, or perhaps in a sense because of this, the new President did take the unprecedented step of inaugurating regular semiweekly press conferences.[12] Baker gives ground for wondering if disillusionment did not in part motivate this departure from precedent. Referring to the "open door" policy with reporters in the early Governorship period, he goes on: "The experience had been difficult and painful but he had considered it a part of his programme for taking the people fully into his confidence. He had found the practice expensive both in time and in strength."[13] It was time-consuming because an interview granted to one reporter meant that others clamored for equal treatment, resulting, presumably, in what seemed an inefficient need to repeat things several times. His health was not sufficiently robust to stand up to unlimited demands upon his energy. Hence he determined to cut out all attendance at public functions for the first year, and, writes Baker: "In pursuance of this new policy of concentration, he both restricted and liberalized the relationships of the President with press correspondents."[14]

By liberalizing these relationships Baker means, of course, that under the Wilson conference scheme reporters had a kind of "right" of access which had not been enjoyed earlier. Even a President like T. R. retained the prerogative firmly in his own hands to see those whom he wanted to see and ignore or even exile others. The restriction came from the fact that the system of regular conferences raised a strong presumption against individual interviews or individual access to the Chief Executive in general—in the name of equal treatment[15]—and also meant the confining of presidential availability to the two semiweekly confrontations.

Discussion of these Wilson press conferences would, until recently, have had to rest on very slender resources of direct information, and the somewhat contradictory accounts of contemporary observers and participants. It was therefore fortunate that the papers of Charles Swem, the President's personal stenographer, when donated to Princeton University Library in 1957, were found to contain what appear to be fifty-seven full or partial transcripts of Wilson press conferences.[16]

In general they were held on Mondays and Thursdays, apparently, though the pattern shown in the sample seems rather erratic. Up to December, 1914, all but five of the forty-three transcripts in that period are dated either Monday or Thursday, while from December on, all the remaining ones in the file through 1915 are dated Tuesday. (It can be assumed that even a fairly regular schedule was abandoned in the middle of that year.)[17] One suspects from this that during 1915 Wilson had reduced his meetings with the reporters to one a week, held on Tuesdays. Further point is given to this suggestion in the *New York Times* account of the single conference found for 1916: "President Wilson today resumed his conferences with newspaper correspondents after a suspension since July, 1915. Hereafter he will receive the correspondents every Monday afternoon."[18] This once-a-week schedule seems not to have materialized, from all accounts, but may reflect a similar pattern earlier.

The content of the transcripts raises several questions. To what extent does it appear that these conferences were used by Wilson, who saw his role as that of strong leader, as a part of his effort to educate the public and influence Congress? In general, it is probably true that he was far less inclined to take the kind of deliberate and premeditated advantage of this forum than was his Assistant Secretary of the Navy, Franklin Roosevelt, some years later. The former had a more rigid and narrowly defined conception of the proprieties of the office which seems to have permitted the "teaching" of the public, via the press, but ruled out anything smacking of manipulation of the reporters, or of the public through them.

More specifically, he appeared to *offer* himself for questioning rather than take the initiative in guiding the conferences in some predetermined direction. This by no means destroyed their value to him, but did rule out certain obvious uses to which they might have been put, and left things largely in the hands of the reporters. The conferences represented by the surviving transcripts tend to divide roughly into three major categories. There were those in which the reporters quizzed him repeatedly on one particular subject of immediate interest, such as the Mexican situation, seeking to elicit information or evidence of policy direction, and in which the President fended them off and fenced with them because there was nothing of consequence he was willing to discuss. Second, and similar to the first, were conferences in which a series of subjects would be canvassed in the same relatively unproductive fashion. Finally, there were transcripts in which a more communicative Chief Executive in response to questions, would discourse at length, and in considerable technical detail, on one of the administration's proposals then being framed or debated.

The first two categories are of less interest than the third, which best illustrates the exceedingly useful role some of the conferences played in Wilsonian legislative leadership—if not wholly by his design. In five particularly, the President is seen explaining his proposals to the press at length. Two related to Federal Trade Commission and general antimonopoly legislation, and one each to the tariff, currency reform (the Federal Reserve System), and a ship purchase bill after the war in Europe had broken out.

The conference held on Friday, June 23, 1913, will offer a good illustration. This was the same day on which the President had gone before Congress to ask for legislation setting up the Federal Reserve System. The meeting opened thus:

> Mr. President, just to start off, I wonder whether you are ready to tell us anything in answer to the criticisms of the proposal to make a purely governmental board in command of the currency situation. You don't say anything about that in your message.
>
> No, I don't say anything about that; because I didn't want to discuss the terms of the measure. I simply wanted to urge the necessity for action by Congress. I don't want to be quoted on this, but I want to give it to you men for your own thought: there are only two choices, of course; either to give the central control to the bankers or to give it to the government. I don't see any other.

This introduced a lengthy discussion of the intricacies of the proposed legislation. The questions were long and often technical, and the answers equally so. In reply to one as to why some provision had been taken out of the bill before submission, the President said: "Now, I want to explain to you gentlemen why it was stricken out; because I am giving you the benefit of all I know this morning, without desiring this to be a public discussion at all." This, again, was the beginning of a very long answer of nearly a page and a half in the transcript. All in all, the conference, devoted almost entirely to this single subject, is strikingly similar to some of F.D.R.'s during his first term, when he would take the reporters into his confidence "for background use only" on some pending measure.

In the *Times* the next day,[19] the message to Congress was the lead story, with a lengthy continuation on page two, and the text of the message as well as comment on it. At least a column of the coverage came directly from the news conference, and was introduced: "In the course of the day the President made a splendid defense of the currency bill and met the suggestions and arguments of visitors to the White House. . . ." There then followed a detailed discussion of the measure, drawn from the questions and answers. His press conference thus had provided a vehicle for the President to use to supplement the generalizations in the message itself.

On January 26 and March 12, 1914, the Federal Trade Commission legislation was a major conference topic. At the former encounter, after about half the time had gone by, the discussion shifted:

> Mr. President, have you anything new in [on?] your trust programme?
>
> No, nothing at all.
>
> No new developments?
>
> No.
>
> With reference to this question of holding companies, is it intended to bar subsidiary corporations that are organized to comply with some particular local law?

Again this began a lengthy interchange comprising detailed questions and extended answers. The *Times* of the following day carried a story of some nineteen column inches on page seven, drawn from the discussion, headed: "Trade Commission to 'Smell Around.'" The conference of March 12 followed essentially the same pattern. It netted about four and a half column inches, on page one, headed: "Not to Define Trust Law." In both instances, clearly, the President was able to convey thus to the public some detailed information and explanation on a major legislative project. As the quoted passage suggests, however, at least in the first of these, the result obtained seemed hardly premeditated on his part.

On the shipping bill, at the press meeting of February 2, 1915, the discussion (and the conference) began:

> Mr. President, can you say anything about the shipping bill?
>
> That needn't bother you.
>
> It does.
>
> Well, you must not let it.
>
> It doesn't bother us, Mr. President, we just want to know about it.
>
> It is going through all right.
>
> With some changes, Mr. President?
>
> No changes of any sort that is not consistent with the principle of the bill.

In spite of this rather unpromising beginning, the President was drawn into a long exchange on the legislation and gave fairly full and detailed answers. The *Times* printed a page one, column one story the next day headlined: "Offer to Modify Shipping Bill," which contained some indirect references to the press conference in the first part, and then in the continuation, carried the subhead: "President Outlines His Views," followed by, "In his interview with the correspondents President Wilson. . . ."[20]

In a final example Mr. Wilson deliberately took the initiative in using the conference as a channel of communication to Congress and public. Part way through the meeting of May 15, 1913, he interjected the following, right after an answer on another subject: "There is one question which, if I am properly informed, I would ask me, if I were you!" Involved was a rumor that had been going the rounds that he was willing to compromise on the wool schedule in the tariff bill. Having established the existence of the rumor, he said: "Well, when you get a chance, just say that I am not the kind that considers compromises when I once take my position. Just note that down, so that there will be nothing more of the sort transmitted in the press." This presidential assertion formed the basis of an article headlined "Tariff Compromise Spurned by Wilson" the next day.[21]

There were other occasions on which the President took the initiative. On at least four, in the transcripts available, he opened the conference with a statement he obviously had been considering well in advance. For example: "Well, I will start the ball rolling by saying that these yarns about our sending marines to Mexico City are nothing but yarns." On another occasion he said that Tumulty had reminded him to clear up a misapprehension on the Panama tolls controversy. At the beginning of the conference of August 3, 1914, he talked to the reporters at length on the importance of using discretion, in view of the developments in Europe. Though these instances are partial exceptions to the rule, and though much that was useful for his policy leadership did come out of his encounters with the working press, President Wilson did not apparently view the press conferences as forums to be exploited aggressively by the Executive.

Much has been written about how he actually disliked these twice a week meetings, how he sought an excuse for ending them, and finally found it in the increasingly tense international situation following the sinking of the *Lusitania*. George Creel quotes him in response to a request he resume the conferences: "It is a waste of time, . . . I prepared for the conferences as carefully as for a Cabinet meeting, and discussed questions of the day frankly and fully . . . [but] I soon discovered that the interest of the majority was in the trivial and personal."[22] In the beginning, of course, he had talked of "pitiless publicity" and his desire "to take the people of the country into his confidence."[23]

The transcripts preserved by Swem suggest that the President's reaction was neither as uniformly negative at the time as he himself later recalled, nor consistently favorable either. Neither do they show a man always tense and aloof, as other commentators describe him during them.[24] He was adept at injecting a humorous story or quotation to turn aside a question or imply an answer he did not want to state. Once, when asked whether he would compromise a certain provision of the tariff bill, he told a story of Lincoln's about a little girl grown so sleepy playing with her alphabet blocks at bedtime that she could only say, in lieu of her prayers: "Oh, Lord, I am too sleepy to pray; there are the letters, spell it out for yourself."

There is also ample evidence that the reporters nettled him on occasion. When asked about one matter he replied, "No, that is all 'guff,' pure 'guff'." Then when the question was being rephrased, Wilson cut in: "How many forms are you going to ask the same question in? I have answered it." Again, a reporter referred to something as being in the President's mind and was asked, "When did you discover that that was in my mind?"

On the other hand there were frequent occasions when he took the reporters into his confidence and gave them "off the record" information on some delicate matter. This would suggest an atmosphere of mutual trust, rather than one of muted hostility. No less than ten times in the existing transcripts, the President said "if I may say this just among ourselves," or "That is just for your information," or "I would rather you gentlemen would not quote me on that subject, but I am perfectly willing to show you my mind about it," or "Now, this is just for your own ears, for your own guidance." Here again Wilson's conferences read very much like those of Roosevelt two decades later.

In sum, these Wilson meetings with newsmen were the diametric opposite of the audiences T. R. granted to his favorites. The President under the new scheme gave up control over who could attend (though he did try to banish an occasional offender).[25] Since Wilson also made no attempt to guide the discussions, initiative regarding content as well as attendance passed to the correspondent group. One cannot help but feel that they used this new-found access and freedom with more vigor than tact. They assumed the right to "worry" a particular subject like a dog with a bone, and badger the President for an answer until they either got it or his evident annoyance forced them to desist. Both Wilson's self-imposed rule of passivity at the conferences, and the relative paucity of really newsworthy question subjects in that more leisurely day, aggravated these tendencies.

President Wilson, though he made but modest use of his press conferences, was still strikingly successful in winning public support for his policies and administration. His exceedingly fortunate choice of a secretary "wise in the ways of the press" and able to make up in considerable measure for his own weakness as publicist was partly responsible.[26] Clearly either a President had to be able to manage these matters himself, or he had to provide himself with staff that could supply his limitations. Though Theodore Roosevelt remained his own best guide in public relations, he nevertheless had had as secretary a man well qualified to supplement these considerable abilities. It is interesting to speculate how Wilson's career would have turned out had he been as poorly provided with staff as his unfortunate predecessor, Taft.

Joseph P. Tumulty had been with his boss in the New Jersey State House as secretary and it was natural that Wilson should take him to the White House as well. What the rather austere and dignified President lacked in human warmth and gregariousness was more than made up for by the personal qualities of the genial Irishman. Not that he could wholly make up for the alleged failings of "the Governor," as he persisted in calling Wilson, but at least as far as the reporters were concerned, he could and did maintain close relations with them, gave them aid and comfort whenever possible, and interpreted them to his boss and his boss to them.[27] In a real sense he was the intermediary, the broker, between these two entities whose contacts otherwise remained at best formal and reserved.

It was Tumulty, not the President, one can safely assume, who kept the whole range and pattern of administration publicity and public relations under constant review and who laid the plans for improving them. He held daily conferences of his own with the reporters who frequented the White House and thus kept in touch with their thinking and the issues their queries brought to his attention. He directed the compilation of the "yellow journal" of press clippings and editorial comment which was traditionally prepared in the White House for the President. The daily editions of this "journal" went home with him at night for careful study. He knew how to extract the greatest possible advantage from a human interest story, and was skillful in the art of building up expectations in advance of an impending speech or event.

The President claimed that Tumulty was the one person—other than himself—who played a significant role in the composition of major speeches. He told Ida Tarbell that his method involved, first, a draft written in his own shorthand to save time, which he himself then transcribed and revised on the famous little typewriter. After that, he noted, the manuscript was usually ready for the printer with little if any further change. He rarely consulted anyone else on speeches that were peculiarly his own, like an acceptance speech, but sometimes, "when it seems specially important that I be understood, I try it on Tumulty, who has a very extraordinary appreciation of how a thing will get over the foot lights. He is the most valuable audience I have."[28]

David Lawrence seems to have been justified in writing, "Time and again, Secretary Tumulty revealed the President's views and articulated the administration viewpoint with more skill than the President showed in his conferences with the newspapermen."[29] Without him, Wilson would have been far less successful in dealing with public opinion. Tumulty's greatest importance coincided with the period before April, 1917. This was the era of domestic reform. Skillful handling of public relations was particularly necessary for success. The importance of his intermediary role doubtless became even greater in 1915, when the conferences between the reporters and the President tapered off and virtually ceased entirely. This left Tumulty as the sole remaining link between the two.

On April 14, 1917, eight days after America had declared war, President Wilson signed an executive order setting up the famous Committee on Public Information, with George Creel as its chairman and virtual personification. With brief exceptions, from then on, according to his biographer John M. Blum, Tumulty left public relations matters to Creel. He eliminated his own official daily press conferences and reduced all his work in this area to a minimum, while intensifying his efforts as a buffer between the President and the world, in response to the latter's increasing desire to be left alone. Tumulty did remain an unofficial guide to the reporters, and continued to do his best to keep relations between them and his boss as cordial as the rather difficult circumstances during the war permitted.

Before dealing with the war years themselves, another early Wilson innovation deserves discussion: his revival of the direct presidential address to Congress. This carried a theoretical as well as a practical significance which has only been partially recognized. Wilson obviously could not have lived happily with complete dependence on the press. (Even Theodore Roosevelt had used the swing around the circle to supplement newspaper publicity.) The professor in the White House had developed a personal distaste for the reporters as a group, seemingly, and his whole approach to publicity led to impatience with the medium they represented. Arthur Link, for example, has written that "His chief instruments in achieving a position as national spokesman were of course oratory and public messages . . . ,"[30] implying, by omitting mention of it, a lesser role for the press as such. At least one other commentator seems to doubt that Wilson really ever sought "to win the press."[31]

When the President had dealt with the reporters, as in his experiment with press conferences, he had done so in part because he felt on theoretical grounds that he should, and also because they were there and could hardly be ignored.[32] But he dealt with them in a spirit of passive resignation. His *active* interest in matters of public opinion leadership and the dissemination of ideas he reserved for other channels. Ray Stannard Baker, in discussing the President's problem of reaching the people, concludes: "The radio, if it had been in use at that time, might have proved a godsend to Wilson: for he would have been able to secure direct contact with his public, broadening his influence as the fragmentary reporting of his addresses could not do."[33] Without the radio, of course, the newspapers had to remain a party in some degree to any dissemination of matter from the White House. And yet there were ways of minimizing this intermediary role, as the new Chief Executive seemed to sense very early in his first term. The revival of the Washington and Adams practice of addressing Congress in person was motivated in large measure, it seems clear, by this desire to bypass the press. As he no doubt foresaw, this forum would so concentrate public attention as to eliminate the likelihood that the newspapers would either slight or distort his message.

The first of these personal appearances before joint sessions took place on April 8, 1913, before the special session he had called, and barely a month after he had taken office.[34] It dealt with tariff revision. Wilson's reply to his wife's mention of the fact that Roosevelt had not thought of such an appearance, as they drove back to the White House ("Yes, I think I put one over on Teddy") was significant.[35] Neither Wilson nor contemporary observers were unaware of the importance of what he had done. The *New York Times* commented editorially the next day: "The wonder is that in seven years Theodore Roosevelt never thought of this way of stamping his personality upon his age."[36] Baker comments that Wilson lost no time in following up the advantage he had thus gained, by appearing the very next day in the President's room of the Senate for a conference with the members of the Finance Committee, who would be responsible for the new tariff legislation. "These vigorous innovations occasioned an enormous amount of publicity. The country at large was vastly interested, amused, impressed."[37]

Twice more during 1913 did the President ride to the Capitol to address joint sessions: on June 23, to launch his currency reform proposals, and then on August 27, to discuss the Mexican situation. In 1914 he appeared before Congress four times. Again two of these appearances were designed to highlight major elements in his legislative program: trusts and monopolies on January 20, and revision of the policy on Panama Canal tolls on March 5. April 20 saw him explaining a new turn in the continuing crisis in Mexican relations; on September 4 he delivered an appeal for more revenue. No personal appearances are recorded for 1915, but once in 1916 and three times in 1917, before his second inauguration, he went to discuss the mounting European crisis. The one remaining address to a joint session during his first term came in August, 1916, on the railroad strike then in progress. Thus between March 4, 1913, and March 4, 1917, he made no less than twelve personal appearances before one or both houses of Congress (not including Annual Messages).

David Houston, who spent eight years in the Wilson Cabinet, wrote in his autobiography: "He [Wilson] believes that he can lead better, can get nearer to Congress, and convey his message more impressively to the people by delivering his message in person."[38] Both the substance and pattern of the messages Wilson read before joint sessions lend support to the same theory. Seven during the first term had to do with specific legislative proposals which he doubtless wanted to dramatize in the most forceful possible way in order to focus public attention on Congress and hasten enactment. In the five other cases, there is even stronger evidence that enhanced publicity and direct access to the ear of the *public* were the prime objectives of the journey to Capitol Hill. In each of these latter, there was no immediate legislative objective at all. Hence his purpose could only have been to acquaint the Congress, ostensibly, but actually the public, with his views on a crisis situation in Mexico or Europe.

The pattern with an average of approximately three per year during the first term, in addition to the importance of the subjects, lends further support to the theory that Wilson was making these personal appearances a central element, if not *the* central element, in his strategy for leading public opinion. He went before Congress rarely enough not to lose through boredom the public attention he had first captured, and yet frequently enough to preserve a sense of continuity, as he shifted public attention from one major policy or problem to another. "His appearance before Congress called attention vividly and dramatically to the cause he was championing; it focused public attention," Baker wrote of the tariff message.[39]

The personal appearances continued during the second term. Between the call for a declaration of war against Germany on April 2, 1917, and the onset of his illness in late 1919, the President went to address Congress ten more times, or with about the same average frequency as earlier. Twice he spoke only to the Senate: on woman suffrage and to present the Versailles Treaty. Five times he went to ask for legislation or discuss domestic problems. The remaining occasions saw him using joint sessions as a sounding board for discussion of the Fourteen Points, the war aims of Germany and Austria, and to mark the signing of the Armistice.

A final point on these messages (and a characteristic they tended to share with the later Roosevelt fireside chats) deserves mention. As Richard Longaker put it, "They were not portmanteau messages of the Theodore Roosevelt variety but were brief and contained a single, well-prepared request."[40] T. R. had been in the habit of putting everything but the kitchen sink into his lengthy disquisitions, thereby losing the punch which both Wilson and F.D.R. achieved in their brief addresses, designed usually to highlight only one issue or proposal.[41]

Returning now to the Committee on Public Information, the idea seems to have been Wilson's own.[42] It may well have been foreshadowed by his desire for direct access to the public through visits to Congress, and by a proposal he had once made for a "national publicity bureau." Baker asserts that this latter idea had grown out of his exasperation with the reporters and press in general, and called for "a kind of clearing house for the news."[43] Such a project is always distasteful to newspapermen, for obvious reasons, and nothing seems to have been done about it at the time. Later, after the C.P.I. had been established, Wilson revived the proposal and urged Creel, against the latter's better judgment, to inaugurate the "Official Bulletin," which became one of the many publications of the Committee. It was the President's "conviction that the government should issue a daily gazette for the purpose of assuring full and authoritative publication of all official acts and proceedings. . . ."[44] The idea, Creel says, appealed to him strongly, but he knew that it would stir up a journalistic hornet's nest. Again here the President was seeking a means of bypassing the press and getting verbatim information into the public's hands. Besides circulation to government officials, editors, and other publicity agencies, the *Bulletin* was posted in all military camps and in 54,000 post offices.

The Committee on Public Information has most often been cited as the pioneer effort, par excellence, in the professional public relations industry which became so pervasive following the first World War.[45] More important for immediate purposes, it was a kind of embryonic "propaganda ministry" for the national Executive, which in turn meshed with Wilson's desire to reach the populace directly. As will be seen, the President achieved this latter objective to an extraordinary degree, in view of the then state of the communications arts. Finally, the work of the C.P.I. seems clearly to have had a considerable long-term impact on the stature and development of the presidential office itself.

The ostensible purpose of the Committee was to aid the prosecution of the war by enlisting the support and enthusiasm of the American people, and later of the people of the world. However, a propaganda effort of the magnitude it undertook almost invariably would have a powerful secondary impact by publicizing individuals or agencies connected with the material it presented. To put the matter another way, three courses of action were theoretically open to Creel: the presentation of depersonalized messages emanating from "the government;" the linking of the messages with Cabinet members or agency heads variously involved; or a general tie-in of the appeals and information with the President as national leader and prime mover in the war effort.

There is little question that Creel consciously or otherwise chose the last alternative. The "Creel Committeee" saw the war in Wilsonian terms. This identification of the whole war effort—mobilization, diplomacy, and peacemaking—with Wilson could hardly have failed to impress on the public a heightened sense of the importance of the presidency. And added to the impact of his prior peacetime leadership, it must have carried over and colored attitudes toward the White House and its succeeding occupants, as well.

Creel himself, who had been active in both the 1912 and 1916 campaigns, was the heart and soul of the whole enterprise. Spurred on by his restless imagination, and gathering ideas from any and all sources, the Committee staff collected and exploited a breathtaking array of devices for disseminating its message, which was, broadly speaking, the need for national unity behind the war effort, the righteousness of the cause, and the despicable qualities of the enemy. Among media used were both indirect access to the public (via various commercial media) and more or less direct channels. Typical of the first were news releases, syndicated features, and the *Official Bulletin.*

In the absence of direct channels like radio in 1917, the Committee staff, feeling that indirect techniques would leave some audiences still untapped, produced three brilliant improvisations. In addition to the obvious speakers' bureau, posters, and the like, there was, first of all, a vast program to place pamphlet material directly in the hands of the public. Secondly, the really unique device for direct audience contact was the "Four Minute Men." Enrolling eventually some 75,000 speakers under local and state chairmen throughout the country, this division concentrated at first on getting four-minute messages on war themes to the ready-made audiences in motion picture theaters. Later they broadened their work to embrace audiences wherever they were to be found. Third, there was the National School Service, a twice monthly brochure sent to every school teacher in the country, containing timely messages cast in useful form for class presentation.

The pamphlet program is the easiest to analyze, and illustrates the tremendous circulation given to some of the C.P.I. material.[46] All in all, the Division of Civic and Educational Cooperation distributed more than 75,000,000 pieces of literature ranging from leaflets to weighty research documents. A very substantial portion of this vast mass of material consisted of reprinted Wilson speeches and statements. The clearest example is the dissemination given the President's Flag Day Speech (delivered June 14, 1917) in which he gave what was felt to be a classic statement of the reasons America went to war. This first came out as an appendix to the initial number in the so-called Red, White, and Blue pamphlet series, and was entitled: "How the War Came to America." No less than 6,227,912 copies were circulated. Then as the fourth item in the same series, the Flag Day Address was issued again, this time as the main text of the pamphlet, elaborately footnoted to document the President's recital of the nefarious German aims and activities. This had an even larger circulation of 6,813,340.

A handbook was also prepared to be put into the hands of every Boy Scout in the country (to be kept for the duration of the war for reference). The text began: "Every one of the 285,661 Scouts and 76,957 Scout Officials has been summoned by President Woodrow Wilson, Commander-in-Chief of the Army and Navy, to serve as a dispatch bearer from the Government at Washington to the American people all over the country."[47] Later in the text the Scout is reminded, "Again you are the President's messenger, with a big message to carry." One "message" was the pamphlet containing the annotated Flag Day Speech, and the "dispatch bearers" were enjoined to reach every home with a copy. When interviewing householders they were to "Show them President Wilson's letter on the back of your credential card." Not only did the Scouts thus distribute some 5,000,000 copies of the Flag Day Speech, but unquestionably they must have been impressed themselves, and have impressed their interviewees strongly, with a sense of the preeminent importance of the President in shaping the events of the day and personifying the United States government.

With the Four-Minute men—dubbed broadcasting before radio—problems of analysis become more complex. In exchange for an exclusive privilege of appearing on theater stages at intermission, this division of the C.P.I. guaranteed the managers that they would get no other official demands for their facilities. Every week or two a bulletin was sent out to the several thousand local chairmen for distribution to their rosters of speakers. This outlined the topic, and provided a budget of material for speech preparation with appropriate quotes and catch phrases, and sample four-minute speeches. Speakers were to write their own talks, but follow the guide lines provided; hence one can assume that the emphasis in the bulletin was duplicated closely. Again the degree of saturation must have been phenomenal. Mock and Larson write: "Wherever an American might be, unless he lived the life of a hermit, it was impossible to escape the ubiquitous Four-Minute Men. . . . In New York City alone, 1,600 speakers addressed 500,000 people each week—in English, Yiddish, or Italian."[48]

A careful study of the content of the bulletins revealed that, in spite of the fact that the Four-Minute Men's efforts were not ostensibly aimed at publicizing Woodrow Wilson but rather a wide range of wartime activities, fully one-quarter of all the campaigns were largely or entirely involved in communicating presidential ideas and appeals. Another 20 per cent of the campaign Bulletins were so prepared as to indicate a high probability that the President was mentioned or referred to in the resulting speeches. In a total, therefore, of about 45 per cent of the campaigns, there was a virtual certainty that the speakers mentioned or discussed the President. (A single mention in a speech of but four minutes is enough to be significant.)

In the materials supplied for 90 per cent of *all* the campaigns, at least some mention was made of the President, some Wilsonian passage quoted or message of endorsement included. Creel estimated that the Four-Minute Men gave a total of 1,000,000 speeches to an audience of some 400,000,000. It would be futile to attempt to calculate how many adult Americans heard a Four-Minute Man extol the President from a movie house stage. Nevertheless, if one compares the above audience figure with the total of approximately 60,000,000 adults (21 and over) in the population at the time, and then with the extraordinary extent to which the Chief Executive figured in the materials issued, one must conclude that the Four-Minute Men hammered home the President's commanding role as it had never been done before. And as we have seen, the Four-Minute Men were not the only emissaries of the Committee thus engaged.

Of the ten campaigns in which the speakers were most directly "selling" the President himself, four were entitled: "Why We Are Fighting," "The Danger to Democracy," "The Meaning of America," and "What Have We Won?" These were designed to stimulate war enthusiasm and national unity, and through them, Woodrow Wilson, the President of the United States, must have become the personification of the "war to make the world safe for democracy" in the minds of many. In another of these ten campaigns, set for the Fourth of July, 1918, the Four-Minute Men were given a four-minute message from the President himself to read verbatim. This probably came as close to approximating a presidential radio speech as was possible before the actual perfection of the radio.

Again, on Lincoln's birthday, 1918, the Four-Minute Men were instructed to read the Gettysburg address after first prefacing it thus:

> Ever since the Liberty Bell at Philadelphia tolled its message to the world in 1776 this country has lived for Liberty and Right 'as God gives us to see the Right.' The language of our Presidents from the time of George Washington to this day breathes these highest ideals.
>
> So in this greatest of all wars the President again expresses the noblest of sentiments, emphasizing again and again 'that this is a war of high principles, debased by no selfish ambitions of conquest or spoilation', and 'the cause being just and holy, the settlement must be of like motive and quality.'

Here not only are Wilson and his words emphasized, but the historic role of presidential moral leadership is also. In three other campaigns entitled: "Carrying the Message," "President Wilson's Letter to Theaters," and "Certificates to Theater Members" the Four-Minute Men discussed their own work, and were enjoined to throw the mantle of the presidency around this work and the patriotic theater managers, thus, in effect, capitalizing on the presidential image they were themselves engaged in helping to create.

The story of the last campaign included in the ten was told by William McCormick Blair, director of the Division of Four-Minute Men (and a Republican who supported Hughes, incidentally) in testimony before a House Appropriations subcommittee:

> . . . when the Secretary of the Treasury wished to send out to the people very quickly and directly President Wilson's offer to buy another $50 bond, believing it would greatly increase the number of subscribers, he appealed to our organization and asked if we would send, at their expense, a telegram to our various chairmen so that simultaneously these 35,000 speakers all over the country would make this proposition. That was done and with tremendous results.[49]

The Third Liberty Loan had been lagging and Wilson, on purchasing this additional bond, had challenged the nation to match it.

The National School Service certainly rivals the Four-Minute Man scheme for boldness and daring. It came rather late in the war, the first of its sixteen-page semi-monthly issues being dated September 1, 1918.[50] According to Creel, it was mailed out free of charge to about 600,000 public school teachers with the expectation that through use made of the materials in the classroom, the messages would find their way into 20,000,000 homes. Each issue contained, generally, a "leading article" or two, a summary of major war events during the preceding two weeks, a series of timely shorter articles, boxes containing quotations, and then a considerable amount of material prepared for direct classroom use. This latter was designed to convey to children through stories, projects, and the like, geared to various age groups, the war messages deemed of greatest importance at the moment. Without attempting a detailed discussion of content, suffice it to note that the first number featured on its cover a statement entitled, "Message from President Wilson to School Teachers of the United States" and signed "Woodrow Wilson." Every subsequent number featured the President to a significant extent, often in the news summaries and also in quoted passages and articles. The student was frequently invited to see the war in presidential terms.

Eight issues had gone out when publication was turned over to the Department of the Interior upon termination of C.P.I. activities. That this project was a significant supplement to the communication channels already discussed is apparent. (As a federal effort to influence local school curricula it was unique and startling.) Had the war lasted a year or even a few months longer, the National School Service would certainly have packed a tremendous publicity wallop, particularly in its long-term implications.

The findings presented in the foregoing paragraphs clearly justify the assertion that never before had the presidency been so consistently held up as prime focus of public attention, and never before had a course of national policy been so completely identified with a President. This conclusion can stand regardless of the actual intent of the actors. The question of intent, however, and of the degree of the President's own involvement in the work of the

C.P.I., are interesting subjects of speculation. It seems clear that neither Creel nor Wilson himself saw the role of the committee as a vehicle for the President's political or personal aggrandizement. If Creel's decision to portray the war effort in Wilsonian terms did not stem from this, it probably was the unconscious product of something akin to hero worship. He once wrote the President: "I find it hard always to think of you as a person, for you stand for America so absolutely in my mind and heart and are so inseparably connected with the tremendous events of the time."[51]

The record shows that Wilson himself was by no means unaware of the magnitude of the propaganda effort being mounted by the C.P.I., participated closely in its policy decisions, and kept close track of all similar activities being carried on in the government. Between April 13, 1917, and the armistice, Baker records no less than fifty-six meetings at the White House between Wilson and Creel, or an average of about three a month.[52]

This concern with propaganda policies cannot be taken as evidence that the President had lost any of his earlier aversion to the seamy side of such activity. In fact, one can speculate that the C.P.I. as a publicity medium was particularly congenial to him because through it he could deal with such policy at arm's length. He did not have to devise the over-all strategy, since it seems clear that Creel did most of the initiating of ideas. Wilson's major role, apparently, was to supply much of the content in the form of his wartime speeches, and approve drafts and proposals submitted for his consideration. He had neither to deal directly with the representatives of the media nor concern himself overmuch with the tactical side of the venture.

A brief analysis of the tragic final chapter in Wilson's presidential career will serve as an appropriate conclusion to discussion of the Wilson period. The fight for the League represented a major and in some ways unprecedented challenge to presidential leadership. It also meant a complex tactical problem of using effectively appropriate media of communication. Wilson had displayed throughout his administration an almost unsurpassed ability to enlist the public in the causes he championed. He had succeeded magnificently in relation to the New Freedom legislative program.

Earlier, he had consciously and deliberately developed and carried through a strategy for remolding American attitudes toward the European war and forging a united nation behind his policies. Regarding this campaign he himself wrote, at the time of the declaration of war, "it was necessary for me by very slow stages indeed and with the most genuine purpose to avoid war to lead the country to a single way of thinking. I thank God for the evidences that the task has been accomplished."[53] David Houston quoted a similar comment made by Wilson to his secretary: " 'Tumulty, from the very beginning I saw the end of this horrible thing; but I could not move faster than the great mass of our people would permit.' . . . He, therefore, realized the need of educating the people and steadily pursued a definite course of laying issues before them and Congress. This was the broader objective in his preparedness tour."[54]

Clearly Wilson lacked neither the will nor the sense of strategy necessary for successful presidential leadership in relation to major issues. Where he failed, it seems that his failures were tactical, not strategic, on the whole. Thus it was with the League fight. He did not marshal the necessary means for reaching the people and solidifying their support for his great dream.[55] Obviously the failure of ratification is a far too complex business to be reduced to any one simple explanation. Nevertheless, a persuasive case can be made that the President's failure to confront and solve the public relations problem he faced was a major contributing cause, if not the major cause, of his defeat.[56]

Wilson had been placing steadily decreasing reliance upon the press as a medium for communicating with his constituency, and had allowed his links with the reporter group to become correspondingly attenuated, throughout his period in office. Even before the press conferences were allowed to lapse, he had sought and found other ways of reaching the public which minimized dependence upon the working press and even on the newspapers themselves. The Creel Committee was the culmination of this trend. His leadership just preceding American entry into the war, and during our participation in the conflict, had not suffered unduly as a result of this estrangement, apparently. He could continue to address Congress and thus command public attention, and of course the C.P.I. put him in a position to be about as free of dependence on the newspapers as he wanted to be.

By the time of the Armistice, however, a combination of factors forced the President back to reliance on the newspapers. In the first place, the C.P.I. was wound up as soon as possible after the 11th of November, on the sound theory that the uneasy tolerance of the enterprise by Congress during the war would give way to determined hostility once peace came. Thus this means of disseminating the policies of the White House was lost. George Creel did, however, make every effort to use his agency to pave the way for a Wilsonian peace settlement. In October he wrote to the President that there was "instant need of some clear and complete statement of America's war aims and peace program"[57] and enclosed a Four-Minute Man draft bulletin embodying his ideas. Though there is no written Wilson reply available, the evidence suggests that Creel was not given the go-ahead on his proposal. Again, three days after the fateful Congressional elections of 1918, Creel wrote, "if the defeat is to be repaired, . . . You will have to give out your program for peace and reconstruction and find friends for it."[58]

Meanwhile the indefatigable and, as it turned out, farsighted head of the C.P.I. was doing what he could in a general way to use the waning period of his agency's life to prepare the public for the problems of peacemaking. The last few Four-Minute Man campaigns, which ran into December, 1918, dealt obliquely with the problems of the peace and the proposed league. Also, the last issues of the National School Service did likewise. In one of them the teachers were urged to "encourage pupils to think in international terms" and in another: "In discussion of the formation of the league, the teacher may have different pupils suggest sacrifices that different nations might have to make in order to bring about such a league."[59] These efforts, however, came to an end well before they were to be most needed.

Wilson, it will be recalled, determined to go to Paris himself, and sailed for France early in December, 1918. The public relations significance of this decision was that, in the first place, though it did focus attention and responsibility upon the Chief Executive for whatever was done at Versailles, it denied him the possibility of addressing the people from time to time as negotiations developed, and virtually cut him off from direct contact with his constituents. In this sense the President was forced back on the press as his sole mode of communication with American public opinion. It could be said that Paris represented for him a challenge and opportunity, as well as a problem. An unprecedented number of news writers had assembled there from the United States and from the four corners of the earth, to cover this spectacular climax of the greatest war—and news event—in history.

The details of Wilson's failure to establish satisfactory relations with this vast press corps and exploit the facilities they represented need only be summarized. The President declined to hold regular meetings with the reporters himself and appointed Ray Stannard Baker as his representative to the Fourth Estate. Little information was transmitted to the press by this or any other means, partly because of the unwillingness or inability of Wilson to dramatize the fight he was making, and partly because of the secret nature of the negotiations of the Big Four. He himself seems not to have fully grasped the problem of publicity, and those around him who did were also painfully aware of the physical strain under which he was laboring and reluctant to add to this burden.[60]

Secretary Tumulty watched developments from Washington with growing alarm. Repeatedly he cabled advice and entreaties, but to no avail.[61] The brief return to America in March, ostensibly for the end of the Congressional session, was really a belated effort to enlist American public support.[62] Wilson's feeling that this journey was necessary suggests that he was not wholly unaware of the problem, but also suggests that he was attempting to solve it as he had similar problems before, by the making of formal speeches rather than by exploiting the news columns of the press through the ever present but increasingly frustrated and disillusioned reporters. The latter not only were not handled well but the neglect they suffered may actually have turned them from a potential asset into a liability.[63]

When the Treaty was finally signed and the President had returned to the United States in 1919 to battle for its ratification, it became increasingly evident that the well planned campaign of vilification directed against his handiwork was gaining ground.[64] In the fall Wilson decided—belatedly one can now say—that the only hope was a speaking tour to rally the public to his support. That such an expedient had been useful at the early stages in previous controversies is true. Whether it would have turned the trick if his health had not broken, undertaken so late in the day, is doubtful. Professor Bailey has written poignantly and significantly:

> One of the most fascinating might-have-beens of history is to speculate on what would have happened had there been then, as there was to be in a few years, a nation-wide radio hookup. Wilson had a fine voice and splendid diction. . . . Sitting quietly in the White House, and needing only several half-hour speeches, he might in a series of 'fireside chats' have informed and aroused the people, while at the same time preserving his health and strength. . . . Wilson had to do the job the hard way.[65]

Ironically and tragically enough, Wilson, before he died in 1924, was to broadcast a brief message over the new medium, as a defeated and broken ex-President.

The first two decades of the twentieth century saw the opening stages of a vast and highly significant evolution in the nature and functioning of the presidency. At the hands of Theodore Roosevelt the process of harnessing the enormous potential of the burgeoning media of communication to the needs of presidential opinion leadership began. So too did the attendant shift of the locus of authority and initiative in the whole federal establishment from the hands of Congress to those of the President—though not without a fierce rear-guard defense of former prerogatives on the part of the legislature. The unhappy William Howard Taft did little but represent a period of marking time in the process of White House adaptation to these changes.

Woodrow Wilson's contributions were varied and complex in this area of presidential public relations technique and precedent. He inaugurated formal press conferences, conducted them with some skill, but discontinued them in disgust long before his term ended. He exploited skillfully the publicity possibilities of the personally delivered message to Congress. These innovations, in one way or another, have become permanent adjuncts to the presidential operation. He also was responsible for the most spectacular experiment at governmental propaganda activity in American history. In the nature of things this could not serve as a direct precedent for the future. The Creel Committee did leave, however, as its permanent by-product, a vastly enhanced image of the presidential office which was to affect the conduct and occupants of that office from then on, and was to render even more pressing the problem of adapting the chief magistracy to the demands and opportunities of modern mass communications.

☆☆☆☆☆☆☆

Chapter 4

☆☆☆☆☆☆☆

CONSOLIDATION: HARDING AND COOLIDGE

I

The colorless, do-nothing occupants of the White House in the nineteen-twenties are generally taken to represent the nadir of the presidential office during this century. Using Teddy Roosevelt's categorizations, Harding and Coolidge, at least, were clearly "Buchanan type" Presidents. As before in American history, a period of strong executive leadership had again been followed by an era of passivity and drift. Yet in spite of the persuasive and often cited pendulum theory of the presidency, there is evidence which suggests a counter theme in operation during the twenties. It is clearly arguable that the stature of the office in the eyes of the public, which had been growing since 1900, and was given a powerful further impetus during the Wilson years, at least held its own if it did not actually continue to grow after 1920.

Harding and his Vermont successor were indeed passive in relation to public policy. But they were the inevitable beneficiaries of the rising curve of interest in the presidency fostered by the very existence of the new journalism and the aggressive use made by T. R. and Wilson of the facilities available for molding public opinion. Furthermore, they themselves were active rather than passive as regards further development of White House public relations technique. Presidential leadership of opinion need not be exercised solely by men intent on reform or innovation, but can also be used effectively for partisan and electoral ends by those bent only on preserving the status quo. President Eisenhower did precisely this, using his national prestige and the platform of the White House, and Coolidge, in particular, did the same much earlier.

Warren Harding is probably the outstanding argument available to critics of the presidential nominating system and the whole process of selecting a President. Someone once said that success in lotteries is no justification for them. This was one instance in which the lottery did not even bring success for the players. It would be difficult indeed to find anyone prepared to defend Harding's record as President.[1]

A persuasive claim can, however, be made for the thesis that Harding made significant contributions to the development of presidential techniques for the leadership of public opinion. Almost regardless of what the man inaugurated in March, 1921, did or who he was, the impression he would make on the public was bound to be as great or greater in some ways than any of his illustrious predecessors had made. In 1922, with the general period of Harding's accession in mind, the author of *Behind the Mirrors* wrote:

> We magnified the office of President and satisfied that primitive instinct in us which must see the public welfare and the public safety personified in a single individual, something visible, tangible, palpable. The President speaks and you read about him in the daily press; the President poses and you see him in the movies and feel assured, as in smaller realms under simpler conditions people were able to see their monarch dressed and equipaged in ways that connected him with all the permanence of the past, a symbol of stability, wisdom, and the divine favor.[2]

This seems aptly to characterize the public reaction to the office around 1920. The most colorless and passive President would have reaped this harvest of attention as a symbol if not as a man.

Harding's impact was by no means limited to a role as mere creature of his times and office, however. To an extraordinary degree, editor-publisher that he was, he dovetailed into the contemporary pattern of development in the presidency and the emerging media. In spite of his intellectual limitations and lack of interest in policy, he developed and solidified precedents of considerable import upon which successors could build. As a working journalist he understood the ways of the press with an intimacy that none of his White House predecessors probably shared. He also had a wide acquaintance among the correspondents, spoke their language, enjoyed and felt at home in their company, and hence cultivation of their sympathetic understanding came as naturally to him as breathing.

From the period of his McKinley-type front porch campaign in 1920 onward, this rapport with the working press continued and was strengthened by the considerateness and conscious innovations of the candidate.[3] Pollard points out that definite provisions were made for the reporters in Marion during the late summer and fall of 1920, setting new precedents in this regard. A three-room cottage was built near the Harding home and there the candidate would meet them daily and discuss developments in the frankest fashion. This kind of contact continued after the election during the interregnum. On the Florida vacation of the President-elect, the same friendly and intimate relations persisted, even to the extent of rounds of golf with particular friends among the correspondents. In general, some parallels can be drawn between Harding and the first Roosevelt. Both had a feel for the workings of the press and both were on intimate terms with many reporters and found in them welcome and congenial companionship. The difference, of course, lay in the fact that Harding's attitudes were born of nostalgia for the life work which he had had to give up to enter the White House, while T. R.'s were the intuitions of a shrewd outside observer who had goals to achieve and saw the press as a means to his ends.

By far the most significant Harding contribution was probably the revival of the regular press conference, open to all accredited correspondents. President Harding faced a genuine choice in this area—a choice which, thanks to the way he resolved it, has not really been open as fully to any of his successors. He could, as he did, revive the Wilson idea, or he could have allowed it to die. Though the Wilson precedent did exist, it was hardly a very compelling one in view of the brief duration of the earlier press meeting scheme and the several years it had lain dormant. Once it was revived by the new President, it would have been that much harder for his successor to disappoint the expectations aroused, if Coolidge had been so inclined, and once Coolidge continued the practice without a break, the precedent was too firmly entrenched for change without peril to the changer.

Harding's newspaper background made it natural and virtually certain that he would revive and continue the confrontations with the reporters, if for no other reason than his desire to commune with his former journalistic associates. Fred Essary describes the physical format of the meetings: "At a given hour fifty to one hundred correspondents would be admitted to the office of the Executive, half-surrounding him. The President would arise from his desk and face his examiners. Without preliminaries of any sort the questions would be fired at the head of the Government, a score of them and ofttimes more."[4]

It was announced that the sessions would be held on Tuesdays and Fridays immediately after the Cabinet meetings. The Tuesday conference would take place at 1:00 o'clock and the Friday one at 4:00—to give the morning and afternoon papers equal breaks. The account of the first conference in the *New York Times* notes that: "His [the President's] manner was kindly, and it was evident that whenever he answered any question with what seemed to be shortness he was anxious immediately thereafter to correct any impression that he had been abrupt intentionally."[5]

This twice-a-week schedule plus the use of spontaneous questions and relatively uninhibited give-and-take had been the pattern during the Wilson experiment also. This format was later modified, but until then, the press conferences were exceedingly productive of news, which was handled in a manner rather favorable to the President during his whole period in office and even after his death, when the scandals began to emerge. One can argue that this was the natural reaction of a Republican-dominated press, but it is more likely that the affection of the working press for their journalist-President was the prime reason.

Examination of the *New York Times* during the first three months of the Harding administration suggests both the importance of the conference as link between President and public and the relative success that Harding had in "making news" and keeping presidential activities in the limelight. It should be noted, parenthetically, that it is difficult to do more than make informed guesses about the source of a given news story because the President could not be directly quoted, nor could information be attributed to him in a story. As a result, according to an account printed in the *Times* later in the year, "very often when he [the] phrases 'high officials in the administration,' or 'it was learned at the White House that,' appear in Washington dispatches they refer to topics that have been discussed at the White House press conferences."[6] For the same reason it is often hard to tell whether a conference had even been held on a given Tuesday or Friday. However, sixteen were identifiable in the *Times* for the period checked because they had been productive of news whose form and content suggested the White House as source.

It was during Harding's administration that the "White House spokesman" device was invented.[7] This mythical figure gradually became the standard euphemism for the attribution of press conference news, and became a standing joke during the Coolidge years. From the President's point of view, this veil hung between himself and the newspaper readers gave him some room for maneuver he would not otherwise have had. He was free to repudiate an unfavorable wording or implication attached to something he had said, if not to repudiate the idea itself.

Another way of identifying press conference results was by noting mention of Cabinet happenings in a story. Harding was the first President to reveal frankly and in considerable detail the discussions among his advisors in the twice-weekly sessions. Granting that this was an era during which little of earth-shaking importance was considered in these meetings, it was still a striking departure from precedent for the President to emerge and willingly answer reporters' questions on what had occurred. Apparently his timing of the conference to follow Cabinet meetings was designed to facilitate this kind of disclosure.

This new precedent was another step in the process that had been going on since the days of Roosevelt and was destined to continue, that is, the removal one by one of the barriers between the President and the direct gaze of the public. Gradually, during a half century or so, a situation in which the President operated in aloof, almost monarchical detachment from the public, and even from currents of public opinion, gave place to a state of affairs today when it has become almost impossible for him to confer with persons outside his immediate White House entourage without making the front pages and news telecasts.

One of the best known, probably the only well-known, episode during the Harding relationship with the working press was the famous error which the President made in connection with the Washington Conference negotiations during the late fall of 1921. The Conference, most famous for its agreement on limitation of naval armament, convened on November 12. A four-power pact, dealing with the Pacific area,[8] was also negotiated among the United States, Japan, Great Britain, and France. While the latter negotiations were in progress, a reporter asked the President at his regular news conference on Tuesday, December 20, whether the arrangements being worked out applied to the Japanese home islands as well as to island possessions of the powers in the area. Harding replied that they did not, which was the direct opposite of the view backed by Secretary of State Hughes. A great international stir was caused by this slip, and the President willingly agreed to the unprecedented step of issuing a statement retracting what he had said, in spite of the embarrassment this would cause him. The President's forthrightness in owning up to his error and correcting it further impressed the already favorably disposed reporters.

Most discussions of this episode assert that it was as a result of

Harding's serious slip that the era of free and unrehearsed questioning and discussion was terminated in favor of the rule that questions must be submitted in advance in writing.[9] This was not the case, however. A *New York Times* news item on November 30, nearly three weeks earlier, reported that: "President Harding [had] established a question box for the semi-weekly press conferences at the White House. Hereafter every correspondent will submit his questions in writing before he enters the President's office. These will be given to the President and he will answer them, or not, as he sees fit." The item went on to note that this modified the free exchange pattern, though it was not designed to be unduly restrictive. The reason for the move, it was explained, was the problem of the conflicting interpretations that had been placed on presidential refusals to answer questions in the past, and the presence in Washington of an increased number of correspondents from the United States and abroad drawn by the Conference. This influx had more than doubled attendance at the press gatherings. Verbal questions to pursue further a subject raised by the President would be permitted, however.

Not only did this change of the rules *precede* by three weeks the famous slip, but the error itself on December 20 was committed in reply to a *written* question submitted under the new scheme![10] The true sequence of events, differing as it does from the oft repeated story about Secretary Hughes' irate insistence on the change of rules once the error had been made and retracted, reflects rather more favorably on the President than the accepted version. The change had not really been made on a spur of the moment basis, and represented, one must assume, a rather sophisticated appreciation of certain problems connected with the news conference. Obviously silence can be at times as pregnant with meaning as a specific answer, or at least can be so interpreted. It is a skillful Chief Executive indeed who can successfully take this fact into account and still accept all questions while emerging unscathed. Further, this move apparently represented an early—and, as it turned out, abortive—effort to deal with what was to become a persistent problem by the 1950s, the burgeoning size of the correspondent corps covering the White House.

President Harding initiated a significant innovation (at least it was initiated with his acquiescence) in relation to the growing group of press photographers. The difficulties that this new journalistic clan were encountering in plying their trade caused them to organize a White House News Photographers' Association in June, 1921, and the President's secretary immediately issued identification cards to the members granting them access to all public events and to some private ones at which the President appeared. Harding himself willingly posed for news pictures several times a week, and through his example and perhaps his precept as well, other government officials became much more willing to do the same when asked—a willingness that had been conspicuously absent earlier.[11]

One Washington newsman wrote that though the President was no more anxious to have his picture taken than anyone else, "he submitted to it because newspaper and magazine readers the world over wanted to see photographs of the President, and he considered it his duty to appear before the camera at frequent intervals."[12] Though documentation might be difficult, it is nevertheless apparent that photography itself, together with the inventions of photoengraving and the motion picture, were becoming exceedingly important supplements to the mass circulation daily in focusing attention on the presidency and expanding the presidential image in the eyes of the public. Whether Harding was conscious of this fact and exploited it or not is less important, perhaps, than his willingness to go along with the obvious trend.

One final point on the relations between President Harding and the press sheds light on a persistent problem encountered by both his predecessors and his successors. There is a built-in ambivalence in these relations. The natural preoccupation of the Chief Executive and his staff is to release news in such a way, in both timing and content, as to secure the most favorable impact. They covet the right to conceal, at least for a time, as well as reveal. The reporters, of course, want *all* the news—meaning the intriguing and, where possible, sordid details—and want it at once. A tension, therefore, as well as a degree of cooperation, is bound to develop between the two.

Though F.D.R. fancied himself a journalist by virtue of his work on the Harvard *Crimson,* Harding has been the only genuine newspaperman in the White House to date. He was therefore in a position to see in his own experience both sides of the President-reporter relationship. In June, 1922, apparently smarting under the prominently displayed reports of Congressional criticism of some Cabinet members, the President, at his press conference, made it clear he thought the press was exercising poor news judgment in giving so much weight to these utterances. The journalistic fraternity immediately bristled. *Editor and Publisher* remarked tartly that President Harding had "cast aside the knowledge that came to him from years of experience on the *Marion Star* and attempted to tell the press of America what is and what is not news from the Presidential standpoint."[13]

About a year later the Chief Executive, speaking at an Associated Press meeting in New York, noted: "I have had my viewpoint about journalism broadened while twisting around occasionally in the executive chair. Frankly, I have never squirmed under the criticism but I have sometimes been appalled at the inaccuracy of statement, and if I were going to give a lecture on journalism my theme would be 'a little less eagerness and much more of accuracy.' "[14] Clearly the conflicting aspects of the presidential and reportorial roles are so central to the very roles themselves that even a White House occupant who has partaken of both cannot reconcile the two fully. The conflict is obviously compounded of self-interest on both sides and also deeply held principles which, at least on the journalistic side, verge at times on self-righteousness.

Other public relations developments during the brief Harding era either were important in themselves or foreshadowed major future changes. The new President, for example, decided to retain the practice which Wilson had revived of delivering messages to Congress in person. Three days before his inauguration, the President-elect told the reporters of this intention, and again, a few days before delivering his first State of the Union Message, he commented on his decision. Personal contact between the two branches, he said, was a good thing. Furthermore, the reading clerk could not be expected to read a Presidential address "in a manner that would impress upon the auditors the points that the President desired to emphasize."[15] The record here as elsewhere does not contain any significant evidence that Harding was conscious of the publicity impact that could be gained by the personal trip to the Capitol, but the practice probably contributed to enhancing the public's awareness of the office and the man. When the Chief Executive confronted the Senate in person to argue against the soldiers' bonus in July, 1921, he must have been mindful that he would thus increase the impact of his views.[16]

Speechmaking and the swing around the circle became part of the Harding repertoire of communication techniques. He gave tacit recognition to the mounting burden on the White House occupant of messages and addresses that had to be prepared and given, by instituting the "speech writer" on the Presidential staff. One Judson Welliver seems to have been the first to hold this position, and he remained in the same role under Coolidge. Welliver had been a newspaperman who had joined Candidate Harding's entourage and came into the White House with him after the 4th of March.[17]

One might attribute this departure to the sloth of the new President in contrast to the industry of Mr. Wilson, who drafted his own public papers. True as this may be, the installation of a ghost writer was unquestionably also a recognition of the rapidly increasing scale upon which the whole office had to be operated, with every succeeding term. According to Ira Smith, the retired White House mail clerk, in his early years of White House service the small clerical force moved at a leisurely pace, in a friendly, intimate atmosphere. "Somewhere in Taft's administration the one-big-family atmosphere faded out, and when Woodrow Wilson became President, the times had changed and we were in a busy office that had little chance for byplay, gossip, or an occasional game of craps in the basement."[18]

The addition of a speech writer to the White House staff, besides making possible an increased output of public presidential pronouncements, also had technical advantages over having the President sweat over his own speeches. Regarding the last cross-country trip made by Harding, which culminated in his death on the West

Coast, it has been noted that: "Many of the nineteen set speeches called for by the itinerary were already in type for transmission by mail, ahead of their delivery. Wilson had lost some of his needed publicity in 1919 because his speeches were not always available for the press in time for printing while they were still news."[19] In addition, the secretarial car on the presidential train carried stenographers, and Mr. Welliver, to be available when needed.

The first use of amplifiers for presidential addresses also coincided with the Harding period in office. Newly invented gadgets of this sort were rigged up for the Harding inauguration in 1921. Their use was successful and vastly more of the crowd in Capitol Plaza was able to hear the new President than had been the case in the past.[20] Also, as Fred Essary points out, "for the first time the observation platform of the President's own car was provided with amplifiers, in order to make rear end speeches audible for a greater distance," during the cross-country swing in 1923.[21]

Harding was not unaware, apparently, of the use to which the swing around the circle could be put for policy ends, in spite of his general passivity in exerting leadership. He had become interested, for example, in the brutal system of the twelve-hour day, which was still in use in the nation's steel mills. In May, 1923, not long before he began his journey west, he wrote to Judge Elbert H. Gary of U. S. Steel, as a kind of last ditch effort to secure modification of working hours in the industry, intimating that one of the speeches he planned to make on his tour would be on the twelve-hour day. This frightened the steel barons into an equivocal and partial retreat. The President, seeking to press the advantage he had thus gained, read this letter and commented upon it in the course of his address in Tacoma, Washington.[22] Samuel Hopkins Adams, who recounts these events, concludes: "The President had supplied the final impetus to end the inhuman twelve-hour day. But he did not live to know it."[23] It seems clear from this episode that both the President and the steel men were well aware of the potency inherent in a presidential appeal to the public.

Mr. Harding himself had only a few contacts with the new medium of radio, but radio's technical feasibility was being proven during his brief period in office. It had its first demonstration reporting the returns of the election of 1920, and the inauguration of March, 1921, was similarly reported. Following occasional presidential radio messages earlier in his term, Harding made a major speech on his trip west, from St. Louis, which was carried over a special wire to New York and broadcast from there, and also by a few other stations. Special plans were laid for a landmark demonstration of the possibilities of the new medium utilizing the President's return from Alaska, in an address scheduled for San Francisco on July 31, 1923. An embryonic "national hookup" was planned covering six broadcast points: San Francisco, Omaha, Chicago, New York, Washington, and Round Hills, Massachusetts. Because of Harding's illness this speech, though prepared, was never delivered.[24]

Two aspects of the death of the President hold special significance for this study. In the first place, the elaborateness of the preparations made to cover his last illness suggests the continuing perfection of news-gathering techniques and particularly the minute surveillance of presidential activities. Oliver Gramling, historian of the Associated Press, described arrangements thus:

> Harding's condition had not yet become critical, but the circumstances warranted preparedness. . . . a special wire was looped to the seventh floor of the Palace Hotel, ten feet from the private back stairway leading to the presidential suite on the floor above. The coast traffic chief, Percy Hall, took charge of the telegraphers at the improvised headquarters. "Never leave the wire unmanned for a second," were his orders. "The man who leaves this room without permission leaves the service."[25]

Interestingly enough, the reporter who was waiting a few feet from the President's door when a distraught Mrs. Harding rushed out at the fateful moment was none other than Stephen Early, destined to serve as Franklin Roosevelt's press secretary.

Then there came the "emotional deluge" as Merlo Pusey described it,[26] with which the nation reacted to the President's death. Pusey, biographer of Charles Evans Hughes, describes the funeral journey by train from Washington to the final resting place in Marion:

> Hughes lay awake in his berth most of the night watching the crowds that lined the tracks and jammed the station of every town through which they passed. Again and again the pall of silence was broken by the strains of "Nearer, My God to Thee" and other hymns. The nation's heart had been deeply touched.[27]

This flood of emotion and spontaneous national mourning for a President who had been in office hardly more than two years, and one whom history would count as perhaps the least successful and admirable of all the White House occupants, would be difficult indeed to explain if one could not cite the unique ability of the office itself to attract and hold rapt public attention, and particularly the impact of developments in the mass media in further stamping the image of the presidency and its occupant on the minds of the populace. More than ever before, thanks to the media and use made of them on the President's behalf, the presidency was destined to blow up the man to heroic proportions and project this image constantly on the national screen.

II

Though Harding's transitional importance was considerable, it was left, paradoxically, to the quintessence of taciturn Yankee Vermont to give lasting form to some of the emerging White House communications practices. As counterpart to the press attention given the drama in San Francisco, coverage of Plymouth, Vermont, where the Vice President and his wife were visiting the elder Coolidge, was increased with the onset of the President's illness. It was a reporter stationed in Ludlow, the nearest point with telephone service, who brought the fateful news by auto to the family homestead in the early morning hours of August 3.

Most would argue that Coolidge as President went little beyond his predecessor as regards the use he made of the office.[28] He possessed, however, more native ability. Yet he appears to have had little insight into the long-term currents that were carrying the America of the twenties toward the precipice. Few books have been more aptly titled than William Allen White's study of Coolidge: *A Puritan in Babylon*. The man was part and parcel of his era, its product in a very real sense, and yet remained an isolated island of parsimony and narrow rectitude in a sea of material indulgence and unleashed emotions. So, at least, runs the conventional indictment.

For all his limitations, the silent New Englander had far more than the average endowment of political shrewdness and publicity sense. Many observers either grudgingly or with genuine admiration echoed Willis Johnson's assertion that "He was a master of public relations. . . ."[29] Perhaps the very ordinariness of the man, the extent to which he mirrored the aspirations of the populace and sensed their moods and short-run desires because they were his own, in turn made him more sensitive than most to the atmosphere in which the presidential office was destined to be conducted in the postwar period. In any event, he appeared to understand intuitively and to accept the demands and working methods of the press representatives, and responded instinctively to the heightened interest in the White House and its occupants on the part of the media, and above all, of the public itself.

Fortunately for the student a complete verbatim file of Coolidge press conference transcripts is available for analysis.[30] Such a collection (available also for F.D.R. and his successors to date) represents virtually the only body of material which shows a President in action under conditions likely to illuminate his mind at work and his techniques. Speeches and statements, which are premeditated and calculated (and often ghost-written), are a poor substitute. Files of correspondence have their usefulness but tend to reveal dealings with other individuals, rather than with the public at large. Minutes of conferences and Cabinet meetings, which might show the President expressing his ideas under conditions of spontaneity, simply do not exist in significant numbers. In short, press conference transcripts stand alone as first-hand records of presidential "action" and reflection.

Coolidge was extraordinarily faithful in discharging what he felt to be his obligations to the reporters. He held office almost exactly sixty-seven of the ninety-six months that would have constituted a full two terms. During that period, according to a count of the transcripts, he held 520 press conferences, or an average of 7.8 per month. (In slightly over 145 months, F.D.R. held 998 press conferences, or an average of only 6.9 per month.)[31] There were few gaps in the chronology; at no time was there a single period of significant length during which the press was not seen. In picking up the Harding precedent of frequent and regular conferences, the new President turned it into a firm pattern of expectations and, for practical purposes, a permanent attribute of the presidential office. This was his outstanding contribution.

Calvin Coolidge was the last President to be dependent largely upon the newspaper press for his contact with the public. For him radio was only beginning to represent a major direct link with the populace, and the rules of the press conference kept the reporter as the sole means of transmitting presidential utterances from the executive office to the outside world. Hence cultivation of the working press remained crucial to successful public relations, as it had been for his predecessors.

No one would expect President Coolidge to have been spectacular in this regard as to either technique or results. Comment by reporters at the time or in after years suggests a considerable range of reaction on their part—some found his press meetings frustrating, a few suggested that the press conference on the existing basis be abandoned altogether, others accepted things as they were and found the encounters useful.

There is a good deal of evidence, however, in the transcripts themselves to the effect that the Chief Executive was well aware, at least in a general way, of the needs of the reporters, made a conscious and continuing effort to meet them, and at the same time did what he could to supplement all of this with some—perhaps rather stiff—social contact between the correspondents and himself. The reporter needs, above all, to secure the makings of a story at regular intervals, hopefully from each press encounter. Repeatedly, Coolidge showed awareness of this. For instance, at the conference held on May 1, 1925, he said:

> Now that Congress isn't in session I am rather aware of the paucity of news, though of course there are a lot of small things that are always developing in relation to our government, and many times they have larger import and interest. I want to be helpful in any

> way I can to guide the press in their efforts for news items. My own thought about the situation at the present time is that I would like it if the country could think as little as possible about the government and give their time and attention more undividedly about the conduct of the private business of our country. If that is a thought that you can develop in any way, I think it would be helpful.[32]

Again, on September 28 of the next year, the President is found saying: "As is quite likely to occur when the Government is running along fairly well, there does not seem to be very much news. I just called Mr. Sanders [his secretary] in to ask if he thought of anything that might be helpful to the conference and that I could discuss. They were not able to think of anything, nor do the questions this morning disclose much of anything."

Coolidge was also aware of the desirability of maintaining an even flow of news day by day, avoiding both glut and scarcity. For example: "Well, I have given you sufficient to write about for today. We will save that for some other time." Again, during one of his extended summer vacations away from Washington, when news was often a bit scant, a reporter said concerning one of his visitors: "Did you have in mind any time for us to see him—this afternoon or tomorrow?" Coolidge replied: "Well, you have my conference today. You don't want to get everything in the paper in one day. There is always going to be another publication the next day. I presume you want to see him today, but I should think tomorrow would be all right."

Coolidge was also well aware of the need to have speech texts available well in advance. Note for instance his reply to a question about his acceptance speech, asked July 25, 1924: "I want to try to get it out to the press as early as I can, in order that you may be able to give it a wide circulation without having to resort very much to the telegraph wire—mailed and distributed." Again on September 22, 1925: "I shall try to get out my address that is to be made at Omaha so that it can have a very great deal of mail delivery." This theme was repeated many times in the transcripts.

Not only did the President understand the general needs of the press, but he had shrewdly assessed, it would seem, the kind of coverage various public utterances from the White House would receive and acted accordingly:

> I will give out as soon as I can my message [to Congress] and my address at Chicago. My thought is that the message will probably come out first, as that would be more desirable to have a general distribution. The Chicago address would not be printed in full, I anticipate, in very many of the papers, while practically all the papers I think carry the annual message. I will get it to you as soon as I can. I think it will be five or six days before its delivery.

Note, along the same general line: "I would especially like to thank the press for the very generous way in which they handled the little Christmas message that I sent out. It was carried in all the papers which I happened to come in contact with, and I am receiving a good many messages of appreciation and compliment on the message."

It seems obvious that this kind of cooperation, oft repeated, since it made the labors of the working press easier, must have gained for the President a considerable measure of their sympathetic interest if not affection. He did not overlook the little things only indirectly connected with the reportorial function itself. In July, 1926, while vacationing in the Adirondacks, Coolidge decided to make a visit to Plymouth (Vermont) and this precipitated the following press conference exchange:

> PRESIDENT: What would the members of the press prefer, to go by automobile or by train?
>
> PRESS: Train.
>
> PRESIDENT: Seems to be unanimous. Well, I think I can arrange to take you over by train, if that would suit you better.

It has been suggested that the President himself preferred auto, but bowed willingly to the preferences of the reporters. Time and again during the conferences, when a trip was in the offing, he was careful to let them know in advance the approximate departure time and other details so they could make their personal plans. In fact, there is general agreement that it was during this administration that concern for the comfort and convenience of the correspondents on presidential journeys reached a new high.

Two or three times the scheduling of the conferences came up during one of them. Daylight saving time was usually the occasion. "Here is a suggestion that I should be very glad to comply with if I can, that on account of daylight saving we have the Tuesday conference at 12:00 o'clock and the Friday conference at 3:00 o'clock," the President noted. The problem became more complex during the summer which the official family spent in the Black Hills, because of the different time zones. The President, through his secretary, took the initiative in setting a time for the Friday conference which would be more convenient for the members, as he put it, "both to get their stories off early and insure their reaching their destination in the East in time for the regular publications on Saturday morning." It was decided that the Tuesday one, for the evening editions, would have to be set at shortly after 9:00 A.M. in order to make the east coast papers. A firm agreement was reached that the news from each conference would be held only for the intended edition.

The social side of the President-reporter relationship was by no means neglected, though one can hardly imagine that such occasions were productive of great hilarity. In May, 1925, we find Coolidge saying, in his characteristically tentative and "low key" fashion: "I don't know whether the men present would be interested to go down [the river] on the Mayflower with me some day. You can talk that over among yourselves. If you think you will, let me know and we shall try and arrange an excursion some afternoon." This was about as close, one imagines, to an enthusiastic invitation as anyone ever expected to get from the Vermonter. Each summer at the vacation retreat, the press would be invited to spend a social time at the lodge or camp itself, with the wives of reporters also invited. Much of the discussion of the arrangements for these affairs—exact time, transportation (and once an injunction that the press bring their rubbers because the grass would be wet)—emanated from the President himself in the course of the conferences.

The photographers as well as the reporters were invariably included in discussion of invitations or arrangements. One experienced reporter suggested that "he probably was the most photographed man who ever occupied the White House. It was a joke among the photographers that Mr. Coolidge would don any attire or assume any pose that would produce an interesting picture. He was never too busy. . . ."[33] His keen publicity sense told him of the importance inherent in the published photograph as well as coverage on the printed page, and he therefore submitted willingly to this branch of the journalistic fraternity, and kept their welfare in mind.

It is interesting to note that there are few mentions of the secretary to the President in connection with publicity manipulation during the Coolidge period. The first presidential secretary, C. Bascom Slemp, was deliberately chosen by his boss not for his knowledge of the ways of the press, but rather for his political skills and particularly, so it is theorized, for his connections with the Southern elements of the Republican party.[34] Slemp became secretary right after Coolidge succeeded to the office, which was less than a year before the 1924 nominating convention. The shrewd Yankee saw that his immediate goal must be to secure that nomination and in order to do this he had no time to lose. Ability to double as a press secretary was secondary to this primary consideration. Edward Sanders, Slemp's successor after the 1924 election, may well have had more conspicuous ability along publicity lines, though his background also was political and Congressional rather than journalistic. With the firm establishment of the twice-weekly press conference under Harding and Coolidge, however, and the consequent opening up of a regular channel of access to the ear and mind of the President himself, the press relations role of the presidential secretary had become secondary and supplementary, rather than central, to the opinion leadership function.

Anticipating later events, the increasing importance of the press secretary under later Presidents reflects a new turn of the wheel. As press conferences diminished in frequency the direct link between President and working press again became attenuated, as it had under Taft and Wilson. The press secretary again became a necessary intermediary. Furthermore, the increasing complexity of the presidency and the vastly larger scale upon which it has had to be operated in recent decades also means far less time for the President to attend to such details himself, and a need for staff assistance. And finally, the advent of electronic media brought need for a whole new range of publicity skills at the disposal of the White House.

In general the Coolidge press conferences meant, for the reporters, an opportunity to see the Chief Executive regularly, to question him about pending matters (even with the written question, the Coolidge conference was a considerable advance over the catch-as-catch-can situation of the past)—all on a basis of equal opportunity for access and no favoritism.[35] "Off record" and "background" information were also imparted. Exchanges of this sort were fairly frequent though far less than they were to become under F.D.R. In a sense, given the rules about nonquotation and nonattribution, the whole conference fell generally into the category of background material. "These conferences are held for the purpose of giving newspaper men just in a brief way some idea of what the President has in mind in order that they may write intelligently concerning the transaction of the business of the Government," said the President at one. On another occasion Mr. Coolidge noted, "these conferences are held in order to give the members of the press a sort of background and enable them to get the facts to use in their own way and on their own responsibility."

An example of "background material" in the narrower sense, from a Coolidge conference, is the following:

> I have had mimeographed and given to the members of the press what I think is an accurate and detailed statement about some of the progress that we are making in aviation. I would like to have you use it as your own material. It [sic] think it is important and will be helpful to you in getting a clear idea of what the Government is doing, what progress it is making. . . . I will be glad to furnish things of that kind from time to time if occasion may arise, if they seem to be something you might want to use.

Another example came in the conference held April 23, 1926. Coolidge talked for what amounted to more than three pages of the transcript about the problem of the "very great pressure being put on members of Congress for more legislation that would put permanent charges of a very large amount on the government." He concluded: "I have given you this somewhat at length in order to indicate to you the [budgetary] difficulties that I am under at the present time."

There are a few instances of "off the record" comments by the President. The distinction here, given the conference rules, is a rather fine one. Something put off the record would be for the information of the reporters present only, and not to be included in a story at all, in any guise. "Here is a question that I am going to answer, but which I am hoping you won't say anything about. There has been absolutely no intimation to me from any source that Associate Justice Holmes would retire from the Supreme Court." Obviously a reporter had heard this rumor and was checking it with the President. Immediately following the end of another conference, the reporters were called back and Mr. Coolidge, obviously with the intent of scotching a rumor that could have been harmful to American foreign relations, said: "I don't think there is any foundation whatever for any rumor of that kind." One final example: "The War and Navy Departments . . . always seem to think that if they can tell me that the expense is for non-military purposes it doesn't cost the taxpayer anything, and that, therefore, I ought to approve it. I am telling you that for your information—not for your publication."

Another obvious use to which press conferences can be put is to boost legislation in which the President is interested. Surprising as it may seem, Calvin Coolidge made considerable use of his conferences for this purpose also. A detailed study of the conferences held during two sessions of Congress was made in quest of mentions of legislative matters which could be construed as efforts to influence the work of Congress.

The first of these was the first session of the 68th Congress, which had been elected in November 1922, convened on December 3, 1923, and adjourned June 7, 1924. This was also the first meeting of Congress after Coolidge had entered the White House. Unquestionably he was aware that its record, and his record in dealing with legislative matters, could affect his renomination. The second session chosen was that from December 7, 1925, until July 3, 1926, the first session of the 69th Congress. This Congress was elected in November 1924, in conjunction with the President's own landslide victory, and was therefore "his" Congress, not his predecessor's. In other words, the two sessions selected had sharply different bases of relationship to the President.

For the earlier period, there was a total of forty-seven meetings with the press during the session, and at twenty-six of these the President replied to a question about the doings of Congress in such a way as to evidence a desire to influence the legislative process. These varied from flat statements in support of a bill and desire for action to indirect endorsements or a brief allusion to a previous favorable statement. Nevertheless, President Coolidge, at 55 per cent of the press conferences during the 1923-24 regular session, sought to exercise a degree of leadership or influence in the legislative process. The figures for the 1925-26 session, during which he held fifty-six press meetings, show that there were significant mentions of legislative happenings at thirty, or 54 per cent of the total.

A more precise indication of the Coolidge use of press conferences for legislative leadership is afforded by study of a particular issue. One of the President's continuing legislative preoccupations was tax reduction—specifically, the so-called Mellon tax plan.[36] Measures to effect tax reduction were introduced in the 1923-24 session, and followed by the Chief Executive with keen interest. In no less than eighteen of the conferences held between December, 1923, and June, 1924, the subject of taxation was discussed by Coolidge, sometimes at considerable length. On ten of these occasions he urged Congress to enact the legislation, in specific terms. For example: "I am very anxious . . . that there should be legislation relative to taxation," "its enactment at the earliest possible time," "I am in favor of the administration's bill," or "You may dwell with such emphasis as you want on the necessity of getting the tax reduction."

On occasion the President asked the reporters point blank to publicize some particular opinion or idea, and often this took the form of asking them to help him *stop* legislation he deemed harmful. For instance: "One of the disturbing factors at the present time to me is the large number of bills pending in Congress calling for tremendous appropriations. . . . I think it is exceedingly important wherever you can to sound a word of warning in that direction. . . . I don't know of any better service you can perform than to sound a word of public warning." In the general context of the conference in which it appeared, there is little doubt that this was not in reply to a specific question submitted, but a gratuitous interjection by the President.

On January 11, 1924, a reporter asked in effect whether the President would veto bonus legislation then being considered, if it were presented to him. "I don't believe it is quite the thing for the executive to make public announcements that he would veto certain legislation . . . though there are certain inferences always of what might be done. You gentlemen are very adroit at that." Someone immediately asked if the press could speculate on that, whereupon Coolidge replied: "I don't need to stimulate you."

So much concern in press conferences with the status of legislation on the Hill is rather hard to reconcile with the Vermonter's generally limited view of his proper role in policy making. One explanation may be that with the institutionalization of the press conference as a regular means for conveying presidential views to the general public (and to Congress) interest groups came to feel that a White House endorsement would have even more value than in the past in building support for a pet project. That President Coolidge received this kind of pressure seems evident from the following:

> I am somewhat embarrassed sometimes by referring to only one or two of the many bills. . . . That is, other people have bills that are not mentioned, and then they come to me and want to know why I have a legislative program that doesn't include their bill. So I have had to explain a great many times that all I have referred to was some incidental bills that have been brought to my attention.

On another occasion:

> A great many people have bills that they are interested in and just because I happen to mention those two bills I don't want it understood that there are not a great many others that perhaps in some

> instances are more important—more important to the people that are interested in them.

Coolidge, in spite of his own minimal aspirations in this area, was apparently drawn into the business of promoting legislation as a kind of useful middleman, rather more than has been the case with Presidents since. Thus the net total of legislative endorsements during his regime may well have approached that of other Presidents much more active on behalf of their own Congressional objectives.

Frederick Lewis Allen in his book *The Lords of Creation* writes: "President Coolidge and his multi-millionaire Secretary of the Treasury had for some years past been giving intermittent aid and comfort to the bull party in the market by uttering soothing words when stocks showed signs of sagging. . . ."[37] Besides legislative endorsement the President seems to have used the White House platform, and the press conferences in particular, to talk prosperity, to keep up business confidence, and generally to create a favorable climate for economic activity.[38] An examination of his conference transcripts supports Allen's point. One example will suffice:

> I have had here at Paul Smith's [his 1926 vacation camp] in the last three or four weeks quite a number of representatives of different industries and commercial activities of the country. If you will review what they have said . . . I think you will see that it demonstrates pretty well that the country is in a prosperous condition . . . and perhaps that would be worthy of a new story on the part of any of you gentlemen that have a disposition to write something of that kind out. It might be a constructive piece of work. I have had interviews with quite a cross section of the different interests. If you assemble those and recall them, I think they would make an interesting news story.[39]

Every President, to some degree, sets the mood of the country by the cumulative impact of his public utterances. Wilson, powerfully aided and abetted by Creel's organization, did this. Theodore Roosevelt had created a general feeling of buoyancy and excitement. His cousin Franklin certainly became the embodiment of the struggle against economic adversity. Given the twice-a-week press conference as a channel of virtually continual communication between President and people, this impact will almost inevitably be enormous.

Unlike Congress, the Chief Executive, aided by the press conference, can remain in the limelight twelve months of the year. Coolidge sensed the publicity advantage which this gave him. While on his extended vacations away from Washington each summer, he hardly missed a single Tuesday or Friday meeting with the reporters. He said, near the start of the first of these lengthy stays, one assumes only half in jest: "I don't know as I can say very much about my vacation. I expect to spend a considerable part of it trying to amuse the newspapermen (laughter)." A careful perusal of this and subsequent periods out of Washington, in the transcripts, shows a continuing concern that the correspondents be kept supplied with something to write about—if no more than trivia connected with his travels.

Writing of his 1926 vacation, spent at White Pine Camp in the Adirondacks, *Time* notes that: "Spokesman Coolidge (with the aid of plentiful padding by newspaper correspondents) has become a garrulous soul. In fact, press dispatches concerning him and his views, have totalled 1,209,739 words in sixty-two days of his vacation."[40] The following year, the Vermonter himself commented on the amount of news generated:

> THE PRESIDENT: . . . there was such a diversity of happenings that I think the newspapermen found sufficient material nearly every day on which to make a story. I heard very little complaint about that. I haven't seen the official figures of the amount of space that went out from the Black Hills. I think a computation was made of the space that went out from White Pine Camp. . . .
>
> NEWSPAPERMAN: I understand it was 2,150,000 [words] this year and about 600,000 more than last year.[41]

This is further evidence of the publicity sense which Coolidge brought to the presidency.

Shifting now to the format of these confrontations with the press, in general they followed closely the precedents President Harding had set when he instituted the written question. For all the seeming rigidity of these conference rules, in practice they were much more flexible than might be assumed. For example, the Harding rules allowed follow-up queries from the floor only when the President had raised a subject drawn from the written questions.[42] A check of the first eighty-odd Coolidge transcripts shows that on the average the reporters asked between three and four questions from the floor during each meeting. Some of these were "supplementaries" but many, perhaps most of them, in effect raised a new subject. Only once did the President reprove a correspondent for plying him with these spontaneous questions, and this man kept rephrasing the same inquiry, trying to elicit an answer. In view of the frequency of these supplementaries, the contrast between the Coolidge era meetings and the later ones of Franklin Roosevelt, for example, is not quite as sharp as it is often painted. Furthermore, frequently the President would inject a comment or announcement on some matter that he had not been asked about.

Regarding reporters' general attitudes, on occasion one would act as spokesman for the group to thank the President for his efforts on their behalf.

> MR. GROVES: Mr. President, I have been asked by my colleagues to express our very great appreciation for your courtesy and consideration during this summer. The newspaper work of course has its difficulties and this has been an important assignment, important to us, important to our newspapers, and important to the public. But your consideration has been constant and I think that the little matter of the trip to Plymouth is an example of the fact that you had our comfort in mind. And especially do we appreciate the manner in which you have ordered the activities of this office, the fact that you have held your conferences regularly twice a week and that you have brought your guests, your important guests, down here so that we might see them at this office instead of chasing them all over the country.

The President's reply to this gracious speech is also instructive:

> I am very much gratified to know that. I know the difficulties that the members of the press have on summer vacations. In fact, it is a tradition of the Presidential office, with the old heads in there like Mr. [Rudolph] Forster [clerk on the White House staff under many Presidents], that whenever the President goes away on a

> summer vacation that it is always very difficult for the members of the press that go with him. Usually there isn't much for them to write about. . . .

Obviously this exchange reflected conventional courtesy, but it is hard to discount it entirely as a true reflection of the general feeling. The reply is particularly revealing. Coolidge had clearly made inquiries about past practice, and had made the decision to change that practice. Again his sensitivity to public relations emerges clearly.

Yet for all the evidence that suggests a fruitful relationship between President Coolidge and the working press, it would be inaccurate to suggest that all went smoothly amid general satisfaction. The essentially ambivalent relationship of the President with the reporters is such that never, in all probability, will both sides find the conferences completely to their liking.

There were in fact several pronounced points of friction.[43] One major difficulty which most commentators cited was the "White House spokesman."[44] This had become the standard way of identifying the President as news source in the Coolidge era. Critics of the President and of the press conference format contended that in this device the Chief Executive enjoyed an unfair advantage. It was obvious to all but the uninitiated what the source of a statement so labeled was, and yet the real author could still hide behind this formal anonymity if he so desired, and even repudiate something he had said. Actually, Coolidge himself began to find fault with this practice, and complained that the reporters were putting quotation marks around the opinions of the phantom "Spokesman." He eventually requested that the practice be changed, and the "Spokesman" thereupon departed into limbo.[45] Later on the President went further and made it clear that news obtained from the White House should not be identified as to source even by circumlocution. In other words, he preferred that even the fact of the holding of the conferences be concealed from public view, as the only way of fully enforcing the nonattribution rule.

There was also friction over the President's frequent practice of reading a question and silently passing it to the bottom of the pack with neither answer nor acknowledgment. Annoyed reporters began noting in print that the Chief Executive had not answered a particular query and imputing significance to his silence. This practice Mr. Coolidge requested stopped. On another occasion he had a tiff with a representative of David Lawrence who had been sent to take stenographic notes of the proceedings. The President made it clear that, again to protect the confidential nature of the conferences, only *his* stenographer was permitted to make such a record. Some commentators say that these White House transcripts were, for a time, made available to the correspondents after the press conferences,[46] presumably to enable them to check the accuracy of their own notes and recollections. Silas Bent claims, however, that the practice was discontinued in 1926 because a statement the President denied making was verified from these notes, after his denial.[47]

Certain fundamental questions about the nature and purpose of the press conference have never been fully answered. Should the President have some protection against a misquotation or ill-advised statement? Should the conferences be private meetings between reporters and the White House occupant, or should they themselves and what occurs at them become news rather than merely the raw material for the preparation of news stories? From the President's point of view, the rules in force during the 1920s did preserve him, to a considerable extent, from the consequences of inadvertence or misconstruction. They also allowed him to open his thinking to the reporters—by giving background information and the like—much more than would be possible once transcripts came to be published for all to read. He could not, however, under these rules, speak directly to the public through the conferences without the newsmen as intermediaries.

From the reporters' side of the table, the rules were seen as hampering the news-gathering process, as giving the President an unfair advantage at times, and as an encouragement to inaccuracy if not downright speculation and fabrication. On the other hand, they did preserve for the working press (though few seemed to see this at the time) a kind of monopoly position which was to be diminished sharply with the advent of full verbatim disclosure during the last decade.

The President himself summarized his feelings about his press relations on a couple of occasions. In a speech at his first appearance before the Gridiron Club, on December 8, 1923, he said:

> I suppose that I am not very good copy. . . . But the boys have been very kind and considerate to me, and where there has been any discrepancy, they have filled it in and glossed it over, and they have manufactured some. They have undertaken to endow me with some characteristics and traits that I didn't altogether know I had. But I have done the best I could to be perfectly fair with them, and in public, to live up to those traits.[48]

And then, the closing words of his last press conference:

> You have been, I think, quite successful in interpreting the administration to the country. I have known that I wasn't much of a success in undertaking newspaper work, so I have left the work of reporting the affairs of my administration to the experts of the Press. Perhaps that is the reason that the reports have been more successful than they would have been if I had undertaken myself to direct them. It has been a pleasure to have you come in twice a week and give me an opportunity to answer such queries as you wished to propound. I want to thank you again for your constant kindness and consideration.

Important as the newspapers were to Coolidge, he was also the first President to come into office after radio had been developed into a practical medium. Gleason L. Archer, in his history of the first few years of radio, aptly suggested: "It is probably true that radio played an exceedingly important part in the career of Calvin Coolidge. In six months [after he became President] the national election would be in its preliminary stages. In that brief time President Coolidge was so to impress himself upon the voters that no serious opposition to his re-election was to manifest itself."[49] It will never be possible to demonstrate conclusively how important the role of radio was in creating the Coolidge myth or implanting it in the public mind, but it was of considerable importance.

From the pioneer broadcasting done by Harding, the development of the medium went forward by leaps and bounds. Aside from technical advances, the whole atmosphere of wonder and excitement that surrounded this modern miracle undoubtedly redounded to the President's advantage. This was a fascinating new toy. Set owners sat far into the night listening to anything and everything, writing down gleefully new stations picked up. The quality of the programs was less important than the sheer joy of hearing voices and music coming through the ether. This was a day of captive audiences which, held to the earphones by a kind of hypnosis, devoured the programs offered and cried for more. To the would-be exploiter of the medium it meant, one imagines, a dependable audience that required little of the skill that later audiences demanded.

It was at this juncture that the shy, dour, unimpressive looking Vermonter appeared on the scene. Radio, said most contemporary observers, was a natural for him.[50] On the stump in 1920 he had been a doubtful asset to the party. Had he had to rely on his barnstorming abilities to make his mark in the very short time before the convention in June, 1924, his success would have been dubious. But he had radio, and what is more, he realized its potential for himself. Senator James Watson of Indiana reproduces in his memoirs a conversation with Coolidge in which he has the President saying: "I am very fortunate that I came in with the radio. I can't make an engaging, rousing, or oratorical speech to a crowd as you can, . . . but I have a good radio voice, and now I can get my messages across to them without acquainting them with my lack of oratorical ability. . . ." Watson goes on to say that Coolidge laughed "about as heartily as I ever knew him to" over what he considered his good fortune.[51] Slemp, in the introduction to his compilation of Coolidge views, writes that radio seemed to have been invented for him.

The President and his immediate advisors, of whom Slemp was one of the most important, exploited this new medium deliberately. Even in the absence of direct testimony to this effect, a look at the radio appearances by the President before the convention met suggests some very shrewd stage management. From August to December, when Congress was to convene, the President rather ostentatiously refused all speaking engagements, pleading pressure of work in picking up the threads of his new job. This did *not* mean that the people of the country learned nothing about their new leader indirectly through the press, but it did mean that their thirst

President Coolidge broadcasting at Kansas City in 1926.
Times Wide World Photos.

for first-hand contact with him was allowed to grow before it was slaked.

The President's first significant public appearance was his State of the Union Message delivered in person to Congress on December 6, 1923. This was the first presidential message to Congress to be broadcast. Secretary Slemp had done everything he could to insure the largest possible radio audience and checked on reaction to it afterward. The chain which sent it out onto the airwaves comprised stations in Washington, New York, Providence, St. Louis, Kansas City, and Dallas. Listeners a thousand miles away reported gleefully that Coolidge's crisp New England accent and even the noise as he turned the pages of his manuscript came through clearly. The impact seems to have been considerable.

Before the convention in June he made five more large-scale, carefully staged broadcasts plus at least three that went out over one or two stations (usually WEAF in New York and a Washington station). The first of the major speeches originated in his study in the White House on December 10 and took the form of what the *New York Times* called a "touching eulogy of President Harding." In February he made his first "political" speech at a Lincoln Day Dinner. This was broadcast to what one source (probably optimistic) estimated was an audience of five million. Then on February 22 he delivered from the White House a tribute to Washington and again was heard by "several million" people. Regarding his next major effort, before the convention of the Associated Press, a *Times* article ran: "Probably never before has the voice of the head of a government been heard by so many people, for unprecedented steps were taken to broadcast Mr. Coolidge's address as far as possible across the country."[52] Finally, on May 11 he made a 300-word speech on behalf of a movement for better homes.[53]

Note that after the State of the Union Message, Coolidge made sure he revisited the homes of eager radio fans at least on the average of once a month. The occasions and subjects chosen were admirably calculated to convey a general impression of the man and his ideas without in the least offending by their partisanship, save possibly the Lincoln Day Dinner talk. His less widely broadcast appearances followed the same line—an address to the D.A.R. in April, his Memorial Day speech, and a speech in connection with an oratorical contest in early June. Several of these broadcasts were from his study in the White House. In other words, he quickly made the transition from the mere broadcast of a set speech aimed primarily at a live audience to speeches aimed exclusively at the radio listeners. This suggests a very rapid and significant recognition of radio as a medium in its own right, rather than as a mere adjunct to the old-fashioned public meeting.

The fact that the President was nominated to run for a full term with 1,165 out of a possible 1,209 first ballot votes at the convention is a rough measure of what skillful exploitation of the mass media had accomplished. Here was the first President in history whom more than a tiny fraction of the populace could actually listen to, and whose voice they could come to know at first hand. Small wonder that the man developed a tangible meaning for millions—more so perhaps than any of his predecessors.

With the nomination in his pocket, Coolidge sought to press his advantage using the same techniques. An article in the *New York Times* of July 18, 1924, under the heading "Coolidge Plans Campaign by Radio" ran in part: "There is no prospect of President Coolidge taking the stump. . . . In the statement of Mr. Butler [national chairman] there is involved no suggestion that President Coolidge will refrain from speaking in his campaign for reelection. On the contrary, he expects to deliver a number of important addresses, beginning with his speech of acceptance and, as he hopes, to the largest audience in all the history of political campaigning." The report goes on to note that these will be broadcast from the White House or from platforms before audiences in Washington, and then transmitted coast to coast.

The *Times* writer then speculates about the impact of radio on campaigning in more general terms:

> In the four years that have passed since the last national fight, the perfection of the radio has opened a way to revolutionize political campaigning. The campaign managers of President Coolidge expect to take advantage of this to the fullest extent possible. . . . It was pointed out yesterday that with the radio as a vehicle for long distance political speechmaking, not only can President Coolidge's public utterances be carried to the firesides throughout the land, but through cooperation of local organizations, to audiences assembled in large halls with receivers and loud speakers. Supplemented by motion pictures, showing the President in action, persons identified with the campaign believe that addresses by President Coolidge, broadcast throughout the country, would prove a great attraction even to audiences that ordinarily do not attend political meetings. . . .[54]

The last suggestion, if nothing else, shows the ingenuity of the Coolidge managers. In August another *Times* article reported a projected test of an idea developed by Dr. Lee DeForrest "which synchronizes the radio voice with the motion picture of a speaker" and might make possible something approaching the kind of appearances which are now achieved by television.[55]

After the election of 1924 President Coolidge continued to broadcast at intervals. One contemporary observer who did a statistical analysis of presidential public statements claims that an average of over 8,000 words per month went out over the air waves.[56] Coolidge himself, though sensing the campaign potential of the new medium, appears not to have felt that regular "fireside chats" or reports to the nation were either necessary or, perhaps, desirable. In reply to a press conference query in February, 1925, he said: "I don't think it is necessay for the President periodically to address the country by radio. The newspaper reporters do very well for me in that direction. . . . There are certain occasions when I am making an address when it is very fine that the country can hear it . . . but it doesn't seem to me that there is any necessity, or that there will be any paricular value, for the President to undertake any periodic addresses of that kind at fixed and certain times."

For Coolidge, one infers, desirable presidential use of radio was limited to the broadcast of general speeches or fixed policy pronouncements like the State of the Union Message. The notion, later embodied in the Roosevelt "fireside chat," of using it for the specific shaping of public opinion for policy objectives did not occur to him. He did, unquestionably, see the potential of radio for projecting the *personality* of the President, as the foregoing discussion seems amply to demonstrate. In short, his exploitation of the medium can hardly be criticized as timid or unimaginative. In view of radio's newness and the complete lack of guiding precedent, his record seems all the more remarkable.

If it had been Harding who introduced the speech writer as a regular fixture on the White House staff, it was his successor who made the most striking use of this new functionary. Coolidge kept Judson Welliver to fill the same role in preparing speeches for him as he had performed for the late President.[57] Welliver was not technically on the White House payroll, but was nominally attached to one of the departments in the executive branch, though he worked full time for the President. (This kind of expedient was characteristic of the staffing of the presidency until recent decades.) In December, 1925, according to *Time*, the President appointed one Stuart Crawford, who had been at Amherst when he was there, as Chief Clerk at the White House. "The 'Chief Clerk' gathers material for and assists the President in preparing speeches and important letters," *Time* went on to say.[58] Thus Coolidge was amply supplied with ghost writing talent.

This speech writing assistance, one commentator suggested, though it made the President's public utterances rather dull, did free him for the more essential parts of his job as Chief Executive.[59] Nicholas Murray Butler offered a similarly divided appraisal:

> It is a misfortune that as President he had permitted so many of his formal addresses to be written for him by members of his staff. These have made him seem prolix, jejune and ordinary to a degree. Curiously enough, these long addresses have put this so-called silent man in the position of using in his public addresses and papers more words during his five and a half years in the White House than were used by Theodore Roosevelt and Wilson together.[60]

Butler went on to cite a compilation done by a Washington correspondent as the source of his estimate.

Charles Merz, in a piece published in the *New Republic* for June 2, 1926, entitled "The Silent Mr. Coolidge," presents an elaborate analysis of the public pronouncements, speeches, and statements of the President. (This is possibly the same set of figures cited by Butler, though it covers only the first three years Coolidge was in office.) Merz found that Wilson had delivered thirteen addresses in the first year of his first term, and seventeen during the first year of his second term (1913 and 1917 respectively), while Coolidge made twenty-eight public addresses in 1925, and in addition, some sixty statements, letters given to the press, and messages to public meetings, issued from the White House. Merz goes on to note the vast flood of statements by the "White House spokesman" which should be added to the not inconsiderable flow of directly attributed utterances.[61] The pattern of groups, nationalities, and so on, to whom messages were directed covered the population so systematically, he suggests, that it appeared the President had some kind of carefully worked out master plan in mind which he followed in spreading his favors around.

Particularly significant here is the enlarging scale upon which the publicity functions of the President were being carried on. In general the quality of presidential papers is probably less important than the impact of sheer volume on the public. A President who nearly doubles the number of public addresses made annually is obviously calling attention to himself and his office far more insistently than had been the case before.

The ghost writer was obviously essential to make this step-up in output possible. The question why the scale of output expanded is harder to answer. In part, during the Coolidge era, it was the publicity sense of the President himself. He apparently sensed that increased activity on this score would redound to his benefit, particularly his electoral benefit in 1924. The scrapbooks of addresses, statements, and the like,[62] contained the following number of items for each of the years Coolidge was in office: 1923—19; 1924—87; 1925—36; 1926—43; 1927—38; 1928—25; 1929—3. It is probably by no means an accident that in the election year 1924 there were more items than in any other two years combined, and the 1924 list discloses few if any out-and-out campaign speech texts. The White House mimeograph machines were obviously made to grind at double what was to become the normal rate in order to help keep the man from Vermont continually before the public, and allowed to slack off once the election was safely won.[63]

It is also probably true, particularly of messages to special groups from the Chief Executive, that as the general tempo and volume increased, and caused heightened awareness of the presidency as a power and influence center in the government, groups in quest of influence sought to tap this source for their own purposes. A presidential statement to a national association meeting, or better still a presidential use of their meeting as platform for an address—whatever the subject—came more and more to be coveted as a sign of prestige, a source of publicity, and hence an increment of power.

In sum, Coolidge was an innovator of considerable importance in the area of communication technique. He did much to solidify the position of the presidential press conference, thus setting a precedent for his successors. In addition, he indicated in his own use of this device some of the purposes to which it could be put. In harnessing the new medium of radio for the purposes of the Chief

Executive, he laid a firm foundation upon which men like F.D.R. were later to build with spectacular results. He stepped up the outflow of statements from the White House, both enhancing thereby the over-all position of the President, and developing the practice of "loaning" the aura of the presidency to groups and claimants, public and private, far beyond former practice.

In the course of all this, Coolidge made it clear that the growing leadership and opinion-forming potential of the office could be used as effectively by a President who sought only to reign as by one who also wanted to rule. The potential was there, the mass media saw to that—in an ever rising spiral. The presidency merely had to keep pace. Coolidge kept pace with these developments, and actually, so the record would suggest, forced the pace here and there in significant ways.

The foregoing developments had their impact in lowering the barriers which traditionally shut most of the functioning of the Chief Executive from the public gaze. Coolidge continued, for example, the Harding innovation of disclosing the gist of cabinet deliberations. His firm institutionalization of the press conferences insured the public a window on the Executive that they had never had before. Radio, as Secretary Slemp noted, put the Chief Executive in direct communication with the people.[64] Coolidge himself was not unaware of what had happened. He wrote in a magazine article: "The excuse for [rear platform] appearances which formerly existed has been eliminated by the coming of the radio."[65]

Finally, President Coolidge, probably more than any of his predecessors, was willing to throw open his private life as well as his official activity to public gaze.[66] He recognized, so it would seem, that in an age of mass communications, the white light of publicity finds difficulty in distinguishing between the public and the private lives of those involved. The most sensible and realistic approach to this problem for the President, is to accept the fact that he must offer up his privacy as a sacrifice. News about his personal doings can pave the way for ready acceptance of his public utterances.

The presidency, by the time Calvin Coolidge left it on March 4, 1929, had been refashioned, in part through his own efforts, into an office which in public relations terms aroused certain rather specific expectations and made certain demands on its occupant. Both would have to be fulfilled or the successor would suffer the consequences. Presidents, more than ever before, had to be willing and able to function—and live—in a glare of publicity, and had to have enough publicity sense, enough skill at turning these developments to their own advantage, to operate effectively under the new conditions. This was the problem which Herbert Hoover faced, and under the hammer blows of the Great Depression, failed to solve.

☆☆☆☆☆☆☆

Chapter 5

☆☆☆☆☆☆☆

RETROGRESSION: HOOVER

Herbert Hoover[1] was a strange paradox from a public relations point of view. He was the unique product of the new age of mass communications, and yet, once in the White House, was less adept at coping with this side of the office than any President since Taft. The reasons for this anomaly seem to lie in his personality, background, and ideas, and also in the pace and nature of communications development. The depression made a contribution but probably a secondary one.

The "Great Engineer"—as he was called first in admiration and later in bitter jest—brought to the White House a tremendous reputation built up by his work in World War I. The wide publicity given to the Belgian relief effort necessarily involved its director. Will Irwin notes that "Newspapers and magazines, scenting a story, began to appeal for 'personality stuff' on Hoover." He was reluctant, but "in spite of himself his fame grew."[2] After Congress declared war, Hoover was called to take over the role of Food Administrator in the Wilson administration, a job destined by its nature to enhance the fame of its holder, whether he willed it or not. As Irwin wrote, "Hoover appealed to the people." A vast campaign to save food and enlist the aid of every housewife in the land was launched in his name. "He mobilized not only business but journalism; gathered into his department as volunteers eminent editors, advertising specialists, poster-artists, cartoonists."[3] Soon this retiring and once unknown businessman's name "was a household word, . . . the root for that new slang verb, 'to hooverize' "[4] to economize in the use of food.

In the 1920 Republican convention Hoover was a contender, though not a strong one. Samuel Hopkins Adams thought his popularity with the mass of the people was so great that had the issue been up to them, he might well have been the nominee. However, "nominations are not managed in that way. . . . Hoover had no organization back of him. His party allegiance was in doubt. The leaders would have none of him."[5] There was no question, however, about his inclusion in the Harding Cabinet. The President-elect exacted the consent of the reluctant old guard to make him Secretary of Commerce, an apparently innocuous office.

Either as a by-product of his policy aspirations for the Department, or by conscious design, Secretary Hoover made of his agency one of the most active, if not the most active, in the executive branch, and one of the most publicized.[6] An idea of the range of activity of the omnipresent Secretary of Commerce is gained from Irwin's description of a contemporary cartoon entitled "View of Washington" which showed multiple representations of Hoover leading American domestic and foreign commerce, nursing the fledgling radio and aviation industries, as patron of waterways, foe of unemployment, etc. Under the Hoover regime the Department equipped itself with a press room and an official to preside over the dispensing of press releases. In 1926 George Akerson, later his press secretary in the White House, joined the Secretary's staff with the alleged role of keeping his chief in the public eye.[7]

Two instances of potent Hoover publicity while he headed the Department of Commerce will suffice. Starting in 1922, the Department sponsored a "Better Homes in America" movement, with Hoover as president and a growing number of local chapters, which by 1927 numbered 3,600. Then there was the unprecedented

Mississippi flood of 1927. President Coolidge placed Hoover in charge of the giant rescue and relief problem. According to a hostile account, following this assignment, "Mr. Akerson did the rest. He organized a survey trip through the flooded area, and accompanied by a large corps of photographers and reporters, he and the Chief floated down the river amid a fanfare of publicity."[8] In fact a Senate Republican leader is supposed to have observed that the 1927 flood ruined the South but elected Hoover President.

In short, before his nomination, this shy Quaker had had one of the longest and most sustained and most spectacular publicity build-ups in the history of the presidency. Only that of Dwight Eisenhower is comparable, in recent times. For more than a dozen years he had been almost continually in the public eye. He became a symbol of all that Americans admire about themselves—his rags-to-riches career, the aura of science (practical applied science) about his profession, his application of disinterested and militantly nonpolitical administrative talents to large charitable and governmental undertakings, and his self-effacing personality. And the national habit of putting persons with just this sort of apolitical reputation into high political office landed him in the presidency.

Was Herbert Hoover really the shy, retiring individual Irwin and others painted him, who struggled to keep himself in the publicity background, or did he have and use on his own behalf what the author of the *Mirrors of Washington* claimed for him as early as 1921, an "extraordinary talent for publicity?"[9] In reading the voluminous literature pro and con, one is tempted to side with the "shy" school, though with reservations. Once the presidential bug had bitten, there is little doubt that his quest for the office overcame much of his reticence, though even this seemed to produce no enthusiasm for publicity as such. It is also doubtless true that throughout his public career Hoover, as a highly intelligent man and a skillful executive, had an intellectual appreciation for the usefulness and potency of public relations. But this by no means supports the assertion that he assiduously publicized *himself* from 1915 on.

The real point is not what Hoover or his disciples did but what was automatically done for and to the man by the operation of the new model newspaper and the whole vast and growing apparatus of mass communications. One correspondent, in a *Nation* appraisal of "Hoover and the Press" makes the point when he writes, "Knowing that the newspapers made him, [Hoover] assumes they can with equal ease destroy him"—this by way of explaining Hoover's sensitivity to press criticism.[10] This is precisely what happened. Hoover was copy of the most desirable and saleable kind for more than twelve years before 1928. The iteration and reiteration of his exploits, and the appetite for still more news of him thus created, eventually had the effect of imprinting a vastly larger than life Hoover image on the American public mind.[11] Whether there was much conscious abetting of this process by Hoover or his associates is largely an academic question. What happened would have happened almost regardless of anything that the man himself might have done.

This giant media-created image plus the affinity of the American political system for such candidate material made his election almost predictable. Hoover himself seemed to sense this. Will Irwin asked Hoover, during the flood crisis, whether he would be a candidate for the nomination if Coolidge was not. The latter replied: " 'I shall be the nominee, probably. . . . It is nearly inevitable.' "[12] It was by no means equally inevitable that Hoover would in fact fit the White House role as well as the public seemed to assume. For one thing, an intellectual appreciation of public relations and the ability to exploit the platform offered by the presidency are not the same thing.

Certain background and personality characteristics of the man contributed to Hoover's difficulties as President. This ground has been traversed many times and there is general agreement on most points among both friends and foes. Walter Lippmann summed up much of the case when he pointed out that the President had had little or no experience in the art of politics before this, his only election to office, and furthermore, he was characteristically "diffident in the presence of the normal irrationality of democracy."[13] Both as a businessman and as a scientist of sorts, Hoover had dealt in facts, which usually could be marshaled to indicate the one appropriate course of action in a given case. He now moved from a realm of rational discussion to the normal and inevitable irrationalities of politics. All observers agree that of politics he knew little, and what he knew he disliked.

If one pieces together scattered information about Hoover's conception of the presidency and of what he hoped to accomplish in it, the result does not resemble Coolidge's passivity. Hoover drew sharp limits around the legitimate sphere of White House and governmental activity, but his conception was nevertheless positive—and especially so once the depression had struck. He sought to bring businesslike scientific management to public affairs; to identify problems, ferret out the facts, and implement the indicated solutions; and he fully intended to inform and educate the public to these ends. What his concept lacked was allowance for sharply differing objectives which no marshaling of facts could reconcile, and the need to lead and shape public opinion not just by exegesis but by simplifying, dramatizing, and endlessly repeating the lessons being taught. Above all he left out of account the human element, with all of man's need for flattery, his willful obtuseness, suspicion, and the rest. The statistics of which he was so fond were no substitute for the human touch.[14]

Reduced to their essence, most if not all of the Hoover difficulties in the conduct of the office were in the realm of public relations. Hoover apologists have often laid the major blame for the problems of the administration at the door of the Democratic National Committee, and specifically its publicity impresario, Charles Michelson.[15] But as Frank Kent pointed out in a pro-Hoover analysis of the Michelson phenomenon, the Democrats did nothing more than make the first move into a vacuum which had long existed, by taking advantage of recently perfected techniques of press agentry. Since time immemorial both parties had dismantled their Washington staffs once the quadrennial elections were over. After 1928 things were different. Thanks to liberal financing by John J. Raskob, a staff was kept in being, Michelson was put in charge of public relations and brought his not inconsiderable skill to bear on the task of discrediting Hoover.[16]

It is unfair to convict Michelson of malicious mischief, unless it can be shown that his techniques went well beyond the accepted practices of American politics—a difficult task. To decry the mere fact that he did the job for which he was hired, with considerable ability, is pointless. Either party *could* have hired a Michelson if it had wanted to. The Democrats merely thought of it first. There is no more curious lack in American politics than that of an articulate voice for the opposition. Supplying one, as Michelson did, was hardly a crime. The whole American political system had habitually left the propaganda function regarding issues and philosophies largely up to private interests. For better or worse, this age-old pattern was beginning to change, and it began changing at a time which found a beleaguered President Hoover as prime target.

At an early stage of Hoover's political career some backers prepared a news release containing a dramatic account of his Boxer Rebellion experiences, and then made the error of showing it to him. He is said to have torn it up with the comment, "You can't make a Teddy Roosevelt out of me."[17] Clearly, the first prerequisite of successful presidential publicity was missing from his make-up —an understanding of the workings of the media combined with a desire and ability to exploit them. Hoover, apparently, was quite conscious of this lack and had no intention of changing his ways or attempting to acquire skills he did not have.

For cultivation of the working press the device of the press conference, pioneered by Hoover's predecessors, was available to him, and at the outset it appeared not only that he was going to use it with ability and sensitivity, but that he would add highly desirable refinements of his own. In a statement at his first meeting with the correspondents, the day after his inauguration, he outlined what he had in mind, prefacing his sketch of the revised ground rules with the comment that "the relations of the President and the press have been a matter of development over a number of administrations, . . . going through one experimental stage to another down to the present time." Means had been found, he continued, for a more intimate relationship, and he felt that things could be developed even further along these lines.

He said that he would like to have the reporters appoint a committee to consult with him on matters of mutual concern. Then the thorny question of attribution was tackled in a forthright manner.[18] Mr. Hoover said he wanted to establish three categories of informa-

President Hoover broadcasting a speech at Marion, Ohio, in 1931. *Wide World Photos.*

tion. The first, breaking precedent, would embrace presidential comments which could be quoted directly. (In the past only special permission, rarely given, had allowed direct quotation—usually of a very brief passage.) Secondly, background information would be made available for use in preparing stories, but not for quotation; it could be attributed to the White House in a general way. Finally, there were things that would be told the reporters in confidence, for their information only. Hoover made it clear that he wanted to eliminate once and for all the infamous "White House spokesman" of the previous administration. He retained the written question rule, but stipulated that queries must be submitted twenty-four hours in advance. At least one observer felt he was much more willing to submit to "supplementaries" from the floor than his predecessors had been.[19]

That these bright initial hopes for a new era in presidential press relations faded as quickly as they did can be laid in part to the onset of the depression with the stock market crash in October,

1929, some seven months after Hoover had taken office. Apparently, however, they in fact lasted only three months, for one pair of authors insists that the innovations were junked at the end of that period.[20] If this assertion is true, the blame can hardly be put on external crises, but must fall largely on the President himself.

Events preceding the inauguration contained ominous signs of what was to happen. As Secretary of Commerce, Hoover had been very popular with the working press, but during the campaign his relations with the reporters in his entourage were not good. He was aloof, and when he did talk with them, he seemed to resent their questioning.[21] Then, following the election, came the extended good-will tour of South America which filled much of the interregnum. It was announced at the outset that all news copy was to pass through the hands of one George Barr Baker, a former wartime censor, who occupied a liaison position with the President-elect. The reporters murmured about censorship but apparently felt they should bide their time and give him the benefit of the doubt.[22]

What happened to the press conferences can be more easily described than accounted for, since the deterioration got well under way while the predepression honeymoon was still in force. For one thing Hoover was extremely sensitive to criticism, and in a President, supreme target of all disgruntled groups in the country, this is a grievous weakness.[23] Contemporary discussions of the press meetings indicate that he took to lecturing the reporters about critical or allegedly misleading stories. More important, he made few moves to establish cordial relations with the members of the working press. The *cause célèbre* represented by the famous Rapidan Camp is the most spectacular case in point.[24]

This was a retreat purchased and constructed at the head of the Rapidan River in Virginia, some 100 miles from the capital. To it the President repaired on weekends with varying groups of advisers or visitors. The reporters were not allowed anywhere near the camp itself, and had to get by as best they might with accommodations a good many miles away. No satisfactory system was ever adopted for keeping them advised about the activities at the retreat, and in fact as time went on they were not even informed when the President was to leave the city for Rapidan, with the result that they were forced to race after the presidential cavalcade in their own cars on short notice in order not to neglect what they conceived their duty: to keep the Chief Executive under surveillance at all times.[25] More than one reporter was killed or injured on the wild rides through the Virginia countryside. All of this was a far cry from the solicitude for the press which Coolidge maintained on his summer vacations, and at other times as well.

Then there was the matter of the President playing favorites. One of the cardinal assumptions underlying the regularized press conference as established by Wilson was the notion that all reporters would be treated alike. Hoover chose to disregard this precedent. A dozen or so favorites had informal access to the White House's inner sanctum—the chief one being, perhaps, Mark Sullivan, who was a member of the early morning medicine ball cabinet.[26] Then there was the practice of entertaining editors and publishers at the White House and at the presidential retreat of a weekend. Coolidge had begun the former practice on a considerable scale and it represented a further recognition of the great power wielded by the magnates of the mass circulation dailies. The discreet flattery represented by White House invitations could be expected at least to do the President no harm in the news columns. With Hoover, however, there were strong suspicions that the purpose went much farther. In at least a few cases, the reporters were certain that members of their group had been disciplined or even fired at the instigation of a presidential host entertaining their bosses.[27] Again, from the working press's point of view, the rule against favoritism was being broken in a most underhanded and malignant way. These White House practices, plus increasing suspicions that the President was guilty of deliberately misleading his press conferences on specific matters, if not of downright falsification, succeeded in turning most of those who covered the White House against him. Clearly, whatever the harm done to the administration by Charley Michelson, far more damage was done by the news stories written by increasingly disaffected and angry reporters.

Gradually the press conferences became less frequent, and as the administration drew near its end they all but disappeared. From

June 1 to November 25, 1932, the President met the reporters only eight times in spite of a nominal twice-a-week schedule, and after September 13 there was not a single press confrontation.[28] Throughout his tenure, writes Eugene Lyons, one of the most worshipful of the biographers: "Hoover repeatedly called off scheduled press conferences, though he knew the pressmen would be bitter."[29] This Coolidge never had done. Furthermore, he ignored questions which had been submitted, in a much more blatant fashion than his predecessor, insisting at times that nothing had been submitted on a given subject, though the reporters later established among themselves on a couple of occasions that the questions had indeed been put. (It has been suggested that the press secretary, not the President himself, was to blame here.)

An examination of the two volumes of Hoover *State Papers* edited by William Starr Myers is revealing on the matter of press conferences, as well as on administration public relations generally. Among the papers or excerpts included are seventy-six items labeled as having come from press conferences (and a good many press releases and similar documents which went out, presumably, from the office of the press secretary on the President's behalf). These seventy-six represent, in all, sixty-eight separate press conferences. Interestingly, in no case is a press conference *exchange* of any kind reproduced. All are statements, often no doubt previously prepared, which were read at the conference. This emphasizes the increasing tendency for the President to read such prepared statements. Many of the later conferences consisted of nothing beyond such a recital.[30]

In only nineteen instances are these statements prefaced with some indication that a reply to a submitted question is to follow. In all other cases the reader is left to assume that both subject and statement originated with the President. Whether he fully intended it or not, or even realized it, Hoover in effect converted more and more of his meetings with the press into mere lectures from which all initiative by reporters, and all give and take, had been eliminated. The working press as a group was reduced—or would have been had they accepted the role—to the position of a mere vehicle for retailing presidential utterances to newspaper readers. The whole essence of the conference as a two-way mutually beneficial relationship became attenuated and eventually virtually disappeared. Under such circumstances the conferences became a liability rather than an asset.

The impression should not be left that the Hoover administration represented nothing but failure and retrograde steps in the realm of presidential public relations.[31] Actually the march of progress in the media and of White House adaptation to it went ahead, if somewhat less rapidly or successfully, as it had under virtually all of the previous Presidents discussed. The most striking Hoover innovation was the elaboration of staff arrangements. The time-honored precedent of having one person who was the secretary to the President gave way to a system of having three bearing the title (with precedence among them left rather ambiguous) and an allocation of duties formerly superintended by the one secretary. George Akerson came over from the Department of Commerce with the new President to handle press relations and appointments. For the first time, therefore, there was a press secretary in the sense that this office has existed in more recent administrations.

Hoover came to need an intermediary of this kind much more than Coolidge had. Akerson further developed the press secretary's role by holding regular *twice*-a-day meetings with the reporters, a practice generally followed since.[32] But Akerson was described as none too able, and his successor, Theodore Joslin, was written off as having even less capacity. Before his appointment Joslin had been among the least esteemed and admired of the Washington correspondents, and upon his elevation he grew pompous and unapproachable.[33]

Hoover's other secretaries were Lawrence Richey, a confidential assistant, and Walter Newton, in charge of relations with Congress. In general, it seems that the elaborate White House staff was allowed by Hoover to shield and isolate him from people and currents of thought that he should have been exposed to. There was, for example, Akerson's overzealous action in allegedly withholding reporters' questions he felt beneath the notice of the Chief Executive. Edmund Starling, former secret service man on the White

House detail, makes the point that the three secretaries "carried work to their boss, and since three men can carry a lot more papers than one man, they kept him snowed under."[34] Implicit in this rather unsophisticated observation is the strong likelihood that Parkinson's law may well operate in the White House as elsewhere, especially with a President enamored of facts, figures, and reports.

The position of ghost writer was continued by the new administration in the shape of one French Strother, later supplanted by George A. Hastings, who had had a career in professional press agentry. Unlike his two predecessors, however, Hoover rather laboriously wrote his own major public papers, leaving the minor ones to Strother, together with editing and similar assistance on the larger efforts.[35] Though the evidence is inconclusive, it is probably true that the President placed too little reliance upon skilled aid in preparing his speeches. Given the imperative necessity for the White House to put its best foot forward in the material fed to the mass media, unless a President is a literary craftsman of outstanding ability, he should swallow his pride and accept expert collaboration. He need not give over the whole job to others, but he should insure, one way or another, that his ideas are packaged as attractively as possible for general dissemination. Lamentable as this necessity may appear to be, prevailing conditions admit of no less.

There were a few other, more or less minor, innovations. Some emanated from the augmented staff rather than from the President himself. Akerson appreciated the importance of the photographers and saw to it, in the reconstruction of the office wing of the White House which went on during the Hoover administration, that a room was set aside for them. In the same reconstruction, the regular press facilities were expanded and improved. It was also during the Hoover period that representatives of business and trade publications were admitted to the press conferences for the first time on equal terms with the other reporters. President Hoover had a telephone installed on the presidential desk for the first time, because, it is said, this would enable him to confer with individuals on the Hill and elsewhere without their having to appear at the White House and run the press gauntlet. Finally, it is noteworthy that White House mail volume rose to new heights. This was due in part, of course, to the depression, but also to the growing tendency of the public to look to the Chief Executive as source of leadership and personification of the federal government.[36]

The onset of the depression redoubled Hoover's determination to use the presidency to supply the leadership which the public more and more insistently demanded. The do-nothing label attached to him in the campaign of 1932, if justified, relates to the *kind* of policy leadership he offered and to his relative ineptitude at influencing national opinion, rather than to any real abdication on his part. His approach to depression problems was to rely as fully as possible on private and local groups and resources rather than on government, the national government in particular. Within this framework, he repeatedly called for efforts by various segments of the economy and the general public, and did all he could to lead and coordinate them. Hindsight would suggest to all but the most ardent Hoover apologists that this kind of remedy was quite inadequate. Hence the strident accusations of doing nothing in the face of growing human need.

As to general techniques of leadership, on theoretical grounds Hoover shrank from any effort to coerce Congress, on the assumption that the Executive had no right to undercut the position of a coordinate branch. Theory aside, he probably had neither talent nor inclination to go to the public over the heads of Congress in quest of support that would force acceptance of a White House policy. That he rarely used his press conferences in this manner seems evident from analysis of the excerpts in the *State Papers*. Only perhaps fifteen of the seventy-six statements included could be classified as reasonably clear-cut appeals to Congress for action, or condemnations of action already taken. Often when he did comment on policy matters that related to Congressional action, these comments were too broad and general to be classified in these terms.

Coolidge, the pioneer in presidential radio broadcasting, had confined himself largely to sending out over the air waves general platitudinous addresses or statements commemorating Lincoln or Washington, Armistice Day, or some association then holding a meeting. Did Hoover, who *did* have policy objectives which he sought earnestly to advance, similarly limit himself?[37] Relying again on the Myers edition of the *State Papers*, a careful listing was made of all the addresses or other statements which appeared to have been broadcast. There are twenty-one of these.

A breakdown of the twenty-one in terms of primary audience or occasion, and motive, is revealing. One would expect to find a substantial number of general addresses to the nation, designed to inform the public or solicit support. On the contrary, the largest single group, twelve of the twenty-one, were little more than glorified "greetings," using radio rather than the more familiar prepared statement read at an association conclave. There were brief talks to national meetings of the 4-H Clubs, Y.M.C.A., Christian Endeavor, and Methodist Church. This was, to say the least, an unimaginative and, as it were, wasteful use of the new medium by the White House. What of the other nine "radio addresses"? Two could have been included in the first group save that they related to public business rather than private concerns: a message to a Governors' conference, and one on the occasion of the ratification of the London Naval Treaty.

Of the remaining seven, four were political in a rather narrow sense of the term—radioed talks to Lincoln Day dinners on two occasions, an address to women working in the 1932 Republican campaign around the country, and an out-and-out campaign speech. The astonishing thing is that only the final three out of the whole group fitted the category which presumably should have been the largest—direct use of radio by the President to communicate his ideas or objectives or appeals to the populace at large. With subsequent history, and particularly the Roosevelt fireside chats in mind, it seems evident that this is the most effective and obvious use of radio by a President, and yet apparently this had not occurred to Hoover and his advisers. As a matter of fact, only the radio speech broadcast March 6, 1932, in which the President appealed to the country not to hoard money, really fits the category. (The other two were appeals for charitable contributions to relieve unemployment distress.)

Aside from the inaugural address, speeches to Congress, to the

Gridiron Club, and outright campaign utterances, there are twenty-four more addresses in the *State Papers* in which the President dealt at least generally with public policy.[38] Only rarely did he discuss specific policy in any kind of detailed terms. Far oftener he confined himself to general principles and broad objectives. Rarely, in other words, did the President use *any* of the media available to him for discussion of the specifics of his administration's policy. Apparently he either could not or would not get beyond the level of highly generalized exhortation, or the enunciation of vague aspirations and moral precepts.

Radio was still being used, and would continue to be until 1933, either as a kind of intriguing novelty or stunt device (as with the greetings to conventions), or as a mere adjunct to the traditional formal address before a live audience. Radio as a presidential tool would not and could not come into its own until it was realized that only speeches prepared exclusively with an unseen radio audience in mind would make possible full exploitation of the medium. Addresses contrived for delivery to a live audience, and only incidentally broadcast, could rarely rise above the level of an interesting bit of news coverage.

The Hoover administration, save for rather minor innovations in presidential communicational technique and staffing, was significant mainly in a negative sense. It served to make painfully plain the fact that no future President could hope to emerge from his White House ordeal unscathed unless he was prepared in talent and temperament to cope with and master the demands of an age of mass communications. Herbert Hoover would unquestionably have succeeded far better as President in the nineteenth century, before the era of the new journalism, and in the days when the chief magistracy could be conducted discreetly, out of the continuous gaze of a demanding and impatient press and public. As it was, he fought losing battles to keep both his negotiations over public policy matters and his private life screened from view. By the end of the second decade of the twentieth century, he was doomed to lose both battles decisively.

Though some of the devices of strong presidential leadership had been pioneered by T. R. and Wilson, and some of the techniques of presidential opinion leadership through mass media had been devised, much remained to be done, particularly in the latter area, before the presidency as it has come to function in the mid-twentieth century would be possible. Thanks in considerable measure to President Coolidge, that unlikeliest of innovators, with assists from his immediate predecessors, an orderly, continuing liaison between Executive and reporters had been established through the press conference. More was required in this direction, however, which Hoover had been able to formulate in part, but not carry through. To Coolidge alone belongs credit for pioneering the use of radio, and here again Hoover added little. The man elected in 1932, whoever he might have been, would have to accomplish somehow the next items on this agenda, if not in the particular way Franklin Roosevelt did, then in some comparable fashion. The clock could not be turned back—and this is the ultimate moral of the Hoover interlude—since both developments in the world of mass communications and mounting demands upon the presidential office decreed that the only movement could be forward.

☆☆☆☆☆☆☆

Chapter 6

☆☆☆☆☆☆☆

LEADERSHIP: FRANKLIN ROOSEVELT

The election of 1932 inaugurated a new period in the development of the presidency. In the following years the "cosmic scene shifters" (in William Allen White's vivid phrase) did indeed "sweat at their toil."[1] Vast and unprecedented changes occurred in the world role of the United States, in its domestic policy, in the scope and responsibilities of the national government, and, as a result of all of these, in the presidential office.

The Great Depression did far more than defeat Hoover and elect Roosevelt. It so realigned national political forces as to make the election of Republican Presidents after 1932 as difficult as the election of Democrats had been before. It launched the nation on the road to the welfare state with a great burst of social and economic legislation. In so doing, it shifted to Washington functions and concerns that had been, since the beginning, the job of the states or of private groups. Any such massive transfer of responsibility to the national government inevitably meant new responsibility for the President. Franklin D. Roosevelt inherited this situation, and himself instigated many of the subsequent changes.

On top of all this came the Fascist menace in Europe and the Second World War. Total American involvement intensified the focus on the national government and its administrative apparatus, and on the President himself. Some at least of this, too, like the domestic consequences of economic upheaval and reform, would remain as a legacy for the future. In 1945 the United States emerged into a world unrecognizable as the one that had gone to war six years earlier. Now two superpowers remained in a bipolar state system. America, as one of these two giants, found herself catapulted from relative isolation into the agonizing role of free world leadership. More than any of the other changes over the preceding dozen years, this became the peculiar burden of the Chief Executive. The occupant of the American White House became, symbolically and actually, the leader of the free world.

A new-model Presidency was shaped and annealed in the heat of these developments, through the impact of the Dutchess County "aristocrat as democrat."[2] Before his twelve years ended, the office had gone far along the road toward becoming an institution; it was no longer a one-man operation functioning through a few borrowed clerks. The presidency as preeminent source of leadership for national opinion also came into its own during these years. The outline and model for this role was still that which T.R. ("Uncle Ted") had set some thirty years before. But the scale, complexity, and media available had developed enormously, especially since 1932. And perhaps more important, Franklin Roosevelt, displaying all of his uncle's skill, recaptured much of the spirit and flexibility the latter had displayed in dealing with the press and public, while at the same time exploiting the new opportunities which time and technology had made available.

No straight chronological account could do justice to this hothouse growth of new presidential techniques and enormous expansion of the scale of the White House enterprise. Accordingly, the chapters that follow will reconstruct developments during the last three decades in the analytical terms suggested by the multidirectional evolution that took place. First, a case study of the "selling" of social security legislation by F.D.R. will be presented, to suggest in concrete terms the kind of presidential virtuosity in dealing with policy and public opinion which had become possible as the combined result of technical development and Roosevelt's skill. In the ensuing chapters, press-related developments, growing staff involvement in White House public relations, and finally the electronic media will be treated.

Any study of presidential leadership of opinion must become in essence a study of the *words* of the President—the content of his public utterances. Through them the Chief Executive exerts influence over the public and the Congress (in large measure), and ultimately over the shape of national policy. Beyond the words themselves are the subsidiary questions of their transmission and the techniques for accomplishing this, and at times, the further question of the process of preparing the words. The prime focus in this chapter, however, will be on the words of the President.[3]

Franklin Roosevelt was the first national leader to identify himself with the social insurance cause, and did so long before his nomination or election as President.[4] Contemporaries like Frances Perkins and Rex Tugwell testify to this early and deep-seated interest.[5] Once installed in office, he was at last in a position to implement his ideas on the national level. The context of the early 1930s was obviously favorable, even though social insurance was a drastic departure from normally accepted federal policy.[6] Some states had already enacted limited schemes including systems of old age pensions. The depression had focused attention on the plight of the potential beneficiaries of social security to an unprecedented extent. However, in the country at large, there probably was neither general willingness to accept such a scheme, nor even understanding of the basic problems. Between avid proponents and vocal or latent opponent groups lay the vast inarticulate majority whose attitude must have been compounded of indifference and vague suspicion toward any such departure from the individual self-reliance of the American creed.

The first step, therefore, for Roosevelt was to arrive at a judgment of the state of the popular mind and the implications of this for his future tactics. Anne O'Hare McCormick wrote that early in 1933, though he had set people to work collecting data, the President "postponed action on the ground that the country was not ripe for the scheme." "I believe we'll be social-minded enough in another year," she has him say, "to make a beginning in a great social reform which must be carefully adapted to our special conditions and needs." She goes on to note that he realized "a nation has to be educated to the point where reforms can be assimilated naturally, without dangerous spasms of indigestion."[7] Lest it be thought, as some did, that F.D.R. was showing excessive caution, Tugwell, hardly one to drag his feet in regard to reform, wrote the President on February 24, 1934, that unemployment insurance as a problem required much further study and should be put over to the 1935 session of Congress.[8]

Roosevelt did begin making a few tentative moves. Miss Perkins noted that early in 1933 he had encouraged Senator Wagner and Representative David J. Lewis to go ahead in Congress with an unemployment insurance bill, with its educational impact in mind. She also says that he urged her to discuss the matter in as many groups as possible. In December, 1933, he told the Federal Council of Churches to stress in their teaching the ideals of social justice and that people have a right to demand from their government opportunity for a more abundant life. The first overt move the President made came at a special off-the-record press conference for business paper editors in February, 1934. In response to a question about his plans for a social insurance program, he talked at some length on the general subject, saying at one point: "Now, the country is not educated up to all of those things yet."[9] It is probably significant that he began educating the public with this particular group.

Much of the credit for accomplishing this education was in fact due to the Townsend movement and similar groups, and not to the President at all. Miss Perkins gives credit to the ferment produced by the California doctor and his people.[10] Yet it was late 1934 and early 1935 before the Townsend scheme for $200 a month for all over 60 had developed momentum, whereas the press conference noted above had been held months earlier.[11] Furthermore, the Townsendites were plugging only for pensions, whereas equally important in the final legislation was unemployment insurance, and it also included aid to the blind, to dependent children, and other groups. Roosevelt felt that this combined approach would maximize political impact and ward off opposition from both Right and Left.

The President's first public move regarding social legislation was timed with the 1934 mid-term elections in mind. On the 8th of June, ten days before Congress was to adjourn, the President transmitted to the two houses a message in which he discussed his objectives in general terms but at considerable length, noting toward the end: "Next winter we may well undertake the great task of furthering the security of the citizen and his family through social insurance."[12] (Ickes noted in his Diary, entry for April 27: "The President closed the Cabinet meeting today by giving us his views on what he has in mind with respect to social insurance. It is evident that he has thought very deeply on the subject.")[13]

Twenty days after the message to Congress, in his first fireside chat of 1934, the President discussed his social insurance plan in subtantially the terms he had used to Congress, taking great care to counteract any revolutionary overtones that might become attached to the proposal. He carefully pointed out that it was not "Fascism" or "Communism" or "Socialism." The very next day the President issued an executive order setting up a Committee on Economic Security to bring in detailed recommendations. This was a Cabinet group whose public relations role was to have considerable importance.

Shortly thereafter the President set off on one of the trips of which he was fond, combining the traditional swing around the circle with the inspection of administration projects, and vacationing. While away from Washington he by no means laid aside the advocacy of social welfare. In a brief talk in Puerto Rico he discussed the similarity of the social and economic problems faced in the island and on the mainland. His speeches en route were extensively reported in the continental press, including this one in Puerto Rico. On August 3, at Bonneville Dam, he referred directly to "security for old age, security against the ills and the accidents that come to people and, above all, security to earn their own living."[14]

A further step-up in activity followed the President's return to Washington. On September 27 he addressed a message to the Women's Conference on Current Problems in which he mentioned, among other things, the growing tendency "to talk over methods of improving the economic and social lot of our citizenry."[15] Three days later, on the 30th, he included in his second fireside chat of the year a reference to the fact that the British were farther advanced in matters of social security than the United States, chided reactionaries for raising the cry "unconstitutional" over every innovation, and concluded: "I prefer and I am sure you prefer that broader definition of liberty under which we are moving forward to greater freedom, to greater security for the average man than he has ever known before in the history of America."[16] On October 19, in an address at the dedication of a Veterans' Hospital at Roanoke, Virginia, the President suggested to veterans that the time had come to extend the kind of benefits they had been enjoying more broadly to other citizens lacking "the essentials of modern civilization."

On November 10 a press release from the White House discussed the developing studies of the Committee on Economic Security and announced the appointment of an advisory council to aid in its work.[17] A letter to the United States Conference of Mayors dated the 13th specifically mentioned prospective Congressional consideration of unemployment insurance and old age pensions; then came the White House Conference on Economic Security. In an extensively reported address to this group the President outlined in some detail what the forthcoming security proposals would involve and some of the principles upon which the system would rest. The President thereupon left for Warm Springs for Thanksgiving, pausing at various points en route. At Harrodsburg, Kentucky, he concluded his brief speech by looking forward to the "fulfillment of security, of freedom, of opportunity and of happiness which America asks and which America is entitled to receive."[18]

In January Congress met and the educational campaign culminated with a discussion of social security in the State of the Union

"All the News That's Fit to Print"

The New York Times.

LATE CITY EDITION

NEW YORK, FRIDAY, JANUARY 18, 1935. TWO CENTS

'YOU STOP LYING,' HAUPTMANN RAGES AT FEDERAL AGENT

LEAPS TOWARD THE STAND

Story of Raid on Cache in Garage Provokes Court Outburst.

Hauptmann Friend Says He Saw Bills in His Radio

REICH TO GET SAAR MARCH 1, AGREEING TO DEMILITARIZE IT

League Awards the Whole Area Under Conditions Resulting From Versailles Treaty.

LAVAL IN MINORITIES PLEA

EXTENSION OF NRA TO TEST NEW IDEAS URGED BY WILLIAMS

Head of Recovery Board Tells Retailers More Experience Is Needed for Permanent Plan.

PAYS TRIBUTE TO WEALTHY

They Enrich Treasury at Own Risk, He Says Assailing Radical 'Hangers-On.'

ROOSEVELT OFFERS HIS SECURITY PLAN FOR JOBLESS, THE AGED AND WIDOWS; PROGRAM SPLITS CONGRESS PARTY LINES

SHARP RIFT OVER DETAILS

All Parties Hail Theory, but Criticism Rises on Methods of Aid.

PRESIDENT URGES SPEED

Bills Are Introduced at Once to Carry Out His Sweeping Proposals.

Old-Age Benefit Plan

Cost of the Security Program

CITY PARKS TO GET NEW ARTISTIC TONE

ARSENAL IS ON PROGRAM

SMITH HAILS CHANGE IN TAMMANY SPIRIT

LLOYD GEORGE ASKS BRITISH NEW DEAL

FAVORS BIG PUBLIC WORKS

Import Duty on Beer Is Reduced One-Half; Roosevelt Sanctions Tariff Board Decision

Roosevelt makes headlines: *New York Times* coverage of message to Congress on social security legislation. Note another F.D.R. story (on beer), also a story on N.R.A. *Courtesy New York Times.*

Message on January 4, followed thirteen days later by the message to Congress transmitting the administration proposals. To coincide with the latter, the White House gave out a statement to the press summarizing the report of the Committee on Economic Security. Thereupon the President shifted tactics and media. Between the introduction of the bills and the signing of the Act in August, he discussed the subject publicly only once—in a fireside chat April 28, plus a brief mention in his May bonus veto message. From January on he placed prime reliance on the press conference. One can only speculate as to the reasons for this change, and the factor of sheer coincidence cannot be ruled out. However, it is plausible to argue that up to this point his intent had been to educate the *public* on his objectives—almost with a saturation campaign—in the expectation that by the time Congress met a favorable climate of opinion would have been created which would manifest itself in the behavior of the men on the Hill. He may have judged that addressing the public directly rather than indirectly through the press meetings would serve this purpose better.

His shift to the press conference forum might well have stemmed from a desire to continue the process, but more discreetly and indirectly. Now the play was up to Congress. A heavy-handed effort to continue belaboring the public might well have been viewed by the legislators with disfavor.[19] The twice weekly press meetings, however, offered a flexible device for keeping the issue before both legislators and people, and for intervening tactfully in the legislative process itself if that should become necessary. Any assumption that Roosevelt habitually browbeat Congress in order to lash it into more vigorous efforts on behalf of his program does not seem to be borne out here. Most press conference discussions of pending bills were handled with tact.

A canvass of all of F.D.R.'s press conference transcripts from 1933 through August, 1935, was made in quest of discussions of social security and closely related matters. Beginning in February, 1934, through the signing of the Act, there were no less than twenty-five such mentions. Many were brief interchanges in which the President declined to comment or disclaimed knowledge of the point raised, but many of the later ones were obviously carefully calculated uses by him of the conferences to advance the social insurance idea and the legislation itself.

The special conference for business editors already mentioned was an example of his masterly skill at painting the issue in colors that would be most appealing to the audience at hand. He began his lengthy answer to the query about his plans by saying that the country had been headed in the direction of such legislation for twenty years. He stressed the contributory aspects of the scheme as he had it in mind, and that it should be actuarially sound. The government's role was portrayed as only that of paying the administrative and overhead expenses. Throughout he carefully minimized the magnitude of the whole effort and rang the changes on aspects that would make it palatable to business.

There were scattering brief references to social security at press meetings during the spring of 1934. Apparently the reporters gradually came to suspect that a message of some sort would be forthcoming on the subject, but the President did not say yes and he did not say no, turned some queries aside with a joke, and kept their interest whetted. Even after the June 8 message to Congress, and right on through the fall, questions asked on the subject received brief answers at best. Perhaps he felt that the reporters should not be encouraged to speculate or indulge in the flights of fancy, and that he should keep the initiative, which he could best retain with carefully prepared public statements. He might, in other words, if not careful, have gotten bogged down in efforts to answer the charges or refute the wild assumptions of others, when he wanted to concentrate on portraying the problem in his own terms.

By the turn of the year the suspense began to mount and press conference questions were coming hot and heavy. The subject was raised on the 4th of January, and again on the 5th at the budget seminar for the press. On January 9 the President clearly did begin laying the groundwork to secure maximum publicity for the submission of the report of the Committee on Economic Security to Congress. He was asked if he had chosen the date for the message, and replied that he had just been talking to Secretary Perkins, who hoped to have the report available the next day, whereupon he would talk over the timing with Congressional leaders. He then went on "thinking out loud" as he put it, to the effect that he would have Miss Perkins get a press synopsis ready which would be available to the reporters in confidence twenty-four hours ahead of time. He promised to check with Steve Early on the details of this plan, and to have his accompanying message also in their hands as early as possible. Obviously he was following his standard tactic of meeting the reporters' desire for advance information, while at the same time helping the cause of social security along by insuring that the press would carry full and well-prepared coverage.

Two days later he was asked again about the message and the report and replied that he was to confer on it right after the press conference. The conference on the day after the message went up found the President discussing the program at some length, and exerting gentle pressure on Congress to move expeditiously without making damaging alterations. When asked how soon he would like to see the measure passed, he replied carefully that action by state legislatures would be needed to implement the scheme, hence the sooner the better. The next question reflected the disappointment of some members of Congress at the modest character of the provisions in comparison with the Townsend demands. In reply the President emphasized sound financing and the fact that only the federal contribution to pensions was fixed, that the states could expand their contribution if they desired—the matter of generosity was as much in their hands as in Washington's. Further brief interchanges occurred on January 23 and January 25, in the first of which the President denied that the payroll tax provision would interfere with recovery.

On February 1 the President apparently felt that the time had come for one of the "seminars" frequently encountered in the conference transcripts at which pending or projected proposals were discussed at great length either off the record or for background use only. The immediate occasion was another question reflecting the demands in Congress for a more generous pension or annuity scheme. The President replied:

> If you want, I will talk to you just to give you a little bit of information–Just off the record on this thing. As the thing stands, I cannot even talk as background, coming from here. It is in the very parliamentary stages of discussion on the Hill but, if you want, I will talk to you off the record just to give you a slant on the Security Bill as I see it in the present form.

He again minimized the government's contribution to the various aspects of the program, and then came to the pension-annuity part. Here the Townsendite pressure was strongest. In a discussion which occupied some three and a half double-spaced pages in the conference record, he explained in detail the "actuarial" problems and financial burdens involved, particularly in any further liberalization. Toward the end, after consultation with Steve Early, the President agreed to let the reporters use what he had been saying as background material. Apparently he had decided the moment was ripe for a vigorous—but discreet—defense of the basic compromise which his program represented. The press conference "background" device allowed him to do this without appearing to exert undue pressure on Congress at this early stage.

On February 27 Mr. Roosevelt brushed aside a query about the progress of the bill, apparently again not wishing to be in the position of unduly hurrying Congress. Some six weeks later, however, on April 12, there was another "seminar" on social security in which, for the first time, the President exerted some rather direct pressure in relation to the lagging measure. A day or two before, Speaker Byrns and Chairman Doughton of the House committee in charge of the Security Bill had been called to the White House to discuss the lack of progress.[20] Upon being asked by a reporter about that conference, Mr. Roosevelt began: "Well, there were two questions raised at that time which will probably come up in the form of amendments in the House, and there is no reason why there should be any secrecy as to the attitude of the administration on those two amendments." One would have eliminated the state contributions to old-age pensions and the other was designed to knock the unemployment insurance provision out entirely. He opposed the first, the President said, because the twenty-eight states which now had pension systems would be relieved of a burden they had already assumed; and if the federal government took over completely, "a vast Federal army in all of the forty-eight states" would be required to administer it. Regarding the second amendment, he noted that this program would take burdens off the relief agencies and provide a cushion against future economic depressions.

It seems clear here, and in many references to social security in his speeches, that Roosevelt's concern was to convince the moderate middle opinion in the country that the program was sound and actually conservative in relation to traditional American values. The arguments the President emphasized might also have been chosen to take some of the edge off a pretty direct demand that Congress quit tampering with the program in unacceptable ways and pass it. It would be hazardous to draw too far-reaching a conclusion from the fact that the legislation did pass the House eight days after this press conference, but it would be surprising if there were not some connection between this and the President's comments on the 12th. It is of course also probable (though again unprovable) that the overwhelming vote of 372-33 stemmed in part from the educational campaign the White House had been conducting for more than a year.

Twice more the President intervened, with apparently decisive results, by press conference pressure. On May 22 he delivered in person a vigorous veto of the soldiers' bonus legislation. Apparently, irritated Congressmen then suggested attaching the bonus matter as a rider to social security, pending in the Senate. When asked about this in his May 24 conference with reporters, the President minced no words:

> Anything that is extraneous to the Social Security Bill will be vetoed. That is easy. Of course, that is one of the greatest steps in progress we are taking today. I consider the Social Security Bill probably the major Act of this Congress and to attempt to load it down with something that has nothing to do with it—it is perfectly obvious what the answer must be.

Again, while the measure was in conference after having passed both Houses, deadlock developed over an amendment allowing companies with their own pension systems to be exempted. Here too the President put his foot down hard in answer to a press question on July 24. Wrangling continued on the matter for a while longer, but on August 9 Congress completed action and sent the bill to the President for signature.

At the President's meeting with reporters on June 7, an interesting exchange had taken place which, though not on the social security legislation itself, developed into what was doubtless a calculated assist toward its passage. A Canadian correspondent asked the President what he would say was the social objective of his administration. The reply ran in part:

> . . . to do what any honest Government of any country would do: to try to increase the security and the happiness of a larger number of people in all occupations of life and in all parts of the country; . . . to give them assurance that they are not going to starve in their old age; to give honest business a chance to go ahead and make a reasonable profit, and to give everyone a chance to earn a living.[21]

Upon being asked, F.D.R. agreed to direct quotation of this passage after he had had a chance to look it over. Later in the day the statement was mimeographed and handed out as a press release. Here, in other words, is an instance—by no means unique—in which the press conference doubled as a channel for a more or less formal presidential pronouncement.

On the 14th of August the Social Security Bill was signed. At his press conference earlier that day, Mr. Roosevelt said the signing would be opened to press photographers because "with so much other news going on, people do not realize that the Social Security Bill went through and is getting signed, and I want to give it all the publicity I possibly can because it is of such importance."

This signing ceremony and the statement then issued would seem to complete the story. Actually, however, there were six more direct references to the now completed legislation, in public speeches or statements during 1935 alone. One came the 24th of August in a radio talk to the Young Democratic Clubs; another appeared in a letter to the clergy of America dated September 23: "I am particularly anxious that the new social security legislation just enacted . . . shall be carried out in keeping with the high purposes with which this law was enacted."[22] The third came in the course of an address in Los Angeles on October 1. The fourth, during a radio speech on behalf of the 1935 Mobilization for Human Needs; the fifth in a talk at Atlanta on the 29th of November; and the sixth in the course of a speech on agriculture, December 9, in Chicago. The index to the 1936 volume of the *Public Papers and Addresses* lists numerous additional references during that election year.

There were probably at least three reasons for these frequent mentions of the Act whose final passage one might have thought would have ended the President's active championing of it. In the first place, a presidential election was in the offing. Undoubtedly he felt he could strengthen the image of his administration by keeping this unprecedented legislation before the public. Secondly, the legislation was not destined to begin providing benefits for a long time to come. The first consequence of its enactment for most of the public would be the payroll deduction system which would begin on the 1st of January, 1937. Thus the President faced a problem in keeping interest alive during the waiting period, and forestalling disillusionment. The Republicans did a good bit of campaigning in 1936 against the whole system and, during the last two weeks of the canvass, inspired the use of factory notices and pay envelope inserts telling workers their pay was soon to be docked and hinting they might not ever see the money again.[23] Continued concern with popular opinion about social security by the President was clearly justified.

Aside from this, Roosevelt no doubt sensed that here, as with any legislative innovation which represents a major reorientation of public policy, final enactment would by no means remove all doubts and opposition. The "selling," in other words, probably needs to go on in such a case for a long time afterward, at least until the benefits in the hands of recipients become sufficiently tangible to solidify support. This point raises the whole intriguing question as to just what the process is whereby this kind of innovation does become accepted by a democratic public, and what the contribution of opinion leadership such as Roosevelt's really is to the fostering of such acceptance.

The political leader bent on shaping opinion in favor of some new policy departure must do more than merely reason with his audience and parade arguments in the manner of the college debater. His more basic problem, Roosevelt seems to have sensed, is to meet the innate popular aversion to change and tendency to cleave to that which is familiar. In the main, publics resist innovation. Therefore, in the months-long educational campaign to prepare the ground for the introduction of social security legislation, F.D.R.'s tactic was much more than mere repetition, though this was useful, no doubt, in lending familiarity to the ideas involved. He attempted also to clothe the apparently unorthodox in the garb of the familiar. Over and over he insisted that what he was going to propose was not alien to American values, but a mere fulfillment or rediscovery of elements already present.

Thus in his June 8 message to Congress first broaching the social insurance idea publicly, he wrote:

> Our task of reconstruction does not require the creation of new and strange values. It is rather the finding of the way once more to known, but to some degree forgotten, ideals and values. If the means and details are in some instances new, the objectives are as permanent as human nature.[24]

Further on in the same message, he relates the project to the familiar symbol of the Constitution as a logical extension of the aspirations set forth therein: "If, as our Constitution tells us, our Federal Government was established among other things 'to promote the general welfare,' it is our plain duty to provide for that security upon which welfare depends." Later he points out that: "This is not an untried experiment. Lessons of experience are available from States, from industries and from many Nations of the civilized world." Then the first theme recurs: "This seeking for a greater measure of welfare and happiness does not indicate a change in values. It is rather a return to values lost in the course of our economic development and expansion."

The President also inserted a direct answer to those who questioned whether American notions of individualism and free enterprise were to remain intact: "Ample scope is left for the exercise of private initiative. . . . We have not imposed undue restrictions upon business. We have not opposed the incentive of reasonable and legitimate private profit." And in the last paragraph, the basic theme once more:

> We must dedicate ourselves anew to a recovery of the old and sacred possessive rights for which mankind has constantly struggled —homes, livelihood, and individual security. The road to these values is the way of progress. Neither you nor I will rest content until we have done our utmost to move further on that road.

In his fireside chat of June 28, 1934, President Roosevelt again hit virtually the same themes: the refurbishing of old values rather than the creating of new ones, fulfilling the Constitution rather than flouting it, and preserving individualism and free enterprise. Early in the speech he talked of "saving and safeguarding of our national life,"[25] and asserted that "much of our trouble today and in the past few years has been due to lack of understanding of the elementary principles of justice and fairness. . . ." Then the individual-Constitution theme: "Plausible self-seekers and theoretical die-hards will tell you of the loss of individual liberty. . . . Have you lost any of your rights or liberty or constitutional freedom of action and choice? Turn to the Bill of Rights of the Constitution, which I have solemnly sworn to maintain and under which your freedom rests secure." The President later on quotes himself on long established values (referring to the June 8 message). To illustrate the "fulfillment of old and tested American ideals" he uses the kind of highly effective yet homey illustration of which he was fond: the then current remodeling of the White House, to which he likens the adoption of social insurance. After describing the alterations planned he recalled that:

> . . . the structural lines of the old Executive office building will remain. The artistic lines of the White House buildings were the creation of master builders when our Republic was young. The simplicity and strength of the structure remain in the face of every modern test. . . . If I were to listen to the arguments of some prophets of calamity . . . I should fear that while I am away for a few weeks the architects might build some strange new Gothic

> tower or . . . perhaps a replica of the Kremlin or of the Potsdam Palace. But I have no such fears. . . . Our new structure [social insurance] is a part of and fulfillment of the old. All that we do seeks to fulfill the historic traditions of the American people.

These examples show a careful process of grafting social security onto the stalk of traditional American values. The example just cited, when read in full, represents a carefully contrived interweaving of all the themes cited. Other references to social security in other public statements took a similar form. Even after the legislation was passed, in his radio address to the Young Democratic Clubs of America on August 24, 1935, we find the President referring to individuals and organizations "who are now crying aloud about the socialism involved in social security legislation,"[26] and reminding his listeners that "Government cooperation to help make the system of free enterprise work, to provide that minimum security without which the competitive system cannot function, to restrain the kind of individual action which in the past has been harmful to the community—that kind of governmental cooperaton is entirely consistent with the best tradition of America."

Obviously no campaign of opinion leadership by the White House occupant is a one-man show. At least three categories of assistance were brought into play to supplement and underscore the utterances of Roosevelt himself on social security. There were the efforts of members of his Cabinet like Secretary Perkins, the work of a "study commission" appointed for the dual purpose of draftsmanship and publicity, and the crucial supporting role played by the President's own staff, especially his press secretary.

Secretary Perkins' was probably by all odds the most important supporting role in the unfolding of the social security campaign. In her memoirs, *The Roosevelt I Knew*, she wrote: "I myself made over a hundred speeches in different parts of the country that year, always stressing social insurance as one of the methods for assisting the unemployed in times of depression and in preventing depressions. We stimulated others to talk and write about the subject."[27] She also carried much of the burden of the day-to-day development of the program both before and after the setting up of the Committee on Economic Security. In fact, she asserts that the idea for the Committee itself originated with her, an assertion borne out by a memorandum in the Hyde Park files. Dated June 29, the same day as the announcement of the establishment of the Committee, it transmitted to the President a draft of the appropriate executive order plus a plan to be followed by the Committee in its work and a list of suggested persons for appointment to the Advisory Council.[28] Miss Perkins chaired the Committee, made up of the Secretaries of Agriculture and Treasury, the Attorney General, and Harry Hopkins as relief administrator. This Cabinet study group idea was particularly acceptable to the President, she suggested, because it would remain under his control and would "not be likely to get off into the kind of political discussion and publicity that might breed doubt and delay."[29]

Harry Hopkins, with whom, incidentally, Miss Perkins had some basic disagreements as the program developed, also joined in the public discussion and educational campaign. In a well reported speech on November 11, 1934, at a dinner of the Federation for the Support of Jewish Philanthropic Societies, Hopkins discussed the pending program in terms similar to those the President himself had been using: "Unemployment insurance, old age and sickness benefits, care of children have been provided in almost every civilized country in the world. To say that our industrial system cannot provide for this security is, indeed, to admit defeat. A very modest proportion of the total national income would give this security."[30] At one of his own press conferences, nearly a month earlier (October 12) Hopkins had handed out a statement listing some dozen studies being made by the Committee on Economic Security.[31]

As for the Committee itself, in general, setting up such a group, periodic releases concerning the progress of its work, culminating in its final report, all combined into a very valuable publicity and educational strategy. Edwin E. Witte, Executive Director of the Committee, at one point wrote Stephen Early, the President's news secretary (in his capacity as informal coordinator of general administration publicity), as a follow-up to some previous contacts with the White House. He informed Early that though the Committee had decided not to employ a full-time public relations man or indulge in extensive publicity, some newspaper stories had been released through Hopkins' Federal Emergency Relief Administration and through the Department of Labor, and that the question of publicity would be kept under discussion.[32] This letter indicates that the Committee was well aware of its publicity role. It also indicates the interest of the President's press secretary, and through him, presumably of the President himself, in this phase of the Committee's activity.

Direct publicity by the C.E.S. was probably less significant than its role as focal point for the mobilization of group support for the program. Groups like the Fraternal Order of Eagles and the American Association for Old Age Security had long been working for the adoption of various social welfare measures. Support of this kind was consciously mobilized, for the most part through the establishment of advisory groups to the Committee. Professor Witte noted that in addition to the over-all Advisory Council on Economic Security, there were appointed: a Medical Advisory Committee; a Committee of Actuarial Consultants organized at the suggestion of the actuarial societies and the insurance companies; a Public Health Advisory Committee; a Hospital Advisory Committee; an Advisory Committee on Public Employment and Public Assistance; a Committee on Child Welfare; and a Nursing Advisory Committee. He concluded: "It is literally true that just about everybody who had ever written anything on social security and representatives of all interested organizations were drawn into the work of the Committee on Economic Security."[33]

The Advisory Council included individuals "representing labor and industry and just about every other interested group, with President Frank Graham of the University of North Carolina as chairman . . . [and] was of great value in acquainting the organizations represented and the public generally with what was under consideration. . . ."[34] Finally, there was the two-day National Conference on Social Security held in November, 1934,[35] which brought to Washington some hundred and fifty people known to be interested for a series of addresses by leaders in the movement like Paul Douglas[36] and others. The full- or part-time participation of every known expert and specialist in the areas involved, both from within and outside government, had been enlisted for the Committee staff.

All in all, the C.E.S. was admirably suited to supplementing the President's opinion leadership on behalf of social security. Its role in marshaling all possible organized support was made the more necessary because, as Witte pointed out, the wildfire spread of the Townsend scheme (there were a couple of thousand Townsend clubs by 1935) deprived the social security program of the support of some of its potential beneficiaries, the elderly.

Secretary Early, and a few others who might be categorized as White House staff, also participated in the social security campaign. For example, Louis Howe, who by then had little time left to serve his beloved Franklin, wrote a magazine article appearing in April, 1934, in which he cited unemployment insurance as among Roosevelt's immediate objectives.[37] Early, as noted, was involved in his role as coordinator of administration-wide public relations, as well as via his obvious White House responsibilities. He and his co-worker Marvin McIntyre were apparently relied upon, at least during the crucial first years of the life of the Social Security Board, for publicity advice.

An October, 1935, memo from Vincent Miles of the Social Security Board to McIntyre transmitted a copy of his first speech on the Act, which he wanted looked over.[38] Again in July, 1936, Arthur Altmeyer, another Board member, wrote: "Just a note to express my appreciation for your [Early's] helpful suggestions. I wonder whether you or Mr. Hassett would look over the enclosed bulletin and tell us what you think about the publicity policy that is outlined therein. It will serve as the 'bible' for all of our people in the field and we don't want to start off on the wrong foot." Even Mrs. Roosevelt, who in a real sense was part of the President's staff, was involved. An August, 1936, note from "Missy" LeHand, his personal secretary, to the President read: "Mrs. Roosevelt wants to remind you to speak to Gov. Winant [Chairman of the Board] telling him that he should let go to non-partisan meetings all the people he possibly can, in order that they may explain the Social Security Act. This is not campaigning." Obviously this chit helped prompt a letter from F.D.R. to Winant dated ten days later, in which he made precisely this point.

A final example, one of the few available, suggests vividly Early's public relations role and the kind of advice he no doubt often supplied orally. Rarely does an exchange between the President and his press secretary survive on paper. This one did because, apparently, the President was out of the city, probably campaigning. Involved was the resignation during the 1936 campaign of John Winant, in order to be free to fight back against Republican misrepresentations of the new program. Early telegraphed his boss:

> At seven forty five this evening, I received for you the following letter from Governor Winant of the Social Security Board. . . . The Governor is releasing the letter tonight at eight o'clock. It offers an excellent opportunity for you to make a statement on social security in the nature of a reply or acceptance of the Governor's resignation. But, I suggest this be timed as a follow-up story and not written for immediate release. The Winant story is big enough to stand alone tonight. Steve.[39]

There are at least three indicators of the effectiveness of Roosevelt's leadership effort on behalf of Social Security to supplement the judgment of Miss Perkins when she wrote:

> It is interesting to note that the public educational work in the year and a half preceding the introduction of this bill had been sufficient to insure wide backing from the constituents of the congressmen. . . . The House Committee and other members of Congress began to hear from [them] . . . in favor of the social security bill, and it was soon obvious that it was going to be moved along.[40]

If the members of Congress were hearing from the folks back home to the extent suggested, then the President's campaign had clearly reached the grass roots.

Had "scientific" opinion polling been in existence even a year earlier than it was, we should know a great deal more than we do[41] about the way in which opinion shifted and developed on this issue.

The earliest poll results discovered on the subject date from December, 1935. At intervals thereafter other samples were also asked whether they favored government old age pensions. Of the first sample, 89 per cent replied that they did, and subsequent percentages ranged up from that to 94 per cent in January, 1939. In December, 1937, 73 per cent replied, when asked, that they approved of the social security tax; and in July, 1938, 89 per cent replied that they approved of "the present Social Security laws." Though non-governmental groups like Townsend's followers played some part in winning approval for a *pension* measure, the impact of the administration's educational program in all probability represents at least the difference between the roughly 50 per cent who said in 1936 that they favored the Townsend scheme and the much higher percentages cited above.

An approximate measure of the actual amount of publicity gained by presidential statements on the subject can be obtained through a content analysis of a sample of the mass media. Though such an investigation on a large scale would be impractical, a study of coverage in a reputable newspaper or two should give a rough index of what must have obtained throughout the news media. Table 1 summarizes the results of such a study using the *New York Times*. Eighteen presidential utterances were chosen, comprising all speech and press conference references to social security which were sufficiently clear-cut to raise a presumption that they could have been considered newsworthy.

The White House secured consistently prominent featuring of releases, messages, and press conference mentions of social insurance. All but two of the eighteen received front page coverage. In half, social security, or a speech in which the new program was featured, was the basis for the lead story (in the column eight position), frequently with a two-, three-, or even four-column headline. In every instance in which there was a text of a statement or address, that text appeared in full in addition to the story concerning it.

Two compilations of column inches were made. First, the space embraced by both stories and texts was computed and totaled. (The fireside chats and annual message, for example, of course, dealt with social security only in part.) Using 160 column inches as the total for a *Times* front page, the equivalent of nearly ten such pages of matter appeared in the *Times* between June, 1934, and August, 1935, dealing with this subject in at least some degree. Space devoted to social insurance and the President's proposals specifically and directly amounted to just over 900 column inches. It thus seems apparent that throughout the period the issue was a lively subject of news interest in the judgment of the *Times* editors, and was featured accordingly. A combination of the intrinsic interest of the subject, and more than that, the skill and persistence shown by the President in *making* it news, lay behind this editorial judgment.

As a means of checking the usefulness of this analysis of coverage in the *New York Times,* coverage of the same items was noted in the *Providence Journal.* It turned out that the *Journal* actually covered every one of the eighteen items, allocating front page space as often as the *Times.* Five times the story ended up as the feature story (page one, column eight) in both papers. The *Journal* published nine message or statement texts as against twelve for the *Times.* In short, the correspondence between the two newspapers in handling social security news was very close indeed, and doubtless suggests the pattern of national coverage at least in the better papers.

In addition to the evidence of opinion polls and the content of the media, several of the most thoughtful students of the New Deal are convinced that the Social Security Act played an important if not crucial role in forging the so-called "Roosevelt coalition" which from then on remained the basis of Democratic electoral strength.[42] James MacGregor Burns, for one, analyzed the situation on the eve of the 1936 campaign, and noting the various administration programs already in effect, cites the remarkable "sweep and variety of the groups" being helped. Among these new programs of services and benefits, "Most important of all—in a long-run sense—was the social security program, which began operating in 1936."[43]

Rex Tugwell described the genesis of the social insurance scheme and its impact thus:

TABLE 1

New York Times COVERAGE OF MAJOR ROOSEVELT PRONOUNCEMENTS ON SOCIAL SECURITY

Date	*Statement*	*Page*	*Col.*	*Text Pub.*	*Total Col. Inches*	*Col. In. on S.S.*	*Ref. to S.S. in Headline*
1934							
June 8	Message to Congress	1	8	Yes	79*	79	Yes, 3 col.
June 28	FIRESIDE CHAT	1	8	Yes	87	18	Yes (subhead)
June 29	Release, setting up C.E.S.	1	8	Yes	48	48	Yes, 2 col.
Aug. 3	Bonneville speech	1	8	Yes	56	3	No
Sept. 30	FIRESIDE CHAT	1	8	Yes	126	4	No
Nov. 11	Release on C.E.S.	1	4	Yes	24	24	Yes, 1 col.
Nov. 13	Letter to Mayors' Conf.	1	8	Yes	48	11	Yes (subhead)
Nov. 14	Speech to Nat. Conf. on E.S.	1	8	Yes	108	108	Yes, 3 col.
1935							
Jan. 4	Annual Message	1	1	Yes	171*	9	Yes, 3 col.
Jan. 9	*Press conference* mention	None					
Jan. 17	S.S. message to Congress	1	8	Yes	502*	502	Yes, 4 col.
Jan. 18	*Press conference* mention	1	1	No	35	3	Yes (subhead)
Feb. 1	*Press conference* discussion	1	6	No	31	22	Yes, 1 col.
April 12	*Press conference* discussion	1	4	No	35	14	Yes, 1 col.
April 28	FIRESIDE CHAT	1	8	Yes	118	8	Yes, 2 col.
May 24	*Press conference* mention	1	7	No	17	8	Yes (subhead)
July 24	*Press conference* discussion	6	3	No	3	3	Yes
Aug. 14	Statement at signing	1	4&5	Yes	38*	38	Yes
					1,526	902	

> When Franklin began to think about this conception, it took hold of his imagination and he proliferated ideas so rapidly—and for once so openly—that none of those about him could keep up with him. Washington for weeks was devoted to speculation about the various possibilities after the infection began to spread. And the talk spread out to wider and wider circles. Franklin did nothing to check it. . . . It was not long, however, until social security had a hold on people's minds that demanded attention.[44]

He then goes on to assert that "Very possibly the putting forward of this issue was the most potent political stratagem of Franklin's whole career." He feels this issue cemented the loyalty of progressives of all sorts to the New Deal. For them social insurance had been an article of faith for many years. Most important of all, however, was the impact on labor, still skeptical of Roosevelt.

> . . . before the elections of 1936 labor was fairly committed to the New Deal. The Labor Relations Act of 1935 was hardly responsible for the change; its provisions were not such as to win labor's loyalty. It was social security that was overwhelmingly convincing to the working population. . . . Politically, social security consolidated a support that from then on could be counted on.

The Wagner Act was of great and vital interest to the labor leadership, but it was the prospect of benefits under the security legisla-

---

Notes to Table 1

The dates are of the statement or press conference; press coverage usually appeared the following day.

The pages and columns given are of the article dealing with the statement.

The next column indicates whether or not the text of the item was published in full.

The "total column inches" applies to the story plus continuation and the space occupied by the text of the statement if it appeared.

The next column represents an estimate of the proportion of space actually devoted to social security in instances in which it was one among several subjects the President discussed.

The last column indicates whether or not reference to social security appeared in the main headline (or in one of the lower decks of headlines—"subhead"), and the column width of the main headline.

* An additional article or articles appeared on the same subject but are not included in the tabulation.

tion that really caught the attention and cemented the support of the rank and file.

Arthur Schlesinger's view is substantially the same as Tugwell's and Burns's. Labor, he writes, had been drifting gradually in the Democratic direction, certainly since Wilson's day, though with a good deal of uncertainty during the 1920s. "The legislation of 1935 completed the identification of the cause of labor with the New Deal. The Social Security Act and the W.P.A. clinched the loyalty of the ordinary worker; the Wagner Act, the loyalty of the trade unionists."[45]

It must have been the public utterances and calculated educational campaign by the President, and by those who took their cue from him, that produced much of this result.

This case study in leadership of opinion has a multiple usefulness. By updating the example of Theodore Roosevelt's similar effort on behalf of the Hepburn Act, it suggests both the similarities inevitably discernible in the tactics of all "strong" Presidents and the broad range of new possibilities that had opened up during the intervening third of a century. Note the channels F.D.R. utilized to reach and educate the public. They included newly available means of direct presidential access through the radio and the skillfully devised instrument of the "fireside chat;" the refurbished device of the press conference, which owed something to "Uncle Ted" but much more to developments since; and the more traditional channels via the newspaper press, and the activity of White House staff and Cabinet people.

Besides exhibiting the resources of the White House in their range and variety, this analysis in depth of the "selling" of social security serves to make concrete a dimension of the process of leading opinion that otherwise remains abstract and implied. The discussion thus far of the President's ability to shape policy through the development and channeling of public opinion has highlighted the growing breadth of available technique. But public relations tools, like the tools of any trade, are effective only when they are brought together and manipulated in concert by skilled hands toward a particular end.

To what extent can one assume that Roosevelt here, or any President, really plans and executes, consciously and deliberately, the sort of educational strategy that can be inferred from the circumstantial evidence presented? Does coincidence rather than intent and foresight really account for the apparent pattern? It is probably impossible to give a definite answer. Actually, it is doubtless true that the degree of conscious planning varies from case to case, with the magnitude of the issue, and the range of competing demands on the President's attention.

Presidential leadership and preparation of national opinion for American involvement in the two World Wars, for example, unquestionably involved deliberate strategies carefully thought out by both Wilson and Roosevelt.[46] The evidence to this effect is conclusive. F.D.R. is quoted by Samuel Rosenman as having said, after the Quarantine speech backfired: "It's a terrible thing . . . to look over your shoulder when you are trying to lead—and to find no one there."[47] There can be no question that the President read correctly the signs of impending conflagration, as Wilson had read similar signs of near-certain American involvement twenty years before, and did all in his power, deliberately and skillfully, to unite the country to face the inevitable. A leadership problem of this sort is so enormous and crucial that it will admit of nothing less than careful strategy planning.

Individual legislative campaigns also at times acquire a kind of preeminent importance which impels a comparable degree of concern and effort. In recent years, Presidents have had to mount ever more elaborate efforts to secure support for the annual foreign aid appropriations.[48] When, however, the issue is one among several pieces of "must" legislation, attention is bound to be more episodic and publicity strategy often is formulated on the spur of the moment. As the range of presidential policy concern has steadily broadened since World War II, and as White House staff for legislative liaison has taken over more of the day-to-day job of Congressional surveillance, conscious advance preparation by the President of public opinion for pending measures has doubtless become increasingly rare. The tools and the potential are still ready to hand, however, to be used when the urgency is great enough and the stakes high enough to demand their use.

☆☆☆☆☆☆☆

Chapter 7

☆☆☆☆☆☆☆

THE MODERN PRESS CONFERENCE: 1933-1952

Franklin Roosevelt's contributions to the art of presidential communication were so varied and significant as almost to defy summarization. He came closer than any predecessor—with the possible exception of T.R.—to the full exploitation of the newspaper press. Moreover, with extraordinary foresight, he grasped the significance of the new medium, radio, and his skill in the realm of electronic communication is yet to be equaled.

In this chapter the focus will be on the press conference, the traditional point of contact between the White House occupant and the commercial media. These confrontations are of course only part of the pervasive total process of presidential relations with the news-gathering fraternity. The broader pattern of interaction includes coverage of formal presidential utterances, the flow of press releases and statements from the White House, the buttonholing of visitors, and all the other reportorial techniques for ferreting out the news about the Chief Executive, his family, and his staff. Some of this broader pattern will be examined in a later chapter.

Until sometime probably in the 1930s, the news conference was exclusively a liaison between the President and representatives of the printed media. Then the representatives of radio news broadcasting gained admission. After World War II television gradually found its place. The conference format was progressively altered to allow the more direct use of the newly available tools of communication.

I

In opening his first press conference, F.D.R. said that he was about to launch an innovation in White House press relations. "I am told that what I am about to do will become impossible, but I am going to try it."[1] What he proposed was to abolish written questions and permit the kind of spontaneity that had been largely absent under his Republican predecessors. Actually he had ample precedent for this in the practices of his former chief. Within the limits imposed by Wilson's personality and sense of the proprieties, his meetings with the reporters compare strikingly with those upon which the latter Roosevelt was about to embark.

The real uniqueness of F.D.R.'s conference technique lay in the subtle way he conducted the meetings within the framework of this revived precedent. The new President brought to the press conferences two qualities of great importance: an exuberant personality comparable, among incumbents in this century, only with T.R.'s; and a broad conception of the office and its potentialities which, again, had few parallels. These so completely infused everything that Franklin Roosevelt did as to make even the most routine device or tactic appear new and unprecedented and, to many, radical and dangerous.

Enough has already been written about the famous Roosevelt personality and about his Jacksonian-Lincolnian view of the presidency. It is perhaps appropriate to quote again, however, his definition of political leadership in 1932 before the Commonwealth Club: "persuading, leading, sacrificing, teaching always, because the greatest duty of a statesman is to educate."[2] Roosevelt used astutely every opportunity available to educate, and created new opportunities and channels for education where none had existed before. He felt that the office of President called for no less than a maximum effort along these lines, and that it imposed few limits on the incumbent who was so inclined.

The impact of his personality on the press conference is hard to capture. At bottom it was reflected in the feeling so many had in watching Roosevelt as President: that the office had been made for him, and he for the office. One searches in vain in the record of his first days in the White House for any of the sense of newness and strangeness in an alien environment which the awesome burden of the presidency normally generates. From the start he appeared to have a sureness of touch and self-assurance which made the observer feel he had been there for years. He embraced his new role with such zest and relish, such enthusiasm and enjoyment, that his immediate predecessors seemed by comparison like uncomfortable and awkward amateurs. One need only read the descriptions of Coolidge or even Wilson press conferences against the following awed and bemused firsthand impression by John Gunther:

> In twenty minutes Mr. Roosevelt's features had expressed amazement, curiosity, mock alarm, genuine interest, worry, rhetorical playing for suspense, decision, playfulness, dignity, and surpassing charm. Yet he *said* almost nothing. Questions were deflected, diverted, diluted. Answers—when they did come—were concise and clear.[3]

The ebullience and charm which the Hudson River squire possessed, coupled with a genuine and omnivorous interest in, and affection for, people, profoundly colored his relations with the reporters. Fresh from the disappointments and bitterness of the Hoover administration, they greeted his announcements of changed practices, and his easy camaraderie at the first conference, with spontaneous applause.[4] So great was their enthusiasm for him that observers—notably the employers of some of the correspondents—insisted that Roosevelt had hypnotized the usually hardened and cynical press corps and made them his sycophants and propagandists.[5] Ashmun Brown, on the other hand, wrote in the *American Mercury* in 1936 that the newsmen themselves, in their flush

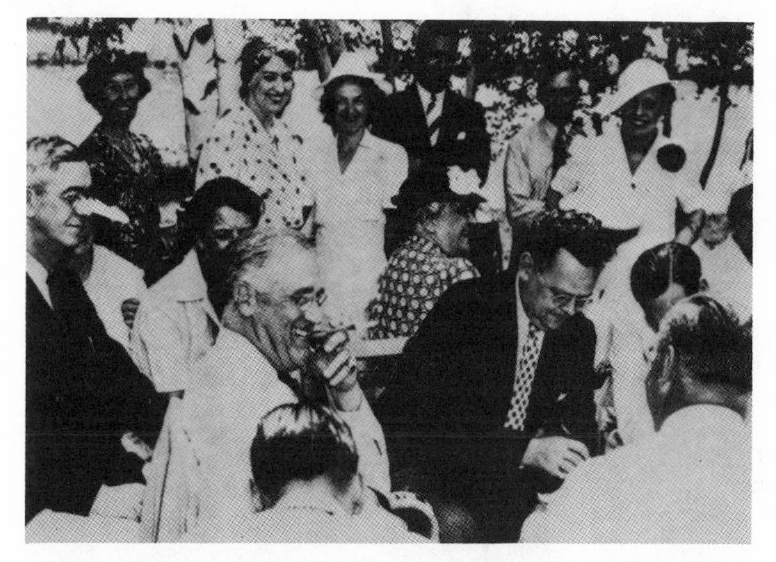

"The old master." Franklin D. Roosevelt enjoys a chat with reporters at Hyde Park. *Wide World Photos, courtesy Franklin D. Roosevelt Library.*

of initial enthusiasm, created a Roosevelt myth and believed it—until, he feels, the gloss began to wear thin and disillusionment grew during his fourth year in office.[6] Leo Rosten, a more detached observer, also lays the blame for the early inflated press reports of the President's skills and virtues to starry-eyed newsmen, and subsequent disenchantment to his inability to live up to the superhuman image they had created.

Raymond Clapper, writing in mid-1934, estimated that 60 per cent of the reporters were for the New Deal and 90 per cent "for Mr. Roosevelt personally."[7] (Early in 1936 Rosten polled some eighty reporters and found 64 per cent for F.D.R. and 31 per cent Republican in leaning.)[8] Clapper goes on to summarize the reasons—a list which could be duplicated, with variations, in other contemporary assessments:

> . . . the personal contacts between Mr. Roosevelt and the press are pleasant. He is on extremely intimate terms with the newspaper men who are regularly assigned full time to the White House. . . .

Roosevelt and Harry L. Hopkins at press conference in Warm Springs, Ga., 1939. *Courtesy Franklin D. Roosevelt Library.*

> On vacations and when he is travelling they are practically members of the family. He calls them by their first names, knows their little jokes, and when one of them appears in the morning with a hangover he is apt to ask for details. They play water polo with him. He has few secrets from them and often will discuss with them the most confidential policies in detail long before any publication is permitted.[9]

In addition, says Clapper, F.D.R. never sends them away empty handed; they admire his political craftsmanship; they believe in his sincerity, courage, and willingness to experiment; and they tend to place themselves in the class of forgotten men who are beneficiaries of the New Deal.

In short, his rapport with the working press rested essentially on three things: his treatment of them as individuals, his sympathy with their professional needs and problems, and their sympathy with his policies. The second of these calls for some further elaboration. F.D.R., more than almost any of his predecessors, was sensitive to the ambivalent nature of the President-reporter relationship. He was well aware that one who helped the reporters with the mechanics of getting news would earn their gratitude. This he did in a number of ways. He kept in mind the need to have something newsworthy come out of each conference. He also carefully framed the schedule so that their interests were served as much as possible.[10] He frequently "put the lid on" weekends (promising no White House announcements) so the regulars could relax.[11]

Perhaps the best illustration of this policy of serving his own and the reporters' interests simultaneously came in the frequency with which he provided "background" and "off the record" information. At his first press conference he had retained the rule that nothing the President said could be put in quotation marks without express authorization. But he did away with most of the vestiges of the "White House spokesman" device of the past. So long as the phrasing was modified, the President could be identified as source. He also established a "background" category of "material which can be used by all of you on your own authority and responsibility, not to be attributed to the White House. . . ." And finally, things given to the reporters present for their own information only would be "off the record."[12]

The importance of "background" (and in a sense of the whole press conference as F.D.R. conducted it) lay in the fact that the reporters, as intermediaries in the communication process, could transmit, in effect, either more or less than they received from the White House; less, in the sense of selective coverage, deliberate omission, or transmission marred by animus; and more by enhancing the prominence, volume, and favorable nature of coverage, providing background for a proposal, explaining, illustrating, placing in context, and generally conveying the fullness and subtlety of the President's intention. Roosevelt, in his relations with the working press, managed to tap these resources of exposition and favorable presentation with great skill, despite growing animosity on the part of publishers.

Gunther was very close to the mark when he wrote that at the news meetings the President "was like a friendly, informal schoolmaster conducting a free-for-all seminar, and indeed the chief function of the conferences was educational."[13] Time after time when a subject was raised prematurely, the President would say that though he could not answer on the record, he would be glad to discuss the matter for background, for the enlightenment of the reporters. When a question betrayed a failure to understand a complex policy problem, he would patiently explain—for background—what was involved and how the administration saw the problem, with copious illustrations of the homey sort he loved. Again, as in the case of social security, and in many other instances, he would fend off questions on a germinating policy until he determined that the time was ripe to begin laying the groundwork for a knowledgeable acceptance of it when it was eventually made public. Then he would lay out the motives and objectives he had in view, the complexities of the problem for which a remedy was sought, why one alternative was chosen over others, and so on.

Illustrations of this kind of background seminar are numerous, particularly during the early months of his first term. At his initial conference, after discussion of the ground rules, the very first substantive matter raised had to do with the banking crisis and action to deal with it. He replied: "I think I can put it this way—and this comes under the second category, 'background information' and not 'off the record,' because there is no reason why you should not use it in writing your stories."[14] Thereupon he explained briefly what was contemplated. Much of the rest of the conference dealt with related matters including the gold standard. His next press conference was held two days later, on March 10. Again banking was top on the agenda, and after some twelve pages of discussion of it in the transcript, someone said: "Doesn't this entire conference fall into the category of background?," to which the President replied that it did.

On the 15th the conference was opened by Mr. Roosevelt: "I haven't any real news, but suppose you would like to have me talk a little bit about the two other measures [besides banking]. Entirely just for background, the general thought has been this:. . . ."[15] A rundown followed of the emergency bills the President expected to get from Congress and some more "constructive" measures he hoped also to have considered. On putting unemployed to work in the forests, a reporter asked whether they would be cutting down trees or planting them. F.D.R. replied, in mock exasperation: "We have to have another class here on it. The easiest way to explain it is. . . ."[16] On the 22nd he discussed, for background, an unemployment relief bill that had been sent up the day before, using this device to answer criticisms voiced by William Green of the A. F. of L. without, as he said, appearing to do so directly. On the 24th he raised the matter of newspapers accepting beer ads (in view of prohibition repeal) and after consulting Steve Early about the reporters using it for background, went on to elaborate. Finally, at the meeting on March 29, "I have something about the securities bill today. . . . What I am saying to Congress in the message —I don't suppose you will use any of this before it actually goes to Congress—is that it applies the new doctrine of caveat vendor in place of the old doctrine of caveat emptor."[17] This prefaced a lengthy commentary on the message and accompanying proposals.

Though the tempo obviously diminished later, the foregoing sample of "background" discussions is far from unique. In several senses the conferences filled an educational function—for the reporters more than for the public directly, but of course the public was the ultimate target. They were genuinely seminar-like, to an extent that has almost never been the case since. It is important to note that the reporters not only were being educated in the motives and objectives of the administration, but were also being briefed on the intricacies of banking, financial policy, farm policy, and a host of other matters, detailed knowledge of which they had never really needed before.

The transition from Coolidge passivity to an era of proliferating government concern in a host of unprecedented areas was a transition that the press as well as the politicians had to make. Covering Washington during the New Deal and after was a far more difficult and technical business than it had ever been before. There is clear indication in Roosevelt's early press conferences of genuine puzzlement on the part of the reporters, who genuinely sought for enlightenment from an apparently extraordinarily well informed Chief Executive. There were few handy sources of information on the economics of worldwide depressions, or government intervention in the economy, or even the nature of the national economy itself. Even scarcer were reporters who had the background to write knowledgeably about such issues. Thus in a very real sense the President was acting the teacher, almost creating at times the reportorial expertise necessary to give adequate coverage of his administration's unprecedented policy ventures.

Two specialized forms which backgrounding took should be noted. These were the budget seminars inaugurated by F.D.R. and the famous, though at the time carefully concealed, Sunday night suppers. Previous Presidents had had mimeographed statements prepared and handed out explaining their budgets.[18] Raymond Clapper described the Roosevelt practice thus, noting first the enormous wartime burdens he was simultaneously carrying:

> After lunch he undertook to explain the war budget in order to assist the Washington reporters who would be writing their dispatches about this complicated array of figures. For two hours he tried to reduce the matter to simple terms for us. He patiently answered questions, some intelligent, some not, and some only repetitious. Though he must have been unbelievably tired and pressed with critical business, he never showed impatience and he stayed with it until all questions were exhausted.[19]

These were off-the-record sessions held in advance of the delivery of the budget message to Congress. By giving the newsmen a head start in writing their stories, the seminar assisted them and earned their good will, while insuring better, more accurate coverage at the same time.

The Sunday suppers, at which Mrs. Roosevelt scrambled eggs in a chafing dish, were not confined to members of the Fourth Estate. But these gentry, including the columnists, were frequent guests. They were to divulge neither what was said around the table nor even the fact that they had been at the White House on such an errand.[20] Sessions of this kind, plus background interviews like those accorded to George Creel of *Colliers* (which then appeared as authoritative accounts of the President's future plans and hopes)[21] obviously supplemented in exceedingly useful ways the off-record and background talks held at the press conferences.

The specific role of "off-the-record" information at the conferences was probably more limited and subtle. Events showed that the President had miscalculated somewhat when he first outlined his intention. It proved impossible to expect that reporters present at a given conference would withhold confidential information from absent colleagues or from their editors. In time, Roosevelt concluded that matters of considerable importance could not really be discussed in this manner without serious risk of a leak. Various commentators have insisted that there is no really valid reason for a President to give out such information anyway,[22] and suggested, as with Theodore Roosevelt, the temptation to sew up a story by discussing it, thereby precluding publication.[23]

Actually, it seems apparent that, at least in the first part of his period in office, Roosevelt turned the "off-record" category into a distinct advantage. As Ernest Lindley has written, "Very often such 'off the record' information is an explanation of why he cannot discuss a particular subject. It is frequently useful in enabling newspapermen to check the authenticity of information which they have obtained elsewhere."[24] Furthermore, it allowed the President to intervene tactfully when a story, particularly in the foreign area, if written on the basis of faulty understanding, might do genuine harm. For example, at one point the President commented off the record regarding some disarmament proposals. When asked if anything could be used for background, he said: "No, I think it is just to enable you not to get stampeded by things coming over from the other side [of the Atlantic]."[25]

The frequency with which the reporters *asked* for "off-the-record" information from F.D.R. should settle doubts about its usefulness to them. Numerous examples are to be found. "As to the European Conferences, can you give us your impression, off the record. . . ." "What do you think of the Morgan show up on the Hill—off the record?" (this the President dodged). "Off the record, Mr. President, can you fill us in on what the situation is on that? Personally I am as ignorant as a nincompoop on it all, and if I could get a little background or off the record. . . . On inflation and deflation of the dollar and so forth."

Turning now from the President's relations with the working press and his use of the press conferences for enlisting their cooperation and support, what about the direct role of the meetings in his political and policy leadership? Clearly the conferences *were* important here—in two ways. First, they served as a forum from which to discuss pending policies and urge their favorable consideration in Congress, or build support in the country that in turn would be translated into pressure on the legislature. But the conferences were also a means of conveying the presidential image to the country, keeping interest in the White House and the doings of its occupant at a high pitch, and thus helping to maintain the public as a receptive audience for more specific appeals.

Speeches and other similar appearances are too infrequent to sustain a feeling of continuing contact and rapport between the Chief Executive and his clientele. White House statements and releases do plug some of the gaps though in a rather impersonal way. But undoubtedly the twice-weekly press conferences of the Roosevelt era did more than anything else to maintain the President in the public eye on a continuous basis and to give the populace a sense of uninterrupted personal contact with him. (The radio provided contact of a more vivid sort, but fireside chats averaged no more than two or three a year.) The importance of such a pattern of warm and constant contact, both in building the impregnable position Roosevelt came to enjoy in the minds and hearts of the bulk of the public and of providing him with a ready and receptive audience, needs no further comment.

The discussion of social security in the last chapter pointed up several characteristics of F.D.R.'s use of the conferences for specific policy leadership. Unlike Coolidge, he often appeared to minimize deliberately his references to a bill while it was being debated, in deference to the sensibilities of Congress. He preferred to rely on careful advance preparation for his major proposals. Another example of this came at the conference of November 7, 1934, in a discussion of work relief policies. (Recall that it was during the 1935 session of Congress, soon to meet, that the policy shift to massive work relief [W.P.A.] took place.)

Q. Mr. President, do you expect any change in the relief policy before Congress meets?

THE PRESIDENT. No. Well, there I can give you something but we will have to make it off the record. I have to keep it off the record because we don't know what the thing is going to develop into.

Q. Do you mean off the record or just background?

THE PRESIDENT. Absolutely off the record so you will know what we are thinking about. It has not got to the stage of background. . . . [Here follows a discussion, in part using concrete Hyde Park examples, of the effect of dole relief on the minds of recipients, etc.] The idea is to see whether, with next year's relief money that is to be divided up between three organizations, really, the CCC camps, public works and Harry Hopkins, to see whether we cannot use all of that expenditure to take people off what we call home relief, that is cash and grocery orders, and put them on useful work instead.

Now, that is the thing we are groping for and we are only in the groping stage.

This passage illustrates several things, besides the use of "background." By replying as he did, the President was able to avoid giving no answer at all or saying "no comment." At the same time he could take the reporters into his confidence and flatter them by giving them a glimpse of the process of policy consideration and formulation. Most important, as with his program of social legislation, he gave them an insight into his motives and objectives which could hardly help enriching their understanding, and their writing, later on when the new proposals were announced publicly. Some hostile assumptions about his purposes might be thus blunted in advance.

In general Roosevelt, in his press conferences, seemed not to be as heavy-handed or inclined to browbeat Congress as is commonly supposed. Coolidge, surprisingly enough, was rather more inclined to issue regular and pointed reminders to the legislators during a session. Suppose, however, instead of something relatively noncontentious like social security, one examines a proposal for which Roosevelt had to fight more vigorously, such as the public utility holding company legislation of 1935, which was bitterly resisted by the industry.

At the conference of February 9, 1934, the President was asked about stock market regulation, and in the course of a background answer he said, referring to the Democratic platform: "Then next is, 'Regulation to the full extent of Federal power of (a) Holding companies which sell securities in interstate commerce.'" On March 2 and November 14 he was queried about utility regulation but disclaimed knowledge of anything pending. On November 21, however, when asked at Warm Springs if there was any other news, he allowed that he had been studying reports and there would be all kinds of interesting things coming out in the next two or three weeks. He suggested an off-the-record discussion, recalling the "perfectly grand" talk he had had with reporters in the same locale before his inauguration about plans for TVA.[26] Two days later this really got into high gear, with a very long off-the-record presidential commentary on electric power, TVA, holding companies, watered stock, and related matters. There was no mention of any pending legislative plan, nor even of any direct role for government in the area, though one was clearly implied. The President, in other words, was thinking out loud about a general problem, for the benefit of the relatively small and select reporter group that had followed him to Warm Springs for the Thanksgiving holiday.[27]

On December 14, back in Washington, and again on December 19 and January 11, there were considerably briefer discussions of the holding company issue at press meetings—still couched in rather general and theoretical terms. The second of these was for background use. On the latter date he began the conference with an attack on misleading utility lobbying. In the face of questions on January 4, 23, 25, and February 1 the President was evasive. On the 7th of February, the Wheeler-Rayburn bill to curb holding companies was introduced in Congress. Queried about this on the 15th, Mr. Roosevelt explained at some length that he had not seen it and did not discuss pending legislation anyway, reminding the reporters not to deduce anything from his disinclination to comment. Later in the same conference, when asked in more general terms about holding company legislation, he obliged: "Well, I will talk entirely off the record about it . . . ," which launched some three transcript pages of discussion.

The bill then lay dormant in Congressional committee for some time and the President was not questioned again about the matter until June 28, in the midst of the struggle on the Hill over the so-called "death sentence" provision for the compulsory dissolution of holding companies. The questioner offered Mr. Roosevelt for comment a rumor that he had lost interest in this particular project. In reply there came a strong endorsement of the legislation—exceedingly strong in comparison with his usual practice: "I am very keen for it and very strong for it. More so than before, if it were possible. And I notice that some people have been talking again about the 'death sentence.'" He went on to deal at length with some apparent misconceptions about this provision, and reiterated the objectives of the administration and the ways provided for their attainment. He then shifted to a discussion of the attendant lobby activity. Asked about a possible veto if the bill emerged in unsatisfactory form, the President cut off the questioner with "I am talking about today, Friday, the 28th of June." Between then and the final signing of the legislation on August 27, during a protracted final conference committee stage, he declined to answer or turned aside questions on the subject at no less than six more conferences.

Reviewing this sequence, it seems apparent that even in an area that generated as much heat and acrimony as this, the President was very sparing in his comments to his journalistic confreres. He had, again, gone to great lengths to explain beforehand the purposes and objectives of the legislation, and even earlier, to explore the setting and ramifications of the problem. Only once, however, did he come out flatfootedly with a public endorsement in a press conference *during* passage, and this came at a crucial point in the Congressional deliberations when, apparently, he felt that drastic measures were necessary. The similarity here with his tactics vis-à-vis social security is far closer than the differences in the receptions accorded the two proposals would lead one to expect.

An outstanding case of the use of a press conference for advance education on a foreign policy issue was of course the famous discussion of lend-lease on December 17, 1940.[28] The bill was then introduced in January and signed by the President on March 11. Very likely the well-known garden hose analogy which the President used in his December press conference did as much as anything else to convey to the public the essence of the method of aiding Britain which he had decided upon, and to gain wide support for it.

The deliberate use Franklin Roosevelt made of his press conferences raises the question of how, mechanically speaking, he accomplished this.[29] Wilson and his successors, by agreeing to deal with all accredited reporters impartially and submit themselves for questioning on subjects more or less of the reporters' choosing, surrendered the kind of control which T. R. had exercised over whom he would see and what subjects he would discuss. As a result, later Presidents had to either let the scribes guide the meetings by their questions, or resort at times to indirect means to insure that subjects were raised about which they wanted to inform the public.

After Roosevelt, as the nonquotation rule was gradually abandoned, this problem became still more difficult to solve. Since only the substance of what he said could be reported, and since both he and the reporters viewed the conferences as private "family" affairs, F.D.R. could rephrase a question to suit his purposes before answering it, or if need be, raise a subject himself. He could thus concentrate on the substance of what he wanted to say, rather than the precise wording, or the means of securing opportunity to say it. Nor, incidentally, need he worry about an occasional bit of profanity, flash of anger, lapse into slang, or touch of earthy humor. All these were kept discreetly behind the veil of nonquotation. Only later did the conferences become public events reported verbatim.

The flexibility thus provided did, in Roosevelt's hands, compensate for much of the loss of presidential initiative which Wilson had sanctioned. But other devices imparted considerable additional flexibility. One of these was the opening statement. Rarely was this the carefully prepared document it later became.[30] Using such openers, he could insure that at least one bit of news would come from the conference if it appeared the day was going to be dull otherwise, and the item he had in mind not too likely to be elicited by a question. Thus he served the needs of the working press and maintained the flow of news identified with the White House. He could also divert attention in this manner from some subject he knew would arise and about which he did not want to talk.[31] And he could insure that adequate time and attention would be devoted to a complex and important matter by raising it first.

The President opened 102 of the first 250 meetings with some kind of announcement, statement, or discussion of a subject which he deemed newsworthy.[32] (This does not include, of course, the few minutes of light banter that went on between him and the regulars grouped around his desk while they waited the signal for the conference to begin.) In an additional eighteen conferences at which he made no opening statement, he interrupted the flow later to interject some unrelated item. All told, then, at roughly half of these first 250 conferences, he did raise subjects himself; during the other half he relied on the questions asked.

The President apparently resorted to another—behind the scenes—device for insuring a particular result: the planted question. During his term in office, it was intimated that other administration officials at times planted questions in order to smoke him out on a particular subject or publicize a pet project.[33] But questions were planted by the White House itself in order to allow the President to say something he wanted to say in answer to an apparently spontaneous query. This tactic was probably not resorted to often. As Raymond Brandt wrote, "such overt action is unnecessary. Mr. Roosevelt has shown no hesitancy in initiating announcements and if he has prepared himself to answer a question which reporters do not ask, he has a way of bringing up the subject."[34]

But there seem to have been occasions when F.D.R. did feel for one reason or other that he would rather reply to a plant than bring something up himself.[35] Henry Morgenthau reports, for instance, that "Franklin" had once announced a budgetary estimate that proved far too low, whereupon, "At a press conference that afternoon Roosevelt had Steve Early plant a question about relief and in reply pooh-poohed the report that he had settled on $500 million."[36] Did the President perhaps feel here that a plant would make his reversal less embarrassing than raising the point himself? Again Jim Farley has him using a plant to deny the validity of a story that had appeared dealing with the third term issue.[37] In view of Farley's well-known ambitions, he might be taken with a grain of salt on this, but presumably the contrived question again enabled the President to avoid taking an embarrassing initiative. The redoubtable Ickes cites another case of a plant to correct a distorted newspaper account of something the Secretary had said at one of his own press conferences.[38] Here, no doubt, F.D.R. did not want to dignify the interagency issue involved by bringing it up himself.

A few memos in the Hyde Park files illustrate the process of question planting. (Obviously this must have been handled orally as a rule.) In 1942 the President had sent Sumner Welles a memo for comment containing a proposal that the White House publicly thank Mexico for providing farm laborers in California. Welles replied with the suggestion that a question be planted at a forthcoming press conference to give the President opportunity to make the appropriate statement, and forwarded a memo on the subject. Thereupon F.D.R. wrote one of the famous "chits": "Memorandum for S.T.E. Sumner Welles suggests that I handle this at a press conference. Will you arrange it? F.D.R." At the bottom of the chit is a pencil notation that the President did use the information on October 20, 1942.[39]

The examples cited above were "plants" in the most obvious sense: a particular friendly reporter being asked to propound a particular question. There is even an example in the Hyde Park files of the actual suggested wording of a proposed plant: "Mr. President, did you notice the annual report yesterday of the American Civil Liberties Union? What has happened to the efforts of the Government to protect civil liberties?"[40] On the other hand, the thing can be done very casually, as Early apparently often did it, by saying in an offhand way that the President had been giving a lot of thought to something lately and might be willing to talk about it if asked.[41] This would obviously bring results in most cases.

This leads to a final point related to the deliberate use of press conferences by the President: advance preparation. The process was far less formalized than it later became, and probably done on a casual and intermittent basis. Normally, Steve Early had a chat with his boss during which he reminded the President of currently hot subjects, and informed him of questions he knew or suspected would be asked. These sessions took place in the President's office just before the conference, or as he was dressing. Lindsay Rogers notes that "In some cases he does prepare himself carefully—always on the financial estimates and occasionally on special subjects such as those covered in the 'horse-and-buggy' conference."[42]

In the Hyde Park papers there are no files that would suggest either the nature or the scope of conference preparation, which again lends credence to the assumption that it was sketchy and episodic. There are occasional memos or other papers relating to the meetings with the reporters.[43] In some instances there are notes from newsmen giving advance notice to the President through Steve Early of intention to ask a particular question.[44] A few are from other officials or even outsiders warning of an impending query.[45] In rare instances there are suggested lines of reply,[46] or queries sent out from the White House to an agency or official requesting information on some matter raised at a recent conference.[47]

When the President was out of Washington and Early or McIntyre had remained to "mind the store," telegraphic communications with the President were often revealing. The following telegram, dated August 31, 1934, is a useful example of the type of guidance Early presumably gave his boss before a press conference:

> Newspapermen here already pressing as to whether Richberg goes out on Sept. 1st . . . stop In some instances at least these inquiries come from quarters pretending to see another victory for [Gen. Hugh] Johnson comma if Richberg goes out stop Think important that more than casual announcement be made by President at todays press conference stop Much has been made of Johnsons quote victories quote dash Presidents refusal to accept his resigna-

> tion comma his walkout and explosion comma his salary increase stop Hence something should be done for Richberg. . . .[48]

There are a few recorded comments by F.D.R. himself about the handling of matters at forthcoming meetings. Regarding a candidate in New York state in 1942 he noted: "I shall say, perhaps in a press conference, 'I shall vote for Bennett' . . . I shall stop there."[49] Ickes records in his diary: "He told me to send him a letter setting forth the facts which he would bring up himself at his own press conference."[50] The point has also been made that he often deliberately held big stories in order to break them at a press conference.[51] In other words, in addition to the briefings by Early, it is evident that Roosevelt often planned in advance the things he wanted to emerge as news, and the way he would insure that those subjects were raised. He must also have asked himself before most conferences what he could count upon as a newsworthy subject to insure that the visiting scribes would not go away empty-handed.

He could plan thus casually[52] for his press conferences in part because during most of his twelve years in office he had to deal *either* with domestic affairs *or* war direction and foreign policy. Not until after the war did the two become simultaneous and constant burdens on a President's time. There was also Roosevelt's fabled knowledge of the workings of the government, which he loved to display for the newsmen. Rarely must it have been necessary for him to bone up on a governmental program or the work of an agency. Finally, the less often conferences are held, the more time must be spent in coping with the backlog of potential questions. F.D.R. held his twice a week, Truman on the average once a week, and Presidents since 1952 about every two weeks or so.

The Roosevelt press conferences, although unique, powerfully influenced subsequent presidential practice. A pre-existing institution was rescued from the doldrums and disrepute into which it had fallen, and used with unsurpassed skill and subtlety. The link thus forged between the White House occupant and the people at large was destined, in an era of big government and frequent world crisis, to become indispensable to future Chief Executives.

Harry Truman and his successors had to cope with the vast expansion of the Washington press corps, the rapid development of the media, the continued growth of the President's domestic and worldwide responsibilities, and the mounting pressures from press and public for the revelation of more and more of the process of governing—demands hard to resist because made in the sacred name of democracy and freedom of the press. Later developments in presidential press relations had a quality of inevitability. The presidency no less than other institutions has been shaped by external forces as well as by the personalities and plans of its occupants.

II

The transition from Franklin Roosevelt to Harry Truman on April 12, 1945, differed in some ways from any previous vice presidential succession. Truman had been Vice President for less than three months. He knew next to nothing about the gigantic issues he would have to face or the conduct of the presidency, save what could be learned from the press or by an observant Senator.[53] He succeeded a man whose length of tenure, virtuosity, and disinclination to delegate had made the office almost nontransferable. In twelve years Roosevelt had wrought a transformation in the presidency, but he had done so on a highly personalized basis. White House practices, precedents, and channels that had developed since 1933 were emanations of his own personality and the habits of his long-term associates, rather than formalized routines which could be readily utilized by a successor.[54]

This was certainly true of the Roosevelt press conference. Yet Harry Truman had little choice but to rely upon patterns set by his predecessor. He held his first press conference on April 17, five days after taking office, and the only immediately obvious difference was the fact that he stood to address the reporters and receive their questions. Otherwise the new President said he would follow the conference rules which F.D.R. had established. It was soon evident, however, that the resemblance between the practices of the two men was to be only superficial.

During the opening months of his tenure President Truman won the affection of the reporters as he did of the community at large.[55] This came in part from sympathy and fervent good wishes in the carrying out of an almost impossible task, but also he was liked for his humility, unassuming manners, and down-to-earth qualities. Though he did not cultivate the newsmen in the apparently conscious way F.D.R. had, they continued to like him as a person, however acrimonious his relations with the press as a whole became.[56] In his case, however, personal affection was not linked with as much admiration of his policies and craftsmanship as it had been with Roosevelt. Thus he reaped far fewer public relations advantages from his dealings with the working press as individuals. That they were a more sophisticated and worldly-wise group by 1945 than they had been in 1933 should not be forgotten, either.

President Truman never seems to have developed as extensive informal contacts with the reporters as F.D.R. This required the kind of subtlety and deviousness, as it were, which Roosevelt possessed, and which his more straightforward and literal successor did not. Perhaps, after the war, the reporters themselves became more sensitive to competitive advantages gained by colleagues, thereby making any individual interviews imprudent. At least the violent reaction to Truman's interview with Arthur Krock in 1950 would suggest this.[57] The press conference format, too, tended to change in ways that made free and easy camaraderie increasingly difficult.

Mr. Truman's decision to hold the conferences only half as often as Roosevelt had was doubtless significant. At his very first encounter with the fourth estate, he announced: "Due to the fact that I have such a terrific burden to assume, I am going to have only one press conference a week. I shall have one in the morning and one in the afternoon—turn about—week about."[58] This was undoubtedly a short-term expedient born of his reaction to the crushing weight which had suddenly fallen on him, and perhaps was a reflection also of his nervousness at the thought of these recurring ordeals. It probably did not represent a considered decision as to the most desirable schedule for the future.

President Truman talks to the press, 1948. *Dorothy Girton, Democratic Digest; courtesy Harry S. Truman Library.*

The once-a-week schedule did continue, and represented a sharp departure from precedent. Wilson, Harding, Coolidge, and even Hoover, as well as F.D.R., had all operated on a twice-a-week basis. The consequences of this change, though perhaps subtle, were considerable. The sense of continuity of contact between press, public, and President must have been markedly reduced. Though the flow of press releases increased under Truman over the Roosevelt output,[59] these were not a full substitute. The implications of this change for the new President are hard to assess, because the image conveyed by his press meetings was not as consistently favorable as with his predecessor. To some extent his humanity, his determination and fighting spirit came through, but there was a less attractive side to the image projected. At times the President seemed impetuous, ill-informed, cocky, and quarrelsome.[60]

This comparison of Roosevelt and Truman images provokes speculation about the qualities that are most likely to endear a President to the people.[61] They are not necessarily attracted by humble origins and an Horatio Alger-like rise, nor by the kind of pugnacity, tendency to occasional error, or salty language which characterize themselves. On the contrary, the sense of security, the father image if you will, which they seek in a Chief Executive is apparently better satisfied by a self-conscious patrician of the Roosevelt type, precisely because he *is* different from the general run, and because he appears to lack the imperfections and foibles they see in themselves. Favorable reactions to the detached and grandfatherly Eisenhower and the vigorously youthful, intellectual, and semipatrician Kennedy bear this out. The picture President Truman projected to the country through the press conference and other channels was at best a doubtful asset. It probably generated less receptivity to policy leadership than Roosevelt had.

What use did the Missourian make of his press conferences for the enlistment of Congressional and popular support for program objectives?[62] Here, as elsewhere, the new President modeled his conduct to a considerable extent on that of his predecessor. He generally declined, for instance, to comment on legislation while it was in the process of consideration on the Hill, as Roosevelt had, or to discuss possible vetoes. Yet he too was from time to time drawn into the vocal advocacy of a bill, especially at crucial junctures in the struggle for its passage.

When his legislative leadership via the press conference is examined more closely, however, some rather striking differences of tone and style become apparent. With Roosevelt one got the impression that he followed carefully worked out strategies of public appeal when a major policy was at stake. And these plans generally involved careful advance preparation of press and public opinion. His successor appears to have less frequently devised and followed such self-conscious plans of campaign, though he was capable of doing so when occasion seemed to demand it.

To secure a more concrete basis for comparison two policy issues have been examined in the Truman press conferences. One of these, perhaps the outstanding monument to his statesmanship and ability as a leader, is the adoption of the Marshall Plan. The other, which might be taken to exemplify his weaknesses as a political leader, is health insurance.

Frequent references can be found in the press conference records to the Truman Doctrine and then to the closely related European Recovery Program, beginning in February 1947 (when the British first notified the United States that they could no longer carry the burden in the eastern Mediterranean).[63] Most of these, in the regular press meetings, were, to say the least, uninformative and usually very brief. The President only once took the opportunity to make a significant contribution to the public and legislative discussion of the Marshall Plan proposal. That came in January, 1948, when most of the conference was devoted to a Congressional threat of drastic cut in Plan funds, and turned into a general canvass of the proposals.[64]

Unlike F.D.R.'s day, reporters' questions were usually followed by brief, one-sentence answers rather than by any extended explanatory monologue. At only one point (in answer to whether he thought the full amount being requested to start the program was essential) did he approach Roosevelt's practice, concluding his reply: "I am—I feel very strongly on the subject. I think the welfare of this country and the welfare of the world is at stake in this European recovery plan." This particular conference was probably highly informative and effective, but was also unique in the development of this and most other policy situations during the Truman administration.

President Truman conspicuously did not try to "educate" the reporters as Roosevelt so often did. In a few instances the wording of a question about the European situation virtually invited some such background briefing, but the President almost never took these proffered opportunities. For example, on May 15, 1947, after quizzing the President about the pending appointment of the Greek aid mission head (which elicited a rare general comment from Mr. Truman on the importance of people being willing to take on such an assignment), one of the newsmen asked: "Mr. President, all of the 'dopesters' around you are saying that this is just the first step, the Greek-Turkey plan, and that there will soon be other countries that will have to be bolstered against Communism. Can you comment on that?" To this the President answered: "We will meet that situation should it arise." Such efforts as Truman made at explanation and elucidation at his press conferences were made almost invariably by a prepared statement carefully drafted in advance, which he read (amid many pleas that he slow down!) but which he would rarely expand upon in the ensuing question period. Almost invariably, when asked to comment on something that had been the subject of a speech or statement, he would tell his inquirers to go back and read the document.

While the President did not use his regular press conferences to build support for the Marshall Plan, he did in this one instance adapt another and closely related device very effectively for the same purpose. It had been customary for Roosevelt to hold special off-the-record "press conferences" with various groups such as members of the American Society of Newspaper Editors and the Radio News Analysts. Truman continued these annual meetings, and during the gestation of foreign aid policies in 1947 and 1948 he made exceedingly good use of them. The first such occasion came on April 17, 1947, some five weeks after the Truman Doctrine message, and involved the newspaper editors. The President opened the meeting with a long informal discussion of administration foreign policy, which he prefaced with an expression of appreciation: "I think the press has given the country a completely clear and fair statement of that situation [aid to Greece and Turkey], and the necessity for it. I might say a word or two to you, off the record if I may, as to the development of that situation." Toward the end of the ensuing long extemporaneous talk he said, "We must continue that bipartisan foreign policy for the welfare of ourselves and the welfare of the world, because our own welfare is mixed up in the welfare of the world as a whole. . . . And you gentlemen can help us prepare to meet that situation. . . . Now I have been exceedingly frank with you gentlemen in stating the situation. I thought you were entitled to know what is in the mind of your President."

On May 13 the President held a similar session with the Radio News Analysts. In late September, following the Marshall speech at Harvard in June, he read and gave out long prepared statements on the Marshall Plan proposals at his regular press conferences of the 25th and 29th. Then on the 30th, and again on October 17, there were two more off-record special conferences for the editors of business and trade papers and for the National Conference of

Editorial Writers. During the latter he said: "I want to bring that home to you so that when you write your editorials, try and get all the facts in relation to the foreign policy before you make up your mind. . . . You have a tremendous influence on the welfare of this country."

On April 23, 1948, three weeks after the Marshall Plan legislation had been signed, at an off-record meeting with the National Conference of Business Paper Editors, and on April 23, 1949, for the Newspaper Editors Association, the President did further educational work on behalf of the European Recovery Program, by then in operation. At all these gatherings he presented the administration's case carefully and at length. Note also the timing of the discussions. The first two followed hard upon the Truman Doctrine speech, which initiated the whole development of foreign aid policy. Two more came in the fall of 1947, timed to prepare the way for the special Marshall Plan session of Congress. The last two doubtless were designed to help complete the foreign policy revolution involved, following passage and initial implementation.

Why did he select these forums rather than the regular press conferences? Several reasons suggest themselves. Most obviously, foreign newsmen as well as Americans became increasingly numerous at presidential press meetings following the war, which made off-record discussion impractical, and such comment on foreign affairs virtually out of the question.[65] He may also have felt that on unprecedented issues like the Truman Doctrine and Marshall aid, which required bipartisan support, convinced editors, editorial writers, and columnists would carry more weight than reporters, however carefully briefed. The regular press conferences, in addition to their more polyglot membership, had also become too large and amorphous, and infused with too much of a hit-and-run atmosphere, for the lengthy discussion of such intricate issues.

But why, in the case of domestic proposals, was he so loath to explain and educate at regular press conferences? In the Truman Library files there is a letter from an experienced Washington reporter to Press Secretary Ross in which essentially the same point is raised. If the President would elaborate somewhat more in answering questions, particularly follow-up questions on the same subject, he would convey a clearer impression of his policy and of his thinking, the writer said in substance.[66] This letter, and questions in press conferences asking for elaboration, suggest that the reporters also felt the lack of explanation in depth. If the President had felt able to comply—either on or off the record—he would have served both his own interests and those of the reporters.

The nature of the problem can be sharpened by an examination of press conference references to the proposal for a system of national health insurance. Mr. Truman first mentioned this idea as a kind of postscript to his long, twenty-one-point message to Congress on reconversion, September 6, 1945.[67] The following November 19, the foreshadowed special message on health insurance was actually sent up.[68] It is important to note that the President announced this unprecedented and controversial proposal without any significant advance preparation. No references at all were found in the press conference transcripts for 1945.

Nothing significant happened on the subject, by way of Congressional consideration or action. This the President made an issue in the 1948 campaign, mentioning health insurance repeatedly in castigating the Eightieth Congress.[69] Only once, however, in a speech at Los Angeles, did he go into much detail about what he proposed. The release of a report by the Federal Security Administrator (which Mr. Truman had requested in January, 1948) at his press conference of September 2, plus these campaign mentions, revived the issue and eventuated in new recommendations to Congress, transmitted in April, 1949.[70]

During 1949 there was an exchange at the budget seminar in early January about the inclusion of funds for implementing the proposal if adopted, and later in January a brief exchange which elicited only the information that the health insurance message was in preparation. On February 24, some six or eight weeks before the message was to be sent up, the President was asked about its prospective content, and said it would be confined to health. Then—

> Q. The whole national health program would be involved, rather than the—just the one angle there?

> THE PRESIDENT. That's right, the whole national health program, and it will be stated very plainly, so there won't be any argument about it.

Again this appears to have been a logical opportunity for some discussion of administration plans and motives in advance of the message, but he chose not to take it.

A month later, on March 24, a question was posed as to when the message would be ready, and garnered the reply that it was still being prepared. On the 31st a nearly identical exchange took place. Neither time did the President discuss the proposal. On April 21, following submission of the plan to Congress, a reporter inquired if Mr. Truman contemplated a follow-up radio talk to go with the program, and the President said it was under consideration. None apparently was delivered. On May 5 a similar brief dialogue took place, though this time the questioner wanted to know if a tour in support of health insurance and other administration proposals was in the offing. He was told that none was planned. On May 26 Mr. Truman rather brusquely cut off an inquiry about his support of specific bills like health insurance with: "I am for all of them." And finally, on June 9, a reporter, apparently hoping that a different tack might bring better results, mentioned the recent dropping of Dr. Fishbein by the A.M.A. as perhaps indicative of a rise in public support for the health plan. The President merely replied that apparently it was discovered there were physicians not in sympathy with Fishbein.

The foregoing catalog of press meeting mentions of health insurance during 1949[71]—when the proposal was most prominently a part of the President's legislative program—may represent an extreme example of Truman press conference technique. It is not wholly untypical, however, and raises again the question: why was he so reluctant to explain and "educate" on an issue of this kind? (Only in connection with the rather special case of the Marshall Plan did he ever do so at any length.) His reluctance cannot be traced to a changed press conference format, because until 1950 they operated more or less as they had under Roosevelt. Clearly there was a personal disinclination or inability on the part of Mr. Truman to use the meetings as Roosevelt had.[72]

Unlike his predecessor, the Missourian approached the conferences more as one would approach an ordeal, or at best a contest of wits,[73] than as an opportunity to be exploited. (In a preconference aside to Romagna, the shorthand reporter, in July 1949, he said: "I am getting so I dread these press conferences.") He did not look upon them as chances to open his mind and motives to the press, and through them, to the public. While F.D.R. was so conspicuously in charge of the conference at all times, Mr. Truman was either disinclined or unable to exert similar control.[74] There were occasions, as with the famous "red herring" reference to Communists in government, when he allowed reporters to put words in his mouth, to his later discomfort.[75] He would rarely reword a question to suit himself before answering it.[76] Also, his unwillingness to be evasive and penchant for quick yes and no answers had the same effect. A "yes" to a question meant accepting the wording of the query as it had been framed by a reporter, perhaps with the conscious intent to entrap.[77] He appeared to take the questions one at a time without seeing that the cumulative impact of a perhaps discontinuous series might be damaging.[78]

One commentator came close to the heart of the matter when he wrote: "To really make something out of a press conference you have to have some ham in you. There is no ham in Mr. Truman."[79] Roosevelt was a consummate actor. Tom Corcoran is quoted as having once said to the President that the difference between him and T.R. was that F.D.R. never faked—in speech delivery and the like. Roosevelt leaned forward and replied: "Oh, but Tommy, at times I do, I do!"[80]

Means of control like the question plant and the opening statement gained importance as the press conference evolved during the 1950s. In spite of this, Mr. Truman and his staff did not apparently make even as much use of plants as Roosevelt had.[81] They did, however, develop considerably the practice of opening conferences with set statements.[82] A rough measure of the increased importance of these can be gained from the fact that the President opened approximately 47 of the 75 conferences he held during 1946 and 1947 with such a statement, and 37 of the 71 held in 1951 and 1952; or 63 per cent during two of his early years in office, and 52 per cent in the last two years.[83]

These statements, when they dealt with matters of importance, were often carefully prepared by a staff group, in contrast to the presumed Roosevelt practice. John Hersey was given opportunity to describe one such process in 1950, when the subject was the atomic bomb. The idea for this statement originated, he noted, not with the President, but at a meeting of Acheson, Harriman, and members of the President's staff. They were considering how the President could best address the country on this subject, when, "One of the White House staff remarked that a carefully prepared statement, which the President could read at his press conference on Thursday, might help communicate to the public the seriousness of the situation. The others agreed." A Truman staffer and a representative of the State Department then proceeded to the painstaking task of drafting it.[84]

This instance was probably more or less typical.[85] It illustrates both the elaboration of the process of preparing and using such statements, and the Truman approach to the exploitation of the press conference generally. The President and those around him, clearly, were coming more and more to view the encounters as opportunities to address the public directly—a subtle but significant change from the Roosevelt era. Mr. Truman, in his own way, used the conferences to lead opinion, but the style and approach were different. F.D.R. loved to play a lone hand, to be mysterious and indirect, and to do it all in an outwardly casual manner. The Missourian was far more at home working with staff through a formalized procedure.

In general, the Truman period saw the institutionalization and formalization of the press conference. In part because of the work habits of the President, but also because of trends already noted that were external to the White House, both the tone and the format of this means of presidential communication had changed considerably by 1953. The increasing use of statements carefully prepared on a staff basis was one aspect of this change. The formalization of the process whereby the President prepared to meet his associates of the fourth estate was another. Both the once a week schedule and increasing White House burdens dictated this latter change. Also, save when a real cause célèbre was on the agenda (e.g., the firing of MacArthur), the one and two-subject conference was bound to disappear. Conferences inevitably came to cover a widening range of matters in a progressively more superficial and general way.

The preconference briefing process seems to have developed gradually. One Truman biographer claims that it was after the difficulty over the Wallace Madison Square Garden speech in 1946 that the President decided to meet with his staff for a preparatory session.[86] Before that, apparently, the press secretary had handled most of what was done himself. At the start of the conference of August 23, 1945, for example, the stenographer recorded Charlie Ross saying, as he sat at the President's desk just before the reporters came in: "I don't think of anything else. THE PRESIDENT. Well, you watch me, and if I get off on the wrong line— . . . ." When staff sessions were initiated they involved a collective effort, led by the press secretary, to brief the President on all the likely questions that could be anticipated, and give him what help he desired in framing a line of reply.[87] Here could be decided, also, what if any prepared opening statements might be used.

When Roger Tubby became press secretary, toward the end of the Truman tenure, he instituted a further refinement, which he had brought over from his experience in the State Department. There General Marshall, as Secretary, had inaugurated a system of using written briefing material instead of relying wholly on oral preparation. In the White House this meant the compilation of perhaps forty possible questions as much as two days before the conference. These were farmed out for the gathering of answer material where necessary, and then the night before the conference, the President would have available a notebook containing the resulting information to take home and study. A half hour before the conference, various of the top White House staff aides, the press secretary, and at times departmental representatives would gather around the President's desk and go over the tougher problems with him.[88] Here, again, what had been a one-man show was being turned into a carefully managed group effort.

As the correspondent corps increased in size, the traditional oval office conference site became physically inadequate. It had hardly been a comfortable arrangement for the bulk of the reporters in

Roosevelt's day. He may well have retained it partly because of his personal problem of mobility, but also because the discomfort and crowding would keep attendance down somewhat and help retain the intimate flavor. President Truman, however, was sensitive to the crowding, and, as his difficulties with the press grew, sensitive also to the disadvantage involved in not always being able to see or identify his questioners. Nor could the press always hear his answers distinctly.[89]

Perhaps spurred on by a letter from David Lawrence suggesting a change of location and the introduction of microphones, such a shift was made to the so-called Indian Treaty Room of the Executive Office Building nearby.[90] The first conference was held in this new room, in which seats could be provided for about 230 reporters, on April 27, 1950, and then, because of the bad acoustics, microphones were introduced at the May 4 meeting.[91] This apparently simple change of location had highly significant ramifications. It relieved much of the space pressure on attendance; and since the reporters entered first and awaited the President's arrival, instead of the reverse as before, it cut down drastically the preliminary banter between him and the front row regulars, thus foreshadowing a more formalized interpersonal relationship.

In a less subtle sense, the rule instituted with the change, that reporters must now rise to address a question and preface it with their name and affiliation, sharply reduced the possibility of quick spontaneous interchange at the meetings.[92] There could now be few supplementaries and impromptu interjections. The whole tone was shifted in the direction of a rather stiff interpellation, far removed from "family" gatherings, as F.D.R. like to call them.

There was also the indirect impact on transcript preparation and direct quotation. In Roosevelt days, though stenographic notes were taken by a White House aide, these were not even regularly transcribed until 1938, when this became necessary in connection with the publication of the first volumes of the President's public papers.[93] F.D.R. was very sensitive about transcripts. In 1935, in response to a request, he sent the text of some remarks at one conference to Congress but declined their suggestion that he supply them with such texts of all his press meetings, on the ground that it would inhibit the free interchange with the reporters.[94] Under Truman the practice developed and was condoned of reporters bringing stenographers of their own into the conferences.[95] With the shift to the Indian Treaty Room and the use there of microphones, it was only a question of time before the idea of recording the President's voice was thought of. According to a letter written by Press Secretary Short, dated June 16, 1951:

> Recording was begun about the first of this year for the purpose of assisting the White House press in checking their notes of press conferences. . . . About three weeks ago, the President authorized direct quotation of certain remarks at a press conference and, upon request, we authorized broadcast of that portion of the recording.[96]

He then goes on to note that up to that first broadcast, a standard office dictating machine was used. Thereafter more elaborate Signal Corps equipment was introduced which would reproduce better on radio.

In July, 1951, letters were written to the Congressional Democratic leaders offering to supply them with conference transcripts, and these offers were accepted.[97] Note the reversal here of the position Truman's predecessor had taken. There was little advantage left in keeping transcripts under close wraps. An inevitable development was the release of far more of the conferences for direct quote than had ever been permitted before. F.D.R. almost never allowed quotation of more than a phrase. With the recording of the Truman meetings, the release of portions for radio meant the release of whole sentences and paragraphs.[98] Thus was radio increasing its impact on the conferences, which, until the admission of radio representatives in the Roosevelt era, had been the exclusive property of the newspaper press.

Though all of these changes seem, individually, of minor consequence, their cumulative impact was considerable. By the time President Truman left office the highly informal, personalized, almost casual press conference of the past had become an increasingly routinized, institutionalized part of the presidential communications apparatus. Preparation became elaborately formalized, as did the conduct of the meetings themselves in their new setting, with a growing array of electronic aids. Finally, the nature of the meetings as private encounters between the Chief Executive and the newspaper representatives was rapidly changing into a semi-public performance (soon to become completely public) whose transactions were increasingly part of the public record.

☆☆☆☆☆☆☆

Chapter 8

☆☆☆☆☆☆☆

THE MODERN PRESS CONFERENCE: 1953-1964

I

The handing on of the press conference from President Truman to his successor involved less difficulty than had the transition from Roosevelt to Truman, for by this time the conference procedures had become more or less routine.[1] There was, however, a period of uncertainty between the 1952 election and the opening days of the Eisenhower administration. For the first time since the transition from Wilson to Harding, serious doubts were raised about whether the incoming President would hold press conferences on the traditional basis at all. But for the presence of James Hagerty at candidate Eisenhower's side, virtually from the day of his return to the United States to seek the nomination, these rumors might have come true.[2] At least some of the men around the President-elect displayed a considerable lack of appreciation for the role of the press in the conduct of the mid-twentieth-century presidency. One is reported to have said, after surveying the west wing lobby of the White House and press room: "I can't see why you fellows need so much space. . . . The General is going to require more room for his staff. Besides he won't like having visitors questioned just outside his door."[3]

Ike's own past relations with the working press, though of long standing, did not necessarily prepare him for dealing with the reporters as President. He had of course been covered avidly while in Europe during the war and on N.A.T.O. assignment, and, like Hoover before him, had become one of the most widely known and admired Americans of his generation.[4] Most commentators thought they detected a cooling off of the very cordial feelings the General held toward newsmen as a result of his campaign experiences with them. In Europe he had been hedged about by the normal protections accorded the military in such situations. But he is quoted as having summed up his campaign exposure to a far less inhibited correspondent group: "Some of those guys aren't reporters at all. . . . They sound more like district attorneys."[5]

Rumor had it that he was therefore reluctant to continue the traditional White House press encounters, and did so only at the urging of his press secretary. His first conference (not held until February 17, nearly a month after the inauguration) went only part way to reassure the reporters. There was much grumbling in its aftermath, particularly at the fact that "He filibustered for twenty minutes and gave us ten," as one wire service man put it, referring to the long prepared statement at the beginning. Also, the President, whether unwittingly or not, took to himself the prerogative of ending that conference without waiting for the usual "Thank you, Mr. President." These symbolized to the reporters infringements of rights to which they felt entitled.[6] At the second conference, doubtless after some intra-White-House soul-searching, things went quite differently and much more to the liking of the scribes—including the recapture by Merriman Smith of his right to close the meeting.[7]

The President-reporter relationship was probably not as important to Eisenhower as President as to some of his predecessors. The nonpartisan position he enjoyed in the affections of the American people made him largely immune to any public expressions of reporters' animus, as he was to similar expressions from the few politicians who dared utter them.[8] The reporters, fully aware of this, were disinclined to court disfavor by saying harsh things about him,[9] while the proprietors of the media were heavily Republican in sympathy.[10] Thus the working press had little choice but to handle Ike more or less favorably.

Actually, thanks in part to Jim Hagerty, relations with the working press never deteriorated seriously, though Eisenhower kept his distance from them.[11] The press conference itself, by the time he inherited it, offered far less opportunity for the Chief Executive and the correspondents to get to know each other than before the move to the Indian Treaty Room. The new President, following Truman's practice, entered after the newsmen had assembled, launched the meeting immediately, and when the time was up he was on his way out one door while they made a break for the other. Gone was any opportunity for preliminary chitchat or for introductions or personal words at the end.

Roosevelt had held conferences on the average of 6.9 per month; Truman cut that figure to 3.5. Eisenhower held a conference about every two weeks, bringing the monthly average to 2.0.[12] Thus the reporters saw the President at most once a week, usually less often, and sometimes there were long stretches when they did not see him at all. All press conferences were customarily canceled in the late summer when the President was out of Washington on vacation. This occurred for more than two months each in 1953 and 1954. For more than five months, from August 4, 1955, until January 8, 1956, during the heart attack convalescence, there was no conference, and then for nearly two months—June and July, 1956—there was another hiatus covering the ileitis operation. Long gaps were less prominent during the second term.

These long periods, though bridged to some extent by the assiduous activity of Secretary Hagerty,[13] did sharply diminish opportunity for the development of rapport between Mr. Eisenhower and the newsmen. Unquestionably, too, the gaps annoyed the reporters, who tend to feel they have a right to quiz Presidents in person at frequent intervals. This pique was particularly evident during vacations when the President remained incommunicado save through his press secretary. Both Roosevelt and Truman ac-

President Eisenhower confers with James Hagerty, his press secretary, during a press conference, as a reporter rises to ask a question. *Wide World Photos.*

cepted the responsibility of seeing the press even when on vacation.[14] Yet the post-heart-attack press conference, held at Key West on January 8, 1956, was the first Ike ever scheduled outside of Washington.[15]

Probably neither the reporters' dissatisfaction nor the reduced conference schedule did Ike serious damage. His press conferences, supplemented by television and other appearances, effectively projected the kind of impression that people already had, which they approved and admired. Some observers even insisted that his frequent lack of information about an issue could actually redound to his benefit. Admissions of ignorance,

> coming from the Chief Executive, . . . are astonishing, clearly unprofessional replies. And yet, in that they make further questioning useless, and sustain the image of the President as a man of sincerity and good will, they have been marvelously effective.[16]

Formalization of the press conferences had caused the steady decline of opportunity for sharp supplementary questions, and initial queries often had to be long enough to brief the President on the subject raised. Further, as more of the conference appeared verbatim on the public record, and the range of questions widened, the President was bound to become more general and noncontroversial in his answers. Ike, of course, had almost a compulsion to avoid controversy of any kind.

How much did Mr. Eisenhower use his press meetings for legislative and opinion leadership? Clearly, he placed less emphasis generally on legislative innovation than had his two predecessors. Since he held far fewer conferences, it was feasible to canvass all the transcripts during a sample year for expressions of opinion on pending legislative projects. The year chosen was the twelve months starting with November 1, 1956, embracing the Congressional session from January to August 1957.

Ike held only one press conference before Congress convened (November 14), and did not see the fourth estate again until January 23, well after his State of the Union and Budget Messages had been delivered. Obviously there was no effort to use the weeks before the first of the year for advance preparation of opinion, save for a very general discussion of "modern Republicanism" at the November 14 conference. Nor was opportunity desired, apparently, for discussion with the press of the Annual Message, either before or after its submission. From January on, however, at all but two of the twenty-one conferences held before the end of the session, the President was led by a reporter's question to make at least one statement of legislative endorsement, or to discuss his attitude toward some bill or amendment.

During January and early February he spoke twice on behalf of his Middle East Doctrine resolution.[17] Two matters which came in for frequent discussion later were foreign aid and the civil rights bill. The President strongly endorsed the former at his press meetings of March 7 and 27 and April 3. Then, after a hiatus until the end of July, he reverted to the subject on July 31 and on August 7. On August 14 he called a special impromptu press conference to announce the signing of the foreign aid authorization legislation, and to plead for the appropriation of the full amount of funds authorized—implying a threat of a special session of Congress if this were not done. On August 21, the last press conference before adjournment, he spoke out again strongly for general foreign aid appropriations. Civil rights legislation came up for discussion in no less than a dozen of the twenty-two conferences, sometimes more than once. On two occasions the President deplored budget cuts affecting the U.S. Information Agency, in strong terms, and he spoke out twice in support of his aid to education proposals. He advocated some half dozen other pieces of legislation at least once.

This pattern hardly represents the aloofness from legislative leadership often associated with Mr. Eisenhower. At his conference of November 14, 1956, he uttered one of his more famous disclaimers of intent to browbeat Congress: "I am not one of the desk-pounding type that likes to stick out his jaw and look like he is bossing the show."[18] Yet by and large he displayed greater willingness to discuss and endorse pending bills than either Truman or Roosevelt. However, discussing proposals with reporters is not necessarily effective intervention in the legislative process, as Coolidge's experience suggested. Ike's intervention with regard to the civil rights bill was a case in point. Some of his comments were a good deal less than helpful. His endorsements were often lukewarm, and he made it clear that he really preferred progress through education rather than legislation. At times he disclaimed either knowledge or legal competence when particular parts of the bill were the subject of a question.

A couple of exchanges on federal school aid legislation occurred at the press conference of July 31, 1957, just after the administration bill was killed in the House. When the first question had been asked and answered with another endorsement of the now defunct bill, May Craig offered the pointed and perhaps significant comment: "The friends of the school bill say that you failed to use your influence, and if you had, you could have got the bill you wanted. . . ."[19]

On some occasions he achieved considerable success in using the press conference to advance administration measures. Foreign aid in 1957, and at other times during his term, is one example. The 1958 session saw a determined push, reasonably successful in the end, to secure a reorganization of the national defense setup. This subject came up at seven different press conferences during that year. On April 2, when the opening question of the conference raised the matter again, Mr. Eisenhower drew a laugh by beginning his answer: "How long am I allowed for this talk?" and then going on for nearly two pages in the transcript.[20]

It is probably safe to say that the issue closest to the President's heart during all of his tenure in office, and particularly in the latter years, was "fiscal responsibility." By this he meant a balanced budget, keeping spending within prudent limits, and thereby minimizing the threat of inflation. At several press conference discussions of "modern Republicanism" this theme, or parts of it, emerged. He really began to bear down at his first press meeting following the Republican defeat at the polls in 1958.[21] From then on, at every opportunity, Ike hammered home his theme. Cabell Phillips, writing in the *New York Times Magazine* on August 16, 1959, asserts that "By actual count, he referred to it [fiscal responsibility] twenty-two times in his press conferences up to the end of July."[22] This represents something approaching a saturation campaign, and a highly deliberate, premeditated one, if the President's own words on November 5 are to be credited: "For the next two years, the Lord sparing me, I am going to fight this as hard as I know how."[23]

The Eisenhower record of using press conferences to lead opinion is, in summary, a curious mixture of vigorous advocacy on some topics with an essentially passive approach on others. In general, he waited for questions to come to him and did no more than Truman to guide the meetings in predetermined paths. He tried to answer all questions, even if the answer turned out to be a lengthy and grammatically complex evasion. This self-imposed rule no doubt caused some of his difficulties in dealing with legislative issues. On civil rights, for example, a "no comment" reply, such as Roosevelt and even Truman sometimes used, might have been less embarrassing than admissions of ignorance and doubt.

Yet Eisenhower's fondness for the long, general, perhaps vague, but apparently helpful answer may have been one of the strengths of his conference technique. Sometimes when the reporters asked the President to give them the benefit of his thinking on something, the lengthy replies were informative in a manner recalling F.D.R. Probably the more sophisticated news corps of the 1950s was not "educated" as often in this manner as their counterparts in the 1930s. However, with the release of press conference transcripts and, by 1955, full television coverage, the public, rather than reporters, was the actual audience the President faced in the Indian Treaty Room.[24]

Explanations of the current state of the disarmament debate, or the need for continued foreign aid, may not have added much to the reporters' knowledge, but couched in the rather simple—if structurally complex—language of Mr. Eisenhower, their impact on the populace at large was doubtless quite different. The Eisenhower technique met, if unintentionally, the needs of the new era. In Roosevelt's day and in Truman's, conference exchanges had often been sharp and uninhibited, at times slangy, flippant, or a bit profane. Roosevelt realized this, as he indicated in his letter declining to send transcripts to Congress. "I no longer would feel like speaking extemporaneously and informally, as is my habit, and it would bring me a consciousness of restraint. . . ."[25] Truman was less conscious, however, of this problem, even though the conferences under his auspices were losing much of their private quality.

In addition, before the admission of the public, the participants shared a common body of knowledge about current happenings which could largely be taken for granted; but many of the questions and answers would have been unintelligible to a wider audience. The fact that the reporters had to provide factual background for Eisenhower's benefit meant that the TV viewers were briefed at the same time. And if the reporters were not always impressed or enlightened by the President's ponderous earnestness, such answers were far more likely to impress the citizens than a brief snappy comeback. Seriousness and apparent sincerity are political virtues in the eyes of the electorate, just as the appearance of cynicism or flippancy is anathema. And Ike could no more help exuding sincerity than Truman could help taking the stance that came most naturally to him.[26]

The evidence suggests that President Eisenhower used the planted question rather more than the previous administration, but placed somewhat less reliance on the prepared opening statement.

James Hagerty, in an interview, emphasized that the initiative in questioning lay with the press, yet the President often had matters he urgently wanted an opportunity to discuss. He said, half jokingly, he had even thought of putting up the kind of board used in churches to display hymn numbers, and spelling out the most urgent topics in the view of the White House.[27] At the end of the conference of June 18, 1958, the stenographer caught the President saying, just after "Thank you, Mr. President," "No one gives me an opportunity to talk about defense."[28] And again in 1959 (May 13): "THE PRESIDENT. Mr. Horner, I can't thank you too much for asking that question. [laughter] I have gone back to my last two or three conferences and I said, 'These people have been conspiring to keep me from insisting that this country is hurting itself by too much spending.' "[29]

The question plant, used from time to time to remedy these situations, is well illustrated by the following, at the meeting of April 29, 1959: "Mr. Hagerty indicated yesterday that you might have some comments that you would like to make about the labor bill which was passed by the Senate and is now going to the House. Would you care to, at this time?"[30] Hagerty made a distinction to the author between the practice he had followed and the out-and-out plant, in which a particular reporter is asked to propound a particular question. He said his practice, rather, was to say something to the effect that: "I think if you ask the President about this, you'll get a decent answer."[31] Presumably this was often done, as it had been by Steve Early, either at the press secretary's own conferences or in the presence of a group of the White House regulars. Also, on occasion, the wire service people, the network representatives, and the regulars would be called in the morning of a press conference at which a prepared statement was to be read by the President. This would give the organizations thus briefed a chance to get appropriate background information ready, and presumably, at times, prepare in advance further questions on the subject to pose to the President.[32]

Prepared statements were used as they had been by Truman, but rather less often.[33] During his whole administration, Ike read one or more to just over 50 per cent of all his press meetings. There was a marked falling off in frequency as the administration progressed, especially during the second term. In 1957 statements were read at only about one-fifth of the twenty-five held during the calendar year.

On the whole, the process of institutionalization and formalization of the conference operation went ahead steadily between 1953 and 1961. Most trends initiated during the Truman years were picked up and carried forward, with hardly any interruption or change of direction. The preparation of the President for the conferences was handled on a very similar though somewhat more elaborate basis, under Hagerty's direction. The press secretary began as soon as one conference was over to get ready for the next. He compiled possible question subjects, using his own detailed knowledge of the current news, and particularly his own twice-a-day meetings with the reporters. (He also had transcripts made of his press conferences to which he could refer.)[34]

Armed with his question list and such information as he had felt it necessary to solicit from departments and agencies, Hagerty met for breakfast at 7:00 or 7:30 A.M. on press conference morning with senior White House staff people, read the questions aloud, and collected further material for possible replies. At times Cabinet officers or their public relations representatives would attend also. Then half an hour or so before Mr. Eisenhower was due to leave for the conference room, Hagerty would lead the top staff people into the President's office for the final "rehearsal." The process must have bordered on briefing at times because of the scant attention the President paid to the daily papers, compared with his predecessors.[35] Hagerty himself claims that with this system—which had been in use with Ike since well before the election in 1952—they could and did bat 900 in spotting the questions that would come up.

Even before 1952, the evolution of the conference format had made it difficult, if not impossible, for the President to go off record or provide semiconfidential background information. Yet this is an important aspect of President-reporter communication. To fill the resulting gap, there gradually developed the now familiar "background dinner" and other sessions held for select groups of reporters and columnists by high government officials, and at times by members of the White House staff.[36]

Some of this kind of thing was done on a less formal basis by men around Roosevelt, but it was not until during World War II that the practice really developed, initially at the hands of General Marshall and Admiral King. They "instituted it by confiding to select journalists some of the most delicate secrets of a nation at war."[37] The practice grew rapidly following Truman's accession. He continued to do some backgrounding himself, but only at the special off-record press conferences discussed above, and at budget seminars. Beyond these, he had few informal contacts with newsmen at which he could explain his policies and motives as Roosevelt had done. Nor do his staff people seem to have talked with newsmen very often for background purposes.[38] Department heads, however, did. Acheson, it is said, held upwards of 1,000 such sessions.[39]

Under Eisenhower, background meetings and dinners continued to flourish at the departmental level. The President himself, however, was even more cut off from direct contact with the press than Truman had been. He no longer held the special press conferences with editorial groups, and the budget seminars were conducted after 1952 under the auspices of Secretary of the Treasury Humphrey.[40] About his only opportunity for informal discussion of his plans and problems with the working press came at rare social gatherings in Denver or at Augusta. White House staffers did not talk very much with the press off the record, and so did not fill much of the increasing vacuum.[41]

Hagerty, who did do a good deal of backgrounding himself, nevertheless appears to have been concerned about the opportunities thus being lost for the President to sell his policies to the reporters.[42] In the summer of 1959 Ike inaugurated, at his suggestion, what turned out to be a series of four background dinners at the White House for groups of about a dozen top press representatives each. But the furore and jealousy these caused forced the abandonment of the experiment. They failed for the very reason that the press meetings themselves could no longer be used for backgrounding. The whole process of presidential press relations, as well as the substantive news generated by the White House, had itself become public property—a new American spectator sport. Roosevelt's Sunday night suppers could be kept discreetly veiled. Ike's little dinners were trumpeted from the housetops.

Thus by the end of the Eisenhower administration, backgrounding as a process was no longer conducted by the President to any significant extent, but had been delegated to his subordinates. This development paralleled the general institutionalization of the process of presidential communication. The magnitude of the problems that faced the President was so great by the end of the war that he could no longer handle this job himself. But the complete cutting off of the President from informal private discussion with select reporters was a serious loss to the White House.

The formalization of the press conferences and the process whereby they increasingly became public property went hand in hand. No sooner had the Eisenhower people settled into the White House than Hagerty made a concession on the matter of conference transcripts. The newsmen had been supplying themselves with unofficial records through a stenographer they brought to the meetings. The new press secretary agreed to allow them to hire a professional stenotyping firm to come in and do the job, thereby making possible an accurate transcript within two or three hours of the end of the session.[43] This, in turn, encouraged the *New York Times* and a few other papers to print the proceedings in full, with the questions directly quoted and the replies in indirect discourse, to get around the no direct quote rule still in effect. (A few of the last Truman conferences had been similarly published.)

Nonquotation was not destined to survive very long.[44] As early as December, 1953, Secretary Hagerty allowed the broadcast of a press conference over the radio using the tape recording.[45] This was a long step beyond the Truman practice of releasing a few sentences. The newspaper press reacted with misgivings to this, while radio and TV people applauded. Hagerty's only reason for delaying video coverage was the problem of film and lighting. He firmly believed all media should have the right to use their chosen means of news dissemination (and doubtless felt the President could not help but benefit). Until the fall of 1954 it would not have been possible to film conferences for later broadcast on TV without a large array of very bright, hot lights. At that point, however, fast film was developed that could be used without such special arrangements, whereupon he and the President gave the go-ahead.[46]

The first conference filmed for television took place on January 19, 1955. All reason for requiring indirect discourse for presidential replies had by then evaporated. As a matter of fact, the White House had authorized direct quotation throughout the conference on November 3, 1954, a couple of months before the television premiere. The one step which Hagerty did not see his way clear to taking was direct live televising, which he felt was too dangerous.[47] The screening of film versions, however, ran into the reluctance of the television industry, once the first enthusiasm had subsided, to devote the time required for broadcasting the entire film. As a result, the practice was widely adopted of showing only brief exchanges in the course of regular news roundups.[48] Thus virtually the last barrier, but not quite the last, between the public and the live conference had been breached, and these presidential meetings had become almost, but not quite, the equivalent of TV "fireside chats" with the reporters playing the somewhat reluctant part of stage props.

II

The transition following the election of 1960 brought a reappraisal of presidential press relations. In the short space of fifteen years the press conference had been transformed beyond recognition. President Eisenhower had little apparent interest in these developments, but the new President who took over in January, 1961, was of a far different breed. One must go back to the two Roosevelts to find a Chief Executive with John F. Kennedy's consuming interest in the press and skill at public relations.

Despite advice in a Brookings Institution study[49] and from other sources, there was an early decision that, as regards the press conferences, the march of events should not (perhaps could not) be

The first presidential press conference at which full picture coverage was permitted, January 19, 1955. Photographic equipment is set up at back of room as reporters await the arrival of President Eisenhower. *Wide World Photos.*

stopped or deflected.[50] The new administration accepted the conference institution as it was handed on to them, and took the logical next steps in its evolution. A new locale was found at the auditorium of the New State Department building, as attendance had outgrown the Indian Treaty Room.[51] Jim Hagerty had stopped just short of live televising, and it was natural that Mr. Kennedy, who had benefited so conspicuously from his TV debate performances, should take that next and culminating step.[52] (The new conference room had been designed for the installation of television cameras.) The only significant turning back of the clock was a decision to abandon the rule requiring reporters to give name and affiliation before posing their questions.[53] It was hoped, no doubt, to capture a bit of the former informality, and the new President already had a wide acquaintance among the press.

Preconference White House preparation was developed under

Kennedy even beyond the elaborate Hagerty system. When asked to describe his practice, Pierre Salinger, Hagerty's counterpart in the new White House group, began by noting his establishment of what he called an information council.[54] This had a somewhat fluid membership drawn from the public relations officials of the various departments and agencies. It met the day before each presidential press conference under his chairmanship, and compiled the familiar list of possible questions. Some members of the group might come prepared with position papers on particularly hot subjects. In the State Department, for instance, the public relations staff had its own elaborate system for doing State's share of the preparatory task. Starting the Monday before a Wednesday conference, fifteen or twenty potential questions were drawn up and farmed out to Department desks for suggested answer material. This came to Department Press Officer Lincoln White by noon Tuesday, and was ready to be taken by the Assistant Secretary for Public Affairs to Salinger's meeting later that day.[55]

On the day of the conference, either at breakfast or at lunch, depending on whether it was scheduled for morning or afternoon, the Secretary of State, the Vice President, staff people including Salinger, Sorensen, Feldman, Bundy, Heller, and perhaps others would gather with the President to go over the accumulated material. These sessions lasted around an hour and a half, and might be followed by a quick call for another memo on some subject. Finally, in an anteroom just off the stage of the auditorium, the Secretary of State awaited the arrival of the President for a quick last-minute word on developments up to the minute.[56] Though this procedure varied in detail from week to week, with the inclusion of different people as problems changed, it obviously represented the ultimate in the institutionalization of the morning bedside chats Steve Early had had with his boss.

The conferences themselves also became productions, far closer to a Hollywood epic than to the informal family gatherings of a scant two decades before. The new administration's first, on January 25, saw the use of two TV cameras on the platform, on either side of the President, two more out in the auditorium, two "shotgun" microphones to pick up questions, a pulpit-like lectern for

President Kennedy making the first live telecast of a presidential press conference, January 25, 1961. This photo was made from a TV screen in New York as the President faced a battery of newsmen in Washington. *Wide World Photos.*

President Kennedy approaches the rostrum before the telecast press conference of January 25, 1961. Pierre Salinger, press secretary, is at left; reporters stand at right. *Wide World Photos.*

Kennedy press conference on the situation in Laos, in State Department auditorium, March 25, 1961. Lincoln White, State Department press chief, stands near the maps; Pierre Salinger, White House press secretary, is seated at right. *Wide World Photos.*

the Chief Executive, an attendance of 418 reporters—said to be 107 more than Ike ever had—and an estimated television audience of some twenty-four million.[57] The reporters grew to feel that they were extras in the recurring drama.[58] As Merriman Smith pointed out, relatively few took notes during the conference.[59] So efficient had the transcript system become that the first five or six pages were ready for use by the time "Thank you, Mr. President" was uttered,[60] and stories could be written from the conference by newsmen who had not even bothered to attend. The point had almost been reached, in short, at which the only real excuse for holding the conferences was the vast unseen audience.[61]

The fact that the President took his place before the assemblage on an elevated stage separated physically from the press in the pit robbed the meetings of even the traces of informality which had survived up to 1961. The introduction of live televising and accompanying innovations were greeted by the newspaper reporters with injured outcries. F.D.R.'s conferences were again recalled with the nostalgia which distance lends.[62]

But most of the changes had been virtually forced upon the White House by the march of events. The constant increase in the size of the correspondent corps might have been ignored and the meetings kept in the oval office, but this would have provoked a rising chorus of favoritism charges as space limitations excluded more and more reporters. Actually the newly relocated conferences with their average attendance of some 350 were not as unwieldy as was feared.[63] The extra space in the larger quarters plus the reduced pressure to take notes encouraged a seating pattern that divided the assemblage roughly into three groups. The reporters who seriously intended to ask questions were either regulars with "assigned" seats in the first row or found space in one of the first three rows. Other reporters who came largely to observe took seats in the next four or five rows, and behind them sat the nonjournalistic visitors. The progressively relaxed rules for admitting the latter underscore the increasingly public quality of the whole affair.[64]

Experienced reporters noticed that the President rarely called on anyone back of the first three rows,[65] and my observation of the conference of April 3, 1963, confirmed this. Twenty-four newsmen were recognized, and only two were seated farther back. (One of these apparently had arrived too late to get down front and Mr. Kennedy noted this and called on him by name.) Thus what took place was a kind of "inner conference" comprising the approximately seventy in these first rows, less than a quarter of the 327 people present in the room that day. The existence of this inner conference group meant that the mass quality of the affairs under Kennedy was more apparent than real. The actual participants represented a relatively limited and manageable group.

The advent of new media and their representatives had added to the pressure of numbers, but also meant other kinds of pressure on the conference format. Movie newsreels, radio, and television each in turn had demanded the right to use its particular tools. Refusal would not only have earned hostility for the White House occupant, but would have cut him off from important channels of access to the public.[66]

Was it true, then, as the authors of the Brookings study insisted, that the press conference could be viewed as the President's to do with as he saw fit?[67] The answer seems to be: in theory, yes; in practice, probably not. The new Chief Executive saw that the regular meetings with the Fourth Estate had an important role in his press relations, though a far different role from that they had filled for Franklin Roosevelt. Kennedy accepted the news conference frankly for what it was by 1961: a channel of direct communication with the public that in recent years had moved closer and closer in function to the fireside chat.[68]

Richard Rovere makes the essential point about the Kennedy conference format:

> The White House knows . . . the structural flaws of the press conference. It insists, nevertheless, that the President will make as much use of TV as he can. He feels he must attempt direct communication with the people because, in the first place, he wishes to awaken and arouse them, and because, in the second place, he fears that a predominantly Republican press will not deal objectively with him and his views.[69]

The President decided to make a virtue of necessity. The conferences, having become public spectacles, could no longer be used for semiconfidential briefing of the press. So be it. Use them to reach the public, over the heads of the proprietors of the printed media.[70] The corollary to this decision was the development of surprisingly successful alternative ways of reaching the reporters themselves with background information.

The Kennedy conference schedule and pattern of use followed closely the Eisenhower precedents, though with some significant variations. During his period in office he held sixty-three, or an average of 1.85 per month. Ike's average was a shade higher—almost exactly 2.0. Under present conditions, with the enormous burdens a contemporary President must carry and the elaborate preparation system thus made necessary, a once-a-week schedule may well be the maximum frequency realistically possible, and twice a month defensible.

The matter of live conference telecasting was apparently a subject of considerable concern to the White House. On February 1, 1961, after the first two Kennedy meetings had been given live coverage, Salinger announced that the next two would be taped, to avoid overexposure from too frequent live broadcasts. This concern apparently dictated an irregular pattern of interspersing live with taped screenings until early 1962. Starting on March 21, however, all conferences were opened to live coverage. This was done after a discussion with the networks at which the prerogative of deciding on live coverage was shifted to them from the White House.[71] One can only speculate as to the reasons for this change in strategy. Perhaps, as the number of stations using the broadcast decreased, the White House decided that live coverage had to be allowed most of the time to sustain the networks' interest in carrying the conferences at all.

President Kennedy used his press meetings for legislative leadership with few inhibitions. One brief example suggests his vigorous technique. One of his major policy innovations centered on the Trade Expansion Act of 1962, designed to broaden the government's authority in negotiating trade agreements and to facilitate links with the European Common Market. Trade policy, from the days of the tariff, has always been highly sensitive. Thus the President faced a difficult battle in Congress. What use did he make of the press conference device to win his point?

At two conferences with the reporters before Congress met, he was asked about the rumored trade liberalization plan.[72] Mr. Kennedy took these opportunities to do much the kind of thing F.D.R. used to do "for background" at similar stages of policy development. Toward the end of his reply on November 8 he noted, "we are considering the matter and we will come to the Congress in January and make our recommendations."

The proposal was first broached in the State of the Union Message, January 11, 1962, was mentioned again in the Economic Report on January 22, and formed the basis of a special message sent up three days later. Twenty-five presidential press meetings were held in the period between the State of the Union Message and the final passage of the trade bill. At no less than ten of these the Chief Executive found opportunity to plug the program. Three times Mr. Kennedy introduced the subject himself with an opening statement in which he urged passage. At the last of these conferences he said: "I want to emphasize once again how deeply I am convinced that the passage this year of the trade expansion bill, on which one House will vote tomorrow, is vital to the future of this country."

Here and in other instances President Kennedy took full advantage of the press conference in dealing with Congress. He seized opportunities to lay the groundwork for this bill in advance of its introduction, and he prodded the legislators repeatedly while it was under consideration, not infrequently contriving the opportunity to do so. Among recent Presidents his technique compared most closely with Roosevelt's, though adapted to a vastly different conference format.

The use made of opening statements during the Kennedy administration is significant. Truman and Eisenhower opened about half of their sessions with some kind of announcement. Only a few times did President Kennedy fail to make either a statement or a series of brief announcements.[73] Not infrequently the statements were of great importance. Notable was the lengthy discussion of American policy in Laos on March 23, 1961, and the angry denunciation of the steel price increase on April 11, 1962. Obviously the President realized that the press conference is a superb means for addressing the nation as a whole with maximum impact. The process of statement drafting was painstaking and elaborate, centering often on Theodore Sorensen.[74]

Mr. Kennedy also resorted to question plants. As *Time* put it in November of the administration's first year, Salinger on occasion tipped off reporters "to raise questions that the President wants to answer. Last week, for example, Salinger suggested to ABC's William H. Lawrence that a certain question might get an interesting response. . . . Kennedy had a ready answer to that one—neatly organized on paper."[75] The famous episode which found the President promising to appoint Robert Weaver as the first Secretary of Urban Affairs (if such a department were created), and the first Negro in the Cabinet, apparently had a plant as its point of departure. In this instance the prearranged question was part of the chess game the President was playing with Congress on this issue.

Alan L. Otten, writing in the *Wall Street Journal*, suggests the kind of situation which can tempt a President or press secretary to use planted questions: "At a recent press conference . . . he wanted to reaffirm his opposition to the seating of Red China in the United Nations. The question was never asked, and the answer had to be issued rather lamely as a White House statement the next day."[76] Otten adds that though it is true a point can be covered in an opening statement, even this, or a plant, is a weak substitute "for a forceful reply to the spontaneous question." Secretary Salinger said that during the first year and a quarter Kennedy was in office he planted questions only three or four times.[77] But apparently, according to Otten, Cabinet members sometimes called reporters with tips on policy developments outside their own departments.

Ted Lewis noted, two or three weeks after the Kennedy administration had taken over, that "a President must at times wonder how he can use the press conference to discuss in depth a problem on which he wants the nation to know exactly how he stands and concerning which he needs the support of the people."[78] As a matter of fact, it became increasingly evident that Mr. Kennedy had given up wondering about the press conferences in these terms and had turned to other means. He reverted to the practice of Franklin Roosevelt, and other predecessors, of talking informally and confidentially to reporters, and did so on an unprecedentedly massive scale.[79]

The basis for this *ad hominem* approach to the working press had been well and firmly laid in his days as a member of Congress and during the 1960 campaign. As Theodore White has written, Kennedy had "an enormous respect for those who work with words and those who write clean prose. He likes newspapermen and likes their company. Kennedy would, even in the course of the campaign, read the press dispatches, and if he particularly liked a passage, would tell the reporter or columnist that he had."[80] White concludes that this friendliness and cultivation of the working press "colored all the reporting that came from the Kennedy campaign."[81] If anything, J.F.K. may have been too concerned with the attitude of the press, too sensitive to what individual news writers had to say about him and his policies.[82]

Utilizing this fund of rapport and wide acquaintance among the men who cover Washington and the White House, Kennedy developed a network of private contacts which provided him with opportunities to do an enormous amount of "backgrounding" on his goals and policies. He saw columnists as well as reporters, both friendly and hostile. Even such right-wing pundits as George Sokolsky took to actually praising Kennedy after private sessions with him. Also, on quiet Saturday afternoons, the President sometimes walked into the press room in the White House for an impromptu chat.

Then there were the large-scale, carefully planned, not-for-attribution background sessions at Palm Beach in late December, 1961, and also a year later.[83] The President would have encountered all the risks of wounded pride and jealousy, to say nothing of the problem of sheer numbers, if he had tried to hold any formalized backgrounders in Washington; but the same hazards diminished sharply out of the capital. Only a relatively small group of regulars followed the Chief Executive on vacation.[84] Taking advantage of this fact, and also well aware that the new year would call forth the usual spate of "think pieces" and summaries of the first twelve months in office, the President arranged for a three-and-a-half-hour backgrounder at Palm Beach, where he had gone for the holidays. Half was to be devoted to domestic and half to foreign policy, and those present were asked to agree to divide what they got into two stories, and to use "friends of the President" or some other euphemism as source. In this context he could cover a great deal of ground, could give depth and breadth to the discussion, and in general open his mind in a way never possible at a regular press conference. On December 31, 1962, he held a similar briefing in Florida. This one caused considerable embarrassment because a British correspondent violated the ground rules.[85]

Another device pioneered and used to apparent good effect in the Kennedy administration was a series of off-record luncheons for groups of editors, usually drawn from one state.[86] By April, 1962, 186 had been thus entertained, and the intention was to continue the practice until all fifty states had been covered.[87] In a larger sense, this sort of gathering was a "backgrounder" even though it might not result in any immediate output of news or interpretive columns. (Recall the off-record press conferences Harry Truman held for editorial and similar groups.)

In the realm of semiconfidential communication with the press, Pierre Salinger pointed out that though Mr. Kennedy could not do so in his regular conferences, he, Salinger, went off the record almost every day in his own twice-a-day press meetings. He also emphasized the extent to which top members of the White House staff talked to reporters—this went on almost constantly with people like McGeorge Bundy and Ted Sorensen.[88] In general, Kennedy staffers were a good deal more accessible than those under either Truman or Eisenhower.[89] Formal backgrounding sessions comparable to the budget seminars of an earlier day were still held, though in a more decentralized manner. For example, shortly before a message of major policy import was sent to Congress, the press secretary would call in appropriate experts from the government for the benefit of interested reporters. Regarding the general White House air of informality and helpfulness under Kennedy, one observer wrote: "Reporters roam through the back corridors, enjoying the freedom Eliza Doolittle dreamed of in Buckingham Palace."[90]

What can be said, by way of summary, about the general pattern of press relations under the thirty-fifth President? In effect Kennedy solved the problem of presidential communication with the press, and through the press with the public, by freeing himself at last from the consequences of the self-denying ordinance accepted by Woodrow Wilson. Franklin Roosevelt had dealt successfully with the press both collegially and individually, provoking only occasional flare-ups of jealousy. Kennedy, however, carried individualized and private contacts farther, and indulged in them more freely, than any President since Theodore Roosevelt

—and did so without serious complaint or resistance from reporters.

He was able to indulge this bent for "the private, the informal and the intimate" partly because he had developed the necessary skill and rapport with correspondents before entering the White House. Fletcher Knebel estimated that he saw more than fifty newsmen privately during his first year, and the main reason there had been so little grumbling about it was that "for the first time in memory a President is accessible to almost any reporter who will spend enough time and effort with the staff members to get to him."[91] Since in the long run Kennedy did not play favorites with these interviews, resistance to the practice was minimized. Also, the correspondent corps, as it has become larger and more specialized, has perhaps lost some of its close-knit *esprit de corps* and accompanying sensitivity to "unfair" advantages.

As the press conference has become progressively institutionalized and formalized, the nature of its usefulness to the White House occupant (and to the press) has changed drastically. It has been less and less useful as a channel for dealing with the reporters and correspondingly more important as a forum for addressing the public. In short, the conference has been stripped of its original function, and the President has had to choose between accepting increasing isolation from the reporters or devising new lines of communication with them. Mr. Eisenhower in effect chose the former, Mr. Kennedy the latter. He virtually brought the whole presidential press relations enterprise full circle, back to the days of T.R. The Republican Roosevelt might be astonished by the present size and complexity of the White House press relations operation, but would have felt quite at home with Kennedy's conduct of it.

III

Unlike John Kennedy, Lyndon Johnson is a man of impulse and intuition, and it would be foolhardy to predict the course of his press relations on the basis of his first half year. Like Truman, he was elevated to the presidency suddenly and unexpectedly. His first impulse, naturally enough, was to revert to the practice he had followed as majority leader: highly informal meetings with small groups of reporters. Pierre Salinger seems also to have advised him that President Kennedy had been considering such a tactic to supplement the mass televised conferences.[92]

During his first two months in office, this impromptu conference format held sway. The first, on December 7, and some later ones, were held in the President's office, suggesting the Roosevelt practice of two decades earlier.[93] Others were held at the LBJ ranch, once with a bale of hay for a lectern. Advance notice was not given, and indeed once or twice it seemed that even the President had not expected to turn a casual encounter into a question and answer session. Pressure from at least two directions soon built up for a revival of the more traditional conference. Spur-of-the-moment sessions have many advantages over the more familiar mass encounters—for those fortunate enough to be on hand. Reporters not regularly assigned to the White House, however, began to complain, as did the television networks, whose medium was also excluded.[94]

On February 1, with about two hours' notice, the President called his first conference in something like the Kennedy style. TV filming for delayed broadcast was allowed. The locale was not the State Department auditorium but the somewhat cramped quarters of the White House movie projection room (capacity: about 100). Contemporary comment emphasized Mr. Johnson's reluctance to face the cameras and the massed press, and invite direct comparison with his predecessor's adroit conference style. He quickly gained in self-assurance at subsequent televised encounters and in later ones appeared to enjoy himself thoroughly.

Until the last day of February there were no further press conferences—as if to allow time for stock-taking. Then there followed two more, announced in advance, on the 29th and on Saturday a week later, the first at the State Department but in the international conference room rather than the auditorium, and the second in the White House East Room. Both were televised live. Though still experimenting with locale, the President had at last adopted most of the Kennedy precedents. Finally, on April 16 he held another pre-announced conference, this time in the same auditorium that had become familiar to viewers after 1960. On May 6 there occurred what Tom Wicker of the *Times* called "one of the most colorful news conferences ever held by a President."[95] The setting was the south lawn of the White House and the guests included not merely the reporters but their wives, children, parents, and grandparents. Refreshment tents stood nearby.

The President by no means gave up his snap conferences with small groups after returning to the Kennedy format. In fact, in the three weeks between the last two formal conferences mentioned, he saw the press on no less than five other occasions—in his office, in the White House garden, or for a "walking press conference" around the grounds. So varied did the press meetings become during the first six months of Johnson's presidency that they defy classification or even accurate enumeration. The impromptu session held at the World's Fair in New York on May 9, 1964, was listed by the *Times* as the eighteenth. Yet actually twenty-three instances can be identified up to then in which the Chief Executive invited or allowed questions from a reportorial group.

Some tentative conclusions illustrate both Johnson's uniquely experimental approach and the limits within which any President must still work. For example, no future White House incumbent, as Johnson seems to have concluded, can avoid conferences on something like the Kennedy model. The demands of a complex array of media must be met.

On the other hand, the Johnson experience suggests that there is still much room for variation. Since the mass conference has of necessity become primarily a channel for addressing the public, the most fruitful area for experiment is the re-creation of useful lines of communication with the working press. Kennedy revived the dialogue with the reporters through the numerous private interviews he granted. Johnson not only continued this practice with gusto, but used his impromptu conferences to the same end. He has held them more often than not on Saturdays, when fewer than the normal number of newsmen would be in the White House. Such relaxed encounters invite a freer exchange, make possible follow-up questions on a given subject, and facilitate briefing in depth by the President. At the one on April 25, for instance, Mr.

Johnson opened with an extensive preview of his forthcoming message on poverty in Appalachia. In fact he has made even greater use of opening statements, at both informal and formal conferences, than his predecessor.

In order to put the Johnson style as thus far developed in broad context, it is useful to recall the three major patterns of presidential press relations that have succeeded one another in this century. Under T. R. the keynote was informality and intimacy of contact on a selective basis. Wilson and F.D.R. typified the coupling of a new equal access rule with a continued semiprivate dialogue between President and reporters. The central element since 1952 has been the mass, televised, fully public performance with reporters playing a marginal role. Johnson's remarkable feat has been a blending of many of the advantages of all three of these styles. Whether he will be able to sustain this virtuoso performance remains to be seen. Whether his successors will follow his example or revert to simpler and less demanding styles is even more problematical. At the very least, however, his uniquely uninhibited approach to presidential press relations has broadened the range of available possibilities, and perhaps raised new expectations for the future.

IV

Any effort to appraise the current presidential press conference or to forecast its future encounters many difficulties. Every new administration, and every significant change, calls forth conflicting evaluations and predictions, usually pessimistic. Prescriptions for remedying the assumed maladies are legion. Evaluation is highly subjective, and much of the critical commentary comes from by no means wholly disinterested journalistic sources.

In certain limited areas, however, the elusive data can be reduced to measurable terms. The press and the President, in the last analysis, are interested in the conference in terms, respectively, of the amount of news it produces and the breadth of circulation it gives to White House utterances. How have sharp differences of personality, and evolution toward formal institutional status, affected the amount of news Presidents have made through the conference device?

In order to supply a tentative answer, one year was selected for each President who left a complete transcript file available for analysis: Coolidge, Franklin Roosevelt, Truman, Eisenhower, and Kennedy. For Coolidge the year chosen was 1925, for Roosevelt 1935, Truman 1949, Eisenhower 1957, and Kennedy 1962. Since the most meaningful year in the presidential annual cycle is not the calendar year but twelve months beginning well before the convening of Congress, it was decided to take the period from November 1 through October 31, in each case.

The front page of the *New York Times* was analyzed for the day following the date of each press conference during these twelve-month periods. All news articles which derived in whole or in significant part from the conference were measured in column inches and the results tabulated. Space occupied by multicolumn headlines was recorded, and also, in a few instances, front-page pictures bearing an integral relationship to the conference news involved. Presumably *Times* decisions on newsworthiness would offer at least a rough measure of the amount of important news the President had produced at his conferences during the year selected. The findings obtained are presented in Table 2.

Despite the sharp decline in the annual number of conferences during the last three administrations, the amount of news generated held up surprisingly well. It is natural that Coolidge's total would be the smallest. It is surprising that he was able to make as much news as he did in an era of relative governmental inactivity. Though Roosevelt is clearly the champion, Truman, holding less than half as many conferences, still produced more than two-thirds as much news. When Ike further reduced their frequency, the resulting coverage hardly diminished at all. The Kennedy total is the most impressive of any. With less than a third of F.D.R.'s press encounters, he nearly equaled the latter's output. Apparently the frequency with which conferences are held—and varying formats—have made relatively little difference in news generation. Other variables, of course, can hardly be weighed with exactitude. The steadily broadening range of presidential responsibility has doubt-

TABLE 2

FRONT PAGE PRESS CONFERENCE NEWS IN THE *New York Times*

	C.C. (1925)	F.D.R. (1935)	H.S.T. (1949)	D.D.E. (1957)	J.F.K. (1962)
1. Number of press conferences tabulated	94	92	44	26	26
2. Total number of news articles from conferences	84	104	84	92	126
3. Number of articles with multicolumn headline	4	21	7	3	6
4. Total column inches on page 1 from conferences	1,032½	1,563½	1,156½	1,132	1,386
5. Number of press conferences with no page 1 story	31	24	1	0	0
6. Average number of articles per press conference	.91	1.13	1.91	3.54	4.9
7. Average column inches per press conference.	11.0	17.0	26.2	43.5	53.3
8. Average column inches per article	12.1	15.0	13.8	12.3	11.0

less counteracted in some measure the decline in conference frequency. The reporters have fired fewer questions per subject but covered far more subjects; and in recent years the *Times* has tended to print separate articles for each major policy problem raised.

In Coolidge's and Roosevelt's day, the practice was to group the relatively small number of subjects covered in one—or at most two—articles. After 1945, and especially after 1952, separate articles, subject by subject, became the rule. President Kennedy was led by questions to touch on just about every major current topic, and as a result, even news stories datelined outside of Washington often included the President's comment or reaction.

There is some limited basis in the data for arguing the superiority of certain combinations of personal style, frequency, and format. Both the Roosevelt column inch total and the fact that a fifth of the stories his conferences produced were thought to rate a multicolumn head suggest that his approach was particularly effective.

This reflected in part the greater likelihood, given semiweekly conferences, that big news stories would break at a press encounter with the President making the announcement himself. When the reporters are seen only once a week or every two weeks, this possibility goes down sharply.

Kennedy, with no more conferences than Eisenhower, nevertheless garnered far more stories and column inches, and double the number of multicolumn headlines. General public relations skill must hold part of the answer. Specifically, a President who does his homework as carefully as Kennedy did, and who therefore gets the reputation of being briefed on just about all current subjects, will likely make news in a correspondingly wide range of areas. President Eisenhower had the opposite reputation and therefore either was not asked questions, or, if queried, often disclaimed knowledge.

The combination of infrequent conferences, which cause a backlog of questions to pile up, and the well-rehearsed Kennedy-style performance doubtless produced a serious problem for the conscientious editor. If all the resulting stories were put on the front page, there would be little room for anything else. The average Eisenhower conference occupied more than a quarter of the 160 page one column inches in the *Times*. Kennedy produced news that filled nearly one-third of the same space. Unless such a newspaper is willing virtually to abandon its first page to the use of the President on such days, increasing selectivity must be employed.[96] From the Chief Executive's point of view, the press conference with its present format and biweekly schedule is fast encountering a journalistic law of diminishing returns.

The one clear overall conclusion is the continuing importance of the press conference as a channel of communication from President to public. Changes in format, personality, and private character have seemed to make little fundamental difference. What the President says has always been news, and increasingly so as the public appetite for dramatic copy has increased, and as competition among a number of channels disseminating news has grown. In gross terms, therefore, all that Presidents have needed is some kind of forum, sufficiently formalized to maximize attention and regular enough to create a pattern of expectations, yet flexible and informal enough to supplement the relative rigidity of set speeches and messages to Congress. The press conference, in almost all of its various forms and permutations since its inception, has met these broad criteria fairly well.

☆☆☆☆☆☆☆

Chapter 9

☆☆☆☆☆☆☆

THE WHITE HOUSE STAFF AND PUBLIC RELATIONS

The most striking evidence of the institutionalization of the presidential establishment has been the growth of the White House staff. Official figures credit the "Office of the President" with 45 to 50 employees from 1932 through 1937.[1] About the time of the creation of the Executive Office of the President in 1939 by Franklin Roosevelt, terminology changed and "White House Office" became the heading under which the actual presidential staff was listed. Until 1947 that figure did not exceed 61, but it jumped to 293 the next year.

Until that date, many of the staff aides who worked in the White House were actually, for bookkeeping purposes, employees borrowed from other executive agencies, whose salaries were not charged against the White House at all.[2] This practice, untidy as it may seem, dated to the time of Jackson at least.[3] When Harry Truman took over, even the man who was to be the assistant press secretary during his tenure, Eben Ayers, was still on the rolls of the Office of Inter-American Affairs, whence he had been borrowed in the latter Roosevelt years. To Mr. Truman's mind, this arrangement was somehow not honest and he changed it. From then on, White House personnel became such in law as well as in fact; hence the sharp jump in the total, which for the first time can be taken as reflecting the true state of affairs.

This initial Truman total was actually above the average for the remaining years of his tenure, and in 1952 the figure stood at 245. During Eisenhower's two terms the number began a sharp climb, as one might have expected in the light of the General's dependence upon staff. In 1957, at the start of his second four years, there were 387 in the White House office, and in 1960, 446, or nearly twice the final Truman total. Much was said during the 1960 campaign about the weaknesses of an overstaffed presidency. Seemingly suiting his actions to his words, Mr. Kennedy, as of the end of January, 1961, had only 395 in his immediate entourage. A little more than a year later, however, in March, 1962, the total in the White House office had risen to a new high, 452, but by November 1963 it was only 365.[4]

Obviously the way staff is used is at least as important, and probably more important, than sheer numbers. The figures do demonstrate, however, that the contemporary presidency is a large and growing institution and can no more be imagined functioning without these several hundred people—or most of them—than the President himself can be imagined bereft of the White House. Only within limits are the personal tastes and work habits of succeeding Chief Executives likely to alter the broad outlines of this staff situation. The formalization of the communications aspect of the presidential role, as exemplified in the press conference, has proceeded in lock step with this trend toward the institutionalization of the whole White House enterprise. The question is: to what extent and in what ways has the President come to rely upon staff assistance in the discharge of his crucial duty to teach and persuade?

The President's secretary of course had as one of his multiple roles that of "press secretary," long before this function was differentiated and placed in separate hands under Hoover. And though the role of the speech writer *per se* will be dealt with in the following chapter, the ghost writer concerned with presidential greetings and messages, as well as with presidential oratory, became a White House staff fixture in the early 1920s. In short, Presidents for some decades had been staffing themselves in modest ways to enhance their effectiveness in reaching the public. The New Deal, however, clearly represents a new beginning in this area, as in so many others.

There is not and never has been a White House public relations staff as such. The press secretary and his immediate assistants are the only ones who devote most of their time to these concerns. On the other hand, since the bulk of the President's activity is hortatory or communicational in nature, there are few members of the White House establishment who are not in some degree involved with public relations. Divisions of labor have characteristically been fluid, in part because the various roles of the President flow into one another in a manner that would defy strict compartmentalization. Thus any substantial increase in White House personnel can be taken, in the broad sense, as tantamount to an increase in the President's public relations assistance.

Several major considerations are involved in assessing the role played by recent press secretaries. First, it has obviously changed with the changing background, inclinations, and publicity skills of incumbent Presidents. The press secretary exists to act as his boss's alter ego. The extent to which the White House occupant needs or prefers to rely on his aid, or wishes to act on his own, hence becomes of prime importance. Secondly, shifts in the format and scheduling of the presidential press conference also have an important bearing. Frequent, semiprivate, informal conferences with the Fourth Estate mean that the Chief Executive can become, to that extent, his own press secretary. Biweekly, highly formalized meetings of the sort held during the 1950s can hardly serve the same purpose. Finally, there is the question of the personality and skills of the press secretary himself.[5]

The subtle cooperative relationship between Franklin Roosevelt and Steve Early, born as it was of a long prior association, will rarely if ever be duplicated.[6] The two were in contact off and on from the day Early, as a cub reporter, covered the swearing in of the young Franklin Roosevelt as Assistant Secretary of the Navy in 1913. In a sense, F.D.R. did not need a press secretary. His publicity sense and sense of timing were superb, and his instinctive ability to weigh the news value of a story was the object of repeated comment.

Only under special circumstances do bits of the interplay of advice and discussion between a President and his press secretary survive. For instance, bound in with the press conference transcripts there is a memorandum, apparently never released, on the flight of capital from the United States, dated November 22, 1933. It was dictated at Warm Springs by the President, in case such a statement should be needed. Following the text, the stenographer recorded: "MR. EARLY Unless you have a reason for letting that out *sub rosa*, I would never give it out, not even as background."[7] Many of the subtleties of the interaction between the two men come out here, as well as a glimpse of the intimacy of the relationship. Note the almost blunt offer of advice,[8] and the history of cooperation in the use of the leak and the confidential information categories implied in Steve's comment.

Correspondence between Early and McIntyre during presidential sojourns outside of Washington sometimes illustrates staff functions. During trips and vacations the problem of keeping an uninterrupted flow of White House news on the wires—and thus sustaining the impression of constant presidential activity—became more difficult. One telegram from Early to McIntyre, dated June 1, 1937, reads: "Unless the President has something in mind concerning which I have no knowledge comma I see no reason why there should be a press conference stop Will have message to Congress on National Planning which will make good story without conference stop."[9] Another is undated, but probably was sent in 1937 or 1938, from McIntyre to Early: "Will you check with Agriculture if we can release forest conservation statement up here. Need story badly."[10] Presumably this kind of preoccupation with the pattern of news flow was typical of Roosevelt's press secretary.[11]

Steve Early seems to have held the balance with remarkable skill between serving his boss's best interest and defending before him the rights of the press. James Rowe, who was on the White House staff under F.D.R., insisted that it was Early who really developed the press secretaryship, and that his conduct of it has not been equaled since. He did not become a press agent but remained ambassador from F.D.R. to the press, and from the press to the President. At times he would "put the heat" on Roosevelt to release a story the reporters wanted. (Nor was he, according to Rowe, at all inhibited in tendering advice. When the President decided to shift the date of Thanksgiving, Steve went in three different times to try to dissuade him because of the potential public reaction, and when that came, said, "I told you so.")[12] Early was serving both the press and his boss in the following telegram from assistant secretary Bill Hassett to McIntyre (November 10, 1938): "Steve felt very strongly that in view of Cabinet meeting and full schedule of other business on holiday failure to hold press conference would be construed by correspondents as sidestep."[13]

An example of Steve at his best in this dual role is found in a memorandum to Louis Howe, dated November 2, 1934. A proposal transmitted from the Executive Council by Donald Richberg had urged that the government publish some kind of regular bulletin of official information, thus bypassing the press and transmitting material directly to the public. (Recall Wilson's similar notion. It is quite possible that F.D.R. viewed this idea with favor, initially, for the same reasons.) Howe sent the report on to Early for comment, which was not long in coming. "To date I have been but a mild zephyr, moving gently and creating only a slight and occasional disturbance. If the Government is to publish officially 'The Federal Register,' my barometer would drop immediately to new lows, registering in the cyclone or hurricane areas. In brief, I shall oppose the project with every ounce of energy and power I have. . . ." He went on to predict inevitable and violent opposition from the press. Howe sent this in to the boss the same day, prompting an immediate F.D.R. chit to Richberg: "I do not want any federal paper established."[14] Early's famous temper had already become legendary. This ability to blow off steam no doubt enabled him to survive twelve years of what is perhaps the toughest job in the government, next to the presidency itself.

Stephen Early, Roosevelt's press secretary, briefing reporters on Truman-Attlee talks, December 7, 1950. Early temporarily served President Truman after the death of Charles Ross. *Acme Photo, courtesy Harry S. Truman Library.*

In sum, Steve appears to have been a nearly ideal complement, as press secretary, to a President adept at conducting his own press relations. It was a cooperative relationship in which the press secretary was an extension of the President's personality and both shared in planning and controlling the flow of news from the White House. Early also shared with the President the task of dealing with the media representatives. He was not, as his later counterparts tended to become, *the* spokesman for the President,[15] or the main point of contact with the working press. The press conference schedule meant that the President saw the reporters frequently himself, could deal with them as individuals, and often act as his own spokesman. F.D.R. remained his own publicity strategist, however much he was open to suggestions.[16]

When Harry Truman took over, he called upon his old friend

and fellow graduate of Independence High School, Charles G. Ross, to become his press secretary.[17] The new President could hardly match his predecessor's innate ability at public relations,[18] which meant greater initiative and responsibility for the press secretary and staff. The decision to hold but one press conference a week produced some of the same effect, and so did the continued steady increase in the burdens of the presidency.

Eisenhower, after 1952, and Roosevelt were exceedingly fortunate both in their choice of press secretaries and in the fact that these men stayed in office during virtually all of their administrations. The same good fortune was not vouchsafed to Truman. Two of his press appointees died in office, so that three different men held the position: Ross to December, 1950; Joseph Short from then until September, 1952; and Roger Tubby for the remaining months. None of these men—though appraisals of them differ—measured up in the eyes of observers to the standard set by Steve Early, or Jim Hagerty. Ross who served by far the longest period, though product of a career in journalism as teacher, author of a textbook, and reporter, had been on the editorial side for some time before called to the White House. This lack of recent contact with day-to-day reporters' problems probably helped reduce his usefulness in his exacting new role.[19]

Robert Allen and William Shannon, generally hostile critics of the Truman administration, offer the opinion that as press secretary, "Ross has been a distinct disappointment." They continue: "A press secretary's job is twofold in its nature. He must prep the President so that he will handle himself effectively during his weekly press conference, and he must also dispense important news in such a way as to give it maximum 'play'." Part of Ross's trouble, they felt, in doing this dual job, was that the two men were *too* close, and that Ross was too fond of Truman "to be an imaginative and helpful assistant." They recall the June, 1947, speech by General Marshall at Harvard outlining the Marshall Plan. Truman, on the same day, gave out a great deal of hot news at his press conference. "Thus, without Ross's lifting a finger to prevent this blunder, Truman inadvertently 'scooped' his own Secretary of State right off the front pages."[20]

President Truman with his press secretary, Charles Ross.
Acme Photo, courtesy Harry S. Truman Library.

On the other hand, the close relationship between the President and his friend and aide was interpreted by others quite differently. When Ross died, Margaret Truman wrote that "Charlie was a tower of strength and trust for Dad."[21] Perhaps one of the most balanced appraisals was offered by a former Truman staffer, who felt that if Ross had lived, the President's prestige would not have fallen as low after 1950 as it did, less because of Charlie Ross's skill as an image builder than because the close relationship meant that the President was particularly receptive to his advice. At the same time, the point was made that Ross was not a good organizer. He could not be persuaded to make adequate advance plans for news coverage of the Potsdam conference. This in turn caused no end of trouble for the press staff that remained in the White House. They had the thankless task of fending off the irate reporters.[22]

The Truman press secretaries continued to hold daily press conferences, as Early had, for the White House regulars and any other accredited reporters who wanted to attend.[23] They developed an increasingly elaborate briefing system, already discussed, for the President's own weekly press meetings, and participated in the daily staff sessions over which Mr. Truman presided.[24] The latter, which replaced, in a sense, the morning bedside chats in the Roosevelt era, suggest again the process of institutionalization that went forward between 1945 and 1952. John Hersey was allowed, in 1950, to attend one of these staff meetings. The following excerpts from his account show the working relationship between Mr. Truman and his press aide:

> [When first turned to by the President, Ross tried to lighten the burden of his Chief with a humorous bit he had found in a Washington paper.]
>
> Now Ross got down to work. "Is there anything that can be said about the appointment of an Ambassador to Spain?" he asked. "Smitty [Merriman Smith, the White House correspondent of the United Press] was questioning me about it yesterday, and I promised to check up."
>
> "We're going to appoint Stanton Griffis on January 15th," the President said, "but we don't want to announce it just now."

"Then there is no information on that subject?" Ross said.
"Not a word," the President said.

Ross picked up a document and began, "I have this memorandum—"

"Yes," the President said, interrupting; he had looked at the papers in Ross's hand and had evidently seen what they were—a list of legislative recommendations for the lame-duck session of the Eighty-first Congress, which had just convened. "I'd like to put that out. . . ."

The President swung around to his right, toward Charles S. Murphy, his Special Counsel, who was sitting on the chair beside the sofa.

"Murph," Truman said, "can you see any reason why we shouldn't put that out?". . .

[Murphy raised questions about a couple of items on the list.]

"I can get together with Murphy," Ross suggested, "and go over it with him."

The President said, "You do that—but let out everything you can on that list."

Ross shuffled his papers again. "We have a long draft of a proposed statement on the naming of a Point Four Committee—"

"It's terrible!" the President said. "I read it last night and I wanted to tell you to redraft it. You can cut out every other paragraph without losing anything."

George McK. Elsey, one of the President's Administrative Assistants, . . . said, "Mr. President, I ran across that draft, saw it was unsuitable for you, and briefed it into a more concise statement for you to work on."

He handed up two typewritten pages.

"That's much better," the President said after glancing at Elsey's draft. "I'll go over this. All we need to say about Point Four is that I've been for it, I'm still for it, and I'm going to stay for it."

"That's all I have," Ross said.[25]

This rare and valuable glimpse at the inner workings of the Truman White House, if typical, suggests several things about the relation of staff to public relations activity. Merriman Smith's question to Ross may illustrate the impact of the diminished frequency of press conferences. On November 28, when this staff conference took place, there had been none since the 16th. Presumably, in the Roosevelt years, with conferences twice a week, such a question might have been asked of the President himself. Note the involvement of both Murphy and Elsey (a kind of Jack-of-all-trades in the White House, according to Hersey) in an essentially public relations matter. Though Harry Truman hardly ran the kind of one-man show for which F.D.R. was noted, nevertheless, after appropriate consultation, it was clearly he who called the shots.

A series of factors conspired to give James Hagerty wholly unprecedented prominence as Eisenhower's press secretary.[26] Ike is often credited with having a keen publicity sense, and with having condoned if not conspired in his own self-advertisement during the decade preceding his election in 1952.[27] It seems abundantly clear, however, that he had little real taste for or detailed knowledge about the ways and means of cultivating the mass media. In this regard he compares more closely with Herbert Hoover than with any other President in this century. Unlike Hoover, however, he was supplied, very early in the game, with a press secretary of outstanding technical qualifications.[28] He is supposed to have said, just after the heart attack, "Tell Jim to take over,"[29] a phrase which the record suggests had been uttered in effect, if not in fact, much earlier.

Hagerty, in short, worked for a man who was only too glad to leave both the grubby details of public relations and, apparently, much of the high strategy to a subordinate. Furthermore, on three occasions, Jim represented the sole link between the presidential sick room and the anxious public.[30] As such he held the center of news interest to the unheard of extent of having *his* press conferences reproduced verbatim in the *New York Times*. Finally, Eisenhower held news conferences on the average of only twice a month, and at times not at all for many weeks. This, coupled with the President's own disinclination to see reporters except in the conferences, left Hagerty the sole link with the curious world, in times of health as well as sickness. It is probably significant that he saw the reporters twice a day, rather than once, as before 1952.[31]

The conclusion of many observers was that Eisenhower's press secretary came far closer to being a kind of press agent for his boss than had any such White House aide in the past.[32] Stan Opotowsky insisted in a series written for the *New York Post*: "Hagerty is press agent, pure and simple, and his job is to make his client look good at all times. So he cheerfully admits to the techniques which his detractors fervently damn."[33] It has been argued that he carefully channeled favorable announcements from the executive branch—e.g., the successful launch of a rocket—through the White House, but not the unfavorable.[34] He allegedly kept the reporters so busy with "Hagerty-made news" that they did not have time to dig out embarrassing things.[35] Then there was the technique of taking a brief case of items off on Eisenhower vacation trips, to be doled out, thereby giving the appearance of continuing activity.[36] Opotowsky claims that this need to manufacture the raw material for stories prompted Hagerty to say to his wife at the end of an exhausting day: "I had to scrape the news off the walls today."[37]

Rather than debate the fairness of this kind of indictment, it is more useful to note that in fact Hagerty did little more than streamline practices which had been used by Steve Early before him, and which were too seldom used on behalf of Harry Truman. In an era of massive use of professional public relations by all sectors of the community, it is utopian to ask Presidents, whose only weapon is often their platform for addressing the public, to deny themselves the means of doing so with maximum impact. The problem, if one existed, in the Eisenhower-Hagerty partnership lay not so much in the hyperactivity of the latter as in the near abdication by the former which made it necessary.

There is an amusing and at the same time significant side to the way in which Hagerty's unprecedented prominence as *the* spokesman for the President affected White House news. With increasing frequency the press secretary began substituting "we" for "he" (i.e. the President) in his announcements. For example, three showed up in a Hagerty discussion of the budget in December, 1957: "We still want to do a lot more talking and studying on things we believe necessary and things we believe can be reduced or cut."[38] The use here of the plural did, in fact, refer rather more to the administration as a whole than to the President as an individual. Not so another case. The reporters had gotten wind of the fact that someone—the President, they assumed—had had a nosebleed during a flight to Chicago. Actually it was Senator Dirksen, who was in the presidential party. Replying to the inevitable question, Jim said: "'Oh, you thought it was us, huh? No, it was Senator Dirksen.'"[39]

However comical, slips of this kind do indicate the extent to which Hagerty had become in fact the major and often sole channel of communication between the President and the press (and public). They also underscore the further institutionalization of the press secretary's role. The fiction could hardly have been maintained much longer that the President's was the sole authoritative voice. Robert A. Rutland checked the files of the *Department of State Bulletin*, which carries important foreign policy pronouncements, and found that Roosevelt's press secretary was never quoted in the years between 1933 and 1945. A Truman press secretary was quoted only once. But Hagerty was quoted frequently, both before and after the President's heart attack.[40] In a sense, then, the mythical "White House spokesman" of the Coolidge era had at last been clothed with flesh and respectability.

President Kennedy campaigned and entered office with a hopeful vision of himself as another Roosevelt, and the conduct of the communications side of the office resembled the New Deal era more than either intervening administration. Pierre Salinger, his youthful press aide during the campaign and thereafter, told the author (a point also noted by others), that the President was really a master of public relations in his own right, and therefore quite capable from a technical standpoint of acting as his own press secretary.[41]

Thus Salinger's role was a very different one from that of his predecessor, and his prominence as spokesman for the Chief Executive correspondingly less.[42] The President had the inclination and contrived the opportunities for dealing personally with the reporters to an extent far beyond either Truman or Eisenhower. In these informal contacts he could and did personally brief the newsmen on the background of his policies.

Salinger, however, was a man of great ability.[43] Having been replaced by his Chief in some of the traditional functions, he broadened the scope of his responsibilities in other directions. The author of "The Kennedy 'Image'—How It's Built" which appeared in *U. S. News and World Report* doubtless had Salinger particularly in mind when he wrote: "Mr. Kennedy and all of those around him work intensively to create the 'image' that the White House wants to build. Madison Avenue advertising experts could take a lesson from the White House."[44]

This image building effort was truly awe-inspiring, and the press secretary's role was a central one. For example, during 1961 he traveled from coast to coast and made no less than twenty-nine speeches. Then there were the briefing sessions held for Congressional staff people. Individuals were invited from the offices of the Representatives and Senators, on a bipartisan basis, to hear talks by Cabinet officers and others, who discussed current policy problems. The obvious assumption behind this scheme was that these staff aides were highly important and influential cogs in the legislative machinery and therefore to be cultivated, to say nothing of the fact that they might be expected to carry the message with them on their visits back home.

One of Salinger's most imaginative ideas was a special briefing for the press secretaries of the fifty state governors. These officials were invited to Washington in February, 1962, again on a bipartisan basis. The thirty-five who came were guests at an evening reception at Blair House. The Vice President attended and greeted them (in place of the President, who was in Florida). The next morning they breakfasted in the White House staff dining room, toured the mansion, and then went by bus to the State Department, where sessions had been arranged with General Lyman Lemnitzer (Chairman of the Joint Chiefs of Staff), Ed Murrow (head of the U.S. Information Agency), Under Secretary of State George Ball, and the Assistant Secretary of Defense in charge of civil defense. They also had a session of shop talk on the role and problems of the press secretary, and a luncheon at which Vice President Johnson again was the speaker.[45] In short, an amazingly comprehensive strategy was employed for exposing key people from all over the country to the President, to administration officials, and to the major elements of the Kennedy program—a strategy that, as *U. S. News* suggests, pretty obviously paid off in the high popularity ratings Kennedy earned in the polls.

Another area into which Secretary Salinger moved with vigor was that of coordinating the activities of the various executive agencies in the interest of an integrated administration-wide public relations policy. Here he was not breaking new ground so much as improving on the practice of his predecessors. Even T. R.'s Secretary Loeb did a bit of this on a very informal basis. Thus before noting the Kennedy administration practices, a look at earlier precedents is in order.

Pendleton Herring wrote of the New Deal in 1935: "Never before had the Federal Government undertaken on so vast a scale and with such deliberate intent, the task of building a favorable public opinion toward its policies."[46] No effort will be made here even to sketch the growth of federal press relations staff generally.[47] The sole question of immediate concern is the role of the White House, and particularly the presidential press secretary, in inspiring and coordinating this effort.

Most commentators agree with Delbert Clark that "President Roosevelt assigned his secretary, Stephen T. Early, to organize press services in the various departments and important non-Cabinet agencies. . . ."[48] (The major disagreements came on whether this was a *bona fide* information dispensing program or an insidious propaganda plot.)[49] Apparently Roosevelt and his staff came to the conclusion that the public utterances of the President himself could and should be supplemented with a broader educational effort. This meant the coordination of the more important speechmaking of top administration officials, the proper staffing and coordination of the public relations offices that had already begun to appear in the departments and agencies, and the development in conjunction with the departments of other means for bringing the New Deal message to the public. There was also a series of experiments with information-coordinating offices and agencies, culminating in the Office of War Information.

Secretary Ickes, for example, gives various glimpses of the use made of Cabinet members. The entry for February 16, 1937 (during the Court fight) reads in part: "He [the President] outlined several things that he would like to have me say when I speak before the joint session of the Texas Legislature on Friday."[50] In the same entry there is mention of another speaking engagement F.D.R. wanted him to fill, and talk on the same subject. Ickes also noted that Press Secretary Early usually read and approved his speeches. Regarding a prospective radio debate with Frank Gannett on the subject of press freedom, the Secretary wrote: "I find that the President and Steve Early are both enthusiastic over the prospect of his joint discussion and so I have accepted."[51]

Early also filled the role of personnel officer for executive branch publicity offices. According to Raymond Brandt, the President, through Steve, "replaced the party hacks in press agent's jobs with trained newspapermen who enjoyed the confidence of their former colleagues."[52] Some critical observers maintained at the time that the administration thus virtually stripped the correspondent corps of its best talent.[53] The resulting system, Brandt goes on to note, meant that: "While there was propaganda galore, access was given to the real news in the executive agencies."[54] In other words, besides providing a vastly important supplementary apparatus for publicizing the administration and its aims, this refurbishing of the government press offices also earned reporters' gratitude by making their work easier.

Correspondence at Hyde Park between Colonel Edwin A. Halsey, Secretary of the Senate, and Steve Early revealed the apparently prevalent White House practice of using—as Congressmen long have for their own benefit—the circulation of *Congressional Record* reprints for propaganda purposes. Note the following letter from Early to Halsey, dated May 19, 1938:[55]

> Dear Eddie:
>
> You did such noble work last year with the summaries which we furnished you concerning activities and accomplishments of various government agencies that I am having similar material prepared this year. Here is the first installment—TVA accomplishments. I will leave it to you to handle this in the way in which you are so adept.
>
> Other installments will follow and I should have all of the

> material in your hands within a week. I shall send duplicates to Charlie Michelson for his guidance. Assuring you of our very great appreciation of your cooperation, I am
>
> Very sincerely yours, . . .

Other correspondence reveals clearly the modus operandi. Halsey would see to it that these blurbs were entered in the *Congressional Record* by a friendly member of Congress. They could then be reproduced very cheaply for mass circulation. (Early notes in a letter to Secretary of Agriculture Wallace, urging him to take advantage of the scheme, that reprints could be secured from the Government Printing Office "at a cost of $62.26 and $40.11 respectively per 10,000 copies.")[56] Distribution was apparently accomplished by the Departments—as Early said to Wallace, "through your usual sources"—or they were sent out franked by friendly Senators and Representatives. Postcards with brief messages and reprints of presidential fireside chats and statements were also prepared for distribution by members of Congress. The letter to Wallace drew a reply which described former distribution of material "not only through our regular channels, but also through the National Emergency Council and the Democratic Congressional Campaign Committee." The writer went on: "In response to your suggestions, however, we are now rechecking our distribution with a view to exploring fully the possibilities of more widespread dissemination of information as you suggested." Secretary Early had also written in the same vein to the Civilian Conservation Corps, Farm Credit Administration, Federal Alcohol Administration, Federal Deposit Insurance Corporation, Federal Housing Administration, Federal Power Commission, Federal Trade Commission, the Secretaries of the Interior and Labor, Maritime Commission, National Labor Relations Board, Federal Emergency Administration of Public Works (PWA), and at least eight others.

The Roosevelt administration was the first since Wilson's to experiment with agencies to institutionalize coordination of information functions. One of the first steps taken in this general area was the establishment of the Division of Press Intelligence as part of the N.R.A. in August, 1933, to provide the national government with a comprehensive clipping service.[57] This was Louis Howe's idea, apparently, and the resulting news and editorial summaries were called "Louis Howe's Daily Bugle."[58] A month before, the President had set up the Executive Council to coordinate the New Deal attack on the depression. Then in November, 1933, the National Emergency Council was formed as a more compact group to do essentially the same thing—though the Executive Council continued to exist more or less separately until it was merged with N.E.C. in October 1934.[59]

The National Emergency Council marked the real beginning of formalized efforts to coordinate administration public relations. In March, 1934, the United States Information Service was created as one of its divisions "to function as a central clearing house for information on all phases of governmental activity."[60] (Out of its program grew the publication of the *U.S. Government Manual.*)[61] And in July, 1935, the Division of Press Intelligence was transferred to the jurisdiction of the N.E.C. This latter agency, after an early flurry of activity, was finally abolished as of July 1, 1939, with the transfer of its functions and those of the U. S. Information Service to the Office of Government Reports in the newly created Executive Office of the President.[62]

With the advent of World War II President Roosevelt was faced with the same sort of problem which had prompted Wilson to set up the Creel Committee: the conflict between military censorship and the enormous appetite of the media for news and information. The solution found, after a period of growing confusion and pressure upon the President to act, was the establishment of the Office of War Information in June, 1942, under the capable direction of veteran newsman Elmer Davis.[63] Into it were put the O.G.R., the Office of Facts and Figures (which had been set up the previous October to furnish the public with information on the defense effort), and other information activities that had grown up under the aegis of the Office of Emergency Management and the Coordinator of Information.[64]

The emphasis in O.W.I.'s work was quite different from its predecessor's of twenty-five years earlier. Both Wilson and Roosevelt had faced long periods of national division and indecision over

American involvement in war. In 1941, however, Pearl Harbor (plus the shock produced earlier by the fall of France) brought swift and solid unity behind the national effort. Thus the kind of domestic propaganda campaign mounted by Creel was far less necessary, even if politically feasible—which it probably was not by the 1940s. O.W.I. therefore became "in the main an organizer and coordinator, rather than a primary source, of war news."[65] Elmer Davis noted emphatically that the job of his agency was to give the people the news about the war (the good with the bad), and the background necessary for its interpretation. His staff were not going to act as press agents for the government, he insisted.[66]

The emphasis throughout was therefore on coordination, rather than on the preparation of original material. The Creel Committee had been virtually *the* central government news room. By World War II the public relations offices of the agencies concerned were far more elaborate and well established. Hence they continued to function, with the O.W.I. attempting to insure cooperation and provide a degree of central direction. O.W.I. did issue a few pamphlets, but so hypersensitive was Congress to any suggestion of propaganda on behalf of unpalatable causes that in 1943 O.W.I. was forbidden to issue any more. In effect Davis was told that all material must be filtered through the press and other media. With radio available, however, F.D.R., unlike Wilson, already had a channel of direct access when he needed it. Fund cuts were made for the domestic branch in 1944 lest the agency be used to influence the election.

In sum, there obviously was little of the emphasis on the presidency as such which had characterized the outpourings of the Committee on Public Information. Only once, apparently, did O.W.I. issue biographical material on F.D.R., and then only for foreign distribution. Yet this one incident was cited as justification for the 1944 fund cuts.[67]

The Truman experience with the coordination of administration-wide publicity was not very successful. There is little in the record upon which to base either a description of the practices followed between 1945 and 1952 or a judgment of their effectiveness. Jack Redding of the National Committee Staff has alluded once or twice to problems of coordination between the Committee and the White

House.[68] Interviews with former Press Secretary Tubby[69] and Eben Ayers suggested that little was done beyond what Steve Early had pioneered, and in fact it seems that even the Roosevelt era practices were not followed up. Contacts with the agency press people remained informal and *ad hoc*. Another interviewee noted that at the start of the Korean War, a suggestion was made for the setting up of an O.W.I. modeled on World War II experience, but only informal attempts at information coordination were undertaken.[70]

An outstanding example of lack of intra-administration coordination under Truman was the speech on foreign affairs by Secretary of Commerce Henry Wallace in late 1946, which led to his resignation. According to accounts, the Secretary showed the speech to the President himself in the course of an interview, but it was not seen by any of the White House staff before delivery.[71] The wide discrepancies between what Wallace said and the policy of the President and Secretary of State created a furore, not only because Wallace was a member of the administration, but because Mr. Truman unfortunately had said in a press conference that he had read and approved the speech. (Or at least what he said was so interpreted.) Jonathan Daniels noted that the aftermath of this serious contretemps led to a revision of all White House speech clearance procedures.[72] Eben Ayers confirmed that during the early part of the Truman administration people did get to the President with matters which should have been cleared in the press secretary's office—things the latter therefore did not know about until afterward.[73] This general problem was solved in time.

Allen and Shannon cite a more routine example of apparent lack of coordination. It involved the release by the State Department or the White House, on the same day, of: a presidential message to Congress on E.C.A., the text of Secretary of State Marshall's report on a London Conference of Foreign Ministers, the text of the administration's European Recovery Plan bill, and a 227-page memo explaining aid policy. "As a result, only a few major papers carried the text of the Truman and Marshall messages, and the other two important documents, each representing months of expert work, were elbowed out of the papers altogether." They suggest that "A simple phone call from Ross to Michael McDermott, press chief of the State Department, could have prevented this senseless jamming-up."[74] The next day the White House had no news to give out, and the State Department only one insignificant item. These may be isolated instances but there is little evidence that the administration sensed the importance of this sort of coordination or acted consistently to bring it about.

The record of the Eisenhower administration is quite different, and, as might be expected, the key was James Hagerty. When questioned about White House practices following 1952, he noted that he had brought from the Dewey administration in Albany the Public Information Council idea.[75] He had developed this, starting in 1946, with the then deputy state Commissioner of Commerce. According to one student: "The council was composed of the departmental public relations officers. Its principal job was to serve both as a clearing house for the state's public relations problems and as a forum for the exchange of ideas."[76] As Hagerty said of his parallel effort in Washington, the object was to get the public relations men to stay out of each other's way and make sure that they would not "throw out" everything on one day. If the White House had some important release planned, the coordinating machinery could be used to prevent departments from handing one out simultaneously. Also, conflict between Cabinet press conferences and presidential ones on the same day could be minimized. The White House, said Hagerty, wanted to know about it if a department had some big announcement coming out; on the other hand he preferred at times to release something through a department rather than directly.

Publicity coordination under Eisenhower is well summarized by the following from *Time*:

> . . . as no man before him, Hagerty has placed the news systems of all the departments of Federal Government under his sure thumb: he holds regular conferences with departmental press officers, scans departmental news bulletins before they are released—and plays a key part in advising Cabinet members who have got themselves out on limbs and need rescue.[77]

Even officials as exalted as Cabinet secretaries, if general report is to be taken at face value, Hagerty handled in a surprisingly blunt and direct manner. The same *Time* article has him calling Secretary of Agriculture Benson regarding a highly controversial opinion of the Secretary's which had appeared in print, and telling him: "Ezra, you pulled a boner and the thing to do is admit it." Sometimes in White House meetings the press secretary "silenced Cabinet members with a shake of his head." "His nod gives affirmation to important pronouncements by administration officials. . . ."[78] Even the redoubtable George Humphrey, noting the reaction to his "hair curling" depression phrase in 1957, is supposed to have called Hagerty and said: "Jim, it looks as if I put my foot into it."[79] Not only did the press secretary take the initiative in reproaching his erstwhile superiors in rank, but they thus sheepishly sought him out like bad little boys caught in the act. Hagerty also made himself the sole channel of communication between the White House occupants—President and staff—and the outside world.[80]

To supplement all this, Howard Pyle of the staff had the responsibility of compiling for issuance two or three times a week a "newsletter" composed of a single mimeographed sheet, "that compresses into a few terse paragraphs the official 'line' on every public issue that comes up, usually supplemented with pertinent Presidential quotes." It circulated to some 1,000 top government executives for their guidance, and also went to leading Republicans in Congress, Republican governors, and others.[81]

Actually the contrast between the Truman and Eisenhower administrations is not as sharp as the foregoing would lead one to suspect. The record after 1952 is hardly as perfect as the centralized control and elaborate machinery would make one believe. There was, for instance, the great hue and cry raised by the Attorney General's reference to the alleged subversive record of Truman aide Harry Dexter White.[82] (As a result Ike suffered some of the roughest press conference questioning of his career.) According to Robert Donovan: "Hagerty said later that an advance copy of Brownell's speech had been sent to the White House but that the President did not see or approve the text."[83] Either the new administration's clearance system was also far from perfect, or the reaction was seriously misjudged, or perhaps Hagerty (who apparently did read the speech) wanted the episode to turn out the way it did.

Pierre Salinger, when interviewed, laid considerable stress on the information council he had established when his boss first took office. He attributed this largely to the snafu surrounding the crash of the U-2 reconnaissance plane in the Soviet Union.[84] The details of this incident are not important here. Suffice it to say that there resulted a monumental mix-up and a series of contradictory claims from the American government. The pattern of confusion, fabrication, and above all, complete lack of visible coordination was painfully apparent. Though this certainly proved that the Hagerty machinery was not foolproof, it also suggested that no elaboration of staff arrangements can take the place of minimal guidance and concern on the part of the Chief Executive himself.

Returning to publicity coordination under Kennedy and Salinger, the "information council" was obviously not as new an idea as the latter implied. It was made up, under the press secretary's chairmanship, of a somewhat fluid group of information officers, often of high rank. For example, he mentioned the Assistant Secretary of State for Public Affairs as the State Department representative, not the press officer, Lincoln White. The Vice President's press secretary sat in, as well as the appropriate officials of other agencies. The people attending changed somewhat from meeting to meeting, depending on the subjects that were uppermost at the moment. He said eight or ten came to each of the normally twice-a-week get-togethers.[85] The use of this group as part of the machinery for preparing for the President's press conference does appear to be an interesting and probably important innovation.

Under the headline "Cabinet Officers Told to Mention President" there appeared in the *Times* for April 27, 1961, an account of a "suggestion" to the Cabinet that these officials and their subordinates work the President's name more often into their speeches—an obvious effort to tighten up further the system for enhancing the Kennedy public image.[86] Salinger, when this kicked up a bit of a public storm, denied that there was any effort to get more publicity for his boss.[87]

Under Kennedy there was also a concerted effort to enlarge on the Eisenhower practice of channeling important and favorable departmental news through the White House for announcement or use in a presidential press conference.[88] One of the last Kennedy administration innovations came with the appointment of one Paul Southwick, former newsman, to Salinger's rather substantial staff, to be responsible for transmitting "useful news and information from the White House to members of Congress and to make suggestions to Democratic members of Congress, based on White House information, about publicity benefits they might gain from Presidential actions." This, and other prospective duties, foreshadowed the 1964 campaign.[89]

Thus far the role of staff has been examined in terms of the role of the press secretary. The changes of recent years have not altered substantially, save in scale, the essential functions performed. The press secretary today is still his boss's alter ego in dealing with the media and the working press. He is also, and far more obviously than in the past, the actual source of much White House news, and the focal point for such coordination as has been attempted of general executive branch publicity. His continuing importance reflects the fact that no administration has seriously attempted to equip itself either with a formalized "ministry of information" or even with a permanent publicity coordinating agency. (A proposal made to Kennedy for a super-press secretary, who would combine the present position with that of the special assistant for security operations coordination, and mesh all government information policies, was not acted upon.)[90]

The major point at which all White House staff contributions toward informing and influencing public opinion flow together is the machinery for issuing press releases. Save for the press conference, virtually all presidential utterances take the form of mimeographed handouts made available in the executive offices to such press representatives as care to pick them up. Even things like radio-television speeches, which do reach the public directly, are also put out in printed form either before or after delivery. So potent a news source is the White House that releases need only be made available there to secure worldwide circulation.

Part of the mythology of the Roosevelt-haters was that "government by handout" began with his election.[91] A look at the *State Papers* of Herbert Hoover, or the files of the Coolidge period, will suggest that this was hardly the case. Since 1933, however, not only has the addition of ghost writers contributed to a steady increase in the number of handouts, but an ever widening circle of staff aides has shared in the preparation of documents for public issuance. Some have specialized in preparing material for and drafting messages to Congress; others, assigned to deal with labor, economic affairs, federal-state relations, or civil rights obviously contribute directly or indirectly to the outflow of mimeographed material, and hence are also part of the presidential staff for public relations.[92]

The number of releases issued annually since 1933 is given in Table 3; Table 4 offers breakdowns by category for three selected years. Note the enormous totals in Table 3, and the sharp increase, both annual and cumulative by administration, from Roosevelt to

TABLE 3

ANNUAL TABULATION OF PRESS RELEASES

Roosevelt		*Truman*		*Eisenhower*		*Kennedy*	
1933	197	1945	409	1953	463	1961	833
1934	236	1946	513	1954	486	1962	911
1935	192	1947	474	1955	402	1963	649
1936	238	1948	707	1956	501		
1937	175	1949	406	1957	419		
1938	182	1950	535	1958	513		
1939	207	1951	469	1959	557		
1940	291	1952	620	1960	566		
1941	428	1953	42	1961	141		
1942	373						
1943	290						
1944	353						
1945	106						
Total	3,268	*Total*	4,175	*Total*	4,048	*Total*	2,393

The figures for the Roosevelt and Truman administrations were secured from the respective presidential libraries, for the Eisenhower and Kennedy years from the various volumes of the *Public Papers of the Presidents,* compiled by the National Archives and published by the Government Printing Office. Figures include items listed in Appendix A (Press Releases) for each volume, plus the Proclamations in Appendix B. This total appeared to compare most closely with earlier figures.

Truman. Then for Truman and Eisenhower the totals level off, suggesting at first glance that some kind of saturation point had been reached. However, under Kennedy the output rose again. The Eisenhower administration appears to be the one that is atypical, surprisingly so in view of the almost 100 per cent expansion of the White House office force between 1952 and 1960. Apparently internal staff work for a uniquely staff-conscious President accounts for the efforts of these extra people.

It is interesting to note in Table 4 the frequency with which the President is found addressing the public, rather than official bodies like Congress, or individuals in the government (category 2). The *Messages and Papers of the Presidents* edited by James D. Rich-

TABLE 4

BREAKDOWN OF PRESS RELEASES FOR SELECTED YEARS

	Hoover (1931)	*Roosevelt* (1935) (*per cent*)	*Eisenhower* (1957)
1. Messages to Congress, including vetoes, etc.	15	29	8
2. Official letters, etc. (e.g., acceptances of resignations)	3	15	20
3. "Remarks," "greetings," etc. to groups	20	17	16
4. White House statements to general public	47	21	36
5. Texts of formal speeches and broadcasts	14	4	4
6. Miscellaneous	1	14	16
	100	100	100
Total number of releases	89	235	366

Data on Hoover from William Starr Myers, ed., *The State Papers and Public Writings of Herbert Hoover,* 2 vols. (Garden City, N.Y.: Doubleday, Doran, 1934); no press release files, if they exist, were available. Data on Roosevelt from *The Public Papers and Addresses of Franklin D. Roosevelt,* Vol. IV: *The Court Disapproves* (New York: Random House, 1938). Data on Eisenhower from the 1957 volume of *Public Papers of the Presidents,* issued by the Government Printing Office. Totals do not include proclamations, executive orders, or press conferences.

ardson covering the period through Theodore Roosevelt[93] contain virtually nothing of this sort beyond inaugural addresses. Almost all of his selections were messages to Congress, veto messages, executive orders, and proclamations. The recent volumes of *Public Papers of the Presidents* include radio and TV speeches, press conference transcripts, informal remarks, toasts, and a host of items which in earlier years rarely existed among presidential papers at all, or if they did, were not considered part of his official activity.

The fact that complete, serially numbered release files have been kept since 1933[94] itself suggests the extent to which earlier more or less unstructured activity became formalized and institutionalized. This process has culminated in the National Archives volumes of *Public Papers* and their appendices. This process of progressive institutionalization can be perhaps inferred from the fact that the annual Roosevelt totals, especially before 1941,[95] tend to be less than half the average during comparable Truman and Eisenhower years.[96] Though this undoubtedly is evidence of considerably stepped-up activity, it may also indicate a less formalized and more casual record-keeping system, at least during the first two Roosevelt terms.

What is the impact of presidential press releases on the journalistic community and on the public? Do White House handouts often end up in editorial waste baskets? Rough answers can be obtained through a study of the space devoted to a sample of White House releases in the *New York Times*. This was done, using two months—February and March—from the years 1935, 1949, 1957, and 1962. The results are presented in Table 5.

It is apparent that White House releases *are* a potent source of presidential publicity, if coverage in the *Times* is any indication, and if the periods chosen are at all typical. Two-thirds to three-quarters received some notice in each administration, many rated the front page, and not infrequently complete texts were printed. The column inch totals are perhaps most revealing. The increase from Roosevelt to Truman would be expected. The leveling off in the Eisenhower period may represent indirect support for the assumption that the General did indeed practice a more restrained and modest kind of presidential leadership than his predecessors or successors.

TABLE 5

SPACE IN *New York Times* DEVOTED TO PRESS RELEASES
(February and March in the Years Indicated)

	Roosevelt (1935)	*Truman* (1949)	*Eisen-hower* (1957)	*Kennedy* (1962)
1. Number of press releases issued	35	63	58	154
2. Number of releases to which coverage was given	27	45	44	107
3. Number of releases given page one coverage	14	9	17	42
4. Number which included text of release in coverage	20	17	15	35
5. Total column inches of release coverage in period	766	945	944	3289
6. Average column inches for each release covered	28	21	21	30

For the Roosevelt and Truman periods, press release lists were used from the respective Libraries. For Eisenhower and Kennedy, reliance was on the appropriate volumes of the *Public Papers of the Presidents,* Appendices A and B.

The enormous Kennedy total suggests several conclusions. (Note that it was necessary to take 1962 release lists rather than those for 1963, and the choice of an election year may have had some impact.) Much of the wordage released took the form of a veritable barrage of messages to Congress requesting legislative action, underscoring his ardent desire to lead vigorously. Recalling the similar analysis of press conference news coverage (Chapter Eight), where the Kennedy total was only slightly above Truman and Eisenhower, it seems evident that the White House had shrewdly identified this press release area as the one in which stepped-up activity was possible and would pay off. They moved into it with vigor, and with striking success. Clearly, the saturation point in press use of presidential releases had not been reached, and perhaps has not even been reached yet.

A count was also done, for the years 1931, 1935, and 1957, of releases devoted primarily to foreign affairs and those concerned with domestic matters. The results are striking. In the Hoover year, foreign affairs documents made up 17 per cent of the total; in 1935, in spite of the Ethiopian War et al., only 12 per cent; but in 1957, the total was just over 31 per cent, or nearly one-third. These figures bear out the point that since 1945 the White House occupant has been forced by the Cold War to give major concern simultaneously to both areas, which has meant a corresponding net increase in executive activity and public utterance.

This increasing flood of press release material must be interpreted as prima facie evidence of a corresponding increase in the involvement of staff aides in the process of presidential communication.[97] The totals in Table 3 make it apparent that the President himself would barely have time to give even cursory approval to all the statements and documents issued in his name, and must have worked personally on only a tiny fraction of them. Furthermore, staff *initiative* as well as staff preparation and drafting must have come to characterize more and more of the total White House output. Only in the most important cases is the President likely to have made the decision himself that a statement or speech or report should be prepared and released.

Franklin Roosevelt, far more than his successors, retained in his own hands the initiation if not the execution of such publicity maneuvers. For all the intimacy born of long association between himself and Early, McIntyre, Missy LeHand, Grace Tully, and others on the staff, they were not often the source of ideas or initiatives, nor were they privy to his innermost thoughts. As Tugwell has noted, his process of working out the means to an end "went on in his most secret mind. Others got glimpses of the process. A few familiars came to understand something of its basic procedures: but there were not many of these. It sometimes seems that those who were closest to him for the longest time were kept there because they did not probe or try to understand. . . ." And again: "He had long ago learned to conceal from friend and enemy alike his thinking and deciding processes and even many of his convictions. . . ."[98]

F.D.R.'s use of staff for public relations must, therefore, have been far different from Eisenhower's, or even Truman's. It is inconceivable that anyone in the Roosevelt White House could have been in the position Sherman Adams occupied under Ike—holding staff conferences with the President absent, to predigest the current business and supply him later with neat sets of proposals and problem solutions.[99] Nor can one visualize F.D.R. presiding over the kind of staff meeting Hersey described with Truman, and leaving up to collegial discussion the next moves to be made. James Rowe, who served as an administrative assistant in the New Deal era, said that when he had secured a few minutes to talk to the President, and went in with a list of items upon which to get guidance or decision, as often as not the "agenda" would never be reached at all. Roosevelt would take over the conversation and use Rowe as a sounding board to try out some germinating idea or plan, totally unrelated to the immediate concerns which had prompted the meeting.[100] Though frustrating to the staffer, this typified the use to which the President characteristically put aides and visitors alike. They hovered about, as it were, at the periphery of the decision-making process. "Franklin allowed no one to discover the governing principle," as Tugwell noted.[101]

The evidence available suggests that under Truman, and probably under Kennedy, the public relations strategy of the White House was planned and implemented as a joint President-staff operation more than had been the case before 1945. Under Eisenhower, given his devotion to staff concepts and his curious detachment from the day-to-day operation of his office, it seems evident that most of the process was shifted into staff hands.

The files at the Truman Library provide several examples of staff involvement in the process of White House communications planning. One in 1950 suggests the development of a staff proposal which received no more than a presidential O.K., and the way in which staff contributes to the growing flood of press releases.[102] It was triggered by a letter dated April 19 to the President, requesting a message that could be read at the forthcoming meeting of the United States Conference of Mayors. The writer suggested that a specific issue like housing might be emphasized. Matt Connelly (the appointments secretary, to whom, apparently, it first was routed) sent it to Bill Hassett with a note dated April 24: "I believe this is something you should handle." Hassett sent it along to John

April 24, 1950

MEMORANDUM FOR DR. STEELMAN:

Dear John:

Since housing and rent control are under so many different jurisdictions, I thought I would send this letter from Paul V. Betters to you to be handled by your staff, which would have the necessary contacts. It seems to me that the paragraph I have indicated in Mr. Betters' letter opens up the way for the President to make an important statement of policy in a letter to the United States Conference of Mayors.

W. D. H.

wdh-rmh

Letter to the President dtd 4/19/50,

From: Mr. Paul V. Betters,
Executive Director,
The United States Conference of Mayors, #
730 Jackson Place, N. W.,
Washington 6, D. C.

Req message for 1950 annual conference to be held in NYCity at the Waldorf-Astoria, May 11-13.

THE WHITE HOUSE
WASHINGTON

4/25

RPA

This should be checked with Budget and Mr. Murphy. Not much time on it. If ok, a good letter should be prepared.

JRS

THE WHITE HOUSE
WASHINGTON

4/25

Dave

I hate to kick this around any more but it seems so obvious an opportunity for the President to get in some good licks in support of his legislative program I suggest you boys should decide whether you wanted to tackle it.

Please give me your advice soon, since another route will have to be tapped quick if you think that advisable

Russ

THE WHITE HOUSE
WASHINGTON

April 27, 1950

MEMORANDUM FOR MR. NEIL HARDY

Attached is the letter from Paul Betters requesting a statement from the President for the Conference of Mayors meeting in New York, which we discussed on the phone this morning. We will look forward to your sending us a first draft of a letter from the President the first of next week.

Dave

David E. Bell

Attachments

Memos illustrating role of White House staff in public relations. Presidential statement to U.S. Conference of Mayors is used to plug housing legislation. Memos from W.D. Hassett to John R. Steelman, Steelman to R.P.A., R.P.A. to David E. Bell (Budget Bureau), Bell to Neil Hardy (Home Finance Agency). *Courtesy Harry S. Truman Library.*

Steelman[103] the same day: "Since housing and rent control are under so many different jurisdictions, I thought I would send this letter . . . to you to be handled by your staff. . . . It seems to me that the paragraph I have indicated in Mr. Betters' letter opens up the way for the President to make an important statement of policy in a letter to the . . . Conference. . . ."

Thus the original suggestion was picked up and related by Hassett to the publicity interests of the President. Steelman apparently accepted the suggestion. In a handwritten note to one of his assistants he said: "This should be checked with Budget and Mr. Murphy.[104] Not much time on it. If OK, a good letter should be prepared." The assistant, in turn, forwarded the growing file to the Budget Bureau on the 25th: "I hate to kick this around any more but it seems so obvious an opportunity for the President to get in some good licks in support of his legislative program I thought you boys should decide whether you wanted to tackle it." Budget sent it to the Housing and Home Finance Agency, after a phone conversation with the Assistant Administrator, accompanied by a request for a draft letter for the President's signature. On May 2 the draft was returned to Budget and forwarded to the White House, and the last item in the file is the carbon of a letter of transmittal from the President to the Conference official. Here the staff not only followed through on the request involved, but made the decision that the opportunity could and should be used by the President to plug his program.

Another example of staff role came in 1951 in relation to the Administration's proposal for national health insurance. This had been raised by the President as early as 1945 but never given the kind of sustained public advocacy by the White House which hindsight suggests was necessary. A long memorandum dated October 12, 1951, from presidential assistant David Stowe to Mr. Truman[105] begins: "On several occasions during the past months I have discussed with you the desirability of taking action to push the Administration's health program. There is general agreement among the White House staff and interested private persons" that this would be an issue in 1952.

Stowe then goes on to note three possible alternative courses of action: soft-pedal the general health issue; push some peripheral programs in the area but not general insurance; or appoint a study commission to go over the whole problem. Staff discussions had produced the conclusion that the third alternative was the best, and accordingly a draft executive order plus list of possible commission members was enclosed. In a brief note dated October 15 the President accepted the proposed course of action: "The attached looks all right to me. I think the best thing to do is go ahead with it. Let's see if we can find the right people for the Commission."[106] Here broad strategy for selling a proposal to the public was virtually set by the White House staff with minimal presidential involvement.

Kenneth Hechler, also a Truman aide, when interviewed, commented on the type of staff memo represented by this one on medical insurance. He said that one ought not underestimate the role of the President himself. Such a document was often the ultimate result of a request by Mr. Truman at a staff meeting that something be looked into with an eye to getting action started. Thus staff initiative may be more apparent than real. To illustrate, he recalled an instance when the President had told his staff that a good clear statement of American foreign policy was needed. This launched a drafting effort between White House and State Department people, the results of which, after being looked over and revised by the President, became a very successful pamphlet on the subject.[107]

If these examples can be taken as illustrative, what emerges is a close cooperative relationship with ideas flowing in both directions and a continuing role by the President at various stages of initiation and implementation. Until the Eisenhower papers become available there is wholly insufficient evidence to support a conclusion that the practice after 1952 changed drastically. It can be inferred, however, from what is generally known about the General's conduct of the office, that there must have been a considerable change. For one thing, the size of the staff nearly doubled during his eight years, suggesting its increasing importance. For another, the role of Sherman Adams as general manager is well enough documented to justify the assumption that much of the initiative in publicity, as in other areas, must have gravitated into his hands.[108]

Adams, for instance, suggests in his memoirs the considerable role of advisers in deciding what moves Ike should make and persuading him to make them:

> I found early in the game that Eisenhower expected anyone who proposed a speech to him to have the reasons for making it thoroughly thought out, a draft on paper and the trip phased into his calendar. . . . I and the rest of the staff learned that we had to have a finished draft in shape and in the President's hands at least two weeks before it was to be delivered so that he could put it into his desk drawer and brood over it at his leisure.[109]

Armed with such a draft, he and the other staffers involved would secure fifteen uninterrupted minutes with the President, decide who was going to carry the argument, and then make the most persuasive presentation they could, hoping that this and some days of reflection would win them their point.

Apparently this sort of approach was not confined to speeches. Adams, for instance, cites a case in 1955 when the soil bank proposal was being reviewed by the Cabinet before adoption: "*Howard Pyle* outlined a public relations plan to let the public know what the program was all about. . . ."[110] According to *U.S. News and World Report*, a similar and even more clear-cut example of elaborate staff planning was represented in a program called Mission 66. Maxwell Rabb, a White House aide whose job was said to be that of sniffing out problems while they were still small, was responsible. He had decided that the national park system was becoming inadequate and that something should be done. He checked with Secretary of the Interior Douglas McKay, whose department then developed a case that supported this proposition. Next a Cabinet presentation was arranged. (The use of visual aids became a feature of Eisenhower Cabinet sessions.) The interesting point is that this proposal, obviously fraught with publicity and educational implications, was not broached to the President until all the staff work was completed, and only a few days before it appeared on the Cabinet agenda. Ike approved it all, following the Cabinet presentation and discussion.[111]

This state of affairs under Eisenhower, which seemingly found the staff often replacing the President as source of public relations planning, was unlikely to persist under almost any successor, least of all John F. Kennedy. The thoroughly documented genesis of Kennedy's press conference statement on the steel price increase in April, 1962, well illustrates his "task force" approach to decision making in the public relations and other areas.[112]

When steel president Roger Blough made known his mission at his appointment with the President on April 10, the latter's first impulse was to send for Secretary of Labor Goldberg, who arrived before the interview was over. Then, according to Hugh Sidey: "Blough left and Kennedy paced furiously, flopping now and then into his rocker." Bundy and Sorensen came in, Goldberg remained, Associate Press Secretary Andrew Hatcher and staffer Kenneth O'Donnell were present too. Walter Heller (Chairman of the Council of Economic Advisers) was sent for, and a call put in to steel union president David McDonald. "For nearly two hours Kennedy roamed his office, discussing what to do."[113]

Secretaries McNamara and Dillon (Defense and Treasury) were phoned, brother Robert, the Attorney General, was consulted, and former Truman aide Clark Clifford drafted to lend a hand. Various tacks were considered and rejected. "The one great weapon immediately available was an appeal to public opinion. Kennedy had a press conference scheduled for the next afternoon. He could, and he would, lay his outrage before the people."[114] That night material for a conference statement was gathered and discussed over a lengthy breakfast by the President, the Vice President, Secretary of State Rusk, Sorensen, staff member Myer Feldman, Goldberg, Hatcher, and Heller. Sorensen continued to work on the wording, with the President taking a hand, and the finished product was not ready until eight minutes before air time.

Other crises like the Bay of Pigs, and less spectacular decision-making situations, seem to have been handled in the same free-wheeling yet collegial fashion.[115] Kennedy reached out for advice from sources that seemed appropriate to a given task, doubtless accepted suggestions, but remained the pivot of the process and made the final choices. A measure of the intimacy of his continuing involvement in shaping administration public relations was the "barging-in" privilege which Salinger shared with a dozen other aides, and which he is reputed to have used five to ten times a day.[116]

The notion of staff aid to the President in his role as communicator could include, in the broadest sense of the term "staff," an almost infinite range of persons, agencies, and techniques. In certain cases, the members of the President's family were clearly important in this broader sense. Outstanding was of course the assistance rendered by Eleanor Roosevelt to her husband. She herself has written: "Franklin often used me to get the reflection of other people's thinking because he knew I made it a point to see and talk with a variety of people. . . . I felt that [he] . . . used whatever I brought back to him in the way of observations and information as a check against the many official reports which he received."[117]

Apart from this "feedback" role, her multifarious activities unquestionably did much to enhance the Roosevelt image in the country. Her popular column, for instance, entitled "My Day," reached millions of people and was printed in violently hostile papers as well as the more friendly. The editors of opposition organs explained the incongruity of her liberal views beside their conservative and anti-Roosevelt editorials by saying simply that their readers demanded her column.[118] This, plus her lecturing and frequent radio talks, produced an enormous correspondence in addition to the general flood of White House mail. So great was the increase in her mail after "My Day" began appearing that she had to develop a staff of her own to cope with it.[119] She also held her own regular press conferences for the women reporters.

Though Margaret Truman, and the Eisenhowers' handsome son and daughter-in-law, were occasionally prominent during these respective administrations, the first ladies generally remained in the background. Bess Truman held no press conferences and Mamie Eisenhower no more than a few.[120] But not only did John Kennedy bring with him a young, exceedingly attractive, and far less retiring wife, but a small daughter—Caroline—who promptly captured the imagination of the public, and an infant son as well. "Jackie," though she held no press conferences and wrote no columns, was an enormous hit both in the United States and on her frequent trips abroad. She exhibited little if any of Mrs. Roosevelt's interest in causes or public issues, but as an ambassadress representing her husband she generated enormous and almost wholly favorable publicity for him and the Kennedys generally.

Actually the whole extensive Kennedy clan got into the act and became America's equivalent to a royal family, far more than the much married Roosevelt offspring ever did. Attorney General Robert, Peace Corps head Sargent Shriver, and, in a somewhat more equivocal role, Senator Ted shared the limelight by virtue of the official positions they held or sought. The wife and family of the Attorney General came into a share of publicity, particularly when Robert and Ethel carried out a world good will tour which if nothing else was a public relations success. At least one commentator claimed that the White House encouraged much of this and was ever willing to supply appropriate photographs.[121] Another reporter concluded that:

> To the nation's magazines, the Kennedy family has been the greatest boon since paper.
>
> Probably no other group of public personalities ever has captured the attention of the nation as has Boston's clan of colorful Kennedys.
>
> . . . .
>
> Between February of [1961] and January of [1962], for example, there were in the country's periodicals: 194 articles on President Kennedy; 38 on Jacqueline; 21 on Bobby Kennedy; four on Joseph P. Kennedy, the President's father; one on Rose Kennedy, the President's mother; four on Caroline Kennedy, the President's little daughter; two on his son, John Jr.; two on Ted Kennedy, the President's brother; two on Ethel Kennedy, Bobby's wife, and four on their various families.[122]

According to Pierre Salinger, far from inspiring this outpouring, he tried to discourage would-be publishers and bring some order out of the chaos.[123]

The "feedback" of information upon which to evaluate public attitudes has already been broached. Under Franklin Roosevelt the techniques of mail analysis were highly developed. Ira Smith says that whereas daily White House incoming mail averaged some 800 letters a day under Hoover, it jumped to 8,000 during the New Deal Era, "with peak days on which we would go down under a count of 150,000 letters and parcels."[124] The opinion reflected in the letters was carefully analyzed, and had been during the Hoover administration also. One of the new wrinkles added by F.D.R. was the so-called "mail brief," a special study of some particular issue which involved not only a count of the pro and con letters, but also a sampling of excerpts from typical categories of opinion. The President nearly always called for such a mail brief following important policy statements, and they were given to him daily during the first six months of 1940 on the third-term issue.[125]

During the Truman administration special forms were used and the mail count was recorded weekly. The report for the week ending April 29, 1949, ran to three pages.[126] Each page of the form had space for ten subjects down the left margin, and four columns in which to record the disposition being made of mail in that category, the number of letters, the number of postcards, and the total. Some 13,850 letters and 6,150 cards were received during the week. Of the 28 subjects represented (plus two miscellaneous categories) only nine accounted for more than 100 letters or cards each: "Post Office Pay Raise," "Greeks Requesting Admission to United States," "Denazify Germany," "Recognize Italian Colonies in Africa," "Socialized Medicine" (note that the White House staff took over the label sold to the public by the A.M.A.), "Anti-Vivisection" (a District of Columbia issue, apparently), "Cardinal Mindszenty," "Repeal Taft-Hartley Bill," and "Franco Spain."

In five of the 28 categories some effort was made to separate pro and con missives, but only one of the nine most popular was so treated: "Socialized Medicine." It drew 1,298 opposing letters and 3,700 postcards, and only 55 postcards and no letters in favor. These together represented almost exactly a fifth of the week's incoming mail, and suggest either the extraordinary power of the A.M.A. offensive against the legislation, or the almost complete failure of the President's selling campaign, or, more probably, both. On this one issue the mail reports for the months of March through July, 1949, were checked, with substantially the same result. There were virtually no favorable letters, rarely less than one hundred opposing letters and often three to six hundred, plus floods of (doubtless A.M.A.-inspired form) postcards. Six thousand of these were received in the week of May 13 alone. It is hard to escape the conclusion that more vigorous efforts by the President would have improved this amazingly one-sided situation.

An account of the Kennedy practices in analyzing the mail appeared in the press during the July following his inauguration. At the time, the inflow was coming at the rate of 40,000 pieces per week, half of them addressed directly to the President. About 5 P.M. every day a folder of mail was handed to the President, which represented an arbitrary sampling of the total for the day —perhaps every 50th or 100th letter. This sample gave him an idea of how it was running, and he might dictate two or three replies to this budget of letters himself, thus giving his staff clues as to how similar ones should be answered. When opportunity served, he was likely to ask for a further sampling.[127]

Scientific opinion polling came into use during the first Roosevelt term. Were polls used by the White House? The answer seems to be that they were not, in the sense that the President either added such expertise officially to his staff or commissioned polls to be conducted for his use at government expense. There were, however, polls taken by the Bureau of Intelligence of the O.W.I. on basic public attitudes toward the war.[128] The results of commercial polls which might be of interest to the President were also made available for White House use. There are frequent references to polls in the Ickes *Diaries*, especially around election time. In September, 1940, the Secretary recorded that: "The President was interested in newspaper accounts of a poll that has been taken by *Fortune* which will be published in two or three weeks."[129] He had probably received advance information from the Roper organization on, in this case, his standing relative to Willkie. Gallup also furnished advance copies of his results to the White House.[130]

In 1939 Hadley Cantril had started the Office of Opinion Research at Princeton with the intention, among others, of watching trends of American attitude toward the European war.[131] Roosevelt learned about this through a mutual friend, and in talking to

Cantril later, "asked if there were any way I could repeat certain questions more frequently and ask certain others that would be of interest to him." The generosity of a wealthy local Roosevelt supporter thereafter enabled Cantril to set up a special organization, comparable to the existing Gallup one, also in Princeton, to do the kinds of surveys in which the President was interested. "We also established small sample operations," Cantril indicated, "so that we could get quick results (several times I had requests from the White House in the morning and got them the reaction of American opinion by the same afternoon)."

Some of the suggestions for survey questions came direct from the President, some from his close associates. At times speeches F.D.R. intended to give on a certain subject were pretested in this manner in an effort to discover what would be the best and most effective approach to use on American opinion. Cantril summed up the use of his findings:

> President Roosevelt was, by all odds, together with Secretary Stimson the most alert responsible official I have ever known to be concerned about public opinion systematically. I never once saw him "change his mind" because of what any survey showed. But he did base his strategy a great deal on these results.

The files at the Truman Library relating to polls and poll results are singularly thin. They not only reveal no presidential initiative in the commissioning of surveys, but show at best a scant interest on the part of either Mr. Truman or his staff in the results of surveys circulated by the commercial pollsters. A letter to Dr. Steelman, for instance, from the Democratic National Committee, transmitting some of this information, drew only a brief and perfunctory note of thanks.[132] The contempt in which the President quite understandably held the polls following his upset victory in 1948 must have colored not only his own but his associates' attitudes toward this method of feeling the popular pulse.[133]

There is some evidence to suggest that the Eisenhower administration made a good deal more use of polling techniques than had been done before. In May, 1957, Howard Pyle of the White House staff, speaking to a Republican party conference, said that "a previously undisclosed public opinion survey made by the White House since December indicated that what people liked most about the Administration was 'peace,' but that what they liked the least was, paradoxically, the Administration's foreign policy."[134] He went on to say that the poll had been taken under contract by private research organizations in key 1956 voting areas from coast to coast. The findings were to be furnished to regional party officials. The State Department under Secretary Dulles (and to some extent going back to 1944)[135] was also heavily involved in the purchase of this kind of service. A House subcommittee, later in 1957, turned up the fact that since 1951, $350,000 had been thus spent from the Secretary's "emergency fund." Specifically, mention was made of payments of $36,318.75 to the Opinion Research Center at the University of Chicago during the period between June, 1956 and February, 1957.[136]

The kind of use that can be made of such surveys—whether by the White House itself or by an agency like the State Department—in relation to the opinion leadership and legislative leadership activities of the President is suggested by an account that appeared in the *Times* the same year under the headline: "Surveys Dispute Anti-Aid Letters."[137] Five polls taken, presumably as part of the same State Department program, on American reactions to foreign aid expenditures all showed heavy support for the programs. A substantial majority felt that the United States itself benefited from them, as well as the recipient countries. "The findings run strongly counter," the article continues, "to the conclusions that might be drawn and are being drawn by many Senators and Representatives from the 'cut-the-budget' mail now flooding Capitol Hill." Other similar poll results going back to 1951 were cited. (This information, quite possibly leaked deliberately or given out in a "backgrounder" for its value in persuading Congress to accept foreign aid recommendations, was undoubtedly behind the investigation cited above.)

It seems clear that the Kennedy administration made as much and probably even more use of polls. Louis Harris, proprietor of his own very successful market research firm, was first used by Kennedy in his 1958 senatorial race for reelection in Massachusetts, according to Theodore White.[138] Then in the 1960 campaign for nomination and election:

> He was to poll . . . more people across the country than had ever been done by any other political analyst in American history; upon his description of the profile of the country's thinking and prejudices as he found them, were to turn many of John F. Kennedy's major decisions.[139]

Once in the White House, the new President apparently continued to avail himself of Harris's services. According to Reston, for instance, writing in June, 1962, "The White House has watched the decline of its political fortunes on Capitol Hill with some dismay. President Kennedy has been having Lou Harris, his pollster from the 1960 Presidential campaign, checking on sentiment in the country, particularly since the controversy over steel prices. . . ."[140] It was natural that so public relations-conscious an administration should have decided to use scientifically acquired feedback information to analyze the shape of the President's public image and the impact of his utterances.

The use of staff aides in White House communications raises one final and more theoretical question. The President, by the nature of the office he holds, must be preoccupied above all else with persuasion and education. His impact on the broad outlines of policy is largely a product of these communication efforts. They are his stock in trade. At the same time, public relations as a body of technical knowledge and as a profession has seen phenomenal growth in recent years. Hucksterism has been embraced and ever more heavily utilized by all segments of the American national community, including political parties and candidates.[141]

An early and enthusiastic marriage between the presidential office and the streamlined salesmanship identified with Madison Avenue would seem to have been inevitable. Yet, to continue the metaphor, though an increasingly ardent courtship has been going on since about 1933, there is not yet clear evidence that the marriage has been fully consummated. F.D.R. brought into the White House and the Executive Branch a massive infusion of the kind of semiprofessional public relations practiced by former newsmen, including Steve Early. After World War II modern hucksterism shook off this stepchild relationship to journalism and struck off on its self-confident own, armed with the weapons provided by social scientists (referred to affectionately as the "head shrinkers").

President Truman and his entourage were little inclined, it would seem, to embrace the scientific idea merchants. There was the food-saving campaign staged with considerable hoopla by Charles Luckman in 1947, but this rather dubious experiment stood out as an exception to the rule. It was left to the Eisenhower administration to bring Madison Avenue into the White House.[142] The campaign of 1952 was more fully in the hands of the professional public relations men than ever before. The Republican candidate was the kind of lovable, nonpartisan commodity that was highly saleable. And, unlike either Roosevelt or Truman, who were experienced politicians accustomed to planning their own campaign strategy, Mr. Eisenhower's lack of experience made it essential that he place himself in the hands of others.

In the White House, the staff assembled around the President included a good many with a direct or indirect public relations background: Hagerty himself, Emmet Hughes, late of *Life*, Gabriel Hauge from *Business Week*, C. D. Jackson (*Fortune*), Frederic Morrow from the public relations staff of C.B.S., Howard Pyle, who had been a writer and announcer, and of course Robert Montgomery.[143] This array of communications skill did not produce uniformly satisfactory results. "No administration in a generation has been more public relations conscious," wrote James Reston in 1955, "none has experimented more widely with modern public-relations techniques; and none has had a better press. Yet, paradoxically, it is constantly adding to its difficulties by clumsy handling of public statements."[144] Things did improve, but the evidence does not suggest that professional public relations represent the be-all and end-all for insuring presidential success. Perhaps the problem was the general noninvolvement of the President himself. Staff on their own can do much for a Chief Executive, but can undoubtedly do more when he contributes not only acquiescence but leadership and direction.

The Kennedy administration, too, came into office determined to make use of the new skills. Lawrence O'Brien and Timothy Reardon of the Kennedy group both had had careers in advertising and public relations. As one observer wrote in September, 1960, "the young pros [around Kennedy] show an almost brutal realism about the techniques of mass communications. The whole apparatus of persuasion and manipulation—opinion polls, Trendex ratings, and market research—holds few secrets from the Senator's staff."[145] But far from the passive role often played by his predecessor, Kennedy ran the White House as very nearly a one-man show. He was keenly interested in the public relations side of the enterprise and deeply and personally involved. Among the many other consequences of his tragic death was the untimely termination of the most imaginative experiment in White House public relations since the New Deal.

☆☆☆☆☆☆☆☆☆

Chapter 10

☆☆☆☆☆☆☆☆☆

THE ELECTRONIC MEDIA

Francis Chase in the volume he subtitled "An Informal History of Broadcasting" writes of the initial Roosevelt fireside chat, on the banking crisis: "For all practical purposes, that was the first broadcast from the White House."[1] He goes on to note that both Coolidge and Hoover had taken to the air waves, and the latter while in office had spoken over the radio no less than ninety-five times (only nine less than Roosevelt during his first term). And yet so different and compelling were the broadcasts of the new President that earlier efforts could hardly be counted as precedents.

> More than any other individual, Mr. Roosevelt has a feel for audiences, a feel for the microphone which has made the vital core of the nation's activities not the formal reception rooms of the White House—the Blue, Red, Green and East rooms—but the Oval Room, which, oddly enough, doesn't have a fireside.[2]

Again something essentially new in presidential communication technique was created out of a mixture of past practice and the unique skills of a particular White House occupant.

Radio and television were revolutionary developments for the presidential office as for society at large. Until Coolidge, the channels for reaching the public available to a President had remained the same in essence since the days of George Washington: the printed word, or oral utterances to a live audience. Despite wide variations in the skill with which these could be used, and technological changes which overtook the printed medium, no White House occupant could escape the limits thus imposed upon him.

F.D.R. had seen radio's potential for policy leadership during his four years as governor of New York.[3] Frank Freidel noted: "Long since, Roosevelt had grasped the significance of radio as an invaluable political medium for the Democrats which would enable them to break through the paper curtain of the publishers and appeal directly to the voters."[4] The antecedents of the famous fireside chats began with broadcasts in March and April, 1929, designed to advance his programs in the hostile atmosphere of the habitually Republican-controlled legislature.[5] As he himself put it, writing in 1938: "Throughout my Administration as Governor I made very generous use of the radio not only to keep the people of the State informed as to the progress and activities of their State Government, but also, in many instances, to obtain the support of the people for legislation in their interest."[6]

Once in the White House, all was not Roosevelt innovation, however. Radio lent itself to the purposes of the presidential office in various ways, some of which had already been recognized. Calvin Coolidge was clearly aware of its potency for building the "image" of the President—as it might be put today. Hoover followed the Coolidge practices, though, one assumes, more in deference to established expectations than as a means of conscious self-advertisement. Thus a pattern for presidential broadcasting had already been set by 1933.[7]

The Roosevelt contributions were of a more subtle sort. First and foremost was the technique represented by the fireside chats, to be considered in detail below. Important as these became, however, they averaged only about two per year and hence were but a tiny fraction, quantitatively, of the administration's total use of radio.[8] More important in terms of sheer bulk was the new impetus given after 1933 to radio appearances by Cabinet members and other high officials.[9] On March 4, 1935, for instance, the administration put on a two-hour radio program, which had been carefully script-written, to celebrate the anniversary of the first inauguration two years before. This kind of effort, together with the appearances before the microphone of such colorful figures as Secretary of the Interior Ickes, undoubtedly paid handsome dividends.[10]

Most significant in Roosevelt's approach to radio was his clear understanding of its over-all implications. Presidential dependence on the press had meant, over the years, dependence upon a series of middlemen. Wilson had felt this keenly both as a President bent on innovation and as a Democrat facing a more or less hostile press. Radio for the first time put the President and his public in face-to-face contact. Cutting, paraphrasing, quoting out of context, adverse editorial comment, and other alleged newspaper practices which annoyed Chief Executives were ruled out. The audience could receive the message precisely as it was sent. And the press itself, aware that many of its readers were in a position to know exactly what the President had said, handled after-the-fact comment with a new circumspection. As John Franklin Carter put it: "F.D.R. swiftly showed that when he had delivered a major radio address, so many people had already heard it over the air that the newspapers, in self-defense, were compelled to publish an account of the speech, pretty much as it had been delivered."[11]

That Roosevelt was indeed aware of all this is abundantly clear.[12] On May 10, 1933, he received a letter from the president of the National Broadcasting Company dealing with his use of radio to date. Though concerned mainly with the technical aspects of presidential broadcasting, the author noted: "I can honestly say that I have never known a public official to use the radio with such intelligence." F.D.R.'s reply is of greater interest, however. After thanking Aylesworth for his letter and making a technical suggestion or two, he goes on:

> I need not tell you that in my opinion radio now is one of the most effective mediums for the dissemination of information. It can not misrepresent or misquote. It is far reaching and simultaneous in releasing messages given it for transmission to the Nation or for international consumption.[13]

The President again alluded to radio's peculiar importance for the office he held in 1940, in a reply to a letter from Mrs. Ogden Reid:

> I did not speak on the radio the other Sunday evening because I wanted to. I spoke in order to give a report to the people of the United States—to give them facts about the international situation and our situation at home—facts they needed because so many fanciful and confusing statements had been made. . . .
>
> When a section of the press can bring itself to such extravagant falsification it becomes necessary to resort to other media in order to give the people of the country the facts they are entitled to have concerning what their government is doing.[14]

A year and a half earlier, Mr. Roosevelt had written a note to President Frank Graham of the University of North Carolina thanking him for his favorable comments about an appearance by Secretary of Labor Perkins on the university campus. After noting the odds the administration faced in getting its story past the hostile press, he closed: "Sometimes I wish the advent of television could be hastened."[15]

Not only did Roosevelt grasp the unique significance of radio, but his active mind apparently ranged over the steps that might be necessary to preserve its usefulness for himself and his successors as an independent and direct channel of communication.[16] The most obvious threat in his eyes (and the eyes of others) was the joint ownership of newspapers and radio stations. The press had greeted the advent of the radio as a news competitor with ill-concealed dismay. For some time the press-controlled wire services were prohibited from selling their matter to radio, and only threats by the station operators to set up a press service of their own brought a reluctant change of policy.[17] Another obvious ploy was for newspaper owners to buy up radio outlets and control them directly.[18]

(Parenthetically, the denizens of the Congressional press galleries saw to it that radio news commentators were barred, nor were they admitted to presidential press conferences in the early years of the New Deal. In December, 1938, Fulton Lewis, Jr., sparked a move to force recognition of the representatives of radio, which succeeded, over the strenuous protests of the traditional reporters, in April, 1939.[19] Immediately the White House press conferences were similarly thrown open.)

Returning to joint ownership, there were suggestions in 1941, when the FCC finally took up the problem, that the administration had been angling for a probe of these conditions for some years.[20] The data seemed to suggest that there *was* a developing problem. A survey reported by the Commission in 1941, covering 801 radio broadcasting stations, showed that 353 were the only outlet in their respective cities, and that of these, 111 were controlled by the local newspaper—which in turn was the only paper in town.[21] Another survey showed that roughly 300 of the stations in the country were newspaper-owned, double the number so controlled seven years earlier.[22]

It now seems apparent that the inspiration for the FCC probe had come from the President. A former Roosevelt staff member revealed that Roosevelt told James L. Fly (who became chairman of the FCC in 1939) to work on this problem, that it would produce a furore when broached, and that he, the President, would not be able to come publicly to the rescue of the Commission in that event. Roosevelt's motive was his desire to retain radio as an independent channel of communication that would not be affected by the hostility of the press toward his administration.[23] Corroborating evidence of the President's involvement came in a brief memo he dictated to Morris Ernst, dated February 7, 1941: "I still think Jim Fly ought to go ahead with divorcing press and radio. I see no particular need of hearings. A statement of policy does it."[24] The Commission never came up with a clear policy against this kind of joint ownership, but did imply later that it would be taken into account in the granting or renewal of licenses.

Any discussion of Roosevelt and radio must focus on the famous fireside chats.[25] They above all symbolized the recognition of radio as a medium in its own right and not a mere adjunct to the traditional speech to a live audience. Radio, in other words, could not be used effectively by the White House until it was accepted on its own terms. With a few exceptions, it was not so used during the Coolidge-Hoover era. Yet it is obvious that nearly all the problems of communication change when one shifts from addressing a face-to-face audience to addressing a microphone.

As Cantril and Allport point out, a radio audience is wholly dependent upon auditory impressions unsupplemented by the appearance and gestures of the speaker. "The cues for judging the personality of a speaker and for comprehending his meaning have been immensely reduced. The visual-auditory-social situation of the rostrum has been skeletonized until a mere fragment remains."[26] They go on to note that with radio, the audience is no longer bound by the ordinary conventions of at least feigned attention which operate on those gathered in an auditorium. The radio listener need not pay attention unless he wants to. Above all, radio largely destroys the normal interaction between speaker and audience, and among members of the audience. The radio speaker gets no "feedback" from his auditors during his performance, and cannot respond to their reactions. He may lose them entirely and be quite unaware of it. Furthermore, since he will be listened to by solitary individuals and people gathered in small family groups, but rarely by larger aggregations, interaction and mutual stimulation within the audience will also be reduced to a minimum.

Clearly, the skills of the stump orator are not readily transferred to the microphone. Effective radio speaking is an art in itself whose prime characteristic is the great premium placed on the use and interpretation of the human voice. A nationwide radio audience is an infinitely more diverse and elusive target than any auditorium speaker can ever be called upon to face and hit squarely. Hence it was necessary for the President who would exploit radio to do so consciously and carefully with all of its peculiar characteristics in mind. The reward of success, as Roosevelt found, was the ability to communicate instantaneously, with enormous impact, and with precision, to national audiences approaching fifty million. No combination of printed media could possibly do the same.

Freidel notes of Roosevelt as governor that though "He spoke a good bit more rapidly than in later years; [and] his delivery was to grow in mellowness and strength, . . . already it fascinated radio listeners."[27] By the time he had been in the White House for a year or so he had more than mastered the intricacies of the me-

"My friends. . . . We are now in the war." President Roosevelt giving a fireside chat, December 9, 1941. *Wide World Photos.*

dium. His manner of delivery had become the envy, so one observer insisted, of leading professional broadcasters.

> His ability to create a feeling of intimacy between himself and his listeners, his skill in placing emphasis on key words, his adroitness in presenting complicated matters in such simple terms that the man in the street believes he has a full mastery of them, have won him admiration from even his political enemies.[28]

Another student of Roosevelt style quoted a radio official: "above all, [his radio voice] has a tone of perfect sincerity, a quality that we consider supremely essential."[29]

How much conscious attention and effort went into the perfection of this technique is difficult to say. His wife noted that he never had a voice or diction lesson.[30] Journalists Pearson and Allen, on the other hand, writing in 1936, claim that careful study had gone into his radio style and that he listened to recordings of his speeches afterward to check on his delivery.[31] In any event, it is obvious from the comments of those close to him that preparation for an individual fireside chat was painstaking. Sherwood writes that every word was judged for how it would sound on the radio. Punctuation and timing were also given careful attention. By the time it was to be delivered, the President knew a speech virtually by heart. Invariably the final draft would have been read aloud by him to a small group of his collaborators to test its sound and detect any tongue-twisting passages.[32]

In a sense, Roosevelt had turned the practice of his immediate predecessors vis-à-vis radio on its head. Instead of viewing the medium as a mere supplementary channel for a traditional speech, he geared much of his communication effort to radio even when he had a live audience such as the Congress as his ostensible target. For example, in the election year of 1936 the President persuaded Congress to hold the usual joint session in the evening so that when he read his annual message it would secure the peak radio audience available at 9 P.M. but not available at midday.[33] In the same year, apparently at the behest of Jim Farley, the national convention of the Democratic Party was kept in session for five days (in spite of the fact that Roosevelt and Garner were renominated without opposition) "partly because he saw a chance to drench the air waves with Democratic propaganda day after day, and partly because Roosevelt wanted to give his acceptance speech on a Saturday, as he had four years before."[34]

In 1944, when it was time again to deliver his annual message, circumstances found F.D.R. recovering from the flu and unable to go to the Capitol and read it in person. Not to be done out of the usual radio coverage, however, he delivered it, virtually as originally written, over the radio at 9 P.M., nine hours after it had been sent to Congress. For the radio version he added some explanatory paragraphs, which ran, in part:

> Only a few of the newspapers of the United States can print the message in full, and I am very anxious that the American people

> be given the opportunity to hear what I have recommended to Congress for this very fateful year in our history—and the reasons for those recommendations. Here is what I said: . . .[35]

Again recurs the theme of using radio to reach the public directly, bypassing or at least supplementing the newspaper.

As to the fireside chats themselves, what was their schedule and frequency? What can be learned of the process whereby the President developed his strategy for their use? What kinds of subject matter were involved and what general purposes regarding that subject matter were individual chats designed to serve? The answer to the first of these questions is the easiest to document. The President was exceedingly conscious of the need to avoid wearing out his welcome in the living rooms of the nation. When Ray Stannard Baker wrote him in 1935 urging him to keep a vision of high moral purpose before the nation, he replied with a shrewd analysis of the impact and limits of radio. Demurring from Baker's suggestion of more frequent broadcasts, he wrote: "the public psychology and, for that matter, individual psychology, cannot, because of human weakness, be attuned for long periods of time to a constant repetition of the highest note in the scale. . . . There is another thought which is involved in continuous leadership— . . . people tire of seeing the same name day after day in the important headlines of the papers, and the same voice night after night over the radio."[36]

In another letter, to his close friend and associate Frank Walker, he touched on the same matter of pace and timing, here in relation to the Congressional cycle. Walker had written: "may I again suggest that the President is at his best in the heart to heart sort of talks that were given early in the administration. Again, let me say I would like to see that tone renewed." F.D.R. replied:

> You are absolutely right about the heart to heart talks. It is simply a question of the right time. As you know, every administration slips during a Congressional session and generally comes back after Congress adjourns. Congress, while in session is a sounding board —when it is away the President is a sounding board. I hope to make one or possibly two fireside talks between now and May, but there must be a logical occasion and I am looking for one.[37]

(He did not in fact find occasions for two fireside chats in the period he mentions here.) On taking advantage of the lulls between Congressional sessions, it is interesting to note that during his first two terms, eight of the fifteen chats were delivered during such periods.

Aside from glimpses like this, the process whereby the President decided the time was ripe for one of his carefully husbanded fireside chats will probably remain forever obscure. He was continually bombarded by suggestions and entreaties, from within and without the administration, that he go to the people on this or that issue, doubtless often with the argument that he and only he could achieve the necessary results. This sort of advice, in relation to the Court plan, was pressed with eventual success by Tommy Corcoran, according to one student.[38] More often, apparently, various possible speech emphases and occasions would simmer together slowly in his mind over a period of time until eventually he would reach his decision and set the preparatory machinery in motion.[39] In his diaries, Henry Morgenthau cites various tentative decisions by the President "to take the issue to the people."[40] Once, after further reflection and consultation "he decided not to talk on the radio but to write a letter to Harrison and Doughton."[41] Regarding another issue,

> Roosevelt, urged on by Morgenthau, intended to answer the senator [Harrison, who had made a radio speech about it] early in April, but the President was preoccupied by the spending bill, and while he delayed, the Senate accepted Harrison's schedules and the revenue bill went to conference. . . . Roosevelt then asked Morgenthau to prepare a letter for the conference committee which "the man in the street" could understand.[42]

A common assumption about the content of the chats, as about Roosevelt press conferences, was that they were used to plug pending legislation. He could thus go direct to the people and build support for some specific bill he wanted passed. An examination of the texts of the speeches, however (as with the press conferences), shows that his use of them was far more subtle than any such facile theory would indicate. True, they *were* thus employed on occasion. The clearest example is probably the chat on the Court plan, broadcast March 9, 1937. In a few others among the twenty-seven chats, the President did pointedly discuss pending bills: social security, holding company legislation, and some other items on April 28, 1935; a program he had just sent to Congress to cope with the then current recession, April 14, 1938; and wartime economic stabilization legislation on April 28, 1942. But aside from some additional passing references, this exhausts the list of important pleas for such support.

Occasionally a fireside talk found the President dealing with some immediate event or voicing a specific plea for support other than for legislation. There was the passage justifying the "purge" in the primaries of 1938, the plea to the coal miners to go back to work in the course of a justification of government seizure on May 2, 1943, and two speeches opening war loan drives in 1943 and 1944. But only a small portion of the total number has been accounted for. What of the rest?

The great bulk of the fireside chats, and virtually all of them in some measure, fall into what might be called the "report, review, explain" category. Every one of the first six, for example, extending through September 30, 1934, found the President carefully reviewing for his listeners the steps that the New Deal had taken to deal with the depression, the new legislation that had been passed, and the programs that had been set up. They frequently embodied the question: are you not better off than you were in 1932?

One can of course only speculate about motives and purposes in this area, but some inferences are reasonably clear. Only the most conscientious of the press media attempt to set the day-to-day news in context, and yet unless this is done events become a meaningless blur. Roosevelt was a master at setting events in context, using simple, direct language, and relating the policies of his administration to these events. Acceptance of policies and support for leadership, in a democracy, hinge on understanding. Thus by his reviews of events F.D.R. was not merely informing but fostering such acceptance and support.

Also, at the partisan political level, the President's strategy made sense. His reviews of action taken to combat the depression had the effect of etching indelibly in the public mind the fact that the New Deal and Franklin Roosevelt were responsible. So successful was he that two or three decades later, voters still associated the Democratic Party with social security, banking legislation, mortgage refinancing, farm relief, and the rest.[43] This was probably a necessary part of successful political leadership. In the early thirties the federal government, for the first time since the founding of the republic, undertook massive social and economic reforms in areas formerly left to the states or wholly untouched by government. In a very real sense the New Deal thus represented a revolution, which demanded a radical reorientation of public attitudes toward government and its proper sphere. Undoubtedly F.D.R.'s radio talks did much to facilitate this reorientation.

A final point relates more to the tone and atmosphere created by the chats than to their content: their morale-building aspect. The first inaugural, the banking crisis speech, the speech delivered September 3, 1939, at the outbreak of the war, and several during the first dark months after Pearl Harbor obviously were designed to reassure the populace and restore hope and confidence. Both Roosevelt's unmatched radio style and also the phrasing of his talks were ideally suited to this purpose. His calmness, the frankness yet simplicity of his explanations, his frequent use of "we"—*we* can do this together, I need *your* aid—devices like the request that his listeners have a world map ready to follow during his chat of February 23, 1942, all these and other subtle touches combined to produce an effect on his audience that transcended his actual words and ideas. They felt close to him and the problems he and they shared, they were reassured and given a psychological boost.

In summary, Roosevelt's use of radio, particularly in the fireside chat series, represented political leadership via the mass media in its most effective and subtle form. Rarely did he exhort, almost never did he plead; rather, he chatted. His was preeminently the "soft sell"—even when compared with the television speeches of President Eisenhower, who elaborately refused to emulate the so-called strong Presidents. Much credit for F.D.R.'s radio success must of course go to the man himself and his unique skills as a leader. And yet the times in which he led made their contribution.

It is far easier to win popular response in periods of crisis—domestic or wartime—than in periods of relative prosperity and complacency. His speeches in the transition period, from the plea for his Court plan through Pearl Harbor, show this. The tone is different and the impact diminished. He was more often forced on the defensive or seeking support against a recalcitrant Congress.

There is a parallel between the Coolidge-Hoover-Roosevelt cycle in the development of White House use of radio and the successive contributions of Truman, Eisenhower, and Kennedy to presidential telecasting. The latest electronic medium followed hard upon the heels of the earlier and would have come sooner but for the war. Hardly had F.D.R. perfected his use of radio when television had largely taken its place in the White House tool kit. In fact, a scant two and a half years after the death of Roosevelt Harry Truman was making the first presidential telecast from the White House. As with Coolidge and radio, so the Missourian began utilizing television for presidential purposes at just about the earliest practicable date. But he did so with hardly more flair or skill than Coolidge and Hoover brought to the air waves in their pioneering efforts. In both cases, awareness of the potential of the new medium and the will to use it were present from the outset, but the winning formula for its optimum use was far slower to develop.

Mr. Truman, when he was precipitously installed in the White House, had to labor under the burden (among many others) of an unflattering comparison with his predecessor's prowess as a speaker. He himself is quoted by a biographer:

> I appreciated very much your letter of the twentieth. It is the honest frankness of real friends that helps a man improve his delivery over the radio. I don't think there is anybody in the country who had as rotten a delivery as I did to begin with but thanks to good friends like you, who have been honestly helpful in their criticism, I think there has been some improvement.[44]

But poor delivery or not, the new President was catapulted into the role of radio and later television performer willy-nilly. Though anyone with a political background—and Truman was one of the more experienced politicians to sit in the White House—by definition has some familiarity with public speaking, the presidential and vice-presidential selection processes are no guarantee that all incumbents will be amply endowed. And certainly there is no guarantee that they will come equipped with the unique combination of skills and qualities of an F.D.R.

So rapidly did TV supplant radio that only the video portion of President Truman's experience with the electronic media need be dealt with at any length. Though he had been telecast before, his first broadcast from the White House, the first White House broadcast by any President using the cathode ray tube, occurred October 5, 1947.[45] The occasion was the launching of a food-saving campaign for relief abroad presided over by soap company executive Charles Luckman. The format was suggestive, oddly enough, of some of the efforts staged for President Eisenhower by Batten, Barton, Durstine, and Osborn some years later. It involved not a single set speech by the Chief Executive, but a series of brief talks by Luckman himself, Secretary of State George Marshall, Secretary of Agriculture Anderson, Averell Harriman, and the President.

Subsequent major presidential appearances on the air waves, though for some time still referred to as "radio speeches," were ordinarily carried on television as well. The next television broadcast by the President to elicit comment, however, and the first real landmark in White House telecasting, coincided with the outbreak of the Korean War in the summer of 1950. Jack Gould, the *New York Times* radio-television critic, commented:

> President Truman's appearance on television last night will be remembered. For the first time in a period of national emergency, the person at home not only heard the fateful call for sacrifices to preserve his freedom, but also saw the grave expressions of the President as he explained to the country what it would mean. In millions of living rooms . . . history was personalized last night.[46]

The staging of this presidential appearance typified the Truman period in office. As Gould goes on to note, the only "props" visible behind the President in the White House room used as studio were the flag and the seal. "The President spoke standing up before a lectern on which there were two small microphones." His head was bowed over his manuscript most of the time, but periodically he lifted his face and looked directly at his unseen audience.

Generally speaking, in other words, President Truman and his advisers did not make any special efforts to adapt to the peculiar requirements of television. The President continued to read his text at a lectern, much as he would have done had he only been broadcasting over the radio and been invisible to his audience. Presidents before Roosevelt behaved on radio much as they would have before a live audience; Truman approached television, quite understandably, in terms of radio.

This is not to say that there was no deliberate White House effort to exploit the new medium effectively. President Truman did add Leonard Reinsch to his roster of advisers as a radio expert in 1945 upon assuming office.[47] Reinsch came to the White House whenever the President was to go on the air, to superintend technical arrangements and go over speech texts in the light of the needs of radio. According to Merriman Smith, "Reinsch also served as Mr. Truman's radio coach and worked with the President on a wire recorder in advance of particularly important speeches to help improve the President's delivery."[48] Though sessions like this helped, the note of formality and the speed of delivery were never remedied. This role of adviser Reinsch apparently continued to fill when television began to make inroads as radio's competitor.

Other White House staff people, when asked their recollections of the advent of television, could not recall any particular conscious attention paid to it, or discussion of how it could be used to the President's greatest advantage.[49] The impression they give is that video was accepted more or less uncritically and unreflectively as an adjunct to radio without much concern about its special properties and problems. Nor do the files at the Truman Library contradict this impression. There is, for example, a reply from the Director of Special Events of the Columbia Broadcasting System, dated March 16, 1951, to an oral request from Press Secretary Joe Short for a memo on the problems faced by the networks when requested to carry a presidential broadcast.[50] Short wanted to know how the interests of the White House and the industry could be best served simultaneously on such occasions. Note that the conversation and resulting memo did not take place until nearly two and a half years after the initial presidential telecast in late 1947. F.D.R., by contrast, had been in correspondence with the radio networks during his first year of office.

There was also an apparently unsolicited letter from a New York advertising executive written July 14, 1949, following the one major radio-television speech which the President made that year.[51] It is addressed to presidential Secretary Matt Connelly. The author, after disclaiming any quarrel with the content of the speech, wrote, "from a professional standpoint I would like to offer to you a few suggestions which should improve the President's performance before the public." He goes on to make four points. A more interesting background would have contributed to viewer interest and the President might try speaking while seated at his desk. Second, a system of camera directions in the text was needed so Mr. Truman would know which camera would be on him when he looked up from his text at various points. Third, the dead seconds with the camera still on the President after he finished should be eliminated; and fourth, film clips or the like might have been interspersed in the talk to heighten the interest. He concluded: "The President deserves better television treatment next time."

This letter suggests the problems inherent in White House use of television, which were never solved adequately under Truman.[52] Recalling the comments of Cantril and Allport on radio, TV obviously restores some but not all of the features of the live audience situation. The viewer can now react to visual as well as auditory stimuli—and therefore must be given a broadcast of sufficient visual interest to keep his attention on the speaker and his words. Yet TV, like radio, involves no audience feedback to the speaker, and minimizes mutual stimulation within the audience itself. Little was done by the White House before 1953 to take these factors into account.

The most poignant evidence that President Truman had not developed an effective approach was the rash of letters, especially during 1948 and 1949, begging him to give fireside chats, take the people into his confidence, and fight for his programs, as Roosevelt had done.[53] He of course *had* appeared on radio (and television) but he lacked F.D.R.'s skill.

Comparisons between the subject matter of Truman broadcasts and those of Roosevelt are difficult to make. The latter had two major crises with which to deal, the depression and the Second World War. In both instances popular attention was almost wholly preoccupied with the current crisis and with the Chief Executive's leadership in dealing with it. Hence the President's problem of securing attention for his radio discussions in a sense solved itself. As Richard Neustadt pointed out, however, Truman faced a different situation because, "in most years since the Second World War, there has been no 'main' drama like recovery-with-Roosevelt."[54] Rather, many "shows" have run simultaneously. The Missourian, therefore, could not have broadcast a series of talks on essentially a single theme as Roosevelt did in his first two years on the evolving fight against the depression.

Truman's radio-TV appearances of necessity were more episodic and diverse in subject matter—save for those beginning in July, 1950, on the Korean War and related matters (e.g., the firing of General MacArthur). In the years before 1950, typical radio speeches dealt with the 1946 railroad strike, the veto of a price control bill, the veto of the Taft-Hartley Bill, meat shortage and European food needs, and an appeal for the purchase of savings bonds. The talk on behalf of the mutual security program then before Congress, and another on the steel strike, both in 1952, were typical subjects late in his term. In short, partly because of the period in which he was President, but also partly because of his more episodic and less reflective approach to the office, Truman used the electronic media in an emergency, "fire-brigade" fashion. The record suggests that where it is possible, the Roosevelt-type, longer-term strategy, relying on the cumulative impact of a series of talks, is more effective.

Dwight Eisenhower—or more properly, his advisers—worked hard and with no little imagination to find the key to the harnessing of TV for White House use. This effort was clearly foreshadowed by the 1952 campaign. As Stanley Kelley points out, that was the first quadrennial contest in which "television had an audience large enough to warrant giving it an important place in plans for the presidential campaign. By mid-October of 1952, advertising men calculated, there would be some 19,000,000 sets in use and some 58,000,000 viewers. . . ."[55] Furthermore, Ike with his broad infectious grin, his readily communicated sincerity, and his already astonishing popularity, was a natural for projection over the new medium.

A parallel between Roosevelt and Eisenhower is suggested by the comments of some observers. According to Merriman Smith, "Mr. Eisenhower will be long remembered as the chief executive who really broke the ice on television. He took the Roosevelt radio 'fireside chat' and converted it to the audio-visual field, where he projected himself in sound and sight into the living rooms . . . of America."[56] This somewhat overenthusiastic estimate, written during the latter part of the General's first term, might well have been modified a bit by 1960. George E. Allen, friend of Presidents Roosevelt, Truman, and Eisenhower, despite his worshipful attitude toward the latter, thinks that in the 1952 and 1956 campaigns (and inferentially between them as well), Ike had not proved himself the master of TV that Roosevelt had of radio.[57]

There is no question, though, that the Eisenhower administration made a considerably higher mark than Truman for ingenuity if not all-round success. Two members of Ike's entourage were chiefly responsible for this, Press Secretary Hagerty and special assistant and adviser Robert Montgomery. Jim had announced to the reporters as early as late January 1953, "we are in a day of a new medium—television. I would like to work out with television representatives and with you gentlemen a system whereby the President could give talks to the people of the country—possibly press conferences—on television. What we are presently thinking about is something like that about once a month. . . ."[58]

Hagerty also showed his awareness of the potency of the new medium, and the ways it might be exploited, at an early Cabinet meeting. According to *Time,* he talked at length on public relations techniques with the fledgling Secretaries, urging among other

TV cameras shown in action as Eisenhower reports to the nation on the record of Congress, August 23, 1954. *Wide World Photos.*

things that they sell their accomplishments as often as possible by getting on TV panel shows, thus securing valuable free time.[59] This is strongly reminiscent of the hyperactivity of high New Dealers in the supporting use of radio. Merriman Smith, commenting on Hagerty's shrewd over-all appraisal of the potential of video, insists that he was

> determined that as F.D.R. pioneered and profited by the use of radio as a White House instrument, Mr. Eisenhower will take the fullest possible advantage of television to go directly to the people on major topics without having to deal with them through what he regards as middlemen—the reporters, the columnists, the editorial writers, and the commentators.[60]

This sounds strange coming from a former newspaperman working for a Republican President with remarkably favorable press coverage, but again recalls Roosevelt's conception of the value of radio.

By the time the General was well into his second term, his press secretary had fostered the development of an elaborate system to regularize dealings between the White House and the television industry. As Jack Gould of the *New York Times* put it: "A variety of factors—technical problems, TV's economics and perhaps inertia—have led to a situation where James C. Hagerty, White House press secretary, wields great influence in whether the President is seen or not."[61] An informal committee was established in Washington representing the three television networks, with which Hagerty communicated when there was an address in the offing. In so doing he indicated his evaluation of the importance of the speech by either making a formal request for time or not doing so. In effect, then, it was Jim and not the networks that decided the newsworthiness of a given presidential statement. "The Administration can turn television on or off as it deems expedient."[62] This, in Gould's view, conferred rather too much power on a presidential aide.

The other person who shared responsibility for the television policies of the Eisenhower administration was actor-producer Montgomery. Though his addition to the roster of White House advisers followed the Reinsch precedent set by President Truman, his role was much more specifically related to television as a medium, and acquired much greater importance.[63] Montgomery represented a new departure in White House staffing. There was also the quasi-staff role played from time to time by the advertising firm of Batten, Barton, Durstine, and Osborn, who wrote and produced some of the more elaborate video vehicles for screening the President. At last the White House had recognized that so technically complex a medium as this required expert assistance for its effective use.

But this did not, apparently, force itself upon the attention of the President's entourage immediately. "It all began, according to Hagerty, shortly after the first White House telecast. 'We suddenly realized that nobody on the press staff knew much about telecasting. . . .' "[64] Thereupon, lest the confusion of staging that first broadcast be repeated, and after talking it over with the President, Hagerty called Montgomery, who quickly agreed to come to Washington and lend his services. When he arrived he began immediately to develop a routine for handling future appearances which would not only deal with the multiple technical problems of camera angle and location, lighting, and so on, but also help present the President in as relaxed and therefore as effective a manner as possible.

Under Montgomery's supervision, much attention was given to the staging of telecasts. President Truman's reading from a text at a lectern, left much to be desired. Urgent attention had to be given to the visual parts of the total performance. This was particularly important with Eisenhower, whose supreme asset was his warmth and sincerity—qualities upon which television placed particular emphasis.

During the campaign of 1952 Ike had been persuaded to experiment with a so-called teleprompter device which projected the speech text before the speaker a sentence at a time so that he could appear to be talking informally without a prepared text. On at least one occasion, however, the gadget went haywire while the General was in the midst of his talk, to his unspeakable annoyance. Montgomery managed to remove some of the President's hostility to the device, but cue cards containing the gist of what he wanted to say appealed to him more. Eventually Montgomery eliminated both these expedients and substituted brief notes which the President could have before him on his desk and glance at when necessary. Various other devices were tried from time to time to get away from the appearance of reading a prepared speech. According to one observer, some texts were prepared so that "Where the President was to take off his glasses to emphasize the spontaneity of what he was saying, that portion of his script was printed in outsize type he could read without his spectacles."[65]

Not only were efforts made to contrive spontaneity, but also to avoid delivery from a lectern or seated in one position behind a desk with the attendant visual monotony. A talk given in April 1954 was planned so that the President would be seen lounging against the front of his desk—rather than seated behind it—with arms casually folded as he talked.[66] This called for notes on cue cards off camera, and allowed more freedom for the use of gestures and for movement and changes of position.

Examination of a few of the more elaborately staged White

House telecasts will suggest further Eisenhower innovations. Most of these were concentrated in the first term and before the President's serious illnesses. Less effort was lavished on later TV formats, perhaps to conserve Ike's strength. Also, once the election of 1956 was safely won, since he could under no circumstances run for a third term, the incentive to maintain the former pace diminished. Three video productions might be examined: the "round table" discussion screened June 3, 1953, the televised Cabinet session of October 25, 1954, and the report to the President and the nation by Secretary of State Dulles on the evening of May 17, 1955.

Richard Neustadt says Eisenhower's first "fireside chat" to the public, broadcast May 19, 1953, over radio only (so he could concentrate on reading his speech, according to *Time*),[67] was judged as "fairly ineffectual" in Washington. Jim Hagerty would not comment afterward on rumors of an adverse mail reaction to it.[68] This initial experience may have prompted the radically different experiment on June 3. The round table was of course geared specifically to television and involved a discussion by the President of major current policies with Secretary of Health, Education and Welfare Hobby, Secretary of the Treasury Humphrey, Attorney General Brownell, and Secretary of Agriculture Benson. The *New York Times* the next day hailed it as "the first time a President of the United States discussed affairs of state with some of his principal advisors in a television program."

The program was produced by an official of the Columbia Broadcasting System, as it was C.B.S.'s turn to carry the telecast on behalf of the rest of the industry. The *Times* again noted that "He had the assistance of a crew from the New York advertising agency of Batten, Barton, Durstine and Osborn, which had helped the President in his political campaign."[69] The latter supervised the careful staging and rehearsing involved. The President sat at a desk in the corner of the room with Brownell on his right and the other three participants in comfortable leather chairs on his left. Another *Times* writer commented that it constituted the "newest television panel show with a homey, chatty approach to some of the Government's most complex problems."[70] The object of the show was to achieve spontaneity and informality—by careful planning and rehearsals. There was some adverse comment, though Goodman Ace, writing in the *Saturday Review*, felt that B.B.D. & O. had done a slick job and produced a show which "clipped along with pace and movement."[71] The President himself was fairly pleased with the results, though annoyed at the coverage given to the advance preparations and rehearsals, from which, he felt, the press should have politely averted its gaze.[72]

The October 25, 1954, televised Cabinet meeting came near the climax of the midterm election campaign of that year. Among other things this program posed the incidental problem of when a presidential TV appearance is political and when it is not. The idea for the show was apparently Hagerty's, but the President did not give the go-ahead until a little over eight hours in advance.[73] (Actually there is some confusion in the reports about whether the initiative came from the White House or from C.B.S.—in response perhaps to a tip.)[74] In any event, the Democrats were reluctant to accept the theory that it was a nonpolitical presidential appearance as claimed by the Republicans.

The basic fare for the half hour was a report by Secretary Dulles on some recently concluded European negotiations from which he had just that day returned. The program began with a shot of the empty Cabinet room. Then the members filed in and took their accustomed places, whereupon, following a brief introduction by the President, the report on foreign affairs began. "Mr. Dulles' manner of presentation was an 'intimate' one and frequently he fiddled with his pencil as he talked from twelve pages of notes." Five times he was interrupted for questions—by prearrangement, in order to provide both visual and aural variety—as television critic Jack Gould noted. Secretary Benson, by the way, missed his cue to interject a question and the Secretary of State, after a pause, raised the point himself, thereby allowing the show to go on as planned.

This production, like the earlier one, posed a dilemma. Set speeches fall far short of maximum visual as well as auditory impact. Yet these efforts to devise formats that would avoid the set speech left critics still unimpressed. Gould wound up his account of this 1954 program with the comment that "Such television is not good television nor, in the last analysis, sound government." It was not good television for a variety of reasons. It is difficult if not impossible for nonprofessionals to appear genuinely informal and relaxed on the screen. It is also difficult for anyone to be on a show in which one central actor is performing most of the time, while the rest must do little but appear to be paying rapt attention. And above all, it is impossible to pretend that the audience is watching genuine governmental deliberation without either talking over the heads of many viewers or putting words into the mouths of Cabinet officers that sound banal and simple-minded. This October broadcast turned into a caricature of a Cabinet session rather than a faithful depiction of one.

The last of the three programs mentioned, though rather different, was hardly more successful. Again Secretary Dulles had just returned from one of his many excursions abroad, and again the telecast was ostensibly his report to the President and the public. This time, however, it was decided that only he and the Chief Executive would go on. Accordingly, Mr. Eisenhower sat at his desk and the Secretary sat nearby. Most of the talking was done, naturally, by the latter, with the President supplying only introductory comments, an occasional indication of assent and attention by word or gesture, a few sentences of interjected commentary, and concluding words. This time it was the President who had little to do but act as audience. The problem was more serious here, however, because the viewers had two foci of attention: the Secretary, whom they were supposed to watch, and the President, who always commands major attention whenever he appears, even while serving as a glorified stage prop.[75]

It should be emphasized that these examples were only typical of the more ingenious innovations attempted, and not of the general run of Eisenhower's appearances. Far oftener he appeared on the screen alone, as had Truman—though with a good deal more experimentation in setting and mode of delivery than had been undertaken before. For all the efforts of Robert Montgomery, B.B.D. & O., Hagerty, and the rest, it must be said that the kind of winning formula which F.D.R. developed in his use of radio was not found by Ike for television.

President Eisenhower and Secretary of State John Foster Dulles in Eisenhower's White House office during their joint TV-radio broadcast, December 24, 1957, on a recent N.A.T.O. conference. *Wide World Photos.*

As to the content of his appearances before the viewing public, in general Eisenhower fell somewhere between the practice of his immediate predecessor and that followed by Roosevelt in his fireside chats. Though he dealt frequently with momentary crises, and at times appealed for support, he also on occasion reviewed past policy for his listeners and attempted to set current developments in broad context. Truman, on the other hand, rarely canvassed a policy trend, and almost never resorted to the airwaves except when he had some immediate reason.

Eisenhower's first "round table" discussed above was of the policy review type, as was a summary of the just concluded Congressional session on August 23, 1954, and a few other similar broadcasts. The decision to allow filming of press conferences for later screening is relevant here also.[76] Since the infrequent presidential press conference tends to range over the whole spectrum of current government policy and to elicit general rather than specific answers to questions, for the TV audience it compared closely with Roosevelt's reviews of the battle against depression or wartime progress reports. It gave the public a chance to watch the President explaining informally the general policies of his administration and hence, presumably, helped to cultivate acceptance for them.

A final important dimension of the use of television by the administration emerges in the following comment:

> Eisenhower's television style, assiduously cultivated by professionals, had become technically perfect. Television, in fact, provided party managers with the perfect medium for maintaining the Eisenhower image, for what mattered was not the intellectual content of his speeches, but the sincerity and warmth which he communicates to the public.[77]

As with the President's press conference style, which was appropriate for a mass audience (however much it annoyed intellectuals and reporters), so with TV, what mattered was not so much what Ike said as the image he projected when he said it. The public saw him not in partisan terms, but as a kind of nonpartisan father figure. Hence there was an even greater tendency for audiences to discount, perhaps unconsciously, the specifics of Eisenhower speeches, and drink in the reassurance and warmth he radiated. All of his uses of television undoubtedly made cumulative contributions along this line.

The November 14, 1959, issue of *TV Guide* carried an article by one John F. Kennedy entitled "A Force That Has Changed the Political Scene," in which he commented with considerable insight on media developments during the Eisenhower period. In particular the then Senator warned about the impact television could have on the candidate's "image." The actual television debut of President Kennedy as a national figure preceded his accession to office. In fact, the television debates during the campaign probably did as much as anything else to make him a national personality with sufficient appeal to offset the head start enjoyed by an opponent who had been Vice President for eight years.[78] Thus video had already played a major role in the Kennedy administration even before it began.

Television in the 1952 campaign suggests comparison with radio in 1924 in at least one respect. TV then, like radio earlier, was still a new and exciting toy, and campaign programs commanded almost as much attention as top cowboy and comedy shows. But even by 1956 this tolerance for political preemption of regular programs had waned considerably. It was therefore fortunate indeed for all concerned, save possibly Mr. Nixon, that the legal way was cleared for the debates in 1960.[79] They gave a powerful shot in the arm to political television, and opened new vistas for between-election presidential telecasting.

The Kennedy administration's use of television became a close competitor in skill and virtuosity with F.D.R.'s use of radio. In the brief three years beginning in January, 1961, a formula (perhaps *the* formula) for optimum White House exploitation of the new medium was developed. The key feature of this formula was the variety of techniques and formats devised. For Roosevelt, given the limitations of radio, the fireside chat alone could represent optimum effectiveness. Video, however, seemed to demand a series of complementary program patterns, paralleling in a sense the need for visual variety in the staging of a single telecast.

Any scheme for presidential use of television must begin with the orthodox formal speech, and Kennedy's approach, for all its ingenuity, was no exception. On nine occasions he went before the cameras to give a prepared address on a major topic. As in the past, the occasions were carefully chosen with an eye to avoiding overexposure—to which the new President, like Roosevelt before him, was keenly sensitive. Salinger, when questioned on the frequency of Kennedy TV speeches, immediately noted that his boss had gone on the air approximately as often as F.D.R. had with his radio chats.[80] (Roosevelt averaged two a year; Kennedy about three.) Alan Otten noted the same tactical consideration when he wrote that "being held to a minimum is the 'fireside chat' type of public appeal, . . . and other nationwide TV appearances, on the theory that the citizen quickly tires of stilted political speechmaking."[81]

The staging of most of these nine Kennedy speeches matched the simplicity of the Truman era rather than the Madison Avenue flamboyance of some of the Eisenhower efforts. Perhaps the new President, after campaigning against the B.B.D. & O. features of Ike's tenure, was sensitive to a potential charge that he had forgotten his earlier strictures. Clearly the Kennedy people were hardheaded and knowledgeable about the media and their use. A TV consultant, William P. Wilson of New York, is said to have been brought down to help stage the first televised press conference.[82] Also, the *New York Times* reported in October, 1961, that "President Kennedy would receive advice on some of his future telecasts from Fred Coe, New York Television producer . . . [and] long-time friend and admirer of the President."[83] This administration obviously recognized that such staff advice had become essential.

In most of his appearances before the camera, Mr. Kennedy was by himself on the screen and spoke either from his desk or from a stand-up lectern. In a telecast on August 13, 1962, reporting on the state of the national economy, he began seated at his desk, where he delivered a few sentences. He then moved to an adjacent lectern next to which stood a board with several graphs showing economic trends. As he talked, the President used a pointer to indicate features of the graphs while the camera showed a closeup of that part of the chart. Thus some visual interest was added to the presentation of otherwise rather unexciting material. His last television talk, an appeal for his tax bill, was more typical of those that had gone before. The camera first showed him, and continued to depict him throughout, from the chest up, against a plain dark background. He read or spoke from papers before him, with the focus of his eyes divided about half and half between his notes or text and the audience. Though he cited some family income and tax reduction figures, no attempt had been made to provide charts or other visual aids. The talk only lasted twenty minutes, however, instead of the normal half hour for major presidential broadcasts. Thus here, and on earlier occasions, the White House apparently sought to compensate somewhat for visual monotony by minimizing length.

As to content, all of the nine Kennedy TV talks under discussion dealt with a single subject or policy area, and most of them related to some immediate issue. First came a report on his return from Europe, then the Berlin crisis. In 1962 he dealt with nuclear tests and disarmament, the state of the national economy, and the crises over integration in Mississippi and Soviet missiles in Cuba. In 1963 speeches were prompted by integration, this time in Alabama, the successful negotiation of a test ban treaty, and tax legislation. Clearly J.F.K. followed the Truman "fire brigade" use of the set TV speech rather than the broad policy review effort which Roosevelt favored. Perhaps this concentration on single issue and crisis appearances reflected an awareness that other program formats were available for broader, more leisurely policy discussion.

Several program types came under this latter heading. First there were the live televised press conferences with extensive use of set opening statements. These half hours invariably enabled the President to range widely over the governmental waterfront.[84] Then there were informal interviews which the Chief Executive granted on occasion. For example, in 1962, there was one on April 22 with Eleanor Roosevelt for use on an educational television channel; and another with William Lawrence on October 15 for an ABC network program called "Politics—'62."

The outstanding television effort of the whole Kennedy period in office and the appearance which the President himself felt was his most successful, was the so-called "Rocking Chair" interview of December 17, 1962. All three television networks had teamed up to make available an hour of prime time for a review by the Chief Executive of his first two years. The audience saw him sitting in his office in the famous rocking chair with three experienced members of the Washington press corps in comfortable chairs in a semicircle near him. The President, prompted more or less by questions from the reporters, discussed his accomplishments and problems with considerable candor. He was relaxed and articulate, though without any apparent notes or obvious prearrangement of topics and questions. At his press conferences, Max Ascoli noted, there was a "contrived, almost electronic quality" to his performance. But at this session, "the viewer sensed in him the human being, the person . . . the quiet smile sometimes dimly but gently lighting up his features—all this contributed to inspire a sense of confidence and respect."[85]

The general reaction to the program was wholly and even enthusiastically favorable. Clearly, as Ascoli's comments indicate, this informal setting projected the human qualities of the man in a highly effective way. As was so obvious with Eisenhower, the aura surrounding a presidential appearance and the general impression he creates are at least as important as the ideas expressed. But this interview was also an almost unmatched setting for a wide-ranging review of policy, with all the visual interest and attention-holding quality of an informal conversation. In this sense it bade fair to be the perfect television counterpart to the Roosevelt radio chat. But Kennedy had time to hold only one. A second had been planned for December 17, 1963, the anniversary of the first.[86]

The foregoing does not exhaust the ingenuity of Kennedy's use of video. In several cases the White House was able to capitalize on the desires of the media for attractive program material and gain valuable additional viewing time for the President. For example, there were TV documentaries showing the President at work. In preparation for these the inquiring camera had been allowed admission to the innermost precincts of the White House. One, widely advertised and screened from 7:30 to 8:30 on a Monday evening, was entitled "Crisis: Behind a Presidential Commitment." It dealt with integration at the University of Alabama and showed not only the President's role, but the whole context of the crisis: the minute by minute activity of the Attorney General, the Governor of Alabama, and events on the campus. Scandalized TV critic Jack Gould wrote that "the private deliberations of the Executive Branch of Government [were] turned into a melodramatic peep show," suggesting the lengths to which the presidency had been thrown open to public view to please the networks.[87] Yet the publicity and image building impact of shows like this would be hard to deny.

The miracle of electronic communication, during the Kennedy years, not only bade fair to make the President omnipresent at home, but to bring his image to his "constituents" abroad as well. His press conference of July 23, 1962, was carried live (in part) to Europe for the first time, via the pioneer communicational satellite, Telstar. Then the Chief Executive's trip to Europe in June, 1963, according to the *Times*, was to be "covered by the three television networks with at least 22 special reports varying from 15 minutes to an hour." These were to be relayed, so the account goes, back to the United States by Telstar II.[88]

The importance which the Kennedy White House attached to television as a presidential medium, and a rough measure of its effectiveness in bringing the President's words to the public, both emerge in an opinion survey done by the Young and Rubicam Instant Data Service at the behest of Press Secretary Salinger. Two samples of eighty to ninety respondents were telephoned on June 14 and 15, 1962, to elicit reactions to the Kennedy press conferences generally, and to the one held June 14 in particular. Overwhelming percentages liked the conferences and approved the President's conduct of them. About 90 per cent claimed to have seen or heard at least part of a press meeting on television or radio, and roughly a third had seen some part of the June 14 conference, 20 per cent in excerpt on a news roundup, and the rest in the original broadcast. This last tallies with rating service estimates that six million out of fifty million sets are normally tuned in for conference broadcasts.

Little more need be said to confirm the proposition that as Franklin Roosevelt had, in a sense, been the first radio President, John Kennedy was, par excellence, the first television President. Far more than his predecessors, he had explored and exploited with skill and imagination the expanding range of possibilities this new medium has to offer to the incumbent in the White House. But his response to it and its potential was more profound than this. Again like F.D.R. before him with radio, he grasped the ultimate significance of television for himself and for the presidency: the channel it offered for direct, unmediated, instantaneous, and massive access to the public. No amount of skill in dealing with the newspaper press could overcome, in the long run, the fact that he was a Democratic President elected over the opposition of 84 per cent of the dailies of the nation. With television, however, this handicap could be more than neutralized.[89]

White House speech writing has been reserved for this chapter because of its intimate relationship to the use of the electronic media. Little more need be said by way of general justification for the presidential ghost writer. The growth of the office had eliminated by the 1920s any real possibility that the public utterances of the President could be prepared by his own hand save in rare instances. The contemporary Chief Executive must be judged not in terms of what he writes himself, but of how well he directs and synthesizes the efforts of his staff, and infuses them with a sense and appearance of common purpose, which is clearly recognizable as *his* purpose.

So well documented have been the speech-writing practices F.D.R. followed, in contrast to administrations before or since, that major attention must be devoted to his period in office. It is well known that Judge Samuel I. Rosenman, whose volume *Working with Roosevelt*[90] is the best source on the subject, was perhaps the foremost among the large group involved from time to time. Playwright Robert Sherwood, Raymond Moley, Stanley High, Tommy Corcoran, Charles Michelson, to name but a few, were also prominent in this role, and several have left their own accounts.[91]

The first question is why so many literary craftsmen came and went. The answer goes to the heart of the whole relationship between F.D.R. and his staff. Those writers who were most skillful at devising prose which captured the flavor of the President's own writing and speaking style, and who did not allow their own egos, ideas, or ambitions to intrude into the relationship, tended to stay on. Those, like Moley, whose beliefs began to diverge from the President's, or who were least successful in submerging their own personalities, tended to be dropped.[92] John Gunther's characterization of Rosenman suggests the formula for long-term success: "more than anybody, [he] had the knack of expressing FDR's own thought in just the words he himself would have chosen."[93]

Critics of the President often fixed upon his apparently ruthless and petulant dismissal of faithful aides as evidence of his autocratic temperament or worse. An ingredient of ruthlessness may have been involved—though it is also true that the President had a strong personal disinclination to confront such individuals at the moment of parting and usually contrived to ease them out of the picture more subtly. The point seems to be, however, that any political leader must use staff in much the way a craftsman uses tools. So long as they do the job intended they will be retained and used, but when they are no longer appropriate to the task in hand they will be put aside. Only thus, in the case of ghost writers, can the line between the words and ideas of the Chief Executive himself and those crafted for him be rendered least visible and obvious. And the more successfully this is accomplished, the less room there is for the criticism that alien words are being put into his mouth.

In the 1936 volume of his *Public Papers* F.D.R. comments at some length on the process of speech preparation. Usually he first received drafts and suggestions from others when an address was contemplated. These he went over, together with material from speech files on appropriate subjects. Then, laying all this aside, he would "dictate my own draft, usually to Miss Tully. Naturally, the final speech will contain some of the thoughts and even some of the sentences which appeared in some of the drafts or suggestions submitted." He goes on to note the human tendency for incidental contributors of material to give the impression that they virtually wrote the speech. "Such assertions, however, are not accurate. On some of my speeches I have prepared as many as five or six successive drafts myself after reading drafts and suggestions submitted by other people. . . ."[94] Emil Ludwig has given a similar description of how it was done. "He writes his speeches himself; and it appears that he asks for less collaboration in them than any other state spokesman of our time, Mussolini excepted."[95]

Both these descriptions diverge considerably from the detailed accounts in Rosenman, Sherwood, and other sources of unimpeachable accuracy. Why? Was F.D.R. consciously inaccurate? One suspects not. Biographers and contemporaries have often testified to the kind of "poetic license" he apparently took unconsciously in describing past events so that they came closer to the way he wanted to recall them than to the stark truth. Here he is describing speech writing as he liked to think it took place—and had convinced himself it did take place. So close and intimate had the collaboration with the speech writers become, so completely had they immersed themselves in his style and become extensions of his personality, that he *could* depict the total process as largely his own doing with but incidental assistance. This probably represents the ultimate in the successful employment of ghost writers.

Through the eyes of someone like Rosenman or Sherwood, one finds that in fact, though the President almost always outlined in detail what he wanted to say and then dictated a draft or some pages toward a draft, the successive versions were put together by his collaborators.[96] These would then be gone over by him, words changed, ideas deleted, insertions for the next draft dictated, and so on. Yet in the end the final reading copy would be virtually as much the creation of the President himself, would have as much of his own thinking and effort mixed into it, as would have been the case had the approach he outlined in fact been followed. His genius lay not in any extraordinary facility at composition, but in his ability to draw others into intimate and fruitful collaboration, plus his ability to take their work and by careful editing and refinement produce prose that was unquestionably his own and of a piece stylistically with his other major speeches. The results may not have been in the classic tradition of oratory,[97] but as vehicles for political leadership via the air waves they have yet to be equaled.

Two or three further questions present themselves. What impact on policy did these speech writers have? The answer seems to be that though they were hardly inhibited in expressing their ideas, and even slipping them into the draft on their own initiative, such suggestions were not accepted unless F.D.R. was himself convinced they were right. Rosenman discussed this point at some length. He noted that though no speech writer could ever have made Roosevelt compromise on his basic convictions, aides who posed as mere yes men would have been useless. He went on:

> We learned when was the best time to battle with him. Often we would give way and strategically retreat in draft three, only to return again in draft six with greater success. Or we might be successful in draft five, and the President, after a night's reflection, might change it again in draft seven. Of course there are no traces in the finished speech of this kind of development.[98]

When all was said and done, Rosenman makes clear, "the President, after debate pro and con, made up his mind that he would say a certain thing in a certain way. Then, it generally became useless to keep arguing for a change."

Sherwood describes an episode in which the writers slipped a phrase declaring an unlimited state of national emergency into the speech to be delivered May 27, 1941. This idea symbolized the deep feelings of many around the President who were distressed about the hesitancy he was showing. F.D.R. read aloud the draft in which this had been inserted unbeknown to him, and upon encountering it asked, with an expression of artless innocence: "Hasn't somebody been taking some liberties?"[99] The anticipated fireworks did not materialize, however, and the phrase stayed in the speech. Here, Roosevelt's collaborators did provide that little extra impetus needed to bring him to a conclusion he had been hesitating to reach.

What, precisely, were the President and his associates trying to achieve in the exhausting process of writing, editing, and rewriting through which they put every major radio speech? The production of ordinary expository prose need not be so painstaking and time-consuming an ordeal. Laura Crowell, in her careful analysis of the various drafts through which the "Four Freedoms" speech—actually the annual address to Congress delivered January 6, 1941—passed, attempted to decide why particular changes were made and what was the general drift of revision. She found that the effort at continual improvement and refinement took three principal directions:

> 1. To establish and maintain the precise tone desired for the address.

2. To develop the universal aspect of events. Conditions and qualifications were gradually eliminated so that statements became more and more categorical; declarations that might carry unintended slights were eliminated, and lists that might hurt by omission were made inclusive. Thus, the speech was refined to set forth the "eternal simplicities" so strongly believed in by Roosevelt.

3. To build the strongest verbal and syntactical instrument possible for expression of these ideas and attitudes.[100]

A few of the specific points she noted include: the early elimination of an elaborate statistical presentation and substitution eventually of only two summary sentences; the use of the word "our" more than sixty times and "we" more than fifty times to increase the affective power of the speech; the deletion of a qualification on the historic friendliness of the British fleet in the interest of rhetorical effect though at the expense of historical accuracy; and the rewording of a direct quotation from Benjamin Franklin to make it more appropriate, together with a failure to credit its original author.

The effort in Roosevelt's speech preparation, in other words, was usually toward greater simplicity and directness, and the achievement of language best fitted to the kind of homey exposition which the President liked. He was fond of saying that the language must be simple enough to go over with Moses Smith, a colorful Hyde Park character. Frances Perkins recalls that she supplied material containing the sentence, "We are trying to construct a more inclusive society," regarding social security, which found its way into the resulting speech as: "We are going to make a country in which no one is left out."[101] He often resorted to specific examples to get across ideas that would have sounded far more complex presented in the abstract. For instance, instead of discussing public power generation in terms of kilowatt hours and other technical language, he would note how much it cost a housewife to use particular appliances in one locality versus another. The garden hose analogy for lend lease has already been referred to. He demanded the oversimplification of ideas if he felt it was necessary to put them across.

A final question which might be raised but hardly disposed of has to do with the accusation of demagogy. Did Roosevelt's use of oversimplification, his resort to rhetorical tricks on occasion, his use of emotional appeals, and the like, make him a demagogue? In the first place, it seems apparent that the genuine demagogue does not contrive his efforts in so painstaking a manner as did Roosevelt. Genuine rabble-rousing is probably a mixture of calculation plus the emotional atmosphere, even frenzy, of the moment of delivery. The most that can be said of Roosevelt was that he was an actor of considerable skill, who prepared his scripts with studied care. Donald Richberg, not one to gloss over F.D.R.'s defects, summed up the matter rather well:

> There were many who regarded FDR not so much as a conscious demagogue, as a man who appealed, perhaps unconsciously, to the emotions rather than to the intelligence of the public. It should have been evident, however, in many speeches, that he made great effort to appeal to the intelligence of the ordinary man. . . . On the other hand, there were many times when, as a politician, he was well aware that only an emotional appeal would be effective. . . . In my judgment FDR's emotional convictions often led him into obvious demagogueries. But I think in most instances where he was guilty of purely emotional and unfair appeal (which is the essence of demagogism), he did it deliberately. When he was careless with his facts, it was because of an inherent impatience with such exactness of statement and careful shading of expression as make the speeches of so many learned professors both tiresome and ineffective in swaying public opinion.[102]

From the Roosevelt administration on it has been a normal expectation that White House occupants would use literary assistants. The existence of radio and television may account in part for the present-day ready acceptance of what was once viewed as faintly reprehensible. Performers on these media, whether commercial or political, invariably read words that others have written for them. How could it be otherwise? Thus a public which has become habituated to taking ghost writing for granted would hardly insist on the President of the United States being an exception. The author of a 1949 summary of the state of this occult art makes the further point: "Probably the eagerness of the press for advance copies of a public man's remarks and the insistence of the radio on speeches not a bit longer or shorter than the allotted time were responsible for its growth."[103]

In any event, there was little likelihood that Harry Truman would be criticized for following the Roosevelt speechwriting precedent, as he of course did. His practices, however, appear to have contrasted sharply with his predecessor's.[104] The forthright and unpretentious Missourian, like Eisenhower later, had few oratorical talents, nor, specifically, any backlog of experience at literary craftsmanship either alone or in collaboration.[105] Both obviously had made many speeches in their public lives, but neither had been in a position that called for more than a run-of-the-mill effort.

Furthermore, neither had the temperament or personality which made Roosevelt the adroit and skillful speaker—and speech craftsman—that he was, or had a well developed style of his own. They had only a preference for straightforward exposition, and an aversion to the use of rhetorical tricks or melodramatic flourishes. This lack of a personal style, or interest in the finer points of successful oratory, had several consequences. It seems to have meant, for instance, that in the process of collaborative composition more attention was given to the content of what was to be said than to the best way of saying it.

In general it seems to be true that President Truman was somewhat less involved in the drafting process than Roosevelt had been. When a speech text was nearing final form, a meeting would usually be called to go over it for last-minute changes. John Hersey describes one such session at which no less than ten people, aside from Mr. Truman himself, were present. At least seven of these had been involved in the writing. (Rarely did more than two or three work over the actual draft of a Roosevelt talk.) It seems obvious, as criticism of these meetings also suggests, that the larger and more heterogeneous the group, the greater the difficulty of reaching a consensus, and the greater the likelihood that watered-down compromise language would result. This is not to say, of course, that the President took a merely passive part in such deliberation—far from it. But trying to consult so many people inevitably proves cumbersome.

These mass drafting efforts also reflect indirectly the absence of a strong sense of style on the part of the President. F.D.R. used only two or three individuals—at any one time—who understood his style and were adept at phrasing things as the President himself would do it. In Truman's case, literary aides were probably not chosen on so subtle a basis, and there would naturally be a tendency to widen the circle and thus tap varied resources.[106]

The scanty and somewhat contradictory evidence would seem to suggest that General Eisenhower's practice in speech preparation fell somewhere between that of his two immediate predecessors.[107] It also seems to have varied more from speech to speech and from period to period. In general, he apparently preferred to work with one writer at a time, rather than a team of two or three, as with F.D.R., or a large committee of the Truman sort. This probably, on balance, meant more of his own involvement than with Truman, but less than with Roosevelt.

The direct participation of any President in speech writing will of course vary enormously with the importance of the occasion and the topic. With the rising volume of White House output, this doubtless became even more true under Eisenhower. Thus it is quite possible to reconcile the views of commentators like Sherman Adams, who claimed that Ike would often accept someone else's text and edit it, but make little or no prior contribution himself, and those who insist that he labored long and hard over important speeches.[108] Emmet Hughes, for example, in an interview, tended to minimize the President's own role in drafting speech material, though insisting, as all Ike's former aides do, that he did a good deal of editing. In writing of his experience, however, Bryce Harlow insisted that the President *did* hash over the content of an important speech before writing had begun and would frequently dictate long memoranda on material he wanted included.[109]

The variations in the Eisenhower modus operandi probably stem in part from the President's lack of interest in the fine points of rhetoric—which does not contradict the frequent assertions that he could be a meticulous and demanding editor. As Hughes has written, "his greatest aversion was the calculatedly rhetorical device. This meant more than a healthy scorn for the contrived and effortful. It extended to a distrust of eloquence, of resonance, sometimes even of simple effectiveness of expression."[110] Ike, as President, tended to be bluff, straightforward, and self-deprecating, where Roosevelt was artful and at times devious. In like manner, the General had little or nothing by way of a developed oratorical style, while F.D.R. did. This could hardly help meaning that more of the ghost's own style would remain in a finished Eisenhower speech. As speech writers came and went, there would be—and apparently was—a perceptible change in style and tone.

What does the record of the Kennedy administration show in this area? J.F.K. came into office wearing the laurels of a Pulitzer prize winner, as an ardent admirer of Franklin Roosevelt and his eloquence, and determined to exploit fully the power of persuasion inherent in the presidency and the mass media. The speechwriting system he used appeared to differ from that of any of the foregoing Presidents. His reliance was almost exclusively on one key aide, Theodore Sorensen, drawing on a relationship which developed early in his senatorial career.[111] In this role Sorensen seemingly became a kind of combined Rosenman and Sherwood, writ large. So completely had the Kennedy and Sorensen ideas and styles become merged (observers have raised the question of who influenced whom the most) that for practical purposes, and at least for speechwriting purposes, they were virtually one person.

Sorensen was capable, it is said, of producing a complete Kennedy-style speech on very short notice indeed, which would require little editing before delivery. The most impressive evidence of this merger of styles and personalities came during the campaign when the candidate's voice gave out and his chief literary aide had to substitute for him. "Reading from papers in his hand, he gave a typical Kennedy campaign speech, including Kennedy-style jokes and some of Kennedy's favorite quotations. Actually, reporters learned later, the papers were blank. The speech came directly from a mind so saturated with Kennedy's thoughts and approach that it could speak perfect Kennedy."[112] On the other hand, a summary evaluation of speech writing in the Kennedy administration runs to the effect that: "Obviously, many of the Kennedy words are written by Mr. Sorensen (one good source estimates as many as 60 per cent of those committed to paper). But the evidence still is that the President's best efforts are more nearly his own than are those of most public figures."[113]

As the administration progressed, the President developed his own distinctive means of getting a message across—exploitation of his skill as an extemporaneous speaker. He spoke without text not only to live audiences, but also on television as well, when circumstances permitted (for example, at a Madison Square Garden rally for medical care). As Tom Wicker of the *New York Times* put it, in reference particularly to these off-the-cuff talks: "The President probably has no peer in the simple art of political exhortation. Whether he is talking about the economy, the space program, the minimum wage, Arizona's water problems or the Democratic party deficit, he can impart a messianic ring to his voice, a missionary zeal to his words, and a ringmaster's authority to his stabbing forefinger."[114] Wicker cites an appearance before the National Association of Manufacturers in New York. Kennedy had worked hard on his text about the pending liberal trade program, but when delivering it, soon saw that he was not reaching his audience. Gradually he shifted to an off-the-cuff delivery, using only one small card of figures, and spoke for forty-seven minutes—one-third of the time extemporaneously. The impact of this third far outstripped the rest of the speech.

The area of communication embraced by this chapter is perhaps the most crucial, and at the same time the most subtle and difficult, with which Presidents have to deal. Handling the newspaper press will certainly be no simpler in the future than it has been in the past, but there is a far greater backlog of experience in dealing with this kind of journalism, and the guidelines have emerged more clearly. So too with the various staff problems raised in the last chapter. Though complex, they should yield to the efforts of a President who has some flair for administration and a mastery of previous White House practice.

The electronic media and all that they imply for the presidency are a unique challenge for several reasons. The very newness of television, particularly, and the enormous speed of technical development in this area mean that the precedents are few, and those that exist quickly become outmoded. And yet these means of direct access to the public—unthinkable a half century ago—are by far the most potent weapon which any President has to use. (One suspects that even Kennedy and his immediate aides were awed by the impact of his denunciation of the steel price increase.)[115]

The subtleties and difficulties here derive from the overriding importance of presidential personality and skill. In a crisis, the public will listen to the Chief Executive almost regardless of the elegance or inelegance of his prose and delivery. But in the long pull, television inexorably demands that he be an effective and persuasive speaker, and be able at the same time to radiate confidence, concern, warmth, and sincerity. Even if, as an individual, he has the potential to do all of this superlatively, he must have the additional ability to find and concert effectively the talents of the numerous supporting cast which television just as imperatively demands. No President, obviously, is likely to be able to act as his own specialist in the art and science of TV program production. He must use intelligently and imaginatively the skills of others. And since no President can prepare his own script unaided, he must be able to recruit and mesh the efforts of writers who can write prose that will be distinctly his in style and ideas. The ultimate test is his ability to do all of this, while at the same time enhancing rather than blurring his *individual* image as the source of initiative and energizer of public policy. His individuality is a key asset which must not become submerged in a collegial effort by hucksters and ghosts.

☆☆☆☆☆☆☆☆☆

Chapter 11

☆☆☆☆☆☆☆☆☆

A TRIAL BALANCE

Any examination of a living institution like the American presidency must end at an arbitrary and inconclusive point. The Dallas tragedy of November 22, 1963, provides an all too handy date at which to stop and take stock. But even this unexpected change of administrations, judging from the first six months of Johnson's tenure, far from slowing or deflecting the trends of development which have been traced in the foregoing chapters, actually accelerated them along familiar paths.

The transition from the Kennedy to the Johnson style in the press conference and general press relations area has already been touched on. Regarding presidential use of television, the pattern of continuity from the one administration to the other is if anything more striking. Five days after the assassination, Mr. Johnson spoke before a joint session of Congress and the national television audience in "an address that surprised even his admirers with its force, its eloquence, its mood of quiet confidence."[1] The following day was Thanksgiving, and at 6:15 P.M. he spoke to the nation directly for the first time via television, from the White House, "seated in a deep leather chair between an American flag and the flag of his office."[2] Less than a week of his tenure as President had passed before Mr. Johnson made it clear that he could use the electronic media with sensitivity, and fully intended to do so.

These initial impressions were borne out in subsequent weeks. The passage of the tax reduction measure which President Kennedy had worked so long to secure finally came on February 26, 1964, after major efforts by Johnson, and he marked the occasion by following up the signing ceremony with a brief televised talk on the bill's importance from the White House East Room. The most striking symbol of the continuity in the Kennedy-Johnson use of video came two or three weeks later, on March 15. On the 10th, the *Times* had carried a story headed "Johnson Agrees to Network Chat," which noted that the three networks planned to screen the results of a taped, hour-long interview with the new President modeled on the one featuring his predecessor, December 17, 1962.[3] The resulting program, which had been recorded on Saturday, edited somewhat, and then shown early Sunday evening, left little further doubt about the President's ability to use the medium successfully. As Walter Lippmann put it:

> The President has no reason now to worry about himself as a performer on TV.
>
> In his interview on Sunday night, he was never at a loss for words or facts, or for grammar and syntax, and he was immediately and shrewdly aware not only of the meaning of the questions put to him but of how his answers would be taken by the great audience.[4]

The April 23 televised announcement of the settling of the long railroad work rules dispute graphically underscored Johnson's awareness of the potency of TV for instantaneous communication with the nation, and determination to exploit it to the full. It was nearly 6:20 P.M. when he got the word that agreement had been reached, "and he decided he wanted to go on national television—right now," according to *Time*.[5] Frantic preparations at the Washington studio of the Columbia network, and a fifty-mile-an-hour drive from the White House, succeeded in getting the President and the representatives of the two contending parties on the air at 6:45.

The role of the President as leader of national opinion, as it has evolved during the first six decades of the twentieth century, is clearly a permanent feature of the office and of the American political scene. This role, however, invites two sharply contradictory interpretations. Some will ask, especially in the light of the Kennedy (and Johnson) success in harnessing television: Does not the White House now have available an array of communications techniques of limitless and even frightening potential? Have contemporary Presidents perhaps become dangerously powerful, as channels for manipulating the public have opened up to them?

On the other hand, a case can certainly be made that, short of an overriding crisis, Presidents need more than publicity techniques to overcome the enormous frictions in the American political system. The legislative accomplishments of the Kennedy administration seem meager indeed when measured against the amount of effort and virtuosity expended to obtain them. The real question may therefore turn out to be: Is the President's power and capacity to influence events likely to be equal to the ever increasing demands being made upon him?

The one thing that has emerged clearly, whatever its ultimate significance, is the preeminent ability of the Chief Executive to generate publicity and to command public attention. Both his interpretation of the potential of the office and his natural reserve caused President Kennedy to modulate somewhat his use of the enormous publicity power of the White House. But the breezy and uninhibited Texan who succeeded him has apparently felt no compulsion to keep the danger of "overexposure" continually in mind, with results that come out graphically in the following from *Time*:

> In the course of a single breathtaking, nerveshaking, totally implausible week, the 36th President of the U.S. made nearly two dozen speeches, traveled 2,983 miles, held three press conferences appeared on national television three times, was seen in person by almost a quarter of a million people, shook so many hands that by week's end his right hand was puffed and bleeding.[6]

Quite apparently Lyndon Johnson began his presidency on the theory that there is virtually no limit, no brooding danger of ultimate public boredom, which he need take into account in his efforts to mold and marshal public opinion. Johnson, of course, like Coolidge and Truman before him, faced the problem of building his own national image in order to secure his party's nomination and eventual reelection to office.

But whatever a President's theory in this regard, he can consistently hold the center of the governmental stage against virtually any rival. The Congress, with which he must, in constitutional theory, joust for the citizens' attention, is ill adapted to vie with him for first position in the public eye. A phenomenon of the Kennedy era, archly labeled the "Ev and Charlie Show," dramatically underscores the legislative branch's dilemma—which is also the dilemma of the opposition party—in making itself heard. It consisted of periodical televised "press conferences" staged by the minority leaders of the Senate and House, Everett McKinley Dirksen and Charles Halleck.[7]

These affairs were an outgrowth of the need on the part of the Republican party, and particularly the Republican Congressional leadership, for a platform from which to compete with the Democratic White House. The format chosen was a recognition of the tremendous impact of the presidential press conference and the even greater presumed impact of Kennedy's live televising. As Russell Baker wrote in the *New York Times*, Dirksen and Halleck "did not expect to match the White House with its traditional monopoly over the head lines and the television tube, but they hoped to hold a minority share of the communication lines."[8]

Not long after this effort had gotten under way in 1961 its serious weaknesses became evident—not the least of which was the irreverent title coined by a reporter and taken over gleefully by Washington and the rest of the country. The principals were not particularly telegenic, compared with President Kennedy and other youthful New Frontiersmen.[9] In manner, phraseology, and the stridency of their approach to the issues of the day, they seemed faintly old-fashioned. Whether the results would have been happier with more attractive spokesmen whose views hewed closer to the middle of the political road is hard to say. For whatever reason, the show declined after an initial flurry of success born no doubt of curiosity. According to Baker the session of March 15, 1962 was typical:

> President Kennedy's news conference yesterday was attended by 391 persons. For this morning's 'Ev and Charlie Show,' the authorities of the Capitol press gallery had set up facilities for seventy-five reporters. Seventeen showed up.
>
> After the President's news conference yesterday afternoon, all the major television and radio networks had tapes immediately available for unabridged reproduction across the country. 'Ev and Charlie' drew four screen-film cameras to record fragments that may, or may not, yield the Republicans a few seconds of canned film in some of the nation's living rooms tonight.[10]

Such is the enormous advantage enjoyed by the Chief Executive. The blurred public image of Congress is thus further blurred, and the already monumental disadvantages of the out party made worse, in the television age. So despondent had the Republican leadership become as the 1963 session dawned that funds for the continuance of the show were cut off.[11]

Added to this one-sided advantage which the President enjoys in gaining access to the public is his vast image as national leader and even as father figure. Gallup poll findings that Roosevelt, Truman, Eisenhower, and Kennedy all enjoyed popularity in or near the eighty per cent range at high points in their careers bespeak far more than the partisan following that put them in office.[12] A President, once in the White House, quickly assumes a public position far beyond the limits of his electoral majority, even when this was narrow and inconclusive. This would seem to clinch his unchallengeable position and to confirm the worst fears of those who cry incipient tyranny.

However, access to an attentive public by no means automatically confers the power to shape and mold popular attitudes. TV viewers, even of a presidential telecast, though they may hang on his words, need not accept his conclusions. Not only the legislative record since 1960 but the Congressional achievements of J.F.K.'s three predecessors underscore the point that the President is far from invincible, however fully or skillfully he may exploit the mass media. The Kennedy efforts along these lines, which drew from Senate Republican Leader Dirksen "the lament that he had never seen an Administration 'so organized in the propaganda field,' "[13] resulted in surprisingly little forward movement by the Congress.

What, one might ask, explains this apparent anomaly? Why is the "bully pulpit" of the White House, with all its recent electronic embellishments, so much less effective than it ought to be? For one thing, the collective impact of recent innovations in communications has been far more complex than would at first appear. James Burns, an astute observer of the Presidency, wrote, shortly after the assassination:

> . . . the more [Kennedy] spoke and acted in terms of national unity and bipartisanship, the more he dulled his image as a leader moving strongly ahead, and in a partisan direction, at home. As in the case of Presidents before him, his role as chief of state had to preempt his role as party chief and legislator-in-chief.[14]

Presidents, when they address the nation, cannot help evoking their role as *national* leader, symbol, and spokesman, because the media operate continually to cast them in this role. And the more the public comes to see the President as the personification of the *nation*, irrespective of party, the less willing it is to accept the partisan side of his office. The cold war with its recurring crises has also enhanced the President's stature as a nonpartisan national leader and champion in a dangerous world. Both the magnitude of the reaction to President Kennedy's assassination and the mingled feelings of personal loss and fear for the future that it brought suggest the psychological and symbolic importance which the White House occupant has come to have for the nation.

When the Chief Executive then assumes the mantle of *party* leader or protagonist of one group against another, the "President of all the people" image becomes blurred. The American public, which has been taught to think that political controversy is always in bad taste, reacts unfavorably when the preeminent symbol of its yearning for unity and leadership demeans himself. The higher the pedestal to which the man and the office have been elevated in recent years, the greater the adverse reaction to presidential partisanship. The nation followed Harry Truman willingly in foreign affairs, yet reviled him bitterly for moves like the steel seizure and some of his less inhibited public comments. Similarly, the enormous popularity of Eisenhower the general, the man, and the President was coupled with a refusal to see him as a partisan figure or to heed him when he plugged his policies or his party's candidates.

The last months of President Kennedy's life are particularly suggestive, and in a sense ironic. During most of his tenure he seemed to be acutely aware of a need to preserve his image and to husband his broad nonpartisan support. Sidney Hyman and others criticized him for this acute image consciousness and urged him "to forget about his popularity entirely" in the interest of more effective leadership[15] on critical issues. In 1963, events on the erupting civil rights front forced a sympathetic but reluctant President into taking an increasingly clear stand on behalf of the embattled Negro groups. Unquestionably he took his stand fully aware that it was fraught with danger to his image. Reaction, measured by the polls, showed that the public was indeed responding unfavorably. His general popularity went down sharply and a Gallup survey released just before the fateful 22nd of November showed that nearly 50 per cent of several samplings since May felt the Administration was pushing too fast on integration.[16]

Though the point cannot be proved, it seems obvious that entwined with this specific reaction to a policy trend was a generalized uneasiness and even anxiety at having the President thus take sides and abandon impartiality. Ironically, his fateful visit to Texas was part of an effort to recoup this loss; and even more ironically, its tragic outcome, releasing again as it did the floodgates of emotional identification with both man and office, gave back to the President in death the broad base of support and affection which the imperatives of policy leadership had jeopardized while he was alive.

Earlier in the Kennedy period many commentators underscored the same paradox. Russell Baker wrote in the *New York Times* in April, 1961: "Three months of furious activity and image-building have strengthened President Kennedy's personal popularity with the voters but have generated little or no new support for his domestic programs." In the same article Representative Thomas Curtis of Missouri is said to have agreed "that the President's personal popularity was on the rise. 'But it's like that of a movie actor —it's not related to legislation,' he said."[17] A year later another *Times* correspondent wrote that Kennedy's "high popularity rating has not been translated into public support for his programs."[18] And Sam Lubell, just after the 1962 election, noted:

> In every part of the country voters I talked with praised the President. 'He's my boy,' they would say, or 'It's nice to have a young President who does things' or, 'With Kennedy you always know what he thinks.'
>
> But many of these same voters then went on to express misgivings or opposition about parts of the Kennedy program.[19]

This is the point. The vast impact of the mass media in capitalizing on the President as good copy, the President's own exploitation of these possibilities for "image-building," and a general yearning in the public for a nonpartisan national symbol—a yearning reinforced by the anxieties of cold war—have lifted the White House occupant above the sordid arena of partisan politics. Thus any effort to participate in the party or group struggle, as a President must, is as likely to produce shock and disillusionment as it is to enlist active support.

A supplementary—and more orthodox—explanation of the modest legislative achievement of the Kennedy administration is the different constituencies of the President and Congress. The Congress represents the nation in terms of local groups and interests, while the President represents it as a whole and particularly its *national* interests and currents of opinion. Congress thus has a vested interest in promoting local claims and ignoring national claims, while the President seeks to emphasize national goals and problems at the expense of parochialism. Add to this the rural imbalance that is characteristic of the Senate, and, through malapportionment and obsolete district patterns, of the House as well, and the difficulty is compounded.

The President's prime weapon for influencing policy making is his ability to command and influence a national audience. In theory a public which he has convinced will communicate its desires to Capitol Hill, and action will result. But Congress by its nature is far less responsive to national currents of opinion than to local pressures. Furthermore, well over half the membership come from safe seats and are immune to anything but a virtual tidal wave of popular demand. Only events, rarely Presidents alone, can produce opinion of this intensity. Finally, many of the most powerful individuals on the Hill, the committee chairmen, are from the safest districts and hence the most insulated from any White House-generated pressure.

The consequences of recent Supreme Court decisions on legislative apportionment may help make Congress more amenable to the influence the President can bring to bear from the electorate. His basic power position must remain essentially the same, however. He confronts the checks and balances and planned frictions of the American constitutional system, which no degree of mastery of the media nor further expansion of the presidential image can neutralize. Thus, in the last analysis, those who lament the limits of Executive power, rather than those who fear strong Presidents, may have the better case.

Since little is likely to be done constitutionally to strengthen the President's hand, his ability to lead and mold public opinion, for all its inherent limitations, must remain his prime reliance. American parties and the American public will do well to bear this in mind as they act in their mysterious ways to fill the office—and hardly less as they fill the vice presidency. More than ever before in the history of the Republic, the times demand strong Presidents, and more than ever before, the strong President will be the skillful leader of public opinion.

45. Pollard, p. 626, discusses this article.
46. Quoted in Pollard, p. 609.
47. Sullivan, p. 370.
48. Butt, p. 319.
49. Davis, p. 178.
50. Ibid., p. 184.
51. Essay, p. 98.
52. Davis, p. 173; and cf. also Pringle, *Taft,* p. 451.

3. *Innovation: Woodrow Wilson*

1. For Wilson's attitude toward the press see especially: David Lawrence, *The True Story of Woodrow Wilson* (New York: George Doran, 1924); James Kerney, *The Political Education of Woodrow Wilson* (New York: Century, 1926); and the chapter on Wilson in James E. Pollard, *The Presidents and the Press* (New York: Macmillan, 1947).

2. Cf. Leo Rosten, *The Washington Correspondents* (New York: Harcourt Brace, 1937), p. 25, where he describes Wilson's manner at press conferences as resembling "the professor facing a classroom." See also R. P. Brandt, "The President's Press Conference," *Survey Graphic* (July, 1939), p. 448; and George Creel, *The War, the World and Wilson* (New York: Harper, 1920), p. 35. The authors of a psychological study of Wilson, A. L. George and J. L. George, *Woodrow Wilson and Col. House: A Personality Study* (New York: John Day, 1956), make a point which, if valid, may well have underlain all of his dealings with the press and publicity media: "Woodrow Wilson had what can only be described as a horror of being 'selfish,' and of the possibility of behaving aggressively for personal reasons" (p. 160). This was the result, they argue, of a lifelong need to bottle up aggressive impulses which he could not bear to recognize.

3. Baker, discussing the reactions of Wilson during his prenomination Western speaking tour, paraphrases the candidate: "Why could not the press be satisfied with what he said in his speeches?" *Woodrow Wilson: Life and Letters* (New York: Doubleday, 1931), III, 213.

4. Arthur Link writes about Wilson's "disdain of newspapers as agents both of opinion and of news" and goes on to quote to this effect from his correspondence. *The New Freedom* (Princeton, N.J.: Princeton University Press, 1956), p. 83.

5. Baker, III, 367.

6. Frank P. Stockbridge, "How Woodrow Wilson Won His Nomination," *Current History* (July, 1924), XX, 564. Cf. also Baker, III 213 f.

NOTES

1. *Introduction*

1. A careful effort was made to document this point through an analysis of front page newspaper coverage of the presidency versus coverage of Congressional activity from 1885 to the present. This was published as "Presidential News: The Expanding Public Image," *Journalism Quarterly* (Summer, 1959), XXXVI, 275-283.

2. Walter Bagehot, *The English Constitution* (New York: D. Appleton, 1884), p. 101.

3. Richard E. Neustadt, *Presidential Power: The Politics of Leadership* (New York: John Wiley, 1960).

4. Richard F. Fenno, Jr., *The President's Cabinet* (Cambridge, Mass.: Harvard University Press, 1959). See also, for example, Richard P. Longaker, *The Presidency and Individual Liberties* (Ithaca, N.Y.: Cornell University Press, 1961).

5. Amaury de Riencourt, *The Coming Caesars* (New York: Coward-McCann, 1957), p. 6.

2. *Beginnings: Roosevelt and Taft*

1. Silas Bent in his book, *Ballyhoo, the Voice of the Press* (New York: Boni and Liveright, 1927), Chapter III, offers a critical evaluation of this development.

2. Heavy reliance is placed in the ensuing discussion of the press on Frank Luther Mott, *American Journalism* (New York: Macmillan, 1941).

3. The best single source of information on the relations of the

various Presidents and the newspaper press is to be found in James E. Pollard, *The Presidents and the Press* (New York: Macmillan, 1947). See especially his chapters on Cleveland, Benjamin Harrison, McKinley, and Theodore Roosevelt. Among other volumes that contain discussions of presidential press relations before the turn of the century is J. Frederick Essary, *Covering Washington* (Boston: Houghton Mifflin, 1927).

4. Henry L. Stoddard, *As I Knew Them* (New York: Harper, 1927), pp. 62-65.

5. Cf. Will Irwin, *Propaganda and the News* (New York: Whittlesey House, c. 1936), p. 52 f.

6. Oliver Gramling, *AP, The Story of News* (New York: Farrar and Rinehart, 1940), p. 187.

7. Mark Sullivan, *Our Times,* Vol. III: *Pre-War America* (New York: Scribner's, 1930), p. 71 f.

8. Sullivan, p. 72 f.

9. Sullivan, p. 74. Cf. also Robert W. Desmond, *The Press and World Affairs* (New York: Appleton Century, 1937), p. 308 f.

10. Sullivan, p. 75.

11. Sullivan, pp. 80 ff. See also George E. Mowry, *The Era of Theodore Roosevelt* (New York: Harper, 1958), p. 202 f.

12. Essary, p. 87 f; and Charles Hurd, *The White House: A Biography* (New York: Harper, 1940), p. 228.

13. John J. Leary gives one of the best descriptions of this relationship in his *Talks with T. R.* (Boston: Houghton Mifflin, 1920).

14. David S. Barry, *Forty Years in Washington* (Boston: Little, Brown, 1924), p. 268.

15. Sullivan, p. 256. See also Essary, p. 88; Leo C. Rosten, *The Washington Correspondents* (New York: Harcourt Brace, 1937), pp. 20 ff; and Desmond, p. 308, for other mentions of these Roosevelt "press conferences."

16. These meetings are described in Louis Brownlow, *The Autobiography of Louis Brownlow,* First Half: *A Passion for Politics* (Chicago: University of Chicago Press, 1955), p. 399; and in Lincoln Steffens, *Autobiography* (New York: Harcourt Brace, 1931), pp. 509 ff.

17. Henry F. Pringle, *Theodore Roosevelt: A Biography* (New York: Harcourt Brace, 1931), p. 341.

18. John M. Blum, *The Republican Roosevelt* (Cambridge, Mass.: Harvard University Press, 1954), p. 84.

19. Bent, p. 77; Rosten, p. 22; and H. H. Kohlsaat, in his *From McKinley to Harding* (New York: Scribner, 1923), p. 149, all make this point. Leary, p. 130, insists that Roosevelt did not repudiate stories in this manner.

20. Oscar K. Davis, *Released for Publication* (Boston: Houghton Mifflin, 1925), pp. 141-144, gives an account of one such episode.

21. Rosten, pp. 98-103, has an interesting section on "off-the-record" news sources generally. See Pollard's chapter on Roosevelt for a discussion of T. R. in this connection and references to comments by other observers.

22. Davis, p. 124.

23. Primary reliance in discussing Loeb's role has been placed on Louis W. Koenig, *The Invisible Presidency* (New York: Rinehart, 1960), pp. 136-189.

24. Ibid., p. 172.

25. Ibid., p. 173.

26. Irwin, p. 132; and Irwin H. Hoover, *Forty-two Years in the White House* (Boston: Houghon Mifflin, 1934), p. 27.

27. *The Letters of Theodore Roosevelt,* ed. Elting E. Morison, Vol. III: *The Square Deal* (Cambridge, Mass.: Harvard University Press, 1951), p. 1015.

28. Ibid., p. 664.

29. Davis, p. 123.

30. Koenig, p. 176.

31. *Letters of Theodore Roosevelt,* III, p. 479.

32. Ibid., p. 252.

33. Theodore Roosevelt, *An Autobiography* (New York: Macmillan, 1914), p. 415.

34. Ibid., p. 423.

35. Pringle, p. 258.

36. Ibid., p. 339.

37. William H. Harbaugh, *Power and Responsibility: The Life and Times of Theodore Roosevelt* (New York: Farrar, Straus and Cudahy, 1961), p. 241 f.

38. Sullivan, p. 235.

39. Ibid., p. 234.

40. Ibid., p. 240.

41. Archibald W. Butt, *Taft and Roosevelt: The Intimate Letters of Archie Butt, Military Aide* (Garden City, N.Y.: Doubleday Doran, 1930), I, 30. Butt is a valuable source generally on this aspect of the Taft administration.

42. Henry F. Pringle, *The Life and Times of William Howard Taft* (New York: Farrar and Rinehart, 1939), II, 603.

43. Cabell Phillips et al., eds., *Dateline: Washington* (Garden City, N.Y.: Doubleday, 1949), p. 50.

44. See Davis, pp. 156 and 162; Pringle, *Taft,* p. 415; Sullivan, p. 370; and Stoddard, p. 376. W. G. Shepherd, however, in his article "The White House Says," (*Colliers,* February 2, 1928) also insists that Taft held conferences and describes the format in persuasive detail; cf. p. 19.

7. Eleanor Wilson McAdoo, *The Woodrow Wilsons* (New York: Macmillan, 1937), p. 168.

8. Stockbridge, p. 563 f.

9. Ibid.

10. Baker, III, 213.

11. Kerney, p. 262.

12. That Wilson did this on the advice of a group of advisors whom he had constituted as an informal committee to recommend on press relations is suggested by George F. Milton in his book *The Use of Presidential Power, 1789-1943* (Boston: Little Brown, 1944), p. 211. See also John M. Blum, *Joe Tumulty and the Wilson Era* (Boston: Houghton Mifflin, 1951), p. 62, and H. C. F. Bell, *Woodrow Wilson and the People* (New York: Doubleday, 1945), p. 115.

13. Baker, IV, 228 f.

14. Ibid., p. 229.

15. L. Ames Brown, for example, in his article: "President Wilson and Publicity" (*Harper's Weekly*, November 1, 1913, LVIII, 20 ff) makes the point that neither Wilson nor Tumulty played favorites among the correspondents. Louis Brownlow, in an interview granted the author July 24, 1957, said that the President inaugurated the conferences to avoid the problem of favoritism.

16. The Princeton University Library has had Swem's stenographic notebooks for some time, but acquired the collection of his papers including the press transcripts only by bequest in 1957. (See reference to this material in the *Princeton University Library Chronicle*, XIX [1958], p. 180, n. 41.) The Swem notebooks may contain the rest of Wilson's conferences but have never been transcribed. The recently acquired Swem papers, which will be incorporated eventually in the Library's Wilson collection, were used with the permission of Alexander P. Clark, Curator of Manuscripts.

These transcripts, at least four of which are little more than fragments of the conferences involved, seem not to have been made in the regular fashion that transcripts were prepared after conferences of later Presidents. Rather, in the Wilson administration, though a stenographer was normally present to record the proceedings, these notes were transcribed, apparently, only when some special reason existed for doing so. This often was a request by newsmen for a chance to check their notes and recollections, one can assume, since nearly all the fifty-seven bear the injunction: NOT TO BE QUOTED. FOR GUIDANCE ONLY. Only if the transcriptions were going to be used by the press would this be necessary. Careful investigation, including a conversation on the point with Arthur Link, has turned up no evidence of the survival of any other press conference files. The discussion of these conferences to follow first appeared in an article by the author: "The Press Conferences of

Woodrow Wilson," *Journalism Quarterly,* Summer, 1962, pp. 292-300.

17. The theories advanced in the literature for the ending of the conferences boil down to two: that Wilson used the increasingly grave situation following the sinking of the *Lusitania* as a pretext to get rid of what had become a distasteful chore; and that foreign correspondents were admitted and he felt he could not answer questions on foreign policy with them present.

18. *New York Times,* December 19, 1916, p. 1.

19. Ibid., June 24, 1913.

20. Ibid., February 3, 1915, pp. 1 and 4.

21. Ibid., May 16, 1913, p. 2. The article ran 21 column inches. Wilson's famous statement on tariff lobby activity apparently also had its origins in a press conference. Cf. Link, p. 187; and J. Frederick Essary, *Covering Washington* (Boston: Houghton Mifflin, 1927), p. 179 f.

22. George Creel, *Rebel at Large* (New York: Putnam's, 1947), p. 234. Writing in *The Saturday Evening Post* in 1931, Creel quotes the same statement but has him comparing his preparations to that "for any lecture" rather than "for a Cabinet meeting" (quoted in Baker, IV, 232.)

23. Pollard, pp. 630, 635.

24. A different and much more favorable picture of the President meeting the press is given by L. Ames Brown, cited above.

25. This suggestion is made and elaborated in Fauneil J. Rinn, "The Presidential Press Conference" (unpublished doctoral thesis, University of Chicago, 1960), pp. 70, 80. She discusses some of the instances of banishment on p. 75 f. See also Blum, p. 63 f; and Oswald G. Villard, *Fighting Years* (New York: Harcourt, Brace, 1939), p. 292.

26. Pollard uses this phrase (see p. 632). Pollard also supplies a useful discussion of the Secretary's role in his chapter on Wilson. By far the best and most comprehensive source on Tumulty, surpassing in some ways his own book (*Woodrow Wilson as I Knew Him,* Garden City, N.Y.: Doubleday, Page, 1921) is John M. Blum's study, *Joe Tumulty and the Wilson Era.* Many others who wrote on Wilson refer to his skillful discharge of his role.

27. Cf. Blum, pp. 62-65 and passim; also Kerney, p. 264; Lawrence, p. 89 f; Brown; Arthur Walworth, *Woodrow Wilson,* Vol. I, *American Prophet* (New York: Longmans, Green, 1958), p. 277 f; for the vantage point of a reporter, Villard, p. 256 f.

28. Ida M. Tarbell, "A Talk with the President of the United States," *Colliers* (October 28, 1916), LVIII, 5 f.

29. Lawrence, p. 89.

30. Link, p. 149.

31. Bell, p. 83.

32. Bell suggests another motive for inaugurating the press confer-

ences, which fits in with the argument to follow, namely, "as another method by which the people's leader could keep in touch with them." In other words, he saw them hopefully at first, Bell thinks, as a channel for direct communication with the people. One can assume that his disillusionment with them came in large measure as a result of a realization that he was talking really to the reporters, and only to the people through their rather undependable offices. (Ibid., p. 115.)

33. Baker, IV, 235.

34. Primary reliance in the following discussion of Wilson's personal appearances before Congress is placed on the "Authorized Edition" of *The Public Papers of Woodrow Wilson,* edited by Ray Stannard Baker and William E. Dodd, *The New Democracy* (1913-1917), 2 vols. (New York: Harper, 1926), and *War and Peace* (1917-1924), 2 vols. (New York: Harper, 1927).

35. Baker, IV, 109.

36. Ibid., note 1.

37. Ibid.

38. David F. Houston, *Eight Years with Wilson's Cabinet,* 2 vols. (New York: Doubleday, 1926), I, 53.

39. Baker, IV, 110.

40. R. P. Longaker, "Woodrow Wilson and the Presidency" in Earl Latham (ed.), *The Philosophy and Policies of Woodrow Wilson* (Chicago: University of Chicago Press, 1958), p. 174 f. Henry A. Turner writes: "The brevity of these messages practically assured that they would be quoted in full by the leading newspapers." ("Woodrow Wilson and Public Opinion," *Public Opinion Quarterly,* XXI [1957], p. 510.) The forum from which they were delivered made this even more certain, one can assume.

41. A very useful critique of T.R.'s messages and comparison with Wilson's is to be found in Norman J. Small, *Some Presidential Interpretations of the Presidency* (Baltimore: Johns Hopkins University Press, 1932), p. 174 f.

42. Cf. Josephus Daniels, *The Wilson Era, Years of War and After* (Chapel Hill: University of North Carolina Press, 1946), p. 221 f; James Mock and Cedric Larson, *Words that Won the War* (Princeton: Princeton University Press, 1939), pp. 48-51; and Creel, p. 158 f.

43. Baker, IV, 234.

44. George Creel, *How We Advertised America* (New York: Harper, 1920), p. 208.

45. Stanley Kelley, Jr., *Professional Public Relations and Political Power* (Baltimore: Johns Hopkins University Press, 1956), p. 13 f.

46. The material and figures relating to the Committee on Public Information presented in the following pages came from Mock and Larson and Creel's *How We Advertised America.* See also the author's "Wilson,

Creel and the Presidency," *Public Opinion Quarterly* (Summer, 1959), XXIII, 189-202, which article covers some points in greater detail.

47. Pamphlet, Committee on Public Information records, National Archives, CPI1-C6, file of Carl Byoir.

48. Mock and Larson, p. 125.

49. House Committee on Appropriations, Subcommittee on Sundry Civil Appropriation Bill for 1919, Part II, 65th Congress, 2nd Session, *Hearing*, Committee on Public Information, p. 62 (June 1918).

50. A complete file of these National School Service Bulletins is in the regular collections of the Library of Congress.

51. Creel Papers, Library of Congress, Volume I, from a note written by Creel to Wilson, dated December 28, 1917.

52. Ray Stannard Baker, *Woodrow Wilson: Life and Letters,* Vol. VII (*War Leader*) and Vol. VIII (*Armistice*), (London: William Heinemann, 1927-1939). Baker wrote these last two volumes as a day-by-day chronicle of the President's activities, including daily lists of appointments, etc.

53. Letter to Cleveland Dodge, quoted in Baker, VI (1937), 515.

54. Houston, II, 239. Sir A. Maurice Low in his book, *Woodrow Wilson: An Interpretation* (Boston: Little, Brown, 1919) deals at length with what he also sensed as a campaign to inform and educate the people regarding the war. See pp. 182, 205, and passim.

55. Alan Cranston, in his book *The Killing of the Peace* (New York: Viking, 1945) offers impressive documentation for the proposition that the American people were favorably inclined toward the treaty (cf. pp. 48, 94, 103, 126 f, 197, and 241) and that the burden of proof therefore had lain with the Senate group. Seemingly, Wilson did not have to change the minds of the majority, but rather inform and solidify their support. Ira Smith, in his book "*Dear Mr. President*" (New York: Julian Messner, 1949) has this to say: "The [White House] mail demonstrated that most people did not understand the League of Nations, but they were very strongly in favor of the President's objectives" (p. 102).

56. Note Longaker's appraisal (in Latham, p. 78): "The President's greatest personal defeat can be attributed to many things: bad timing, the personal enmity between Wilson and Lodge, the President's over-dependence on public opinion and yet his failure to inform and organize the public."

57. Creel Papers, Vol. II, October 18, 1918.

58. Ibid., November 8, 1918.

59. See Cornwell, "Wilson, Creel and the Presidency," p. 202.

60. Numerous observers have emphasized the problems of adequate publicity and liaison with the working press in Paris and the key role these failures played in the eventual League defeat: Ray Stannard Baker in his *Woodrow Wilson and World Settlement*, 3 vols. (Garden

City, N.Y.: Doubleday, Page, 1922), I, xxxiv, 151, 317; also his *American Chronicle* (New York: Scribners, 1945), an autobiographical study, goes over some of the same ground. See in addition: Bell, p. 289; Creel, *How We Advertised America*, p. 401; Houston, II, 5; Daniel C. Roper, *Fifty Years of Public Life* (Durham, N.C.: Duke University Press, 1941), p. 198; Longaker, in Latham, p. 78 f; and Villard, p. 396.

61. Blum, pp. 171-173, covers these points about Tumulty's activities and also provides a good summary of the problems of publicity in Paris and the United States while Wilson was abroad. See also Tumulty, Appendix, especially p. 518 f, for texts of relevant cables.

62. Robert Lansing, among others, in his book *The Peace Negotiations* (Boston: Houghton, Mifflin, 1921) discusses the return to America in these terms (p. 135 f). For Tumulty's view see Blum, p. 183.

63. Another problem seems to have been the inexperience of the American journalistic contingent. Baker notes that only a handful of them were capable of filing useful background stories when events of a given day were not newsworthy. (See Baker, *American Chronicle*, p. 376.) This suggests both the extent to which the Paris coverage was a pioneer venture for the new journalism, and that the fault was by no means all on the President's side.

64. According to one student of these developments, a nationwide educational campaign against the treaty was put on by the irreconcilables financed by Frick and Mellon money. Thomas A. Bailey, *Woodrow Wilson and the Great Betrayal* (New York: Macmillan, 1945), p. 77 f.

65. Ibid., p. 104.

4. *Consolidation: Harding and Coolidge*

1. Cf. [Clinton W. Gilbert], *The Mirrors of Washington* (New York: G. P. Putnam, 1921), pp. 3-21, for a critical contemporary evaluation of Harding; also William Allen White, *Autobiography* (New York: Macmillan, 1946), Chap. LXXXVI, for a rather touching and more or less sympathetic commentary. The standard (though basically hostile) book on Harding is Samuel Hopkins Adams, *The Incredible Era* (Boston: Houghton Mifflin, 1939).

2. Gilbert, p. 61.

3. James E. Pollard, *The Presidents and the Press* (New York: Macmillan, 1947), pp. 697-712.

4. J. Frederick Essary, *Covering Washington* (Boston: Houghton Mifflin, 1927), p. 90.

5. *New York Times*, March 23, 1921.

6. Ibid., November 30, 1921.

7. Tentative beginnings along this line were made during the period of Wilson's conferences.

8. Merlo J. Pusey in his *Charles Evans Hughes*, 2 vols. (New York: Macmillan, 1952), devotes Chap. 47 (in Vol. II) to this part of the Washington negotiations.

9. Among the authors that make this assertion are: Silas Bent, *Ballyhoo, The Voice of the Press* (New York: Boni and Liveright, 1927), p. 79; Essary, pp. 90, 171; Robert W. Desmond, *The Press and World Affairs* (New York: Appleton-Century, 1937), p. 311; Leo C. Rosten, *The Washington Correspondents* (New York: Harcourt, Brace, 1937), p. 27; Pollard, p. 705 (citing Bent as authority); and Phillips, pp. 53, 66. Only David Lawrence in his article "President and Press," *The Saturday Evening Post*, August 27, 1927, p. 27, seems to be aware of what really happened.

10. Cf. the *New York Times* account printed December 21, 1921: "It was at the regular bi-weekly conference with the newspapermen that the President, in response to a written question as to whether or not the treaty provisions applied to the main islands of Japan. . . ."

11. Phillips, p. 146.

12. Ibid., p. 147.

13. June 10, 1922, quoted in Pollard, p. 706.

14. Reported in *Editor and Publisher*, April 28, 1923, quoted in Pollard, p. 710.

15. *New York Times*, April 6, 1921.

16. Cf. Frederick L. Paxson, *American Democracy and the World War*, Vol. III: *Postwar Years, 1918-1923* (Berkeley and Los Angeles: University of California Press, 1948), p. 304 and passim. See also *New York Times*, July 13, 1921.

17. Irwin H. Hoover, *Forty-Two Years in the White House* (Boston: Houghton, Mifflin, 1934), p. 252. Cf. also Herbert C. Hoover, *Memoirs*, Vol. II: *The Cabinet and Presidency*, 1920-33 (New York: Macmillan, 1952), p. 50.

18. Ira R. T. Smith with Joe Alex Morris, "*Dear Mr. President* . . ." (New York: Julian Messner, 1949), p. 77.

19. Paxson, p. 384.

20. Phillips, p. 77. Hugh Baillie claims that actually Wilson, though he only did so once, during his final tour, was the first President to use an amplifier—with no enthusiasm. *High Tension: The Recollections of Hugh Baillie* (New York: Harper, 1959), p. 52 f.

21. Essary, p. 117.

22. Adams, pp. 369-371. For the text of the Tacoma speech see James W. Murphy, ed., *Speeches and Addresses of Warren G. Harding, President of the United States . . . June 20 to August 2, 1923* (privately published, 1923, copyright J. W. Murphy), pp. 290-295; some of the

correspondence with the steel men is reproduced in the same volume, pp. 296-298.

23. Adams, p. 371.

24. This information comes from Gleason L. Archer, *History of Radio to 1926* (New York: American Historical Society, 1938), p. 317. Cf. also Phillips, p. 76, and S. L. Becker and E. W. Lower, "Broadcasting in Presidential Campaigns," in Sidney Kraus, ed., *The Great Debates* (Bloomington: Indiana University Press, 1962), p. 26.

25. Oliver Gramling, *AP: The Story of News* (New York: Farrar and Rinehart, 1940), p. 304.

26. Pusey, p. 564. Cf. also Mark Sullivan, *Our Times*, Vol. VI: *The Twenties* (New York: Scribners, 1936), pp. 252 ff.

27. Pusey, p. 564.

28. Though there is far more material on Coolidge than on Harding, there are few useful general studies of the Vermonter. Claude M. Fuess was the "official" biographer. His study is entitled *Calvin Coolidge: The Man from Vermont* (Boston: Little, Brown, 1940). A good but critical study of the man and his times was done by William Allen White under the title *A Puritan in Babylon* (New York: Macmillan, 1938). Coolidge's own *Autobiography* (New York: Cosmopolitan Book Co., 1929) is about as brief and cryptic as one would expect, though revealing in places.

29. Willis F. Johnson, *George Harvey: 'A Passionate Patriot'* (Boston: Houghton, Mifflin, 1929), p. x. Cf. also Rosten, p. 34 f; *Time*, September 13, 1926, p. 5; Lawrence; Charles Merz, "The Silent Mr. Coolidge," "Gentleman at the Keyhole," "Feeding the Press," *Colliers*, August 16, 1930, p. 34; *New Republic*, June 2, 1926, p. 51, for a sampling of this kind of comment.

30. These are among the Coolidge materials in the Forbes Library at Northampton, Massachusetts, and are used here with the permission of the Trustees of the Library. The granting of this permission is gratefully acknowledged. See also Howard H. Quint and Robert H. Ferrell, eds., *The Talkative President: The Off-the-Record Press Conferences of Calvin Coolidge* (Amherst: University of Massachusetts Press, 1964).

31. These figures were first used in an article by the author entitled: "Coolidge and Presidential Leadership," *Public Opinion Quarterly*, Summer 1957, pp. 265-278. Portions of the remainder of the section on Coolidge, especially the material on radio broadcasting, are drawn from the same source.

32. All transcripts cited are in the Forbes Library collection.

33. Jay C. Hayden of the *Detroit News*, quoted in the *Literary Digest*, July 25, 1931, p. 8. See also Sherwin L. Cook, *Torchlight Parade* (New York: Minton, Balch, 1929), p. 250; and Rosten, p. 35 for further comment along the same line.

34. See Edward G. Lowry "Next Friends of the President," *Colliers*,

November 24, 1923, p. 13; White, *A Puritan in Babylon*, p. 251; Edward E. Whiting, *President Coolidge: A Contemporary Estimate* (Boston: Atlantic Monthly Press, 1923), p. 199 f; *Time*, January 26, 1925, p. 1; and Smith and Morris, p. 123.

35. In *Time*, October 11, 1926, p. 7, there is a lengthy account of one special interview which Coolidge granted to Bruce Barton. The rest of the press were furious and wrote an indignant letter to the President. The significance of this episode lies in the indication of how far things had moved from the days of T.R.'s "fair-haired boys." With the advent of the regular press conference open to all, the assumption became firmly rooted that none was to have special advantage of any kind.

36. For a general summary of the Coolidge legislative program, with reference also to the tax proposals, see Charles A. and Mary R. Beard, *The Rise of American Civilization* (New York: Macmillan, 1930), II, 701 ff. There is a detailed discussion of the Mellon tax proposals in Harvey O'Connor, *Mellon's Millions* (New York: John Day Co., 1933), Chap. 8. O'Connor says that Mellon launched his proposals in November, 1923, in a tax reform program addressed to the Chairman of the House Ways and Means Committee.

37. Frederick Lewis Allen, *The Lords of Creation* (New York: Harper, 1935), p. 360.

38. For references to this policy of the President's see: White, *A Puritan in Babylon*, pp. 332 ff and passim; James E. Watson, *As I Knew Them* (Indianapolis: Bobbs-Merrill, 1936), p. 249 (Watson suggests the other side of the coin when he has Coolidge saying that if he did try to damp down the speculation he would cause a collapse); John K. Galbraith, *The Great Crash* (London: Hamish Hamilton, 1955), p. 31; and William B. Munro, "The Art of Timely Exodus, A Coolidge Interpretation," *Harvard Graduate's Magazine*, December, 1927, p. 5 f.

39. September 3, 1926, Vol. VII.

40. September 13, 1926, p. 5.

41. September 13, 1927, Vol. IX.

42. See the account in the *New York Times*, November 30, 1921, of Harding's change in the rules.

43. There is a very useful summary of five particular episodes, which largely parallel the ones discussed below, in which the President was moved to comment on infractions of the rules or reprimand the press, in William G. Shepherd, "The White House Says," *Colliers*, February 2, 1929, p. 19. He also gives the particular happening that appeared to have provoked the President to action in each instance.

44. Comment on the "Spokesman" problem may be found particularly in Lawrence and Merz; Lindsay Rogers, "The White House 'Spokesman,'" *Virginia Quarterly Review*, July, 1926; Osward G. Villard, "The Press and the President," *Century*, December, 1925; Prince-

ton University, School of Public and International Affairs, *Conference on the Press* (published by the School, c. 1931;) and Bent, p. 80.

45. Vol. VIII. See also *Time*, May 9, 1927, p. 9, for a description of the end of the Spokesman.

46. Bent, p. 79; and Desmond, p. 312. Shepherd (p. 48) is a bit more specific about the matter: "At one stage someone started the custom of securing the stenographic official report of the President's remarks and using them almost verbatim as a White House statement. The White House responded to this move by withholding the stenographic report from publication, offering it merely as a memory aid for the newsmen."

47. Bent, p. 79.

48. Gridiron speeches are off the record, though Coolidge's are available in a series of four scrapbooks at the Forbes Library, Northampton, which contain what apparently is designed to be a complete collection of his addresses, proclamations, remarks, and statements. This passage is from the copy of his remarks in the scrapbook covering 1923 and 1924.

49. Archer, p. 324. Pages 321-24 give a useful survey of the state of radio around the time Coolidge succeeded to the presidency. Cf. also Becker and Lower, in Kraus, pp. 26-29.

50. For general comment on Coolidge and radio see: J. Frederick Essary, *Selected Addresses of C. Bascom Slemp* (Washington, D.C.: Ransdell, 1938), p. 296 f; C. Bascom Slemp, *The Mind of the President* (New York: Doubleday, 1926), p. 10 f; French Strother, "A Week in the White House with President Coolidge," *World's Work*, April, 1924, p. 586; "Was Coolidge Elected by Radio?" *Literary Digest*, January 10, 1925, p. 61 f; William Allen White, *Calvin Coolidge: The Man Who is President* (New York: Macmillan, 1925), p. 139; and Will Irwin, *Propaganda and the News* (New York: McGraw-Hill, 1936), p. 248 f.

51. Watson, p. 239. Cf. also Calvin Coolidge, "The President Lives Under a Multitude of Eyes," *American Magazine*, August, 1929, p. 20; and Strother.

52. April 23, 1924, p. 1.

53. Cf. Archer, p. 336 f, for comment on this series of appearances.

54. *New York Times*, July 18, 1924, p. 3.

55. Ibid., August 10, 1924, p. 1.

56. Merz, p. 51.

57. Irwin H. Hoover, p. 252. "Ike" Hoover goes on to say that: "Coolidge really wrote most of his own speeches, whereas Harding wrote but few of his." This statement is hard to reconcile either with other commentators' views or with the greatly increased volume of statements emanating from the White House.

58. *Time,* December 7, 1925, p. 1. Ike Hoover (p. 252) also mentions Crawford in this role.

59. Charles W. Thompson, *Presidents I've Known* (Indianapolis: Bobbs-Merrill, 1921), p. 380.

60. Nicholas Murray Butler, *Across the Busy Years* (New York: Scribner's, 1939), I, 413.

61. Merz, p. 51.

62. See note 48.

63. It is also true that there is a marked decline in the number of pages in the volumes of press conference transcripts toward the end of Coolidge's full term, though the number of conferences held does not change materially. Again, the inference is that he saw this means of publicity, also, in terms of electoral success rather than of continuous policy leadership.

64. Slemp, p. 10.

65. Coolidge, "The President Lives Under a Multitude of Eyes," p. 20.

66. In his *Autobiography* (p. 215) Coolidge wrote: "Not only in all his official actions, but in all his social intercourse, and even in his recreation and repose, he is constantly watched by a multitude of eyes. . . . ," suggesting his awareness of the public relations connection between the public and private presidential lives. Hostile as well as friendly commentators have made the same point about his relative lack of concern at publicity given his private life. Cf. *Literary Digest,* "Mr. Hoover's Refusal to be Humanized," July 25, 1931, p. 8, where the point is made that T.R. and Coolidge were past masters of the "human interest" game; and see also Rosten, p. 35.

5. *Retrogression: Hoover*

1. There are numerous biographical studies of Hoover, though few of real merit, and none that could be considered definitive. Among the volumes consulted for this chapter were: Edwin Emerson, *Hoover and His Times* (Garden City, N.Y.: Garden City Publishing Co., 1932); David Hinshaw, *Herbert Hoover: American Quaker* (New York: Farrar, Straus, 1950); Will Irwin, *Herbert Hoover: A Reminiscent Biography* (New York: Grosset and Dunlap, 1928); Eugene Lyons, *Our Unknown Ex-President* (Garden City, N.Y.: Doubleday and Co., 1950); and Harris G. Warren, *Herbert Hoover and the Great Depression* (New York: Oxford University Press, 1959). There are also, of course, the three volumes of Hoover's *Memoirs* published in 1952 (New York: Macmillan).

2. Irwin, p. 176.

3. Ibid., p. 199.

4. Ibid., p. 201.

5. Samuel Hopkins Adams, *The Incredible Era* (Boston: Houghton, Mifflin, 1939), p. 134.

6. Cf. [Gilbert], *The Mirrors of Washington* (New York: G. P. Putnam, 1922), pp. 107, 120 f; Warren, p. 30; Cabell Phillips et al., eds., *Dateline: Washington* (Garden City, N.Y.: Doubleday, 1949), p. 164 f.

7. Warren, p. 31; and A Washington Correspondent, "The Secretariat," *American Mercury* (December, 1929), XVIII, 390.

8. A Washington Correspondent, cited.

9. Gilbert, p. 120. Other commentators who insisted Hoover was a skillful, even Machiavellian, self-advertiser include: Drew Pearson and Robert Allen (*Washington Merry-Go-Round*, New York: Horace Liveright, 1931, p. 58 f); and Harris Warren (p. 30). On the other side of the argument are Eugene Lyons (pp. 28, 216, 262, 293 and passim); David Hinshaw, p. 238; and Will Irwin, passim.

10. P. Y. Anderson, "Hoover and the Press," *Nation* (October 4, 1931), CXXX, 382-384.

11. Several observers of Hoover's career make the point that the publicity buildup, by creating the image of a superman who could do the impossible, greatly complicated the problem for the President, since almost anything he did would fall short of this. Cf. Charles Michelson, *The Ghost Talks* (New York: G. P. Putnam's, 1944), p. 27 and passim; Warren, p. 3; Elmer Davis, "Hoover the Medicine Man," *Forum* (October, 1930), LXXXIV, 195; and "Doubts about Mr. Hoover's Political Leadership," *Literary Digest* (June 14, 1930), CV, 5.

12. Will Irwin, *The Making of a Reporter* (New York: G. P. Putnam's, 1942), p. 409.

13. Walter Lippmann, "The Peculiar Weakness of Mr. Hoover," *Harper's* (June, 1930), CLXI, 5, 6.

14. Cf. the very good summary in Lyons, Chap. III. On p. 29 Lyons quotes Theodore Joslin, one of the Hoover secretaries, who in turn has Hoover say: "This is not a showman's job. I will not step out of character."

15. See Lyons on the impact of Michelson, pp. 249-254, for example. Hinshaw, in Chap. X, "New Lows in Political Vilification," deals with the same subject. Leo C. Rosten (*The Washington Correspondents*, New York: Harcourt, Brace, 1937), a more detached observer, notes the impact of regular news stories and even of hostile photographs, in addition to the work of Michelson. There is, of course, Charles Michelson's own book, cited above, for the Democratic side of the business; and a more or less pro-Hoover account by Frank Kent entitled "Charley Michelson," *Scribner's* (September, 1930), pp. 290-296.

16. Will Irwin, an observer obviously friendly to Hoover, puts the point thus: "the permanent importance of the work of Michelson and

his superiors lies not in the fact that they, as publicity agents for the opposition, helped to defeat a candidate for president. It lies rather in the contribution of a new method to American politics." (*Propaganda and the News*, New York: McGraw-Hill, 1936, p. 301.)

17. Lyons, p. 27.

18. Hoover, *State Papers* (William S. Myers, ed., 2 vols., Garden City, N.Y.: Doubleday Doran, 1934), I, 12 f. James E. Pollard, *The Presidents and the Press* (New York: Macmillan, 1947), contains the most complete discussion of his press relations.

19. This latter portion of Hoover's comments at his first press conference is not quoted in his *State Papers*, but the gist of what he said can be gleaned from numerous sources such as Anderson; Rosten, p. 40; and Ray T. Tucker, "Mr. Hoover Lays a Ghost," *North American Review* (June, 1929), CCXXVII, 661-669.

20. Pearson and Allen, p. 330; Robert W. Desmond, in his *The Press and World Affairs* (New York: Appleton-Century, 1937), p. 314, makes the same point.

21. For discussion of Hoover press relations as Secretary of Commerce see Warren, p. 57 f, and Anderson. On the campaign period, note commentary in Oliver Gramling, *AP: The Story of the News* (New York: Farrar and Rinehart, 1940), p. 349; and Anderson. A somewhat different impression of the campaign period is given in "Reporters Who Travel with Presidents and Princes," *Literary Digest*, September 14, 1929, p. 76.

22. Pollard, 739; Anderson; Frank Luther Mott, *American Journalism* (New York: Macmillan, 1941), p. 722; and Rosten, p. 39. Friendly biographer Emerson (p. 40) gives a more favorable emphasis to the arrangements, listing the press people who went along and noting that "the wireless operators aboard the ship from day to day dispatched to the naval radio station at Arlington near Washington more than seventy thousand words for press publication." Cf. also the friendly comments of Will Irwin in his *The Making of a Reporter*, p. 419.

23. Lyons (p. 40) attempts to assess this sensitivity from his point of view as a Hoover apologist. Warren (p. 58) offers the unique exposure of the President as one reason for the surprising shift in Hoover press relations as between his periods in the Cabinet and the White House. This sensitivity, coupled with the growing burden and anguish of the depression, caused him to lash out at critics by ordering investigations of supposed information leaks, and the like. See Pollard, p. 746 ff.

24. A detailed discussion of the "issue" posed for the press by the Rapidan camp and the way it was used by the President is to be found in John S. Gregory, "All Quiet on the Rapidan," *Outlook and Independent* (August 5, 1931), CLVIII, 427, 434, 435. See also Rosten, p. 41, and Pollard, p. 749 f.

25. Cf. Ira R. T. Smith with Joe Alex Morris *"Dear Mr. President . . ."* (New York: Julian Messner, 1949), p. 142.

26. Head usher Ike Hoover gives an example of the special privileges accorded Sullivan, and discourses on the resulting jealousy of the rest of the press (*42 Years in the White House*, Boston: Houghton, Mifflin, 1934, p. 209 f). For a feature article on Sullivan's career see "An Average American," *Time*, November 18, 1935, pp. 41-46.

27. Cf. Rosten, p. 40; Harold Brayman, "Hooverizing the Press," *Outlook and Independent* (September 24, 1930), CLVI, 125; and Pearson and Allen, pp. 323, 348, for further discussion of this practice and of the reprisals on unfriendly reporters that allegedly resulted.

28. Rosten, p. 46; and Pollard, p. 768 f.

29. Lyons, p. 265.

30. Pollard (p. 741) offers some tabulations of press conference statements, "press statements," and other items labeled simply "statements." Some interesting support is given to general points made about the trend in Hoover press relations. (The figures in Pollard do not square exactly with those just given. There is occasional ambiguity in the labeling of items in the *State Papers,* which may account for this.)

31. For example, Fred Essary wrote in 1933, regarding Hoover: "His statements and other public utterances were more numerous than had emanated from any other Chief Executive and they were published practically in full by every newspaper. . . . He never lacked for a newspaper audience when he cared to invoke one." ("Democracy and the Press," *Annals of the American Academy of Political and Social Science,* September, 1933, p. 117.) The point is not that Hoover's bad press relations reduced the amount of news coverage given his activities. This may in fact have increased. What was damaged badly was the tone and sympathy with which dispatches were written.

32. Pearson and Allen, p. 331; and Brayman, p. 124. Tumulty apparently held such conferences also, during part of Wilson's term in office.

33. On Akerson, see Pearson and Allen, p. 315, and the article by A Washington Correspondent, cited. On Joslin, see Pearson and Allen, p. 318. Joslin was author of a book on his experiences as Hoover press secretary: Theodore G. Joslin, *Hoover off the Record* (Garden City, N.Y.: Doubleday, Doran, 1934).

34. Edmund W. Starling, *Starling of the White House* (New York: Simon and Schuster, 1946), p. 282 f.

35. For a description of Hoover's methods in composing his own speeches, see Lyons, p. 31 f. Ray Lyman Wilbur, also, maintains that he wrote his own speeches during the 1932 campaign. Cf. E. E. Robinson, ed., *Memoirs of Ray Lyman Wilbur* (Stanford, Calif.: Stanford

University Press, 1960), p. 567. On the details of Strother's role see A Washington Correspondent, cited, p. 390 f.

36. Smith and Morris, p. 12; Hoover, *Memoirs,* II, 327. Ira Smith also notes that Hoover arranged "a scientific check of the mail to watch the trend of public opinion on such matters as Prohibition, and then on the efforts that were made to combat the depression" (p. 140).

37. For general comment on Hoover and radio see Will Irwin (*Propaganda and the News,* p. 249), who notes that as with Coolidge, Hoover's radio voice was better than his ability to sway a live audience. Hoover himself comments (*Memoirs,* II, 147) on the medium in rather disapproving tones. Ray Lyman Wilbur discusses radio in the 1928 campaign (Wilbur *Memoirs,* p. 400 f).

38. The numerous others not included involved routine greetings, general comments suited to the particular occasion, or the like, and in any event, addresses with no significant relation to specific policies.

6. *Leadership: Franklin Roosevelt*

1. White is actually referring to a somewhat earlier period. See William Allen White, *A Puritan in Babylon* (New York: Macmillan, 1938), title of Chap. XXVI.

2. The phrase is Richard Hofstadter's. See the chapter on Jefferson with this title in his *American Political Tradition* (New York: Vintage Books, 1954).

3. Aside from press conferences and a few other items, primary reliance has been upon *The Public Papers and Addresses of Franklin D. Roosevelt* with a special introduction and explanatory notes by President Roosevelt (compiled by Samuel I. Rosenman), Vol. I: *The Genesis of the New Deal, 1928-1932*; Vol. II: *The Year of Crisis, 1933*; Vol. III: *The Advance of Recovery and Reform, 1934*; Vol. IV: *The Court Disapproves, 1935*; and Vol. V: *The People Approve, 1936* (New York: Random House, 1938). Hereafter referred to as "PP&A" and the date of the volume.

4. Cf. Arthur Schlesinger, Jr., *The Age of Roosevelt,* Vol. II: *The Coming of the New Deal* (Boston: Houghton Mifflin, 1959), p. 301. During his campaign for governor in 1928, at a speech in Buffalo (October 20), Roosevelt pledged consideration of the subject of old age pensions. PP&A, 1928-32, p. 35; see also p. 455.

5. See Frances Perkins, *The Roosevelt I Knew* (New York: Viking, 1946), p. 106 f and passim; and Rexford Tugwell, *The Democratic Roosevelt* (Garden City, N.Y.: Doubleday, 1957), p. 182.

6. For a broad and sweeping characterization of the pre-New Deal era see Arthur Schlesinger, Jr., *The Age of Roosevelt,* Vol. I: *The Crisis of the Old Order* (Boston: Houghton Mifflin, 1957); and for a useful

account of the background of social security and the 1935 context in which the legislation was passed, see Paul H. Douglas, *Social Security in the United States* (2nd ed.; New York: McGraw-Hill, 1939).

7. M. T. Sheehan, ed., *The World At Home: Selections from the Writings of Anne O'Hare McCormick* (New York: Knopf, 1956), p. 251 f. Cf. Douglas, p. 25 f.

8. Elliott Roosevelt, ed., *F.D.R.: His Personal Letters, 1928-1945* (New York: Duell, Sloan and Pearce, 1950), I, 393. Cf. Oswald Garrison Villard's comment: "It will be wise leadership as well as sound strategy if the President makes use of the next six months to prepare the public mind for his program of advanced social legislation, so that Congress will know the temper of the people as soon as it meets." "Issues and Men: The President and the Dying Congress," *Nation* (June 27, 1934), CXXXVIII, 722 f.

9. This and subsequent press conference transcripts were consulted at the Franklin D. Roosevelt Library, Hyde Park, N.Y., and are used, with other materials in the Library, with the permission of the Director. This transcript is dated February 16, 1934.

10. Perkins, p. 279. For other comment on the Townsend impact see Edwin E. Witte, *The Development of the Social Security Act* (Madison: University of Wisconsin Press, 1962), pp. 35, 86, 95 f.

11. Schlesinger, II, 307. Cf. also Schlesinger, *The Age of Roosevelt*, Vol. III: *The Politics of Upheaval* (Boston: Houghton Mifflin, 1960), p. 40 f.

12. PP&A, 1934, p. 291.

13. Harold L. Ickes, *Secret Diary*, Vol. I: *The First Thousand Days, 1933-1936* (New York: Simon and Schuster, 1953), p. 163. The passage continues: "He is looking forward to a time in the near future when the Government will put into operation a system of old-age, unemployment, maternity, and other forms of social insurance."

14. PP&A, 1934, p. 354. Edwin Witte (p. 17 and n. 19) claims the President also mentioned social security in a speech at Green Bay, Wis., on August 9. The text of that speech (PP&A, 1934, pp. 370 ff) shows no such mention.

15. PP&A, 1934, p. 409.

16. Ibid., p. 422.

17. Not found in PP&A, but included in the press release files at the Roosevelt Library.

18. PP&A, 1934, p. 458.

19. Witte (p. 94 and n. 55) supports this hypothesis.

20. Under White House guidance the legislation had been referred to Representative Doughton's Ways and Means Committee rather than to Representative Lewis' Committee on Labor, which had handled the Wagner-Lewis bill earlier. Paul Douglas wrote (p. 85) that cynics in-

terpreted this maneuver as an effort by the President to avoid the possibility of the Labor Committee reporting out a more radical measure than he wanted. Miss Perkins says, however (p. 296), that this was done because of Doughton's demand that his Committee handle it. Either or both versions may be correct if one assumes that the President's prime aim was to smooth the path of the legislation by avoiding both major changes which would alienate elements in the country and ruffled Congressional feathers. Cf. also Witte, p. 80.

21. PP&A, 1935, p. 236 f. In the transcripts at the Roosevelt Library the words following "profit" do not appear. It is interesting to note that this statement received prominent front page coverage in the *Providence Journal* of June 8, 1935.

22. PP&A, 1935, p. 370.

23. Schlesinger, III, 635 ff, and passim.

24. PP&A, 1934, p. 288.

25. Ibid., p. 313.

26. PP&A, 1935, p. 341.

27. Perkins, p. 278.

28. Roosevelt Library, O.F. 1086, "Committee on Economic Security," Secretary Perkins to F.D.R., June 29, 1934. Cf. Witte, pp. 47 ff for a discussion of the Advisory Council.

29. Perkins, p. 279.

30. Coverage of this speech plus full text appeared in the *New York Times,* November 12, 1934, pp. 1 (col. 6) and 5; cf. coverage in the *Providence Journal,* November 12, 1934, p. 11, col. 8.

31. *New York Times,* October 13, 1934, p. 15; and *Providence Journal,* same date, p. 3.

32. Roosevelt Library, O.F. 1086, November 12, 1934. Cf. Witte's reflection on the same matter some years later (p. 35).

33. Edwin E. Witte, "Twenty Years of Social Security," *Social Security Bulletin* (October, 1955), XVIII, 17.

34. Ibid.

35. Ibid.; and Witte, *Development of the Social Security Act,* pp. 42-47.

36. The author of the study of social security already referred to, and later Democratic Senator from Illinois.

37. Lela Stiles, *The Man Behind Roosevelt* (New York: World Publishing Co., 1954), p. 253.

38. Documents cited in this paragraph are from Roosevelt Library, O.F. 1710, "Social Security Board, Correspondence, 1935-37," dated October 21, 1935, July 17, August 12, August 22, 1936.

39. This has been translated from telegraphic abbreviations in the original, which was the draft Early prepared. The portion following the phrase "make a statement" was not typed like the first part, but in pen-

cil, presumably in his handwriting. Ibid., no date. Winant resigned on September 30, 1936.

40. Perkins, pp. 297 and 298 f.

41. See Hadley Cantril, ed., *Public Opinion, 1935-1946* (Princeton: Princeton University Press, 1951), p. vii and passim for the poll results used below.

42. See for example, Samuel Lubell, *The Future of American Politics* (London: Hamish Hamilton, 1952).

43. James M. Burns, *Roosevelt: The Lion and the Fox* (New York: Harcourt, Brace, 1956), p. 267.

44. Quotations from Tugwell, pp. 335, 336.

45. Schlesinger, III, 424.

46. See Frederic J. Fleron, Jr., "The Isolationists and the Foreign Policy of F.D.R." (Brown University; unpublished Master's thesis, 1961), for an analysis of Roosevelt's leadership of opinion in the period up to 1941.

47. Samuel I. Rosenman, *Working with Roosevelt* (New York: Harper, 1952), p. 167. Burns (p. 355) quotes a letter in which Roosevelt wrote a friend in 1938: "I am in the midst of a long process of education—and the process seems to be working slowly but surely."

48. Cf. James N. Rosenau, *National Leadership and Foreign Policy: A Case Study in the Mobilization of Public Support* (Princeton: Princeton University Press, 1963), especially Chap. III.

7. *The Modern Press Conference: 1933-1952*

1. *The Public Papers and Addresses of Franklin D. Roosevelt* (hereafter cited as PP&A), Vol. II: *The Year of Crisis, 1933* (New York: Random House, 1938), p. 30.

2. PP&A, Vol. I: *The Genesis of the New Deal, 1928-1932* (New York: Random House, 1938), p. 756.

3. John Gunther, *Roosevelt in Retrospect* (New York: Harper, 1950), p. 22 f.

4. Leo C. Rosten, *The Washington Correspondents* (New York: Harcourt, Brace, 1937), p. 49 f.

5. For discussion of the differing attitudes of reporters versus owners and editors, see: Rexford G. Tugwell, *The Democratic Roosevelt* (Garden City, N.Y.: Doubleday, 1957), p. 305; and Gunther, p. 134.

6. "The Roosevelt Myth," *American Mercury,* April, 1936, pp. 390-394.

7. Raymond Clapper, "Why Reporters Like Roosevelt," *Review of Reviews,* June, 1934, p. 15. Cf. also Walter Davenport, "The President and the Press," *Colliers,* January 27, 1945, p. 12.

8. Rosten, p. 191.

9. Clapper, p. 16. Steve Early sent this piece in to the President with a note suggesting he read it. "Clapper gives a true picture." O.F. 36 (Press) Roosevelt Library, Hyde Park.

10. They were held twice a week, one in the morning and one in the afternoon, so that both morning and evening papers would be served equally. He even held them when he was ill, on occasion: "when too ill to go to the executive office, he has met with half a dozen selected reporters in the Oval room of the White House proper to answer questions. These reporters have then rejoined their colleagues to give an account of his physical appearance, after which the President's stenographer reads from his notes the questions and answers of the sick room session." Raymond Brandt, "The President's Press Conference," *Survey Graphic,* July, 1939, p. 448.

11. Cf. Fauneil J. Rinn, "The Presidential Press Conference" (unpublished doctoral dissertation, University of Chicago, 1960), p. 120 f.

12. See PP&A, II, 31.

13. Gunther, p. 135.

14. PP&A, II, 32.

15. PP&A, II, 67.

16. The first sentence quoted appears in the transcript at Hyde Park, but not in the version of this press conference in PP&A, II, 69.

17. PP&A, II, 96. John Maynard Keynes was then only in the process of formulating his theories. For the relation of Keynes' thinking to Roosevelt's behavior see Tugwell, pp. 373 ff, and Arthur Schlesinger, Jr., *The Age of Roosevelt,* Vol. III: *The Politics of Upheaval* (Boston: Houghton Mifflin, 1960), pp. 400-408.

18. Cf. Drew Pearson and Robert Allen, "How the President Works," *Harpers,* June, 1936, p. 12; and Arthur Schlesinger, Jr., *The Age of Roosevelt,* Vol. II: *The Coming of the New Deal* (Boston: Houghton Mifflin, 1959), p. 561 f.

19. Raymond Clapper, *Watching the World* (New York: McGraw-Hill, 1944), p. 103.

20. These have been discussed and described many times. Cf. Clapper, "Why Reporters Like Roosevelt," p. 16; Davenport, p. 47; Henry F. Pringle, "Profiles," "The President: II," *New Yorker,* June 23, 1934, p. 20 f; and Schlesinger, II, 560. Grace Tully, one of F.D.R.'s personal secretaries, said in an interview (in Washington, March 27, 1962) that these were held perhaps on the average of every six weeks, and were definitely for "backgrounding" purposes.

21. Cf. George Creel, *Rebel at Large* (New York: Putnam, 1947), p. 290 f; and William L. Chenery, *So It Seemed* (New York: Harcourt Brace, 1952), pp. 241, 251.

22. Delbert Clark in his book *Washington Dateline* (New York:

Frederick A. Stokes, 1941) makes the distinction between "background" which can be used to enrich the reporter's information, augment his fund of knowledge, and provide him with the reasons for some action, and "off record," for the use of which he insists there is no valid reason.

23. Cf. Lindsay Rogers, "President Roosevelt's Press Conferences," *Political Quarterly* (1938), IX, 366; and Rosten, p. 57.

24. Ernest Lindley, *The Roosevelt Revolution: First Phase* (New York: Viking, 1933), p. 280.

25. Press conference quotations are from the transcripts at Hyde Park unless otherwise noted.

26. For the earlier Warm Springs background session see: Arthur Schlesinger, Jr., *The Age of Roosevelt*, Vol. I: *The Crisis of the Old Order* (Boston: Houghton Mifflin, 1957), p. 454 f; and Lindley, p. 111.

27. Much of this conference is reproduced in PP&A, III, 465-477.

28. PP&A, IX, 604 f. Cf. also Tugwell, p. 553.

29. Many have commented on the extent to which F.D.R. was in command at all times during the conferences and deftly steered them in the direction he wanted them to take. Raymond Brandt (p. 449) notes that: "On several occasions, after a number of intervening questions, he has corrected what might have been a false impression." This suggests the extent to which Roosevelt kept the whole developing pattern of a given conference in view as it progressed. In the transcript of the National Emergency Council meeting of December 11, 1934 (No. 19), F.D.R. gives a valuable insight into his press conference technique in the form of advice to the department and agency heads assembled. See this transcript in Lester G. Seligman and Elmer E. Cornwell, Jr., eds., *The New Deal Mosaic: Proceedings of the National Emergency Council* (Eugene: University of Oregon Press, 1964).

30. Undoubtedly there were times when F.D.R. did prepare his conference comments carefully in advance though perhaps not often on paper. James Martel (in "Washington Press Conference," *American Mercury*, February, 1938, p. 205) claims that there were such "carefully thought out Presidential statements that reveal shifts in the New Deal wind. . . ." Rogers (p. 369) notes careful preparation on special subjects like those involved in the "horse-and-buggy" conference following the invalidation of the N.R.A. Again, as at the conference of November 17, 1933, when the recognition of the Soviet government was announced, documents had been prepared for use at the conference and mimeographed for the reporters to pick up afterward.

31. Grace Tully (interview) made this latter point in discussing his conference tactics.

32. These figures are the result of analysis of the transcripts at the Roosevelt Library.

33. Cf. Brandt, p. 446. Louis Koenig in *The Invisible Presidency* (New York: Rinehart, 1960, pp. 273, 276) notes instances of Corcoran planting questions.

34. Brandt, p. 446.

35. A good many commentators have asserted that question planting was practiced. Cf. Clark, p. 158; Creighton J. Hill, "The No. 1 News Source," *Senior Scholastic*, September 18, 1944, p. 6; Martel, p. 205; Rosten, p. 58; and others. James Reston of the *New York Times* discussed the tactics followed during the Roosevelt era in an interview in Washington, April 4, 1962.

36. John M. Blum, *From the Morgenthau Diaries, Years of Crisis, 1928-38* (Boston: Houghton Mifflin, 1959), p. 278 f.

37. James A. Farley, *Jim Farley's Story* (New York: McGraw-Hill, 1948), p. 229.

38. *The Secret Diary of Harold L. Ickes*, Vol. I: *The First Thousand Days* (New York: Simon and Schuster, 1953), p. 556. See also Vol. III: *The Lowering Clouds* (1955), p. 284.

39. October 6, 1942, O.F. 36B (Press Conference Answers), Roosevelt Library, Hyde Park.

40. July 18, 1939, O.F. 2111 (American Civil Liberties Union), Roosevelt Library, Hyde Park.

41. Reston interview.

42. Rogers, p. 369. See also Charles W. B. Hurd, "President and Press: A Unique Forum," *New York Times Magazine*, June 9, 1935, p. 3.

43. Roosevelt Library, O.F. 36-A and O.F. 36-B.

44. There is, for instance, a memo from Lowell Mellett of the Office of Government Reports to Early, dated September 11, 1940, informing him that a certain reporter "has in mind to ask the President. . . ." Mellett indicated that he did not think the newsman should be encouraged to ask that question. Early penciled on the bottom: "Lowell: I agree: Ray should not. S.E." A reporter's note to Early read in part: "Dear Steve: It's been a week, and I thought I would remind you that I plan to ask that question at tomorrow's conference. . . ." (The Mellett note was in O.F. 53, "Roy Howard," as a cross reference and dated September 11, 1940; the other note was found in O.F. 36-A and dated June 6, 1944.)

45. A memo from Early to the President, dated October 21, 1941, begins: "The Canadian Minister tells me that he understands that you will be asked at your press conference today concerning reports that the defenses of the Port of Halifax. . . ." On another occasion (June 12, 1944) an official at the Treasury sent the President a note with a question tip. (Both of these, and others like them, are from O.F. 36-A.)

46. Note for example a memo from Archibald MacLeish, Director

of the Office of Facts and Figures, dated March 9, 1942, to Grace Tully, the President's secretary: "I am sending you the enclosed in answer to the President's suggestion that I prepare something he might perhaps wish to say about the Detroit riots." Early noted in pencil that the President did not use it. (O.F. 36-B.)

47. On November 1, 1941, for instance, Michael Straus of the Secretary of the Interior's office sent a wire to Secretary Hassett at Poughkeepsie, supplying information in response to a question at the President's press conference of the previous day (O.F. 36-A). In a confidential memo to the President, dated April 6, 1937, Early reminded him that he (F.D.R.) had asked for information from the Attorney General on a point that came up in press conference that afternoon, and proceeded to relay the results of the inquiry. (O.F. 1961, "Donald Richberg.")

48. O.F. 1961, "Donald Richberg."

49. William D. Hassett, *Off the Record with F.D.R., 1942-1945* (New Brunswick, N.J.: Rutgers University Press, 1958), p. 104.

50. Ickes, I, 284.

51. Cf. Bernard A. Weisberger, *The American Newspaperman* (Chicago: University of Chicago Press, 1961), p. 173. For his timing of stories see also Rosten, p. 50; and Clark, p. 89.

52. The casualness with which F.D.R. conducted his conferences was in part a pose, apparently. After one of his first press conferences James F. Byrnes writes that: "His hand was trembling and he was wet with perspiration" (*All in One Lifetime*, New York: Harper, 1958, p. 74); and presidential physician Ross McIntire said that the press conferences "took a lot out of him, and I wanted the number cut down." (*White House Physician*, New York: Putnam, 1946, p. 81.) Obviously he worked harder at the conferences than he was willing to admit.

53. In the first volume of his *Memoirs* President Truman summarizes briefly his few contacts with Roosevelt between the election and the latter's death. (*The Truman Memoirs*, Vol. I: *Year of Decisions*, London: Hodder and Stoughton, 1955.)

54. This comes out vividly in Richard Neustadt's article, "Presidency and Legislation: Planning the President's Program," *American Political Science Review* (December, 1955), XLIX, 980-1021.

55. The first Gallup poll question asked after Truman became President showed 87 per cent approval. John M. Fenton, *In Your Opinion . . .* (Boston: Little, Brown, 1960), p. 32 f.

56. James E. Pollard, *The Presidents and the Press* (New York: Macmillan, 1947), p. 847. Truman himself has written: "I always got along well with the reporters." *Memoirs*, I, 48.

57. Miss Rinn suggests (p. 151) that in connection with the Krock fiasco, the President had broken two "rules" which related to such inter-

views; (1) he had granted one, and (2) he had not insisted that the source of Krock's information be concealed, thus increasing the embarrassment of the other reporters.

58. *Public Papers of the Presidents, Harry S. Truman, 1945* (Washington: U.S. Government Printing Office, 1961), p. 12. The President, in his *Memoirs* (I, 49 ff), discusses this decision and the first press conference he held.

59. According to Anthony Leviero, by the time he had been in office a little over four years, his press releases numbered an even 2,000. It took Roosevelt twice as long to reach this figure. (Anthony Leviero, "Press and President: No Holds Barred," *New York Times Magazine,* August 21, 1949, p. 10 f.) Further discussion of White House press releases will be found in Chapter Nine.

60. For general discussions, using public opinion poll data, of the fluctuations of Truman's popularity see Chapter 6 in Elmo Roper, *You and Your Leaders* (New York: William Morrow Co., 1957); and Fenton, especially Chapters 2 and 3. Obviously it is impossible to segregate the impact of the press conferences on any statistical basis.

61. There is little data available, save for that found in occasional articles, upon which to base more than impressionistic generalizations. Some such information can be gleaned from the voting behavior studies of people like Paul Lazarsfeld, Angus Campbell, and their associates. Note, for example, Campbell et al., *The American Voter* (New York: John Wiley, 1960), pp. 54-59.

62. President Truman in his *Memoirs* (I, 48 f) asserts the importance of the conferences to a Chief Executive but does not mention their use in this connection specifically.

63. Joseph M. Jones in his book *The Fifteen Weeks* (New York: Viking, 1955) presents an admirable summary of this over-all train of events. Cf. also Truman's *Memoirs,* II: *Years of Trial and Hope,* Chapters VII and VIII.

64. Transcripts cited were used at the Truman Library, Independence.

65. Eben Ayers, assistant press secretary under Truman, among others, made this point in an interview, in Washington, March 26, 1962,

66. Letter from Jim Wright of the *Buffalo Evening News,* April 10, 1947 (O.F. 36, Press Conferences, Truman Library, Independence). The same point is made by the author of "The Atlantic Report on Washington" (*Atlantic,* February, 1950, p. 6 f): "What Mr. Truman has never been able to do is use the press conference to explain, elaborate, and interpret, to give broad outlines of Administration policy in language the people can understand." Cf. also William H. Stringer, "Mr. President, Will You . . . ?" *Christian Science Monitor,* December 28, 1946, p. 7.

67. *Public Papers,* 1945, pp. 263-309. Cf. p. 309: "I shall shortly communicate with the Congress recommending a national health program. . . ."

68. Ibid., pp. 475-491.

69. At the Truman Library there is a folder containing a long memo entitled: "Summaries of pre-campaign and campaign speeches 6/4—11/1/48" which lists both major speeches and "whistle-stop" remarks. This was gone through in quest of mentions of health insurance. Some twenty-seven of these were found, some brief mentions, in passing, of the nation's health, others more explicit.

70. Truman, *Memoirs,* II, 22. See pp. 20-24 for general discussion of this course of events by the President.

71. That on June 9 was the last time the subject came up during the year.

72. Ernest Lindley put it this way (in "The Truman Press Conferences," *Newsweek,* October 28, 1946, p. 30): "Truman, although candid, is not discursive. Roosevelt's most valuable conferences were those in which he talked at length on one or two subjects. From these the correspondents, and the public to which they report, got insight into his mind and objectives which they could not have got so well in any other way. Truman doesn't use his conferences for that purpose. Probably it is because his mind doesn't work that way. Unlike Roosevelt, he is not an originator and he doesn't have the habit of thinking out loud."

73. Cf. Douglass Cater, *The Fourth Branch of Government* (Boston: Houghton Mifflin, 1959), p. 36.

74. John Hersey, describing the famous conference of November 30, 1950, in which mention of the use of the atomic bomb in Korea was turned into a cause célèbre, wrote: "The President, who throughout was apparently so busy meeting each question as it came that he neither followed the tendency of the questions collectively nor understood the way the patchwork was being put together [by the reporters], nevertheless seemed to sense that he had somehow been pushed." "The Wayward Press," *New Yorker,* December 16, 1950, p. 86. This description probably applied to Truman's conduct of many if not most of his press conferences. For his own account of the episode, see *Memoirs,* II, 419 f.

75. Jack Bell, *The Splendid Misery* (Garden City, N.Y.: Doubleday, 1960), p. 170.

76. Brandt says Roosevelt "simply rephrased the questions to suit his own purposes and gave an answer after pointing out he had not used the original question."

77. This point is made in the unpublished Memorandum No. 5, on the Presidential Press Conference, prepared by the Brookings Institution for President-elect Kennedy, p. 10.

78. As Douglass Cater put it (p. 36): "But the major fault was that Truman never was able to comprehend both the culling process of the press and the printed impact of his words. More than this, he suffered, as Joseph C. Harsch of the *Christian Science Monitor* once commented, from a habit of thinking 'not consistently aware of the general implications of the specific.' "

79. "Mr. Truman's White House," *Fortune*, February, 1952, p. 78.

80. Donald R. Richberg, *My Hero* (New York: G. P. Putnam's, 1954), p. 280.

81. At interviews with both Eben Ayers, Truman's assistant press secretary, and Roger Tubby, the last man to hold the press secretary position under him, the point was made that few plants had been used. (Interviewing was done in Washington on March 26 and 28, 1962, respectively.)

82. Tubby (interview) stressed the importance of these statements and the relative unimportance of plants, as related matters.

83. Analysis based on transcripts at the Truman Library, Independence.

84. Hersey, "The Wayward Press." In spite of all this care, it was at the same conference that the misinterpreted reference to using the A-bomb in Korea occurred in reply to a subsequent question. (Cf. note 74.)

85. Jack Redding, who was in charge of publicity for the Democratic National Committee, recounts his involvement in a pre-press-conference staff briefing session at which a decision was made to use a prepared statement to deal with a problem that had arisen and would probably be subject of a question. Secretary of Defense Lovett produced a draft that he had brought to the meeting with him, which was accepted and used. (*Inside the Democratic Party*, Indianapolis: Bobbs-Merrill, 1958, p. 219 f.)

86. Alfred Steinberg makes this point in *The Man from Missouri* (New York: Putnam, 1962), p. 352. Cabell Phillips also suggests that systematic briefing did not begin right away. He quotes a White House staffer: "We had a hell of a time during the first few months. . . . After some pretty embarrassing bobbles, Charlie Ross (then Press Secretary) hit on the idea of having a pre-conference briefing. From then on we had a lot less trouble." ("Q and A on the Press Conference," *New York Times Magazine*, February 13, 1955, p. 62 f.)

87. For descriptions of the briefing process under Truman see: Leviero, "Press and President: No Holds Barred"; "Covering the Capital," *Time*, July 9, 1951, p. 54 f; Phillips, "Q and A on the Press Conference"; and Steinberg, p. 352. Tubby and Ayers, in interviews, described the process as it operated while they were involved. In addition to the kinds of materials found in the files at Hyde Park, which were

more or less duplicated at Independence, there were some occasional lists of possible questions (O.F. 36). The papers of Charles Ross, which were also consulted at the Truman Library, did not reveal any systematic collection of this kind of material (nor did the regular White House files).

88. Tubby interview, and interview with Lincoln White, State Department Press Officer, Washington, April 4, 1962.

89. Cf. Steinberg, p. 351; Brookings Memo, cited, p. 8; Rinn, p. 147.

90. February 17, 1950, O.F. 36, Truman Library, Independence.

91. At the April 27 conference the President opened the conference thus, in part: "It occurred to me that it would be more comfortable for you. I know it will be more comfortable for me to be able to see everybody, and for everybody to be able to hear what is said." On May 4, he said: "I changed the arrangement around a little bit, and we have set up some microphones around all over the place so that everybody can hear." Transcripts, Truman Library, Independence.

92. There was much comment on this kind of effect at the time. See for example Arthur Krock, "President and Press in a New Relationship," *New York Times,* April 30, 1950, p. E3.

93. It is said that the White House stenographer had been given strict orders by F.D.R. not to transcribe a word of shorthand unless he or Early ordered it. This order held until 1938. (Brookings Memo, cited, p. 6.) Apparently, however, "bootleg" transcripts were prepared by a stenographer hired by the *Herald Tribune* (Rinn, p. 140).

94. PP&A, IV, 169 f. He also discussed the matter, off the record, at his press conference of May 8, 1935 (Transcript, Roosevelt Library, Hyde Park).

95. Cf. Douglass Cater, "The President in your Living Room," *Reporter,* March 24, 1955, p. 24; and Roscoe Drummond, "Mr. Kennedy's Calculated Risk," *Saturday Review,* February 11, 1961, p. 83. James Hagerty in an interview (New York, May 31, 1962) said that he found this "system" in effect when he took over in 1953.

96. O.F. 36, Truman Library, Independence. Cf. also *Newsweek,* December 28, 1953, p. 61, and July 2, 1951, p. 50; and W. H. Lawrence, "Taping the Talk," *New York Times Magazine,* October 14, 1951, p. 62 f.

97. Letters dated July 13, 1951, O.F. 36, Truman Library, Independence. Replies accepting the offers are included with them in the file.

98. Cf. Rinn, p. 158.

8. *The Modern Press Conference: 1953-1964*

1. A somewhat briefer discussion of this process of institutionalization, much of which is incorporated here, appeared as an article by the

author: "The Presidential Press Conference: A Study in Institutionalization," *Midwest Journal of Political Science* (November, 1960), IV, 370-389.

2. For a discussion of this period of uncertainty see Emmet Hughes, *The Ordeal of Power* (New York: Atheneum, 1963), p. 131; Hugh Baillie, *High Tension* (New York: Harper, 1959), pp. 276-278; Douglass Cater, "The President and the Press," *Reporter,* April 28, 1953, pp. 26 ff; and Merriman Smith, *Meet Mister Eisenhower* (New York: Harper, 1954), p. 266 f. Henry and Katherine Pringle write of Hagerty's role: "In retrospect it is clear that Hagerty had to convince his boss of their [press conferences] value." "Mr. President!" *The Saturday Evening Post,* June 15, 1957, p. 128. Mr. Eisenhower himself skirts the issue in his memoirs. See *The White House Years,* Vol. I: *Mandate for Change* (Garden City, N.Y.: Doubleday, 1963), pp. 108 and 232 f.

3. Pringle. Cf. also Merriman Smith, p. 267.

4. Cf. Dwight D. Eisenhower, *Crusade in Europe* (Garden City, N.Y.: Doubleday, 1948), p. 58 for his description of his European press conferences; and Marquis Childs, *Captive Hero* (New York: Harcourt, Brace, 1958), p. 65 on the same thing, and pp. 64 and 77 for consideration of the "publicity buildup" of the General during the war.

5. Pringle.

6. For discussions of this first conference, see: Jack Bell, *The Splendid Misery* (Garden City, N.Y.: Doubleday, 1960), p. 290; "Ike's First," *Time,* March 2, 1953, p. 68; and "Ike's First," *Newsweek,* March 2, 1953, p. 56 f.

7. "Thank You, Mr. President," *Time,* March 9, 1953, p. 20; and "The March of the News," *U.S. News and World Report,* March 6, 1953, p. 4.

8. According to John M. Fenton (*In Your Opinion . . . ,* Boston: Little, Brown, 1960), the Gallup polls showed that in 1948, 92 per cent of those asked knew who Ike was, and in 1950, he came out at the top of the list of "most admired humans" with another sample (pp. 100 and 93, respectively). While in office, "His popularity rating showed a great deal more stability than either Roosevelt or Truman" (p. 116). See also chapter on Eisenhower in Elmo Roper, *You and Your Leaders* (New York: William Morrow Co., 1957).

9. This question of the gentle treatment accorded Eisenhower by the reporters was much discussed during his period in office. Note, for example: Douglass Cater, *The Fourth Branch of Government* (Boston: Houghton Mifflin, 1959), p. 40; and citations in note 10.

10. Cf. Robert L. Riggs, "The Press and the President," *New Republic,* May 24, 1954, p. 11; and "St. George (Humphrey) Frees the Press," *Progressive,* June, 1957, pp. 14-16. In the latter piece Riggs wrote: "This attitude on the part of the home offices made the White House

press conferences a farce for the first two years under Eisenhower" (p. 14). Note also "T.R.B. Washington Wire," *New Republic,* December 27, 1954, p. 2.

11. Cf. Bell, p. 291; and Smith, p. 71: "He tends to stiffen when he is around reporters, even socially, as though he expects someone to hurl a volley of unpleasant questions at him." Smith gives a rather more friendly picture of Ike in the earlier pages of the same book (p. 4).

12. In addition to this relative infrequency, Mr. Eisenhower refused to follow the past precedent of holding alternating morning and afternoon meetings. Smith, p. 272. On conference schedule see Eisenhower, *Mandate for Change,* p. 232.

13. As *Time* put it: "He took with him on trips briefcases full of executive orders, appointments, etc., and parceled them out daily to make news under the Augusta or Gettysburg dateline." (January 27, 1958, p. 19.)

14. F.D.R. himself wrote that conferences were held "in my study at Hyde Park, N.Y., when I am there, or in my cottage at Warm Springs, Ga." and went on to say that he also continued to see the press on trips. *The Public Papers and Addresses of Franklin D. Roosevelt* (hereafter cited as PP&A), Vol. II: *The Year of Crisis: 1933* (New York: Random House, 1938), p. 40.

15. *New York Times,* January 8, 1956.

16. "The President's Press," *Commonweal,* May 3, 1957, p. 116.

17. Press conference transcripts cited are in *Public Papers of the Presidents* (Washington: U.S. Government Printing Office), 1957 vol.

18. November 14, 1956, *Public Papers of the Presidents,* 1956 vol., p. 1103.

19. Ibid., 1957 vol., p. 576.

20. Ibid., 1958 vol., p. 259.

21. November 5, 1958, ibid., pp. 827-838.

22. Cabell Phillips, "The 'New Look' of the President," *New York Times Magazine,* August 16, 1959, p. 76.

23. *Public Papers of the Presidents,* 1958 vol., p. 828.

24. Cf. Cater, "The President and the Press," p. 21. *Time* commented: "he is turning these conferences into educational sessions from which the public can learn a lot about the President's mind and the nation's business." (March 30, 1953, p. 13.)

25. PP&A, IV, 170.

26. Several observers have commented on the "image" of the President projected at Ike's press conferences. Walter Johnson, for instance, has summed up the matter thus: "Although his sentences at press conferences wandered across the landscape without consideration for syntax, what did come through was the fact that the President was a warm, kindly, decent human being who said simple, friendly things. He could

communicate a belief in homely virtues; and to the public, at least during his first term, this seemed more important than penetrating analyses of issues or the development of far-seeing policies." *1600 Pennsylvania Avenue* (Boston: Little, Brown, 1960), p. 319.

27. Hagerty interview, New York, May 31, 1962.

28. *Public Papers of the Presidents,* 1958 vol., p. 488.

29. Ibid., 1959 vol., p. 384.

30. Ibid., p. 349. See also Pringle, p. 130, for general comment on plants.

31. Hagerty interview.

32. Hagerty interview.

33. For discussions of the Eisenhower use of statements see: Sherman Adams, *First Hand Report* (New York: Harper, 1961), p. 445; and Robert J. Donovan, *Eisenhower: The Inside Story* (New York: Harper, 1956), p. 149, where a staff discussion of the possible use of a statement is mentioned: "Before Eisenhower's press conference the next morning, his staff met with the President to draw up a statement he intended to read to the reporters" (p. 249); and p. 292, where the President himself is represented as considering such a statement as a means of discussing something. At his first press conference he implied an intention of making considerable use of such statements, but the pattern subsequently suggests some change in this plan: "This morning I have chosen four subjects that I think are of immediate interest. . . ." *Public Papers of the Presidents,* 1953 vol., p. 42.

34. Reliance for this discussion of conference preparation is placed on the Hagerty interview, and on the following descriptions of the process: Adams, pp. 72, 74 and 119; Bell, p. 294; Louis Koenig, *The Invisible Presidency* (New York: Rinehart, 1960), p. 372 f; Pringle, p. 130; and "Authentic Voice," *Time,* January 27, 1958, p. 16 f.

35. Of the many, often conflicting, accounts of Ike's newspaper reading habits, perhaps one of the more balanced is to be found in Adams, p. 72. See also Douglass Cater's analysis of the various claims made: "The Folklore of an Electronic Presidency," *Reporter,* July 12, 1956, p. 15. Eisenhower himself, in his memoirs, insists he did read "the better part of at least two newspapers." *Mandate for Change,* p. 233.

36. Cater's *Fourth Branch of Government,* pp. 130-138, has been drawn upon in the following account. Cf. also Richard L. Strout, "Government by Leak," *New Republic,* January 21, 1957, pp. 8-10; and "Washington Wire," *New Republic,* December 24, 1956, p. 2.

37. Cater, *Fourth Branch of Government,* p. 131.

38. Roger Tubby, in an interview, Washington, March 28, 1962, expressed the opinion that a good deal more staff backgrounding was being done during the Kennedy administration than was done either

during the Truman or Eisenhower periods. Cf. also "The President and the Press," *Time,* October 26, 1953, pp. 61 ff. Hagerty (interview) said substantially the same thing as Tubby.

39. "Covering the Capital," *Time,* July 9, 1951, p. 56.

40. Bell, p. 264; Strout.

41. Merriman Smith claims that in the early months of the Eisenhower administration Hagerty attempted to enforce a policy of channeling all "backgrounding" by White House staff through himself (p. 270). Russell Baker makes the same point: "Fourteen Clues to Washington News," *New York Times Magazine*, April 7, 1963, p. 110.

42. For an account of this experiment see Felix Belair, Jr., "President Tries Out New Press Technique," *New York Times*, July 26, 1959, p. E7; and Bell, p. 291.

43. Cf. Cater, *Fourth Branch of Government*, p. 41; Roscoe Drummond, "Mr. Kennedy's Calculated Risk," *Saturday Review*, February 11, 1961, p. 83; and Hagerty interview.

44. Hugh Baillie claims that Ike said before taking office he would allow direct quote if he held press conferences (p. 278). Cf. also Eisenhower, *Mandate for Change*, p. 232.

45. *Time*, December 28, 1953, pp. 7 and 45.

46. Cf. Cater, *Fourth Branch of Government*, p. 41. This series of developments was also discussed by Hagerty (interview). Cf. also Eisenhower, *Mandate for Change*, p. 232.

47. Cf. Sidney Shalett, "We Bring You Now the President!" *Saturday Evening Post*, May 21, 1955, p. 146. Cf. Eisenhower, *Mandate for Change*, p. 232.

48. Douglass Cater, "The President in Your Living Room," *Reporter*, March 24, 1955, p. 23.

49. Unpublished memo No. 5 on Presidential Press Conference, Brookings Institution, prepared for President Kennedy. For an evaluation of the early months of the Kennedy press conference experience see: E. R. Hutchinson, "Kennedy and the Press: The First Six Months," *Journalism Quarterly*, Autumn 1961, pp. 453-459.

50. Brookings memorandum, cited, pp. 14-16. Cf. also Jack Raymond, "Kennedy Ponders News Policy Shift," *New York Times*, November 27, 1960. An excellent over-all summary of Kennedy press conference and press relations technique and development can be found in Raymond P. Brandt, "Kennedy Expected to Expand Press Conferences. . . ," *St. Louis Post-Dispatch*, April 29, 1962.

51. See "Historic Conference," *Newsweek*, February 6, 1961, p. 56; and Hugh Sidey, *John F. Kennedy, President* (New York: Atheneum, 1963), p. 49 for a description of the preparations for the first conference. Cf. also *New York Times*, January 23, 1961.

52. James Reston referred to this, when announced, as: "the goofiest

idea since the hula hoop" ("The Problem of Holding a Political Balance," *New York Times*, January 11, 1961). Young and Rubicam, a New York advertising firm, conducted a poll for the White House on audience reaction to these televised conferences and found a highly favorable response. *New York Times*, July 23, 1962. Cf. also Sidey.

53. *New York Times*, January 23, 1961, pp. 10 and 11. At times he did talk of going back to the Treaty Room (*Providence Journal*, December 10, 1963).

54. Interview with Salinger, Washington, March 27, 1962. What was apparently the first meeting of this group is noted in the *New York Times*, January 25, 1961. See also "How Much Management of the News?," *Newsweek*, April 8, 1963, p. 62. Descriptions of the process whereby Kennedy prepared for his press conferences have appeared in print: Joseph A. Loftus, "Preparation Key to News Sessions," *New York Times*, March 29, 1962; Alan L. Otten, "What Do You Think, Ted?" in Lester Tanzer, ed., *The Kennedy Circle* (Washington: Luce, 1961), p. 5; also Mary McGrory, "The Right-Hand Men," p. 67, same volume; and "The Show-Biz Conference," *Time*, November 17, 1961, p. 39 f. Much of the following is also based on the Salinger interview.

55. Interview with Lincoln White, Washington, April 4, 1962.

56. White interview, and "The Show-Biz Conference," *Time*, p. 39. Sidey (p. 79) cites an instance of this.

57. "Historic Conference," *Newsweek*. Cf. also Russell Baker, "Kennedy and Press' Appears to Be a Hit," *New York Times*, January 26, 1961.

58. For comment on the new conference format directed particularly to this point see: Charles L. Markmann and Mark Sherwin, *John F. Kennedy: A Sense of Purpose* (New York: St. Martin's, 1961), p. 277; Richard Rovere, "Letter from Washington," *New Yorker*, February 4, 1961, p. 111; "Show-Biz Conference," *Time*, p. 39; and Sidey, p. 50.

59. Merriman Smith, interview, Washington, March 28, 1962.

60. E. W. Kenworthy, interview, Washington, April 3, 1962.

61. Rovere suggested that the conference might well be abandoned entirely for this kind of reason ("Letter from Washington," p. 111 f).

62. In addition to the citations in note 58, note the following critiques: Ted Lewis, "TV Press Conference," *Nation*, February 11, 1961, p. 112 f; "Long Time No See," *Newsweek*, November 13, 1961, p. 93; "J. F. K. and the Conference," *Time*, March 24, 1961, p. 44; T. R. B., "Protected President," *New Republic*, December 12, 1960, p. 2; and Gerry Van der Heuvel, "Is JFK Considering Press Parley Change," *Editor and Publisher*, April 7, 1962, p. 74. According to Alan L. Otten the President himself had decided reservations about the existing state of affairs ("Presidential Pressmanship," *Wall Street Journal*, November 29, 1961, p. 18).

63. According to Salinger (interview) there were only 125 reporters accredited to the White House in Roosevelt's day and there are now 1,200. He may have exaggerated the difference between the two periods (there were 475 listed in the press gallery in the *Congressional Directory* in 1935 and 829 in 1961). Whatever the precise figures, the growth has been considerable. Sidey (p. 105) also cites the figure 1,200.

64. The author attended the conference of April 3, 1963, through the gratefully acknowledged assistance of Senator Claiborne Pell of Rhode Island.

65. Stuart Hale of the *Providence Journal* staff made this point to the author and provided other valuable information as he and I sat together at the April 3 conference.

66. *Time* (in "The Pencil v. the Lens," January 25, 1960, p. 55) describes the practice of Governors Edmund Brown of California and Nelson Rockefeller of New York in holding separate conferences for the regular newsmen and the TV people as a way of solving the problem. The results have not, apparently, been completely successful.

67. Brookings memorandum, cited, p. 1.

68. Roscoe Drummond, for example, has written: "By making the Presidential press conference a White House window which opens into the drawing rooms of millions of American voters, he is acting to widen the sense of public participation in government. He is creating a new intimacy between the President and the people." "Mr. Kennedy's Calculated Risk," *Saturday Review*, February 11, 1962, p. 82. Cf. also Sidey, p. 51 f.

69. Rovere, p. 112. One interviewee said in effect that the President rejected the idea of a return to the F.D.R. conference format because he felt in time he would lose the press as a sympathetic intermediary in his communication with the public, and hence needed the TV conference to go directly to the people.

70. The 1961 *Annual Report of the Associated Press* contained the following statement by Frank J. Starzel, general manager, which demonstrates the publicity advantages inherent in the televised press conference: "One Kennedy innovation—news conferences broadcast live on television and radio—required the Washington Bureau to mobilize as many as 35 persons to cover all angles at the speed demanded. This meant writing first bulletins and leads from TV in the bureau—while reporters in the presidential conference room still were locked up. It meant additional newsmen, monitors, deskmen, dictationists, photographers, motorcycle couriers." Cf. *New York Times*, July 23 and 24, 1962 for the first overseas transmission of a press conference telecast via the communications satellite Telstar.

71. Letter from Pierre Salinger to author, June 26, 1962. He did not indicate the reason for making this change save to imply that it was

somehow better for the media to be given the right of making these decisions. He also noted that the new policy had been working extremely well. Cf. also: Jack Gould, "Kennedy Press Conferences," *New York Times*, May 30, 1962.

72. References are to the *Public Papers of the Presidents*, 1961 and 1962 vols.

73. Alan L. Otten, in "Changing Presidency," *Wall Street Journal*, March 15, 1961, p. 1, writes: "But little is being left to luck; the public relations effort is coldly calculated. Presidential press conferences begin with a series of announcements carefully prepared to report good news or give the image of a man of action and good will." See also Markmann and Sherwin, p. 272 (they note that some reporters have resented the time thus taken away from questioning); and W. H. Stringer, "Kennedy Gropes for the Press," *Christian Science Monitor*, November 11, 1961.

74. Cf. Sidey, pp. 58, 78 f, and 297 (steel).

75. "The Show-Biz Conference," *Time*, p. 39. See also reference to what he assumed was a plant in Tom Wicker, "Kennedy Puts on Polished Show . . . ," *New York Times*, February 15, 1962; and "How Much Management of the News?" *Newsweek*, April 8, 1963, p. 62.

76. Otten, "Presidential Pressmanship," p. 18. Cf. also Tom Wicker, "U.S. Backs Taiwan Regime," *New York Times*, October 20, 1961.

77. Salinger interview. Assistant Press Secretary Andrew Hatcher said early in the administration, in discussing the conference format, that: "the president had no desire to plant questions at his news conferences or to speak at great length in support of Administration projects. He does not want to change the free flow of question and answers, Mr. Hatcher said." *New York Times*, March 9, 1961.

78. Lewis, p. 112.

79. This practice has been subject of considerable comment. See: Worth Bingham and Ward S. Just, "The President and the Press," *Reporter*, April 12, 1962, pp. 18-22; Otten, "Presidential Pressmanship;" article prepared by Fletcher Knebel dated January 26, 1962, for the Minneapolis papers he serves; Sidey, pp. 69 and 98; "Fourteen Clues to Washington News," *New York Times Magazine*, p. 110; and Victor Lasky, *J.F.K.: The Man and the Myth* (New York: Macmillan, 1963), p. 3.

80. Theodore H. White, *The Making of the President: 1960* (New York: Atheneum, 1962), p. 337; cf. also Stan Opotowsky, *The Kennedy Government* (New York: E. P. Dutton, 1961), p. 36.

81. Ibid., p. 338.

82. Cf. Bingham and Just, p. 21; J. T. Crown and G. P. Penty, *Kennedy in Power* (New York: Ballantine Books, 1961), p. 25; and James MacGregor Burns, "The Four Kennedys of the First Year," *New York Times Magazine*, January 14, 1962, p. 9.

83. Most of the information about the 1961 backgrounder came from interviews with Salinger and James Reston, Washington, April 4, 1962; but see also Bingham and Just, p. 20.

84. Reston (interview) claimed to have suggested this idea to Salinger.

85. Direct quotes appeared in a British newspaper and the resulting furor forced the White House admission that transcripts had been supplied to some foreign newsmen who were not present. *Providence Journal*, January 11, 1963.

86. For comment on these see Bingham and Just, p. 22; Otten, "Presidential Pressmanship," and "The Show-Biz Conference," *Time*, p. 39 f. There also have been similar luncheons at which the guests have not all been drawn from one state. Cf. Tom Wicker, "Congress' Return to Step up Press Briefings by President," *New York Times*, January 23, 1962.

87. "The Kennedy 'Image'—How It's Built," *U.S. News and World Report*, April 9, 1962, p. 57. Cf. also "Kennedy Fetes News Executives to Hear Views and Give Them," *New York Times*, October 22, 1962; and "President Fears Negro Racists . . . ," *New York Times*, May 14, 1963.

88. Salinger interview. Cf. also "Fourteen Clues to Washington News," *New York Times Magazine*, pp. 106 and 110; and "How Much Management of the News?" *Newsweek*, p. 61. Staff contacts were to be reported to Salinger, however. (*New York Times*, November 19, 1962).

89. Jim Hagerty admitted this also (interview, New York, May 31, 1962).

90. McGrory, p. 58.

91. Fletcher Knebel, letter to the author, dated February 9, 1962. James Reston was sure before Kennedy came into office that such a policy of giving individual interviews would be resented (Bingham and Just, p. 18). Essentially the same point about the reason they in fact have not been the source of trouble was made by Merriman Smith to the author (interview).

92. The following discussion is based almost entirely on a careful analysis of reports in the *New York Times*.

93. Most of the impromptu press conferences as well as the more formal ones have been represented by verbatim transcripts in the *Times*.

94. The *Times* noted unrest among the reporters as early as December 19 ("President Keeps Press on Alert"); and TV industry pressure, December 20 ("President Invites TV Aides to Lunch").

95. Tom Wicker, "President Hints at Extra Session If Congress Lags," *New York Times*, May 7, 1964.

96. Merriman Smith (interview) noted that the volume of stories on conference topics was cut way down when the full transcripts began to

be carried. The data in the table cast some doubt on this generalization, however.

9. *The White House Staff and Public Relations*

1. These figures and subsequent ones are from tables showing federal civilian employment in various issues of the *Statistical Abstract of the United States*, unless otherwise indicated.

2. The following description of the changes brought about by President Truman in this aspect of White House staffing comes from an interview with Eben Ayers, assistant press secretary during the Truman Administration, Washington, March 26, 1962. Cf. also Douglass Cater, "The Power of the President," *Reporter*, May 27, 1952, p. 6.

3. See the various volumes of Leonard D. White's study of American national administrative history, published by Macmillan, 1948-1958.

4. U.S. Civil Service Commission, "Monthly Report of Federal Employment," March, 1962, and November, 1963.

5. Eben Ayers (interview) stressed this last point in discussing press secretaries he had worked with or known.

6. For discussions of this relationship see, for example: James Reston, "The President and Public Opinion," in Morton Gordon and Kenneth N. Vines, *Theory and Practice of American Foreign Policy* (New York: Crowell, 1955), p. 198; Delbert Clark, *Washington Dateline* (New York: Frederick Stokes, 1941), pp. 81, 125, and *passim*; F.D.R.'s own discussion of Early's role in *The Public Papers and Addresses of Franklin D. Roosevelt* (hereafter cited as PP&A), Vol. II: *The Year of Crisis, 1933* (New York: Random House, 1938), p. 39; Robert E. Sherwood, *Roosevelt and Hopkins* (New York: Harper, 1948), p. 207 f; Merriman Smith, *A President Is Many Men* (New York: Harper, 1948), pp. 87, 89, 98, and *passim*; James E. Pollard, *The Presidents and the Press* (New York: Macmillan, 1947), various references in the chapter on F.D.R.; Unofficial Observer, *The New Dealers* (New York: Simon and Schuster, 1934), pp. 222-225. Reliance has been placed on an interview with James Rowe, who was on the White House staff during the Roosevelt years, conducted in Washington, April 3, 1962.

7. Press conference transcripts, Roosevelt Library.

8. Early had little hesitancy, apparently, in interrupting the President during press conferences. John Gunther notes: "Steve Early sometimes interrupted and corrected him at press conferences, even to the point of interjecting sharply, 'Make that off the record.' " (*Roosevelt in Retrospect*, New York: Harper, 1950, p. 45.) Cf. also Smith, p. 89 f.

9. O.F. 253 (Stephen Early), Roosevelt Library.

10. O.F. 259 (Marvin McIntyre), Roosevelt Library.

11. Secretary Ickes, in his *Secret Diary* (Vol. I: *The First Thousand Days*, New York: Simon and Schuster, 1953, p. 328 f) cites an instance in which the liaison between Early in Washington and McIntyre with the President in Florida failed to operate.

12. Rowe interview.

13. O.F. 259, Roosevelt Library.

14. This correspondence is to be found in O.F. 788 (National Emergency Council), Roosevelt Library. The "Federal Register" referred to by Early is not to be confused with the publication of the same name later inaugurated by the government containing texts of executive orders and the like.

15. Cf. Clark, p. 126. He makes the point that, nevertheless, Early was quoted in the press far more frequently than his predecessors, who usually remained anonymous.

16. According to James M. Burns, even Early and McIntyre did not know about the Court packing plan in advance. *Roosevelt: The Lion and the Fox* (New York: Harcourt, Brace, 1956), p. 297.

17. For Ross's background see John Hersey, "Mr. President," II: "Ten O'Clock Meeting," *New Yorker*, April 14, 1951, p. 38. For general appraisals of Ross as press secretary see: Robert S. Allen and William V. Shannon, *The Truman Merry-Go-Round* (New York: Vanguard, 1950), pp. 54-56; Jack Bell, *The Splendid Misery* (Garden City, N.Y.: Doubleday, 1960), p. 250; Jonathan Daniels, *Man of Independence* (Philadelphia: Lippincott, 1950), p. 359 f; and James E. Pollard, "President Truman and the Press," *Journalism Quarterly* (Fall, 1951), XXVIII, 457-468, *passim.*

18. He was not unaware of the importance of this side of the office, however. He told William Hillman: "the President must be a sort of super-public relations man." William Hillman, *Mr. President* (New York: Farrar, Straus and Young, 1952), p. 11.

19. Ayers interview.

20. Quotations are from Allen and Shannon, pp. 54, 55, 56.

21. Margaret Truman, *Souvenir* (New York: McGraw-Hill, 1956), p. 278. Other comment on the reliance of the President on Ross is to be found in: "Mr. Truman, Chairman of the Board," *U.S. News and World Report*, November 25, 1949, p. 20; and "Mr. Truman's White House," *Fortune*, February 1952, p. 74.

22. Ayers interview. Ayers' point about Potsdam is amply borne out in correspondence at the Truman Library between him and Ross during the conference. (Charles G. Ross papers, Box 8, "Trips of the President.")

23. Ayers pointed out (interview) that during the Truman era press secretaries held only one such daily briefing, though two have been held since. Cf. also Allen and Shannon, p. 56. A letter from Ayers to Herbert

Miller, dated April 13, 1949, at the Truman Library, contains a good description of the functions of the press secretary including the daily press conferences. (O.F. 253, Charles G. Ross.)

24. There are numerous mentions and brief descriptions of these in the available literature including: Allen and Shannon, p. 32; Hillman, p. 14; and Alfred Steinberg, *The Man from Missouri* (New York: Putnam, 1962), p. 347 f. They were also discussed in interviews with Ayers and with David Lloyd, a Truman assistant, Washington, April 4, 1962.

25. Hersey, p. 38 f.

26. Only a sampling of the literature on Hagerty can be listed: "Authentic Voice," *Time*, January 27, 1958, pp. 16 ff; a series of six articles by Stan Opotowsky under the title "Eisenhower, Inc., Adams and Hagerty, Mgrs." appeared in the *New York Post* between March 31 and April 6, 1958; Cabell Phillips, "Speaker of the White House," *New York Times Magazine*, August 12, 1956, pp. 12 ff; Richard Gehman, "Hagerty: Voice for the President," *Esquire*, April 1956, pp. 53 ff; and Joseph Kraft, "The Dangerous Precedent of James Hagerty," *Esquire*, June 1959, p. 91 f. In addition there are of course almost innumerable references to Hagerty's role in books dealing with the period, for example in: Bell, Chapter 18; Merriman Smith, *Meet Mr. Eisenhower* (New York: Harper, 1954); and Merriman Smith, *A President's Odyssey* (New York: Harper, 1961).

27. Cf. Marquis Childs, *Captive Hero* (New York: Harcourt, Brace, 1958), pp. 64 f, 77 f, 80.

28. Hagerty told the author (interview, New York, May 31, 1962) that he had started working with Eisenhower on press matters shortly after the latter returned from his NATO command in Europe, and while he (Hagerty) was still on the New York state payroll. (Cf. also "Authentic Voice," *Time*, p. 18.) He of course remained with Ike throughout all of his two terms in the White House.

29. The full quotation, according to Robert J. Donovan, is: "Tell Jim to take over and make the decisions—and handle the story." (*Eisenhower: The Inside Story*, New York: Harper, 1956, p. 367.)

30. The heart attack, which took place September 24, 1955, the operation for ileitis on June 9, 1956, and the slight stroke suffered by the President on November 25, 1957.

31. Cf. Walter Johnson, *1600 Pennsylvania Avenue* (Boston: Little, Brown, 1960), p. 322; and Gehman, p. 53. In spite of Kennedy's frequent informal contacts with reporters, an effort by Pierre Salinger, his press secretary, to cut his own daily meetings with the reporters from two to one in late October, 1961, was abandoned within a week. Again, one assumes, the form and infrequency of presidential press

conferences was responsible for this quick reversal. (Cf. *New York Times*, October 27 and November 3, 1961.)

32. Merriman Smith made essentially this point in discussing the press secretary role with the author (interview, Washington, March 28, 1962).

33. Opotowsky, *Post* series, April 4, 1958. Elsewhere Opotowsky wrote, after noting that in effect the modern press secretary position had been created under F.D.R.: "Under Eisenhower, James Hagerty broadened it from a mere help-the-reporters functionary to a full-scale public relations counsel." *The Kennedy Government* (New York: Dutton, 1961), p. 35 f.

34. Cf. Louis Koenig, *The Invisible Presidency* (New York: Rinehart, 1960), p. 372; Johnson, p. 322; and "A Day in the Life of the President," *U.S. News and World Report*, March 14, 1958, p. 40. (In this last instance, it seems to have been the President who suggested that a statement be prepared for use in the event that a scheduled rocket launching should be successful.)

35. Opotowsky, *Post* series, April 3, 1958.

36. "Authentic Voice," *Time*, p. 19.

37. Opotowsky, *Post* series, April 4, 1958. This has also been referred to as "woodworking:" "Boy, I sure had to dig into the woodwork for that one," Hagerty is quoted as having said. Kraft, p. 92.

38. *New York Times*, December 5, 1957.

39. Bell, p. 306.

40. "President Eisenhower and His Press Secretary," *Journalism Quarterly* (Fall, 1957), XXXIV, 452-456.

41. Interview with Salinger, Washington, March 27, 1962.

42. For general discussions of Salinger and his role as press secretary see: Mary McGrory, "The Right-hand Men," in Lester Tanzer, ed., *The Kennedy Circle* (Washington, D.C.: Luce, 1961), pp. 61, 68 and *passim*; Theodore H. White, *The Making of the President* (New York: Atheneum, 1962), p. 337 f; Opotowsky, *The Kennedy Government*, p. 36; "How Much Management of the News," *Newsweek*, April 8, 1963; and "White House Bon Vivant," *New York Times*, October 30, 1962.

43. For comparisons of Hagerty and Salinger see Opotowsky, p. 36; and McGrory, p. 60.

44. *U.S. News and World Report*, April 9, 1962, p. 56.

45. These details were secured at an interview with Kenneth Barnard (Providence, R. I., April 6, 1962), at the time press secretary to the Governor of Rhode Island, who attended.

46. E. Pendleton Herring, "Official Publicity under the New Deal," *Annals of American Academy of Political and Social Science*, 179 (1935), p. 167.

47. For this see the issue of the *Annals* cited; and James L. McCamy, *Government Publicity* (Chicago: University of Chicago Press, 1939).

48. Delbert Clark, p. 120, and also passim; for other discussions of this assignment of Early's see: Unofficial Observer, p. 225; and a hostile view by Gordon Carroll, "Dr. Roosevelt's Propaganda Trust," *American Mercury*, September, 1937, pp. 1-31.

49. See, for example, Carroll, cited, and two subsequent articles by the same author in the *American Mercury*: "How the WPA Buys Votes," October, 1937, pp. 194-213, and "Propaganda from the White House," November, 1937, pp. 319-336.

50. Harold Ickes, *Secret Diary*, Vol. II: *The Inside Struggle* (New York: Simon and Schuster, 1954), p. 75.

51. Ibid., p. 527.

52. Raymond P. Brandt, "The President's Press Conference," *Survey Graphic*, July, 1939, pp. 446 ff.

53. Cf. Stanley Kelley, Jr., *Professional Public Relations and Political Power* (Baltimore: Johns Hopkins University Press, 1956), p. 15; and Carroll, "Dr. Roosevelt's Propaganda Trust," p. 28.

54. Brandt.

55. This and subsequent correspondence on the same subject referred to were found in O.F. 180 (*Congressional Record*, Material Regarding Administration), Roosevelt Library.

56. Letter dated August 24, 1938.

57. There are some general discussions of this in the Roosevelt era: Delbert Clark, "The President's Listening-in Machine," *New York Times Magazine*, September 1, 1935, pp. 3 ff; James Kieran, "The President Listens In on the Nation," *New York Times Magazine*, October 3, 1937, pp. 1 ff. (The President told Kieran, the latter relates, that he had ten different devices for checking public opinion: the press, his mail, personal conversations, telegrams after speeches, digest of editorials, Democratic party reports, visits by political leaders, reports from aides, discussions with advisors, and trips through the country.) Also Paul Mallon, "Roosevelt's Ear to the Ground," *New York Times Magazine*, January 14, 1934, pp. 1 ff. On the Division of Press Intelligence see Margaret H. Williams, " 'The President's' Office of Government Reports," *Public Opinion Quarterly* (Fall, 1941), V, 550-553; Appendix A of the *U.S. Government Organization Manual* under "Division of Press Intelligence," and Cedric Larson, "How Much Federal Publicity Is There?" *Public Opinion Quarterly* (October 1938), II, 638.

58. Lela Stiles, *The Man Behind Roosevelt* (Cleveland: World, 1954), p. 249 f.

59. One of the most useful sources on both the Executive Council and its successor, the National Emergency Council, is Louis Brownlow, *A Passion for Anonymity* (Chicago: University of Chicago Press, 1958),

pp. 318-325. See also *U.S. Government Organization Manual*, Appendix A. For the proceedings of the NEC see Lester G. Seligman and Elmer E. Cornwell, Jr., *The New Deal Mosaic* (Eugene: University of Oregon Press, 1964).

60. *U.S. Government Organization Manual*, "United States Information Service" in Appendix A. See also Williams, pp. 550 and 553 f.

61. Williams, p. 550. Renamed *U.S. Government Organization Manual* in 1949.

62. Ibid., p. 550 f. See also the various agency titles in *U.S. Government Organization Manual*, Appendix A.

63. There is no single comprehensive study of O.W.I. comparable to the ones done of the Creel Committee. The agency is dealt with, however, in PP&A, Vol. XI: *Humanity on the Defensive* (New York: Harper, 1950), pp. 274-283, which comprise the executive order setting it up and a note commenting on its establishment by the editor of the volume. See also relevant portions of Roger Burlingame, *Don't Let Them Scare You: The Life and Times of Elmer Davis* (Philadelphia: Lippincott, 1961). The Spring, 1943, issue of the *Public Opinion Quarterly* is devoted to a series of articles on O.W.I., including one entitled "O.W.I. Has a Job," by Davis himself; see also "Passed by Censor," by George Creel, Byron Price, Elmer Davis, and William A. Kinney, in Cabell Phillips, ed., *Dateline: Washington* (Garden City, N.Y.: Doubleday, 1949), pp. 199-226. At the Truman Library, Independence, among the Charles G. Ross papers was found the as yet unpublished final report to the President on O.W.I. written by Elmer Davis, and this also was consulted. (It apparently was available to Burlingame for use in his book on Davis.)

64. See Lester G. Hawkins, Jr., and George S. Pettee, "OWI—Organization and Problems," *Public Opinion Quarterly* (Spring, 1943), VII, 16 f and passim.

65. Elmer Davis' final report to the President, p. 27.

66. Davis, "O.W.I. Has a Job," p. 8.

67. This paragraph is based largely on Davis's report to the President.

68. Jack Redding, *Inside the Democratic Party* (Indianapolis: Bobbs-Merrill, 1958), pp. 59, 165, 216, and 223 f.

69. Interview with Tubby in Washington, March 28, 1962.

70. David Lloyd interview.

71. See Harry S. Truman, *Memoirs*, Vol. I: *Year of Decisions* (London: Hodder and Stoughton, 1955), pp. 498-501; Steinberg, pp. 281-285; Daniels, pp. 312-316; and James F. Byrnes, *Speaking Frankly* (New York: Harper, 1947), pp. 239-243.

72. Daniels, p. 314.

73. Ayers interview.

74. Allen and Shannon, p. 56.

75. Hagerty interview.

76. Bernard Rubin, *Public Relations and the Empire State* (New Brunswick, N.J.: Rutgers University Press, 1958), p. 106. See also the rest of Chapter 5 dealing with the Council.

77. "Authentic Voice," *Time*, p. 17.

78. Bell, p. 316.

79. C. J. V. Murphy, "The Budget—and Eisenhower," *Fortune*, July, 1957, p. 230. For an account of the whole episode see Sherman Adams, *First Hand Report* (New York: Harper, 1961), Chapter 17.

80. Cf. the point that Merriman Smith makes in his book *Meet Mr. Eisenhower*, p. 270.

81. Cabell Phillips, "Executive for the Chief Executive," *New York Times Magazine*, June 5, 1955, pp. 11 ff.

82. For an account of this episode see Donovan, pp. 164 and 177-182; and Adams, pp. 137 ff.

83. Donovan, p. 181.

84. Salinger interview. Cf. Theodore H. White, pp. 115-118, for comment on the U-2 incident and its relation to the 1960 campaign.

85. Cf. "How Much Management of the News?," *Newsweek*, p. 62. Apparently the frequency of meetings declined to every other week.

86. *New York Times*, April 27, 1961.

87. Ibid., April 20, 1961. Cf. also Hugh Sidey on this episode (*John F. Kennedy: President*, New York: Atheneum, 1963, p. 153).

88. "Cabinet members are asked to save and forward to the President each week announcements that tell of favorable developments or outline some government action." Alan L. Otten, "Changing Presidency," *Wall Street Journal*, March 15, 1961, p. 1 f.

89. *New York Times*, April 30, 1963.

90. Ibid., December 19, 1960.

91. Cf. George Michael, *Handout* (New York: Putnam, 1935).

92. Listings of major White House office personnel in some recent issues of the *Congressional Directory* are useful in this connection. The staff of the Truman Library have prepared for their own use a listing of all persons who served in the White House during the period with which they are concerned, down to and including clerks and typists, which is a unique source of such information.

93. James D. Richardson, ed., *A Compilation of the Messages and Papers of the Presidents, 1789-1908*, 11 vols. (Washington, D.C.: Bureau of National Literature and Art, 1908).

94. These can be consulted at the Roosevelt and Truman Libraries and presumably also exist for the Eisenhower and Kennedy periods.

95. The larger totals for the latter Roosevelt years are probably attributable to a combination of more careful filing practices and the impact of the War.

96. An interesting sidelight on the institutionalization of the presidency can be gleaned from the press release records covering the period of President Eisenhower's heart attack and subsequent period of recuperation. The attack occurred September 24, 1955, and he held his first Washington news conference following it on January 19, 1956, having been out of Washington most of the intervening period. The monthly press release totals for 1955 and early 1956 are:

January, 1955	34	June	41	November	25
February	23	July	46	December	12
March	24	August	48	January, 1956	38
April	29	September	18	February	29
May	41	October	19	March	29

Note that though the illness and absence of the President reduced the number of press releases to about half the average earlier in 1955, so institutionalized has the White House operation become that the flow of statements (and not medical bulletins either) could continue at a substantial rate.

97. For example, an Eisenhower staffer, Reverend Frederick Fox, was responsible for preparing messages to fill the numerous requests from the 6,500 voluntary associations and agencies in the country which seek a word of blessing from the Chief Executive. Cf. *New York Times*, April 6, 1958, and February 23, 1959; and Robert K. Gray, *Eighteen Acres Under Glass* (Garden City, N.Y.: Doubleday, 1962,) p. 111 f.

98. Rexford G. Tugwell, *The Democratic Roosevelt* (Garden City, N.Y.: Doubleday, 1957), pp. 332 f, 355.

99. There are numerous discussions of these staff meetings, among them: Adams, picture and caption following p. 300; Koenig, p. 375; C. J. V. Murphy, "Eisenhower's White House," *Fortune*, July, 1953, p. 77; and Merlo Pusey, *Eisenhower the President* (New York: Macmillan, 1956), p. 88.

100. Rowe interview.

101. Rexford G. Tugwell, "Franklin D. Roosevelt on the Verge of the Presidency," *Antioch Review* (Spring, 1956), XVI, 62.

102. The following correspondence was all found in P.P.F. 2222 (Conference of Mayors), Truman Library, Independence. Cf. Emmet Hughes, *The Ordeal of Power* (New York: Atheneum, 1963), p. 94, for a strikingly similar episode from the Eisenhower period: "I seized on a request for a Presidential message to the annual conference of the American Library Association—to draft for the President another blunt warning on the ugliness of McCarthyism." See also p. 95.

103. William D. Hassett, a holdover from Roosevelt days, remained as Truman's Correspondence Secretary. John R. Steelman carried the title of The Assistant to the President.

104. Charles S. Murphy, Special Counsel to President Truman.

105. In the files of David Stowe, deposited at the Truman Library, Independence.

106. Ibid. Cf. also the comment by the President in his memoirs: "In a move to offset the propaganda of the opposition an executive order was issued on December 29, 1951, creating the President's Commission on the Health Needs of the Nation. . . ." Vol. II: *Years of Trial and Hope* (London: Hodder and Stoughton, 1956), p. 22.

107. Interview with Representative Kenneth Hechler, Washington, March 28, 1962.

108. There are almost countless discussions of Adams' functioning as "chief of staff." They of course range all the way from the hostile Opotowsky series, cited, to Adams' own memoirs (*First Hand Report*). Robert K. Gray's book, cited, is particularly interesting since it was the work of a fellow White House staffer.

109. Adams, p. 81. But cf. also Hughes, p. 102 f.

110. Adams, p. 213 (emphasis added).

111. "The Presidency: Can Any One Man Do the Job?," *U.S. News and World Report*, November 22, 1957, p. 65.

112. Much of the account below is drawn from Sidey, pp. 293-297. Cf. also Grant McConnell, *Steel and the Presidency—1962* (New York: Norton, 1963); and Roy Hoopes, *The Steel Crisis* (New York: John Day, 1963).

113. Sidey, pp. 294, 295.

114. Ibid., p. 296.

115. Sidney Hyman notes that Kennedy never held regular staff meetings. ("How Mr. Kennedy Gets the Answers," *New York Times Magazine*, October 20, 1963, p. 17). Sidey uses the phrase "task force" (p. 299), and discusses other similar group decisions.

116. "How Much Management of the News?," *Newsweek*, p. 60.

117. Eleanor Roosevelt, *This I Remember* (New York: Harper, 1949), p. 3. Cf. also pp. 4, 56, 125. Other discussions of this role for the First Lady are to be found in: Burns, p. 173; Drew Pearson and Robert Allen, "How the President Works," *Harpers*, July 1936, p. 11; Frances Perkins, *The Roosevelt I Knew* (New York: Viking, 1946), p. 30; and Tugwell, *The Democratic Roosevelt*, p. 304.

118. On the importance of "My Day" see: Burns, p. 266; and Tugwell, p. 527 f.

119. Ira Smith and Joe Alex Morris, *Dear Mr. President* (New York: Julian Messner, 1949), p. 153 f.

120. Margaret Truman, p. 107; and "Ladies' Day," *Time*, March 23, 1953, p. 19.

121. Otten.

122. Paul F. Hoye, "272 Articles in a Year on the Kennedys," Providence *Evening Bulletin*, February 10, 1962.

123. Salinger interview.

124. Smith and Morris, p. 12. Cf. also Ben Whitehurst, *"Dear Mr. President"* (New York: Dutton, 1937).

125. Leila A. Sussmann, "F.D.R. and the White House Mail," *Public Opinion Quarterly*, Spring, 1958, pp. 5-16.

126. O.F. 550 (Mail Reports), Truman Library.

127. *New York Times*, July 5, 1961. Cf. also Hyman, p. 104.

128. It is not possible to be absolutely certain on this point. No evidence was uncovered at the Roosevelt Library that the White House commissioned polls in F.D.R.'s day. On O.W.I.'s activity, see Alan Barth, "The Bureau of Intelligence," and Jerome Bruner, "O.W.I. and the American Public," both in *Public Opinion Quarterly*, Spring, 1943.

129. Ickes, III, 324.

130. Ibid., p. 219. Elmo Roper describes the interest Roosevelt and his intimates showed in the results of Roper polls in his book *You and Your Leaders* (New York: William Morrow, 1957), p. 71.

131. This and the following paragraph are based on a letter from Hadley Cantril to the author dated August 14, 1962.

132. O.F. 505 (Polls) and 505A (Gallup Poll), Truman Library. The Steelman note was found in the former.

133. See the President's comments on the polls and the 1948 election in his *Memoirs*, II, 188 f.

134. *New York Times*, May 3, 1957.

135. Cantril set these surveys up for the State Department and ran them for a year until the end of the war (Cantril letter, cited).

136. *New York Times*, July 2, 1957.

137. Ibid., March 17, 1957.

138. White, p. 51. See Louis Harris' article "The Use of Polls in Political Campaigns," in James M. Cannon, ed., *Politics U.S.A.* (Garden City, N.Y.: Doubleday, 1960), pp. 253-263.

139. White, p. 51.

140. James Reston, "A Year of Frustration for Democratic Congressmen," *New York Times*, June 27, 1962. See also "Private Polling of Voters Hailed," *New York Times*, July 22, 1962; "Kennedy Praised on News Parleys," *New York Times*, July 23, 1962; and Victor Lasky, *J.F.K.: The Man and the Myth* (New York: Macmillan, 1963), p. 562.

141. See for example Kelley; Daniel J. Boorstin, "Selling the President to the People: The Direct Democracy of P.R.," *Commentary* (November, 1955), XX, 421 ff; and Martin Mayer, *Madison Avenue, U.S.A.* (New York: Harper, 1958).

142. In the fall of 1953, Bill Lawrence of the *Times* staff was overheard saying that there was too much B.B.D. and O. in the White House since Ike moved in. (Reference is to Batten, Barton, Durstine and

Osborn, the firm most often used by the Eisenhower people.) ("The President and the Press," *Time*, October 26, 1953, p. 61 f.)

143. Marion D. Irish, "Cipher in the White House," *New Statesman and Nation*, December 7, 1957, p. 762.

144. James Reston, "A Problem in Publicity," *New York Times*, May 25, 1955.

145. Karl E. Meyer, "The Men Around Kennedy," *Progressive*, September, 1960, pp. 19, 20.

10. *The Electronic Media*

1. Francis Chase, Jr., *Sound and Fury* (New York: Harper, 1942), p. 113. For the use of radio in Roosevelt's various presidential campaigns see S. L. Becker and E. W. Lower, "Broadcasting in Presidential Campaigns," in Sidney Kraus, ed., *The Great Debates* (Bloomington: Indiana University Press, 1962).

2. Chase, p. 113.

3. In fact there is much basis to the claim that it was Al Smith and not F.D.R. who originated the idea of using radio in connection with executive leadership. Cf. George Michael, *Handout* (New York: Putnam's, 1935), p. 36 f; and Robert F. Bradford, "Politics and Television: A Fable," in W. Y. Elliott, *Television's Impact on American Culture* (East Lansing: Michigan State University Press, 1956), p. 186.

4. Frank Freidel, *Franklin D. Roosevelt: The Triumph* (Boston: Little, Brown, 1956), p. 31. Cf. also Bernard Bellush, *Franklin D. Roosevelt as Governor of New York* (New York: Columbia University Press, 1955), p. 33.

5. Cf. Freidel, p. 61; and *The Public Papers and Addresses of Franklin D. Roosevelt* (hereafter cited as PP&A), Vol. I: *The Genesis of the New Deal, 1928-1932* (New York: Random House, 1938), p. xl.

6. PP&A, p. 539.

7. In four years Hoover broadcast 95 times, and Roosevelt 104 times in the comparable period.

8. According to Cedric Larson, F.D.R. spoke 125 times on the radio from March, 1933, until the end of 1937 ("How Much Federal Publicity Is There?," *Public Opinion Quarterly*, October, 1938, p. 639) as against the ten fireside chats he made in that period.

9. Cf. Joseph Alsop and Robert Kintner, *Men Around the President* (Garden City, N.Y.: Doubleday, 1939), p. 134; Elisha Hanson, "Official Propaganda and the New Deal," *Annals of American Academy of Political and Social Science* (May, 1935), p. 183; and Louis E. Kirstein, "Radio and Social Welfare," *Annals* (June, 1935), p. 130. A memo from a Publicity Committee chaired by Steve Early to Louis Howe dated November 14, 1933 (O.F. 570, Executive Council, Roosevelt Library,

Hyde Park) reads in part: "Arrangements have been made with a broadcasting company to give us a national hookup once a week." This is part of a very interesting summary of publicity media being utilized and the coverage being received by the administration.

10. Cf. Harold L. Ickes, *Secret Diary*, Vol. II: *The Inside Struggle* (New York: Simon and Schuster, 1954), pp. 75, 527.

11. John Franklin Carter, *Power and Persuasion* (New York: Duell, Sloan and Pearce, 1960), p. 30.

12. For general comment on Roosevelt and radio see: W. L. Chenery, *So It Seemed* (New York: Harcourt, Brace, 1952), p. 250; John Gunther, *Roosevelt in Retrospect* (New York: Harper, 1950), p. 38; Kirstein; Samuel I. Rosenman, *Working with Roosevelt* (New York: Harper, 1951); Arthur M. Schlesinger, Jr., *The Age of Roosevelt*, Vol. II: *The Coming of the New Deal* (Boston: Houghton Mifflin, 1959), p. 558 f; and John H. Sharon, "The Psychology of the Fireside Chat" (Princeton, N.J.: unpublished honors thesis, 1949).

13. Both letters found in P.P.F. 477, (National Broadcasting Co.), Roosevelt Library. The writer of the first was M. H. Aylesworth; the President's reply was dated May 18.

14. P.P.F. 897 (Mrs. Ogden Reid), Roosevelt Library. Letter was dated June 6.

15. P.P.F. 530 (Frank P. Graham), Roosevelt Library. Letter was dated January 21, 1939.

16. References, in addition to those already cited, to Roosevelt's use of radio to bypass the press and reach the people directly are to be found in: James M. Burns, *Roosevelt: The Lion and the Fox* (New York: Harcourt, Brace, 1956), p. 446; A. S. Draper, "President Employs Air, Press to Educate Nation," *Literary Digest*, January 27, 1934, p. 9; Schlesinger, p. 559; Leila A. Sussmann, "F.D.R. and the White House Mail," *Public Opinion Quarterly* (Spring, 1956), p. 16; and B. A. Weisberger, *The American Newspaperman* (Chicago: University of Chicago Press, 1961), p. 173.

17. Cf. Morris L. Ernst, *The First Freedom* (New York: Macmillan, 1946), pp. 152 ff.

18. Cf. James L. Fly, "Regulation of Radio Broadcasting in the Public Interest," *Annals of American Academy of Political and Social Science* (January, 1941), p. 103.

19. Cf. Chase, pp. 131, 133; and Theodore F. Koop, " 'We Interrupt This Program . . . ,' " in Cabell Phillips, *Dateline: Washington* (Garden City, N.Y.: Doubleday, 1949), p. 84 f. James Hagerty, Eisenhower press secretary, also discussed this episode, interview, New York, May 31, 1962.

20. "F.C.C. vs. Press," *Business Week*, July 26, 1941, p. 32 f.

21. Ernst, p. 155.

22. "F.C.C. vs. Press," *Business Week.*

23. Interview with James Rowe, Washington, April 3, 1962.

24. *F.D.R.: His Personal Letters, 1928-1945* (New York: Duell, Sloan and Pearce, 1950), II, 1118.

25. The phrase "fireside chat" seems not to have been invented by the President but by Harry C. Butcher, manager of the Columbia Broadcasting System office in Washington. Schlesinger, p. 559. For a listing and general discussion of them see: W. W. Braden and Ernest Brandenburg, "Roosevelt's Fireside Chats," *Speech Monographs*, November 1955, pp. 290-302.

26. Hadley Cantril and Gordon W. Allport, *The Psychology of Radio* (New York: Peter Smith, 1941), p. 10. The points made in this and the following paragraph are drawn largely from this source, pp. 9 ff. See also Alfred McClung Lee and Elizabeth Briant Lee, *The Fine Art of Propaganda* (New York: Harcourt, Brace, 1939), p. 7, for a discussion of the *advantages* of radio over the auditorium speech.

27. Freidel, p. 61.

28. Draper, cited.

29. Harold F. Gosnell, *Champion Campaigner: Franklin D. Roosevelt* (New York: Macmillan, 1952), p. 221.

30. Eleanor Roosevelt, *This I Remember* (New York: Harper, 1949), p. 73.

31. Drew Pearson and Robert Allen, "How the President Works," *Harpers* (June, 1936), p. 12.

32. Robert E. Sherwood, *Roosevelt and Hopkins* (New York: Harper, 1948), pp. 215, 217, 297.

33. This is commented upon in: Burns, p. 227; Schlesinger, Vol. III: *The Politics of Upheaval* (Boston: Houghton Mifflin, 1960), p. 503; and Seymour H. Fersh, *The View from the White House: A Study of the Presidential State of the Union Messages* (Washington, D.C.: Public Affairs Press, 1961), p. 103.

34. Burns, p. 272.

35. PP&A, Vol. 13: *Victory and the Threshold of Peace*, compiled by Samuel I. Rosenman, (New York: Harper, 1950), p. 43.

36. *F.D.R.: His Personal Letters*, 466 f. Letter to Baker dated March 20.

37. P.P.F. 1126 (Frank Walker), Roosevelt Library. Walker's letter was dated February 4, 1936, and F.D.R.'s reply, February 13.

38. Louis Koenig, *The Invisible Presidency* (New York: Rinehart, 1960), p. 287. Corcoran corroborated this for the author.

39. Both James Rowe (interview, cited) and Grace Tully, who served as the President's personal secretary, thus characterized the process (interview, Washington, March 27, 1962). See also Schlesinger, *The Coming of the New Deal*, p. 559.

40. John M. Blum, *From the Morgenthau Diaries* (Boston: Houghton Mifflin, 1959), p. 315.

41. Ibid., p. 332.

42. Ibid., p. 444.

43. Voting behavior studies conducted in the years since 1945 amply bear this out.

44. William Hillman, *Mr. President* (New York: Farrar, Straus and Young, 1952), p. 222. See also James F. Bender, "The Truman Voice—'General American,'" *New York Times Magazine*, April 29, 1945, p. 17.

45. On September 4, 1951, President Truman spoke over the first coast to coast television hookup. Cf. Robert MacPherson, "Imagine It Was only 10 Years Ago," *TV Guide*, September 9, 1961, p. 26.

46. *New York Times*, July 20, 1950.

47. For comment on Reinsch's role see: Merriman Smith, *Thank You Mr. President* (New York: Harper, 1946), pp. 213, 298; same author, *A President Is Many Men* (New York: Harper, 1948), pp. 143 f; and Alfred Steinberg, *The Man from Missouri* (New York: Putnam, 1962), p. 197.

48. Smith, *A President Is Many Men*, p. 143.

49. Interviews with David Lloyd and Eben Ayers, Washington, D.C., March 26 and April 4, 1962, respectively.

50. Letter, Lewis W. Shollenberger to Joseph Short, O.F. 136-B (Television), Truman Library, Independence, Mo.

51. Letter from David Levy of Young and Rubicam, O.F. 136-B, Truman Library.

52. Richard Krolik of the Schwerin Research Corporation wrote a similar letter of commentary on presidential televising dated September 6, 1950 (O.F. 136-B, Truman Library) in which he said, among other things, "the advantages which television has over radio have not been exploited in the Presidential speeches delivered to date. . . ."

53. There were literally dozens of these letters, no less than twenty-nine in a folder covering August 1948 to March 1949. (See O.F. 136-A, Radio, Truman Library.)

54. Richard E. Neustadt, *Presidential Power, The Politics of Leadership* (New York: John Wiley, 1960), p. 103.

55. Stanley Kelley, Jr., *Professional Public Relations and Political Power* (Baltimore: Johns Hopkins University Press, 1956), p. 161. For further comment on the use of TV in the 1952 campaign, see Becker and Lower, in Kraus, pp. 40-45.

56. Merriman Smith, *Meet Mr. Eisenhower* (New York: Harper, 1954), p. 261.

57. George E. Allen, *Presidents Who Have Known Me* (1960 ed., New York: Simon and Schuster, 1960), p. 261.

58. *New York Times*, January 22, 1953. Ike himself was reluctant to

go to the people via TV, according to Emmet Hughes, *The Ordeal of Power* (New York: Atheneum, 1963), p. 131.

59. "Authentic Voice," *Time*, January 27, 1958, p. 18.

60. Smith, *Meet Mr. Eisenhower*, p. 264.

61. "TV: Hagerty's Role Discussed," *New York Times*, February 28, 1958.

62. Ibid.

63. For discussion of Montgomery's role, see: Sherman Adams, *First Hand Report* (New York: Harper, 1961), pp. 296 ff; Jack Bell, *The Splendid Misery* (Garden City, N.Y.: Doubleday, 1960), p. 308; Leo Bogart, *The Age of Television* (New York: Frederick Unger, 1956), p. 208; Richard Gehman, "He 'Produces' the President," *Good Housekeeping*, November, 1955, pp. 64-67; "Robert Montgomery Presents: President as a Pro," *Life*, April 19, 1954, p. 28 f; and Walter Johnson, *1600 Pennsylvania Avenue* (Boston: Little, Brown, 1960), p. 319.

64. Gehman, p. 66; see also Roger Kennedy, "Television," *New Republic*, May 30, 1955, p. 22.

65. Bell, p. 308.

66. "Robert Montgomery Presents," *Life*.

67. "Age of Danger," *Time*, June 1, 1953, p. 13.

68. Neustadt, p. 71.

69. Quotes from article by Anthony Leviero, *New York Times*, June 4, 1953. Cf. also "Direct to the People," *Newsweek*, June 15, 1953, p. 24 f; and "Panel Show," *Newsweek*, same issue, p. 93.

70. June 4, 1953, article by Joseph Loftus.

71. "Fireside Chit Chat," *Saturday Review*, June 20, 1953, p. 31.

72. Robert J. Donovan, *Eisenhower: The Inside Story* (New York: Harper, 1956), p. 146.

73. " 'Some Cabinet Meeting,' " *Newsweek*, November 8, 1954, p. 25.

74. *New York Times*, October 26, 1954, news accounts and Jack Gould's column.

75. Jack Gould in *New York Times*, May 18, 1955. On this program cf. also Hughes, p. 258.

76. Jim Hagerty had this idea early in the administration, though it was not implemented for some time. (See Smith, *Meet Mr. Eisenhower*, p. 263, and the discussion in Chapter Eight above.)

77. N. A. Graebner, "Eisenhower's Popular Leadership," *Current History*, October 1960, p. 234.

78. Theodore White gives a detailed analysis, including the findings of opinion polls, of the impact of the debates. *The Making of the President* (New York: Atheneum, 1962), pp. 290-295. Cf. also Kraus.

79. A complete record of the joint television appearances of the two 1960 presidential candidates, including the verbatim transcripts of the debates, can be found in Part III, *Final Report* of the Senate Committee on Commerce, Report No. 994, 87th Congress, First Session.

80. Interview with Pierre Salinger, Washington, D.C., March 27, 1962.

81. *Wall Street Journal,* November 29, 1961.

82. Hugh Sidey, *John F. Kennedy, President* (New York: Atheneum, 1963), p. 49.

83. *New York Times,* October 26, 1961.

84. Cf. John Cogley, "The Presidential Image," *New Republic,* April 10, 1961, pp. 29-31; and Charles L. Markmann and Mark Sherwin, *John F. Kennedy: A Sense of Purpose* (New York: St. Martin's Press, 1961), p. 271. Salinger, in an interview with DeeWitt C. Evans, Washington, D.C., March 3, 1964, claimed that he had suggested live televising because of the crucial role he felt the TV debates had played, and in general that television was an ideal Kennedy medium.

85. *Reporter,* January 3, 1963, p. 12.

86. Evans interview with Salinger, cited.

87. *New York Times,* October 23, 1963. Gould also provides some description of how the show was filmed.

88. *New York Times,* June 17, 1963.

89. Cf. Ben H. Ragdikian's excellent analysis of the Kennedy use of television, and its importance as a medium to the President: "Television —'The President's Medium?'," *Columbia Journalism Review,* Summer, 1962, pp. 34-38. James Rowe (interview) said that Kennedy had made this point to him in explaining his decision to live televise his news conferences.

90. Samuel I. Rosenman, *Working with Roosevelt* (New York: Harper, 1952).

91. See Robert E. Sherwood, *Roosevelt and Hopkins* (New York: Harper, 1948), especially pp. 213 f; Raymond Moley, *After Seven Years* (New York: Harper, 1939); Stanley High, *Roosevelt—and Then?* (New York: Harper, 1937). On Corcoran, see Koenig, *Invisible Presidency,* pp. 249-298, and Charles Michelson, *The Ghost Talks* (New York: Putnam, 1944), especially pp. 12 f and 56 f. In addition, the speech writing process and related matters are discussed in: Joseph Alsop and Robert Kintner, pp. 89 f, 155 f, 185 f; Gunther, pp. 122 ff; James Roosevelt and Sidney Shalett, *Affectionately, F.D.R.* (New York: Avon, 1959), pp. 236 f; and Schlesinger, II, *The Coming of the New Deal,* p. 559 f. A master's thesis done at Cornell University by Lois Jean Wilson entitled "A Discussion of the Use of Ghost Writers by Some of the Great Presidents" (September, 1961) is useful on the general subject and for the Roosevelt period as well.

92. On Moley, cf. Schlesinger, *The Coming of the New Deal,* p. 549, and Rosenman, p. 104. F.D.R. himself in discussing speech writing notes the problem of writers who claim more credit for the result than they really deserve. PP&A, Vol. V: *The People Approve* (New York: Random House, 1938), p. 391.

93. Gunther, p. 122.
94. PP&A, V, 391.
95. Emil Ludwig, *Roosevelt* (New York: Viking, 1938), p. 284.
96. Schlesinger, *The Coming of the New Deal,* p. 559; interview with Grace Tully, cited.
97. *New Yorker,* "Notes and Comments: Course in Ghostwriting at American University," February 23, 1952, p. 23.
98. Rosenman, p. 10.
99. Sherwood, p. 297.
100. Laura Crowell, "The Building of the 'Four Freedoms' Speech," *Speech Monographs* (November, 1955), p. 283.
101. Frances Perkins, *The Roosevelt I Knew* (New York: Viking, 1946), p. 113.
102. Donald Richberg, *My Hero* (New York: Putnam, 1954), p. 280 f.
103. Harry Gilroy, "Survey of the Ghost Writers," *New York Times Magazine,* March 27, 1949, p. 20.
104. Among the relatively few commentaries on Truman era speech writing are: John Hersey, "Profiles," "V—A Weighing of Words," *New Yorker,* May 5, 1951, pp. 36-53; Charles G. Ross, "How Truman Did It," *Colliers,* December 25, 1948, pp. 13 and 87 f; Merriman Smith, *A President Is Many Men,* pp. 29 f, 37; Steinberg, p. 355; Harry S. Truman, *Memoirs,* Vol. I: *Year of Decisions* (London: Hodder and Stoughton, 1955), pp. 29 f and passim; and Wilson, p. 108 f. Interviews with Eben Ayers and David Lloyd; and with Roger Tubby (Washington, D.C., March 28, 1962).
105. Cf. Jack Redding, *Inside the Democratic Party* (Indianapolis: Bobbs-Merrill, 1958), p. 52.
106. Among the Truman speech writers were White House special counsels Charles Murphy and Clark Clifford, staff members George Elsey and David Lloyd, Samuel Rosenman in the beginning, Press Secretary Ross, and others.
107. Even less descriptive information about the Eisenhower practices has found its way into print than was the case with Truman. There are brief mentions in Sherman Adams' book and in Robert K. Gray, *Eighteen Acres Under Glass* (Garden City, N.Y.: Doubleday, 1962). Wilson, p. 4 f is useful, as is "Behind Each Eisenhower Speech: Men Who Do the Writing," *U.S. News and World Report,* January 7, 1955. Useful information was also obtained in an interview with Emmet Hughes (New York, May 31, 1962), and a lengthy letter from Bryce Harlow, dated March 13, 1964. Hughes' book, cited, is helpful.
108. Adams, p. 81 f.
109. Hughes interview and Harlow letter.
110. Hughes, p. 25.

111. Sorensen first joined the Kennedy staff in 1953. On the former's speech writing role see: James M. Burns, *John Kennedy* (New York: Harcourt, Brace, 1959-60), especially pp. 122-24; Theodore White, p. 324; Wilson, p. 117 f; Alan L. Otten, "Sorensen's Role," *Wall Street Journal,* January 5, 1961, p. 1 f; and Alan L. Otten, "What Do You Think, Ted?" in Lester Tanzer, *The Kennedy Circle* (Washington, D.C.: Luce, 1961).

112. Otten, in Tanzer, p. 7.

113. Tom Wicker, "Kennedy as a Public Speakah," *New York Times Magazine,* February 25, 1962, p. 71.

114. Ibid., p. 70.

115. Cf. Bagdikian, p. 35.

11. *A Trial Balance*

1. Tom Wicker, "Johnson Bids Congress Enact Civil Rights Bill. . . ," *New York Times,* November 28, 1963.

2. Tom Wicker, "Johnson's Thanksgiving Address Asks Nation . . . ," *New York Times,* November 29, 1963.

3. By Val Adams, March 10, 1964.

4. Walter Lippmann, "The President Is Formidable on Television," Providence *Evening Bulletin,* March 17, 1964.

5. "The Presidency, The American Dream," *Time,* May 1, 1964, p. 19.

6. Ibid., p. 17.

7. See Russell Baker, "' Ev and Charlie,' or a G.O.P. Lament," *New York Times,* March 16, 1962; and Remy Zimmerman, " 'Ev and Charlie Show' Contrasts Sharply to Kennedy News Briefing," *Brown* (University) *Daily Herald,* March 23, 1962.

8. Baker.

9. As James Reston put it: "Compared with the youthful President Kennedy, Senator . . . Dirksen and Representative . . . Halleck looked like a veteran Shakespearean actor and W. C. Fields." *Providence Journal,* January 9, 1963.

10. Baker.

11. *Providence Journal,* February 4, 1963. Senator Dirksen assured the curious that other sources of funds would be found.

12. An American Institute of Public Opinion release dated February 20, 1964, gives the following "popularity ratings" registered between two and three months after assuming office: Truman 87 per cent, Eisenhower 67 per cent, Kennedy 73 per cent, and Johnson 75 per cent.

13. Baker.

14. James MacGregor Burns, "The Legacy of the 1,000 Days," *New York Times Magazine,* December 1, 1963, p. 118.

15. Sidney Hyman, "Presidential Popularity Is Not Enough," *New York Times Magazine,* August 12, 1962, p. 65.

16. American Institute of Public Opinion release dated November 20, 1963: too fast 46 per cent, not fast enough 12 per cent, about right 31 per cent, don't know 11 per cent.

17. "Lawmakers Find Kennedy Sells Himself, But Not Aims," *New York Times,* April 14, 1961.

18. Tom Wicker, "Republicans Attack Kennedy with New Optimism," *New York Times,* June 27, 1962.

19. "Endorsement of Kennedy Seen But Not of Domestic Program," Providence *Evening Bulletin,* November 10, 1962.

INDEX